AN ELECTION IN FINLAND

Party Activities and Voter Reactions

BY PERTTI PESONEN

New Haven and London, Yale University Press

1968

AN ELECTION IN FINLAND

Party Activities and Voter Reactions

Foreword

It has often been remarked that the early development of the study of social anthropology in England grew out of that nation's far-flung imperial involvements during the nineteenth century. It might also be surmised that the extraordinary growth of market research in the United States during the 1920s and '30s reflected that country's preoccupation with questions of buying and selling. I would suggest that the early and persistent concern of the Scandinavian countries with the study of political behavior reflects the profound commitment of those nations to the pursuit of democratic government.

To my knowledge, the first major publication to appear under the title of "Political Behavior" was that of Herbert Tingsten of the University of Stockholm in 1937. In the thirty years that have ensued, his pioneering lead has been followed throughout Scandinavia—by Westerståhl and Särlvik in Sweden, Rokkan and Valen in Norway, Stehouwer in Denmark, and Allardt in Finland. The present work by Pertti Pesonen clearly falls in this short but distinguished tradition.

Dr. Pesonen's study provides an opportunity to assess the changes in the study of political behavior which have come about over these thirty years as a consequence of the application of the sample survey technique. Tingsten's analysis was based entirely on aggregative data provided by the election statistics of various countries in Europe and elsewhere. Pesonen's data come from a panel survey of a sample of the electorate of Tampere with a small contrasting sample of a rural community. The movement from aggregative to interview data entails substantial scientific gain though it also involves significant loss.

Critics of sample surveys are wont to argue that aggregative data are superior to interview data because they are freer of error—both sampling error and reporting error. There is point to this criticism, of course, but to my mind the great strengths of aggregative data are that they can be broken down to very small geographical units and that, having been systematically collected over decades, they have time depth. Sample surveys will never overcome the first of these disadvantages and even though sample surveys of major elections are now becoming regular, government-supported undertakings in some countries, notably Sweden, it will be some years before these series will permit the analysis of long-term trends.

The analyses which Tingsten reported thirty years ago illustrate very well the distinctive quality of aggregative data. His formulation of "the law of the social center of gravity" is a brilliant example of the imaginative use of data from small electoral districts differing in social class composition. His analysis of the voting of men and women shows the development of the female vote through time following the extension of the franchise in various countries.

In my opinion the advances in aggregative analysis of the vote since Tingsten have been rather disappointing. The number of scholars who have given serious consideration to this type of analysis is quite limited and their analyses seldom go beyond a description of trends. One does not find many attempts to identify and explain regularities or cycles in historical voting data. The reasons for this may be various. Many students of politics do not consider themselves competent to undertake quantitative analysis. In some cases, particularly in the United States, electoral data have been in such chaotic disarray as to discourage inquiry. No doubt the sheer weight of the work involved in the manipulation of highly detailed data has been discouraging. Happily, all of this is now changing. Political scientists and historians are now informing themselves about the methodologies that once were the domain of the psychologist and sociologist. Data archives are developing in numerous university centers. The increasing capacity of electronic computers is making possible the reduction of great volumes of data that would once have seemed beyond comprehension. There is reason to anticipate a substantial leap forward as these new human and mechanical resources are brought to bear on the archives of electoral data that have been accumulating over the years.

Gratifying as these advances may be, the inherent limitations of aggregative data still remain and the independent contribution of sample surveys will be no less important to the understanding of political behavior. The virtuosity of the survey method for the study of the vote is admirably demonstrated in Dr. Pesonen's study of Tampere. In place of the limited array of sorting variables available in aggregative analysis (sex, age, occupation, urban-rural residence), Pesonen has a wealth of information about his respondents, not just about their socioeconomic circumstances, but regarding their political experiences, attitudes, and acts. Most significantly, of course, he has the report of the individual's partisan choice in his vote, which is seldom available except through personal interview. In contrast to some of the early voting studies, which as V. O. Key complained took politics out of the study of the vote, this study is concerned in detail with the essentials of political life in the industrial city in which the survey was taken—the parties, the political press, the candidates, the campaign, the interplay of party loyalties and short-term forces, and the final voting choice.

The importance of Dr. Pesonen's study is not simply in the fact that it provides a full-scale documentation of popular participation in a Finnish election but also in the contribution it makes to a growing number of election studies in the democratic nations of Europe and America. These studies do not merely duplicate each other; each one reflects the unique qualities of the political system in which it is done and the specific interests of the individual researchers. Over the last twenty years, however, there have developed a common methodology and a set of concepts which form a common core in these various studies. As a result a body of data from different national origins is accumulating which holds great promise for comparative analysis. Early attempts to find regularities across national political systems and to assess the influence of differences in political institutions have begun. They should in due course lead to a more sure understanding of the popular vote than we currently possess.

One further word is in order. Although the use of aggregative data for political analysis and the more recently developed survey studies have to this point been carried out almost totally independently of each other, it is now time that these two research traditions come into closer contact. Aggregative data are valuable to the survey researchers both as historical background and to provide additional dimensions to his contemporary analysis; survey data offer new insights to the aggregative researcher for the interpretation of historical trends and regularities. A new level of development in political analysis should emerge from the imaginative exploitation of the opportunities such combinations of data offer.

ANGUS CAMPBELL

Ann Arbor, Michigan
August 1967

Preface

The study of voters seems to be developing in a truly comparative direction; several recent publications exemplify this trend. A good single illustration is the 1967 International Conference on Comparative Electoral Behavior, one of the academic events celebrating the University of Michigan's sesquicentennial year. Scholars from twelve different countries presented and discussed research in progress on their native electorates and found valuable insights for their new comparative efforts.

No place could have been more suitable for assembling such a gathering than the Institute of Social Research in Ann Arbor. Its Survey Research Center has been instrumental in bringing about the current comparative trend for two reasons: the quality of its work and the interest of its personnel in research on and by other countries. Because I had the privilege of analyzing my Finnish data there during a six-month stay in 1962 and an additional two months in 1963, I wish particularly to acknowledge my gratitude for the Center's facilities and inspiring atmosphere.

The phases of any continuous development ought to be categorized with caution. Yet it is obvious that the study of voters falls into three main periods. There were the pre-survey studies on political ecology and turnout; then *The People's Choice* by the Columbia University team had a cumulative aftermath, especially in the United States and Britain, which for some time best symbolized the behavioral approach to political research; and now we have reached the stage of internationalization of electoral research. The third stage builds upon remarkable information, including *The American Voter* from Michigan's Survey Research Center, and also seems to re-emphasize election statistics.

Two books reporting ecological studies of voting behavior appeared in Finland in 1956. An electoral survey of university students, published in 1958, showed reassuring similarity with what was known about the Anglo-Saxon countries. Thus Finnish electoral research was activated during the development's second phase. In 1957 plans were drawn up by the Finnish Political Science Association to organize the country's first research team of political scientists to do a large-scale analysis of the country's elections. Although those hopes proved unrealistic, they did have the indirect effect of helping to get support for starting the smaller project with which this book deals. The Finnish edition appeared in 1965 under the title *Valtuutus kansalta* (A Mandate From the People).

The present version contains revisions and additions, though long passages are translated directly from the Finnish.

The enthusiasm and helpfulness of numerous people made it possible to gather the material for this study. This was very true of the interviewers, mainly municipal social workers and university students. Valuable information was kindly provided by political parties. The surrounding aura of good will is well exemplified by the willingness of three newspapers, *Aamulehti, Hämeen Yhteistyö,* and *Kansan Lehti,* to allow the use of their original 1958 photographs in this book. For the interview data utilized in the secondary analysis I wish to thank the Finnish Gallup Institute and Professor Warren E. Miller of the Survey Research Center.

The actual writing of the book was done mainly at the Institute of Political Science of the University of Helsinki. Professor Jan-Magnus Jansson deserves special thanks for arranging this opportunity. Angus Campbell, director of the Survey Research Center of the University of Michigan, provided unsurpassable hospitality and encouragement during my stays in Ann Arbor. Helpful arrangements were also made in 1962 by Dean Ralph A. Sawyer and Professor Arthur W. Bromage.

Four foreign friends—Professors Campbell, Miller, Philip E. Converse, and Stein Rokkan—kindly read large sections of the manuscript and made fruitful comments. In Finland, Antti Eskola and Onni Rantala also gave helpful criticism.

I have received grants from Suomen Kulttuurirahasto (Finnish Cultural Foundation), Suomalaisen Yhteiskunnan Tuki (Support of the Finnish Society) foundation, and the Chancellor of the University of Helsinki. My two trips abroad were supported by an ASLA grant (U.S. Public Laws 584, 79th Congress, and 265, 81st Congress) and by the Rockefeller Foundation. Large parts of the work I wrote as a research associate with Finland's Social Science Research Council.

I am deeply grateful for the financial support and for the persistent confidence and generous helpfulness on the part of everyone whom I had occasion to bother on behalf of this work. Furthermore, one real reward of all scholarly activity seems to be the resultant cooperation with charming ladies, such as Dr. Veronica Stolte Heiskanen in Finland, who advised me patiently on my English, and Mrs. Jean Savage in New Haven, whose green pencil made admirable touches on the manuscript.

Tampere, Finland
April 1968   PERTTI PESONEN

Contents

List of Tables and Figures

FIGURES

List of Abbreviations

AL	*Aamulehti* (Morning Paper), Conservative daily in Tampere
Agr.	Maalaisliitto (Agrarian Union)
Cons.	Kansallinen Kokoomus (National Coalition, Conservative Party)
FPDU	Suomen Kansan Demokraattinen Liitto, SKDL (Finnish People's Democratic Union)
FPP	Suomen Kansanpuolue (Finnish People's Party)
HS	*Helsingin Sanomat* (Helsinki Telegraph), independent daily in Helsinki
HY	*Hämeen Yhteistyö* (Cooperation of Häme), FPDU paper in Tampere
KL	*Kansan Lehti* (The People's Paper), SDP paper in Tampere
KU	*Kansan Uutiset* (The People's News), main organ of the FPDU and SKP
MK	*Maakansa* (Country People), main organ of the Agrarian Union
S.D.Opp.	Social Democratic Opposition, Independent Social Democratic Electoral Alliance
SDP	Suomen Sosialidemokraattinen Puolue (Finland's Social Democratic Party)
SKP	Suomen Kommunistinen Puolue (Finland's Communist Party)
Swedish	Svenska Folkpartiet (Swedish People's Party)
US	*Uusi Suomi* (New Finland), main organ of the Conservative Party

Symbols:

–	Magnitude nil
0	Magnitude less than half of unit
··	No information, data not available
·	Category not applicable

1. Elections and Political Parties in Finland

THE CONSTITUTION

Two sharp political breaks divide the history of Finland, the wide and sparsely populated northerly country between the East and the West. Having belonged to the realm of Sweden for six centuries, Finland was annexed to her eastern neighbor during the era of Napoleonic wars: Czar Alexander I of Russia was pressured by Napoleon to attack Sweden in 1808, and a year later the Finnish Diet of four estates pledged its loyalty to the Russian Emperor. This union lasted slightly longer than the Imperial House itself, until the October Revolution shook Russia in 1917. The Parliament of Finland declared independence on December 6, 1917. And the country maintained its independence during World War II, when it fought two wars against the Soviet Union and one against Germany.

It would be erroneous to presume that the development of Finland's governmental institutions was radically altered by the dramatic transfers from the West to the East and then to sovereignty. As a matter of fact, the constitutional history of Finland is characterized by a remarkable continuity. The Swedish Instrument of Government of 1772, supplemented by the Act of Union and Security of 1789, was effective in Finland until 1919, or 110 years longer than in Sweden. The republican Form of Government Act of 1919, in turn, is now the only fundamental law that remains and has been applied continuously of all those constitutions adopted in Eastern and Central Europe in the aftermath of the First World War.

The Swedish era rooted Western culture firmly in Finland. The Church of Rome and, since the Reformation, the Lutheran state church have left a marked impact on the country. In 1362 the eastern part of the realm was formally recognized to have equal political rights with other parts of the kingdom. Important principles of Swedish administration and judiciary, which gradually developed thereafter, have endured in modern Finland; thus the framework of the legal system and some actual laws of today date back to when politics were shared with Sweden. The kings coined the rather meaningless name "Grand Duchy of Finland" in the sixteenth century in order to add another item to their royal titles. This designation, however, gained real significance in 1809, when Finland was "elevated to the rank of a nation among nations" with autonomous statehood. The new Grand Duke, the Czar of Russia, promised not to violate the old rights of the Finns, and all questions relating to this protectorate were submitted directly to the Czar rather than through his Russian ministers. A strong national identity developed in Finland during the era of autonomy. It arose out of such factors as the necessity to create rapidly a central administration; the cultural, linguistic, and political national awakening, especially in the 1860s; and, from 1889 onward, the resistance to Russification known as the Struggle for Constitutional Rights.[1]

The present fundamental law of Finland consists of several acts. The two most important are the Form of Government Act of 1919 and the Parliament Act of 1928. The latter follows essentially the Parliament Act of 1906, whereby the traditional diet of four estates voted itself out of existence, thus passing an exceptionally radical reform of political representation. Suffrage was then made universal for citizens of both sexes over 24 years of age, which increased the size of the electorate from an estimated 125,000 to 1,273,000 persons. The number of chambers was decreased from four to one, and proportional representation was made the basis of Finland's electoral system in 1906. After independence and the civil war of 1918, the focal constitutional issue concerned the choice between a royal domain and a republican form of government. In the Parliament elected in 1919 a large majority endorsed the republic.

The Form of Government Act incorporates two seemingly contradictory principles of the distribution of power. Even before that law, the Parliament Act of 1906 was amended during the very first month of independence to make the Cabinet politically responsible to Parliament. Undoubtedly the fifty cabinets which have ruled Finland since

1. For additional historical background the reader is referred to the articles by Eino Jutikkala ("The Road to Independence" and "Between the World Wars") in Urho Toivola, ed., *Introduction to Finland 1960* (Porvoo-Helsinki, Werner Söderström Osakeyhtiö, 1960) and to those by Pentti Renvall ("The Origin of Finland's Autonomy") and Jan-Magnus Jansson ("A Century of Finnish Government") in *Introduction to Finland 1963* (Porvoo-Helsinki, WSOY, 1963). Recent books on Finnish history include Eino Jutikkala and Kauko Pirinen, *A History of Finland* (New York, Frederick A. Praeger, 1962); John H. Wuorinen, *A History of Finland* (New York, Columbia University Press, 1965); and Wuorinen, *Scandinavia* (Englewood Cliffs, Prentice-Hall, 1965). See also articles and the bibliography in *Finnish Foreign Policy* (Helsinki, The Finnish Political Science Association, 1963).

have felt the significance of the parliamentary system of government. But, when the republicans won their struggle over the monarchists in 1919, the head of the state was given significant powers. The election of the President was also stipulated to be independent of Parliament and parliamentary elections. Like the Fifth French Republic, the Finnish government is an example of a mixture of British parliamentarism, on the one hand, and the American presidential system, on the other.

Leaving the judicial branch of government out of consideration, let us briefly summarize the structure and functions of the Parliament, the Presidency, and the Council of Ministers.

The Parliament (in Finnish *eduskunta,* in Swedish *riksdag*) is unicameral and has 200 members. It used to be elected for three years, but since 1954 a four-year term has been instituted. It convenes every year on February 1, without any special summons. The President, also, has the right to summon it as well as the right of dissolution. Actually, the so-called extraordinary sessions have lost their significance, because the effective length of the annual sessions has become about 250 days. Dissolutions, too, are considered the exception rather than the rule, but they remain a real possibility and are sometimes utilized in Finnish politics. There have been 24 elections of the unicameral Parliament (eight between 1907–17, nine between 1919–39, and seven from 1945 to 1966). But officially the different parliaments are recognized annually; one speaks of the 1962, 1963, 1964, and 1965 legislative sessions and never of the 23rd Parliament. The three Speakers are elected and committee posts filled at the beginning of each session, and that is also the time for submitting private member motions. However, the main bulk of legislation and important financial matters are initiated by the government. Normal legislative procedure includes reports from a special committee and from the Grand Committee, which reviews all such reports, plus three stages in plenary meetings, whereas the budget passes through one stage only. Party groups are recognized in the seating arrangement of members and in the opening of important debates, and the principle of proportionalism is followed when committee chairmanships and memberships are filled. The power to amend the constitution rests with Parliament, and no popular initiative or referendum supplements its legislative work.

The President of the Republic is elected for a period of six years by an Electoral College of 300 members. The electors—who are popularly elected in the same way as the members of Parliament—meet on February 15 to elect the President. As a majority is required, the first President, K. J. Ståhlberg (1919–25) later failed to gain reelection with 149 ballots in 1931 and 150 ballots in 1937. Other presidents have been L. Kr. Relander (1925–31), P. E. Svinhufvud (1931–37), Kyösti Kallio (1937–40), Risto Ryti (1940–43, 1943–44), C. G. Mannerheim (1944–46), J. K. Paasikivi (1946–50, 1950–56), and Urho Kekkonen (1956–62, 1962–   ). Thanks to the existence of an emergency procedure for urgent constitutional changes, Parliament has been able to alter the normal electoral method in some of the above elections.

Traditionally the heads of the state have been thought to be above politics. Thus the 1956 election was the first that was preceded by campaign speeches made by all presidential candidates. But the President is a powerful figure. He has the right to dissolve Parliament, to initiate legislation and to approve legislative proposals passed by Parliament or to veto them (to be set aside pending the next parliamentary election), to issue decrees which complement the acts passed by Parliament, to negotiate treaties with foreign powers, and to appoint ministers and all other high-ranking state officials. In the exercise of his executive powers, the President makes his decisions in the presidential council, the weekly meeting of the Council of Ministers over which he presides.

The Council of Ministers, or Cabinet, prepares and executes political decisions. It is led by the Prime Minister and includes the heads of ten ministries. Usually certain ministries also have assistant heads, and there may be ministers without portfolio, but the total number of ministers may not exceed fifteen. The Cabinet is in a tricky position between the President and Parliament. Conflicts with the President have sometimes led to its resignation, and it falls automatically if lack of confidence is voted in Parliament. A vote of confidence is not taken in connection with its appointment, but such a vote follows an interpellation (to be signed by at least twenty members of Parliament) and is possible when the annual report of the government is considered or when the Cabinet asks for it. Because they are based on party coalitions, many cabinets have resigned because of internal difficulties. The ministers carry both legal and political responsibility for their participation in the President's official acts, as well as for other official activity of their own. The decisions of the Council of Ministers are made in plenary meetings presided over by the Prime Minister (separate from its meetings as the presidential council), and considerable decision making has been delegated to individual ministers or to nonpolitical government officials.[2]

2. More comprehensive descriptions of Finnish governmental institutions and constitu-

The Cabinet submits its resignation after presidential or parliamentary elections, and the political composition of the legislature naturally establishes the parliamentary basis of government coalitions for its electoral period. In theoretical discussions concerning the representative role of legislators there are two opposing views, one preferring "instructed delegates" and the other stressing "the interest of the whole." The Parliament Act of Finland defines the latter stand and stipulates that "every Member of the Parliament is obliged to act according to justice and truth in the exercise of his mandate. He should observe the Constitutional Laws and is not bound by any other instructions." As might be expected under the system of proportional representation, Finns often speak about the just and accurate representation of all prevailing opinions—which obviously does not quite concur with the Burkean idea of the interest of the whole—while references to actual decision making and to majority rule are rare. The Finnish name of the legislature, *eduskunta,* is difficult to translate literally, but a "representative body" or a "unit acting on behalf" are close English approximations; whereas the word for a member, *kansanedustaja,* is definitely "the people's representative." Generally, one might find in the political culture of Finland some inherited tendency to approach the executive branch and its officials with solemn respect. But elections of the unicameral Parliament, which institution was created in 1906 largely to safeguard national interests and to advance popular requests against Russian claims, remain the central device to effect the rule of the people in Finland.

THE CONSTITUENCIES

Article 4 of the Parliament Act phrases the broad principles of Finland's electoral system as follows:

> Members of Parliament are elected by direct and proportional suffrage; for these elections the country shall be divided into electoral districts numbering a minimum of twelve and a maximum of eighteen.
> When local circumstances necessitate an exception to the propor-

tional law include Nils Andrén, *Government and Politics in the Nordic Countries* (Stockholm, Almqvist & Wiksell, 1964), pp. 63–90; *Democracy in Finland* (Helsinki, The Finnish Political Science Association, 1960); Paavo Kastari, *La Présidense de la République en Finlande* (Neuchatel, Editions de la Baconnière, 1962); Veli Merikoski, *Précis du droit public de la Finlande* (Helsinki, Suomalaisen lakimiesyhdistyksen julkaisuja D:1, 1954); and *The Finnish Parliament* (Helsinki, Suomen Eduskunta, 1957).

tional procedure, one or several districts, besides the number indicated above, can be established for the purpose of electing a single
Member of Parliament.

At elections every elector shall have the same right to vote.

The right to vote cannot be exercised by proxy.

Detailed provisions relative to districts, to dates, and to the procedure of elections shall be given by special law.[3]

Furthermore, the voting age was lowered to 21 in 1944, and all electors
are eligible for election to Parliament except those who are in active military service and the chief judges of the country.

The electoral districts, here referred to as constituencies, have numbered fifteen or sixteen in all elections. "Local circumstances" have necessitated only two single-member constituencies. The country's most northerly communes formed the one-member Lapland constituency from 1907
to 1936, and the Aaland island and archipelago has been a single-member
constituency since 1948. In general, the Election Act has aimed at dis-
tricting the country into geographically functional units. It requires that
"a city and borough belong to the same constituency as its surrounding
rural area." However, in 1952 the capital was separated from its province
(Nyland) by an act obviously justified by the steady growth of Helsinki
and its surroundings. In general, constituency boundaries have followed
those of administrative provinces; a desire to avoid unnaturally hetero-
geneous constituencies or large differences in size has caused the division
of some provinces into two and sometimes three parts. At present, Nyland, Turku, and Häme are the only administrative provinces which
form two multimember constituencies; nine other constituencies are as
such identical with administrative provinces. Thus the total number is
fifteen (since the 1962 election and from 1939 to 1951); between 1907-36
and in 1954-58 there were sixteen constituencies.

The constitutional provision that there shall be "a minimum of twelve
and a maximum of eighteen" multimember constituencies signified originally a compromise between two conflicting points of view. An emphasis
on maximum proportionality would have required that the whole country be one single constituency, while a strong emphasis on local representation called for small constituencies, each electing only three members. Constituencies returning approximately twelve to twenty-one members were finally allowed in order to avoid "excessive centralization" and

3. The translation is quoted from *Constitution Act and Parliament Act of Finland*
(Helsinki, Ministry of Foreign Affairs, 1959), p. 30.

to guarantee relatively good proportionality in representation.[4] For example, in 1958 the smallest multimember constituency (Northern Vaasa) elected eight and the largest (Helsinki) nineteen members to Parliament. In the 1966 election the range was from nine (North Karelia) to twenty-one (Helsinki).

The government allocates the 200 seats among the constituencies before each election. This is done strictly in proportion to their population. But actually, because of local differences in the structure of families, the procedure violates slightly the principle of equal suffrage. In 1958 there were 15,160 enfranchized inhabitants per one representative in Helsinki but only 11,230 electors per one representative in Eastern Kuopio (the present North Karelia) constituency. In Northern Häme, with which this study mainly deals, the number was 13,908. On the other hand, because there is no residence requirement for the candidates, Helsinki has been actually overrepresented in the Finnish Parliament. Only 6.0 per cent of the population lived in Helsinki in 1930, but 23.0 per cent of the 1,800 members elected between 1919 and 1939 were residents of the capital. Yet most Helsinki representatives had been born elsewhere, and often political activity had caused their migration. Of the same 1,800 members, a total of 343 (or 19 per cent) came originally from an outside constituency.[5]

The Finnish "returning officer" is the constituency's central election board, a five-member body appointed partly by the government and partly by the municipal council of the city where the board holds its meetings. There are also local election boards, which are responsible for administering the polling in their so-called voting districts. Their number was 4,983 in 1958 (see Table 3.1). Such districts had on the average 520 enfranchised inhabitants, 1,790 in urban but only 360 in rural communes.

THE ELECTORAL SYSTEM AND VOTING PROCEDURE

Finland has adopted Victor d'Hondt's method of proportional representation according to the highest average. Because it is applied separately in each constituency there is no way to utilize surplus votes on a multi-constituency or national level. Within the constituency, the votes cast for each "electoral alliance" are divided by 1, 2, 3, etc., and the quotients

---

4. *Eduskunnan uudistuskomitean mietintö* (Report of the Commission for Parliament Reform) (Helsinki, 1906), pp. 64, 118, 125.

5. Martti Noponen, *Kansanedustajien sosiaalinen tausta Suomessa* (The Social Background of the Members of Parliament in Finland) (Porvoo-Helsinki, WSOY, 1964), pp. 206, 231.

rank-ordered until the constituency's seats have been distributed. In other words, the proportional distribution of seats is indicated by the dividers (1, 2, 3, etc.) which give the average number of votes needed for one seat by each electoral alliance. Partly because Finnish legislation does not recognize political parties, the Election Act refers to electoral alliances and not to parties. The number of candidates that each party is allowed to nominate—or formally the maximum number of lists of candidate that are allowed to be grouped in one electoral alliance—equals the number of seats to be filled in the constituency.

TABLE 1.1. Calculations for Distribution of 13 Parliamentary Seats among the Parties in Northern Häme Constituency in 1954

Parties	\multicolumn{6}{c}{Votes divided by}	Seats
	1	2	3	4	5	6	
Finnish People's Democratic Union	39,189*	19,594*	13,063*	9,979*	7,837	6,531	4
Social Democratic Party	45,864*	22,932*	15,288*	11,466*	9,172*	7,644	5
Agrarian Union	16,396*	8,198	5,132	4,099	3,279	2,732	1
Finnish People's Party	11,216*	5,608	3,738	2,804	2,243	1,869	1
Conservatives	25,363*	12,681*	8,454	6,340	5,072	4,227	2
Total	138,029						13

* Quotient elects a member.

Let us quote the election results of Northern Häme constituency in 1954 in order to illustrate how proportionality is achieved in practice. This constituency was entitled to elect thirteen representatives, and five parties nominated candidates there. Table 1.1 shows that the Social Democratic Party gained five, the Communist FPDU four, and the Conservatives two seats; the Agrarian Union and the Finnish People's Party each got one seat. We might continue the calculations and speculate that had there been a fourteenth seat it would have gone to the Conservatives with an average of $25,363/3 = 8,454$; the fifteenth in order would have been the Agrarians ($16,396/2 = 8,198$), followed by the FPDU ($39,189/5 = 7,837$), the Social Democrats ($45,864/6 = 7,644$), etc.

As was mentioned above, in Finnish legal terminology one speaks of electoral alliances rather than of parties. Occasionally groups which have been unknown in politics form such alliances, and it often happens that two or more political parties unite to form a joint alliance in some constituency. It is true that such cooperation decreases radically their total number of nominees, but on the other hand it may serve as an advantageous safeguard against the tendency of d'Hondt's method to favor large parties. In our example, the three small parties would have gained jointly a fifth seat from the Social Democrats (with the average 52,-975/5 = 10,595), and even the two-party coalition of Agrarians and Finnish People's Party would have utilized enough surplus votes to capture the "last seat" of the constituency (with the average 27,612/3 = 9,204). Calculations of this kind are naturally somewhat unrealistic because one does not take into account eventual voter reactions—either positive or negative—to parties' cooperating in joint electoral alliances. However, we can safely conclude that this type of cooperation may influence the distribution of seats considerably.

Let us illustrate the possibilities with the success of the Social Democratic Opposition (League) in 1966. In 1962 this party ran alone in all constituencies and received 100,000 votes. This would have meant eight seats if the whole country were one single constituency, but in reality the "threshold" for one seat was passed in only two constituencies. Then the party began to cooperate with the Communists and placed its candidate with the FPDU electoral alliance in each constituency. The small party now gained seven seats with the national total of only 62,000 votes. The Finnish People's Party, in turn, would have obtained eight seats alone in 1962, but collected five more through coalitions which it had formed with either the Agrarians or the Conservatives.

It is seldom possible to forecast which party in a joint electoral alliance is going to benefit most. But a far more important aspect of the Finnish system is that one cannot even guarantee the election to Parliament of any individual candidate. This is a marked difference from typical list systems of proportional representation. Finland's unique feature is the simple fact that, although votes are first counted for the parties (electoral alliances) as a whole, each ballot is cast for just one individual candidate. In the case of the example given in Table 1.1, all five parties had nominated the maximum number (thirteen) allowed in the constituency. Thus a voter had 65 individual nominees (formally, lists of candidate) to choose from, each signified with a number (from 2 to 66). His task was to write any one of these numbers inside a printed circle on a small ballot paper, to fold the paper, get it stamped, and drop it into the ballot box. The votes thus cast for the numbered candidates first indicated how many votes each electoral alliance had received, as was shown in Table 1.1. After the count had established how many seats each alliance won in the constituency, the votes further determined which individual candidates filled the seats and who became the "vice-members." Thus, in Finland, the electorate solves those intraparty contests for the ranking of nominees that the nominating conventions decide in most applications of the list system of proportional representation. It is true that many countries permit voters to change the order of candidates whose names are printed in the party list, but in most cases this right has little practical significance. The Finnish voter is also permitted to write any other name on the ballot, if none of the nominees appeal to him, but such votes are as a rule very few and therefore wasted; only 20 "write-in ballots" need to be added to our Table 1.1.

The formal procedure of nominations is simple. A candidate's name will appear on the final combination of the lists of candidate if at least 30 electors of the constituency form an electors' association, signing the statement that they have decided to unite in order to support the election of their candidate. One such association can propose only one candidate (since 1954); therefore the term list might sound confusing.[6] The electors' associations may further announce their joining with other associations to form an electoral alliance under a given title. There are sometimes candidates (lists) outside the alliances, but no such "wild" candidate has ever gained election to Parliament. In fact parliamentary candidates are nominated mainly by the district organizations of political parties. This is a private party affair without public control or regulation. It is also possible, although not very common, to nominate the same person in several constituencies. If he happens to be elected in more than one constituency, he will be declared a representative of that constituency where he has the highest "comparison number" (party vote divided by the ranking of the candidate within the electoral alliance). A government commission on electoral reform recommended in 1964 that a person not be nominated in more than one constituency, but this did not lead to immediate legislative action. Sometimes parties nominate their candidates

6. Until 1935, an electors' association could announce a list of candidates with either one, two, or three names. Separate announcements by each electors' association grouped the lists into electoral alliances which corresponded to the party lists in list systems of proportional representation. The Election Act of 1935 permitted no more than two candidates' names on one list, and in 1954 one-person lists became compulsory. Because the term "list" was not abandoned, legal terminology now uses the seemingly inconsistent concept, "list of candidate."

quite early, which they are free to do, but the deadline is only six weeks before an election. The lists of candidate are submitted to the central election board 40 days prior to the election.

The beginning of July has been traditionally the time for regular parliamentary elections in Finland; the elections of the College of Presidential Electors take place in January; October is the month of local elections for setting up the municipal councils for a period of four years. However, the Election Act was changed in December 1965, to the effect that parliamentary elections henceforth take place on the third Sunday and Monday in March rather than at the beginning of July. If Parliament is dissolved, elections are administered on the first Sunday and the following Monday of that month which begins 60 days after the dissolution's promulgation. All elections are held over two days, in order to facilitate participation and insure a high turnout. Automatic registration of electors serves the same purpose. Proxy voting is not allowed, but absentee ballots ("excerpts from the register of electors") can be obtained in advance from local election boards to be used on voting days at any polling station—and since 1956, also abroad and in hospitals.[7]

Polling stations are open for nineteen hours: on Sunday from noon until 8 P.M. and on Monday from 9 A.M. to 8 P.M. The ballots are counted locally soon after the voting ends, and national election returns may be summarized roughly by midnight. However, the final responsibility of counting the votes is vested in the central election boards, which control the local count and also receive, before counting, all absentee ballots from other constituencies. Often such absentee ballots decide a constituency's "last seat" and, furthermore, are significant in the intraparty contests between candidates. Consequently, the counting of votes keeps the press in suspense for several days, although preliminary election results are known on Tuesday.

We have mentioned above numerous aspects of the laws that have been adopted in order to make voting easier. Moreover, participation in elections is often called a "citizen's duty" in Finland, not only by private organizations and the press, but also by public officials. Recent turnout figures, too, prove that the prevailing norm favors participation. An amazingly high percentage of the newly enfranchised electorate (70.7) turned out in 1907. Participation did go down rapidly (to 51.1 per cent

7. For a more detailed description of the system, see Klaus Törnudd, *The Electoral System of Finland* (Helsinki, Institute of Political Science of the University of Helsinki, 1966, mimeo.). See also Jansson, "Post-War Elections in Finland," *Bank of Finland Monthly Bulletin, 36* (April 1962), 22–27.

TABLE 1.2.   Parliamentary Elections in Finland from 1936 to 1966

| | | S.D. | | | | | Swed- | | |
	FPDU	Opp.	SDP	Agr.	FPP	Cons.	ish	Others*	Total
Votes (in thousands)									
1936	·	·	453	263	74	123	131	131	1173
1939	·	·	516	297	62	176	125	121	1297
1945	399	·	426	363	88	255	134	34	1698
1948	376	·	495	456	73	320	144	16	1880
1951	391	·	481	422	103	264	137	15	1813
1954	434	·	527	484	158	257	140	8	2008
1958	451	34	450	448	115	297	131	19	1944
1962	507	100	449	528	137	347	148	86	2302
1966	503	61	645	503	153	327	142	36	2370
Vote (in per cent)									
1936	·	·	38.6	22.4	6.3	10.4	11.2	11.1	100.0
1939	·	·	39.8	22.9	4.8	13.6	9.6	9.3	100.0
1945	23.5	·	25.1	21.3	5.2	15.0	7.9	2.0	100.0
1948	20.0	·	26.3	24.2	3.9	17.1	7.7	0.8	100.0
1951	21.6	·	26.5	23.2	5.7	14.6	7.6	0.8	100.0
1954	21.6	·	26.2	24.1	7.9	12.8	7.0	0.4	100.0
1958	23.2	1.7	23.2	23.1	5.9	15.3	6.7	0.9	100.0
1962	22.0	4.4	19.5	23.0	5.9	15.0	6.8	3.8	100.0
1966	21.2	2.6	27.2	21.2	6.5	13.8	6.0	1.5	100.0
Elected Members									
1936	·	·	83	53	7	20	21	16	200
1939	·	·	85	56	6	25	18	10	200
1945	49	·	50	49	9	28	14	1	200
1948	38	·	54	56	5	33	14	–	200
1951	43	·	53	51	10	28	15	–	200
1954	43	·	54	53	13	24	13	–	200
1958	50	3	48	48	8	29	14	–	200
1962	47	2	38	53	13	32	14	1	200
1966	41	7	55	49	9	26	12	1	200

FPDU   =   The Finnish People's Democratic Union (1944–), in-
                     cludes the Finnish Communist Party (SKP, 1918–).

S.D.Opp.   =   The Social Democratic Opposition (1958), the Social
                     Democratic League of Labor and Small Farmers (1959–).

SDP   =   The Social Democratic Party of Finland (1899–, 1903–).

Agr.   =   The Agrarian Union (1906–65), the Center Party (1965–).

FPP   =   The Finnish People's Party (1951–65), the National

in 1913), but from then on it varied: for example, in the 1930s between 62.2 and 66.6 per cent; a new high was reached in 1945 with the turnout of 74.9 per cent; in 1954, 79.9 per cent of the electorate voted and the record, achieved in 1962, is now 85.1 per cent.

Finland does not have by-elections. Those candidates in each electoral alliance whose personal votes rank next to the elected ones are declared vice-members. Should a permanent vacancy occur, the vice-member becomes a legislator. In the "long Parliament" of 1939–44 there were twenty-four replacements: seventeen members died before 1945 and seven resigned.[8] A resignation for any other reason than loss of eligibility must be approved by Parliament.

THE SYSTEM OF MULTIPLE PARTIES

As one would expect, where proportional representation is practiced, Finland has numerous political parties. Many features of the Finnish multiparty system are unique, but scholars also stress the mutual resemblance of the Scandinavian countries. According to one Finnish author: "it is justifiable to speak of a special Nordic party system. This system is characterized by the fact that at least five parties are represented in the popular assembly," namely: (1) the extreme left; (2) the workers' parties representing moderate socialism; (3) the party formed of farmers and country dwellers; (4) the bourgeois center party which aspires to represent a kind of liberalism; and (5) the bourgeois right, the upholders of conservatism and national tradition.[9]

Table 1.2 presents the spectrum of Finland's multiple parties. It summarizes the results of all parliamentary elections since World War II and for comparison the last two elections during the 1930s. The seven

8. Noponen, *Social Background*, p. 293.

9. Göran von Bonsdorff, "The Party Situation in Finland," *Democracy in Finland*, pp. 18–19; see also Wuorinen, *Scandinavia*, p. 56.

	Progressive Party (1918–51), and the Liberal People's Party (1965–).
Cons.	=	The National Coalition (Conservative Party, 1918–).
Swedish	=	The Swedish People's Party (1906–).

* The Patriotic People's Movement (98,000 votes and 14 seats in 1936, 86,000 and 8 in 1939); the Small Farmers' Party (23,000 votes and one seat in 1936, 28,000 and 2 in 1939); the Swedish Left Wing (8,200 votes and one seat in 1945); the Liberal League (12,000 votes and one seat in 1962); the Smallholders' Party (1959–) (50,000 votes in 1962, 23,000 votes and one seat in 1966), etc.

major parties are the following, in the order they are seated in the parliament from left to right:

The Finnish People's Democratic Union, or FPDU, has occupied the extreme left since 1945. Its Finnish name, *Suomen kansan demokraattinen liitto,* is ordinarily used in the abbreviated form SKDL even in many English texts. This group refuses to be called a political party but wants to be known as an organization for cooperation. When it entered the scene in October 1944, its name actually introduced an important international catchword of the late 1940s, "people's democracy," signifying a "peaceful" road to communism. Its dominating nucleus, the Finnish Communist Party (*Suomen Kommunistinen Puolue,* SKP), was founded in Moscow in August 1918, by Red leaders who had fled east after the lost civil war. In the 1920s the communist movement participated under various names in Finnish elections, and its success ranged from 14.8 per cent of the vote and 27 seats in 1922 to 10.4 per cent and 18 seats in 1924.[10] Communist activity was outlawed in 1930 and thus forced completely underground. The first result of the newly founded FPDU was quite impressive: 23.5 per cent of the vote and 49 seats in Parliament. A serious repercussion was suffered in 1948 with 20.0 per cent of the vote; since then the popular support of the FPDU seems to have stabilized between 23.2 per cent (in 1958) and 21.2 per cent (in 1966).

The Social Democratic League of Workers and Smallholders is the product of a split in the Social Democratic Party. The opposition wing of the party ran separate slates in four constituencies as "Independent Social Democrats" in 1958, and after the election its new Parliament group of three members was joined by eleven Social Democrats from other constituencies. The party was then founded in 1959 and became rather influential in trade unions; but in the election of 1962 it failed badly, and the party is likely to be shortlived, despite the fact that in 1966 it obtained seven seats with the assistance of Communist votes (see p. 9).

10. A careful history of the first decade of the SKP has been recently published in Finnish: Ilkka Hakalehto, *SKP ja sen vaikutus poliittiseen ja ammatilliseen työväenliikkeeseen 1918–1928* (SKP and Its Influence on Political and Union Labor Movement) (Porvoo-Helsinki, WSOY, 1966). See also James H. Billington, "Finland," in Cyril E. Black and Thomas P. Thornton, eds., *Communism and Revolution* (Princeton, Princeton University Press, 1964), pp. 117–44; Erik Allardt, "Social Sources of Finnish Communism: Traditional and Emerging Radicalism," *International Journal of Comparative Sociology, 5* (1964), 49–72; and John H. Hodgson, *Communism in Finland: A History and Interpretation* (Princeton, Princeton University Press, 1967).

The Social Democratic Party of Finland (*Suomen Sosialidemokraattinen Puolue*, SDP) was founded in 1899 and adopted its present name in 1903. It became the first modern mass party in Finland and won an unexpected 80 seats in the first unicameral Parliament. For nine years its popular vote increased gradually (from 37.0 to 47.3 per cent) to give it in 1916 the only majority (103 seats) ever held by one party in the Finnish Parliament. After the civil war the party accepted Finland's independence and democratic institutions, thus becoming a major opponent of the Communists; in 1919 it again did better than expected and won 80 seats (with 38.0 per cent of the ballots). It was handicapped in the 1920s by Communist competition for the labor vote (only 25.1 per cent and 53 seats in 1922), but rose up to 39.8 per cent of the votes cast in 1939. Against even stronger leftist competition since 1945, the Social Democrats gained between 25.1 per cent (in 1945) and 26.5 per cent (in 1951), until opposition within the party became an additional nuisance in 1958. Another recovery of the SDP was recorded in 1966 when the party received 27.2 per cent of the popular vote.

The Agrarian Union (*Maalaisliitto*) was founded in 1906 and united with a parallel group in 1908. Its beginning was modest, only 5.8 per cent of the votes and nine seats in 1907, but in 1919 it entered the ranks of large parties by winning 19.7 per cent of the vote and 42 seats. It has been the largest nonsocialist party ever since. Its relatively best showings were in 1929 (26.1 per cent of the vote, 60 seats) and in 1930 (27.3 per cent), but it received 24.1 per cent as late as 1954 and 23.0 per cent in 1962. That was the last parliamentary election in which the party participated under the old name. In October 1965, it followed the example set earlier by its counterparts in Sweden and Norway and changed its name to Center Party (*Keskustapuolue*). It carried 21.2 per cent of the vote in 1966 even though it failed to get any of the city vote in that election.

The Finnish People's Party (*Suomen kansanpuolue*) took part in only four elections, those between 1951–62, but it must be considered as one link in a longer chain of parties. The Young Finnish Party emerged in the 1890s as a kind of liberal party. It held from 23 to 29 seats in the unicameral Parliament; the National Progressive Party (*Kansallinen edistyspuolue*) was founded in December 1918 to a large extent as its successor. The Progressives received 12.8 per cent of the vote and 26 seats in 1919, but their support decreased to 3.9 per cent in 1948. The Finnish People's Party, in turn, succeeded the Progressives in 1951 and was able to collect 7.9 per cent of the ballots in 1954. The party was dissolved in October 1965, and on the same day its members joined with those of the Liberal League (another successor of the Progressives) to start the Liberal People's Party (*Liberaalinen kansanpuolue*). This carried 6.5 per cent of the votes cast in 1966.

The National Coalition (*Kansallinen kokoomus*) is Finland's conservative party. It, too, was founded in December 1918 and continued to a large extent the work of the Old Finnish Party. The Old Finns met with success in the 1907 election (27.3 per cent and 59 seats), but lost ground rapidly during the Russian era (17.6 per cent and 33 seats in 1916). Conservative support has since remained on or below the last-mentioned level. In 1936 the Conservatives received only 10.4 per cent because of competition with an extreme right wing, the Patriotic People's Movement. Since World War II the Conservative ups and downs have been almost inverse to those of the Finnish People's Party: the party had 17.1 per cent of the votes in 1948 but only 12.8 per cent in 1954.

The Swedish People's Party (in Swedish, *Svenska folkpartiet*) was founded in May 1906. It replaced the Swedish Party which had been inspired in the 1870s by the Finnish Party, active since the 1860s. It held from 21 to 26 seats during the Russian era and as late as 1922 gained a Parliament group of 25 members. For two decades following World War II its representation had been stabilized at fourteen seats, until a further loss of two seats in 1966. Its relative share of the popular vote (record was 13.5 per cent in 1910) has decreased gradually, and since 1936 (11.2 per cent) with consistent regularity from one election to the next (lowering to 6.4 per cent in 1962 and 6.0 per cent in 1966).[11] Because Finland's Swedish-speaking population is concentrated mainly around the southern and western coasts, the Swedish People's Party sets up electoral alliances in only four constituencies (Helsinki, Nyland, Southern Turku, and Vaasa). It can also rely on the fact that the only member from Aaland joins its Parliament group.

In contrast, the support of other major parties is not equally localized, and they have run in each multimember constituency. However, even their fortunes are unevenly distributed throughout the country. The FPDU, the SDP, and the Conservatives did gain at least some representation

11. Accounts of Finland's political parties include, for example, Andrén, *Government and Politics*, pp. 82–90; von Bonsdorff, *Democracy in Finland;* Jaakko Nousiainen, "The Structure of the Finnish Political Parties," *Democracy in Finland*, pp. 28–43; Marvin Rintala, *Three Generations: The Extreme Right Wing in Finnish Politics* (Bloomington, Indiana University, 1962); and Wuorinen, *A History of Finland*, pp. 236–52, 418–36.

in all constituencies in 1958, but in 1962 the Social Democrats lost their only seat in Lapland, and in 1966 the Conservatives had a similar loss in that constituency in the northern and eastern sections of Finland where the situation is reminiscent of a Communist-Agrarian, two-party system. In the capital, Helsinki, the Agrarians have never gained representation, not even in 1966 when the party made considerable efforts under its new name to get a candidate elected there. This illustrates the rural base of Agrarian support; in 1958 it received 36.3 per cent of the votes in rural areas but only 1.6 per cent in the cities.

To return to the Scandinavian analogy, we notice at least four considerable peculiarities in the Finnish system. (1) The Communists, or the FPDU, receive an exceptionally large share of the votes in Finland, which makes Finland—together with Italy and France—one of the three European democracies where the Communists poll about a quarter or a fifth of all votes. (2) The Social Democratic Party has never gained a dominant position comparable to that of *Socialdemokratiska arbetarparti* in Sweden or *Arbeiderpartiet* in Norway, or even to the *Socialdemokratiet* in Denmark. Therefore labor parties as a whole have been weaker in Finland than in Scandinavia; the election of 1966 gave the combined socialist parties their first majority (51.1 per cent) of the popular vote. (3) The Agrarians have maintained an exceptionally strong position in Finland despite the country's industrialization and urbanization which, to be sure, was slower in starting than in other Scandinavian countries. (4) The Swedish People's Party adds to the Finnish system a politically organized ethnic element which has no counterpart in the other countries, as Finland is the only officially bilingual Nordic country and equal rights for the Swedish minority are protected by the constitution.

The gain of the Social Democratic Party from 19.5 per cent of the votes cast in 1962 to 27.2 per cent in 1966 was a landslide by Finnish standards. Ordinarily, the overall distribution of the popular vote among the parties changes little from one election to another. Many examples might be given to illustrate this tendency toward stability. Thus in the nine elections from 1919 to 1939 the leftist vote (SDP alone or with the Communists) varied between 37 and 42 per cent; in the six elections from 1945 to 1962 the variation was between 46 and 49 per cent. In the latter six elections, the Conservatives and Progressives (or Finnish People's Party) polled together 20 or 21 per cent.

Let us not forget, however, that there have been four kinds of net changes in the distribution of party vote in Finland:

1. One does find genuine electoral victories in repeated contests between established competitors, and some surges have been followed by such counterswings as the Communist defeat in 1948 and the comeback of the Social Democrats in 1966.

2. Changes in the party system have caused reorientations among the electorate. It was possible to vote for the Communists in the 1920s, and again after 1945, but not in the 1930s. On the nonsocialist side, two new parties were founded in 1918, and the Progressives added fresh followers in 1951 and again in 1965. An extreme right wing was active in the 1930s. The Agrarians changed their name in 1965, etc.

3. Occasional "flash movements" have resulted in rather brief support for new parties. These are exemplified by the 8.3 per cent vote for the Patriotic People's Movement in 1936 and the 2.2 per cent received by the Smallholders' party in 1962.

4. Some consistent trends have extended over long periods of time. These include the steady growth of the Agrarian Union from 1907 to 1930, the decline of the National Progressive Party, and the decrease in the votes cast for the Swedish People's Party since 1936.

The role played by different parties in the Finnish governments is not directly related to their parliamentary strength. First of all, none of the eight presidents of the Republic has represented the left: two were Progressives (Ståhlberg, Ryti); three Agrarians (Relander, Kallio, Kekkonen); and two Conservatives (Svinhufvud, Paasikivi); whereas one (Mannerheim) had a nonpartisan background when he undertook this position "above the parties." Furthermore, during two considerable periods socialist parties have also been excluded from Cabinet coalitions. The first one lasted until the twentieth year of independence. After the civil war there was one homogeneous Social Democratic minority cabinet led by Väinö Tanner in 1926–27—causing bitter internal debates about "minister socialism" within the socialist ranks—and the Social Democratic Party was accepted in Cabinet coalitions for the first time in 1937. Since then many coalitions have depended on the "red ocher" cooperation of the Social Democrats and the Agrarians. The second period of exclusion affected the Communists for an 18-year period. The FPDU was represented in three cabinets from 1914 to 1948 but thereafter was not considered "ministrable" until it was able to get three of its ministers in the majority government formed after the election of 1966. The Conservatives have played at times an important part in the cabinets, but after

World War II they actually have become fully "acceptable" only since 1958. The Progressives were a much more important government party than their meager parliamentary basis would indicate, as they held eight of the twenty-two prime ministerships between 1919 and 1943 (with six of the fourteen different persons who then were prime ministers). The Agrarian Union has had the best tactical position in government negotiations, and it has been a partner in almost all coalition cabinets. Soon after President Kekkonen took office in 1956 the Agrarians became unquestionably the dominating party in Finnish politics for almost ten years, either leading coalition cabinets or—between 1959 and 1961—ruling the country by two minority governments of their own.

The Political Situation in 1958

The present study analyzes the parliamentary election that took place in Tampere, Finland's second largest city, on July 6 and 7, 1958. For its background it seems useful to describe more closely some aspects of the general situation which prevailed in Finnish politics immediately preceding that election.

The Parliament elected in March 1954 for a term of three years decided to represent the Finnish people for four years.[12] At the end of the lengthened term the country was in unusually serious political and economic difficulties. Thus, from May 1, 1957, till May 1, 1958, Finland had four prime ministers, and the Cabinet had a total of six different compositions. There had never been such frequent Cabinet changes, except at the beginning of independence and at the end of World War II in 1944–45.

The economic growth of Finland had slowed down. The total national production was in 1957 only one per cent greater than in 1956, although the corresponding growth of the previous year had been 2 per cent, in spite of the general strike in March 1956 (the growth in 1954 and 1955 had been 10 and 6 per cent respectively). Lack of demand became a handicap in the middle of 1957, in such industries as leather, rubber, food, and textiles. The Bank of Finland conducted from the beginning of the year strict money and loan policies in order to prepare for a devaluation, which came into effect on September 15, 1957. The first half of 1958 saw

12. Law on changing Article 3 of the Parliament Act. This law was ratified by the new Parliament in 1954 by a two-thirds majority, as required of constitutional legislation. It was passed originally in 1953.

an industrial production 20 per cent lower than the first half of 1957, and economic activity as a whole was 5 per cent lower than it had been during the corresponding period of the previous year.[13]

The economic difficulties meant fewer working possibilities. At the beginning of 1958, there were 12,700 persons unemployed, or 7,300 more than in the previous year; and the total of unemployed plus persons in employment relief works was 53,700, or 15,400 more than in the beginning of 1957. At the end of March the number actually unemployed was smaller, but by then there were already over 78,000 registered unemployed. After that employment increased so slowly that even at the end of June the unemployment registers included more than 20,000 names, or 16,000 more than in 1957.[14] An additional difficulty was created by forced vacations and shorter working weeks. For instance, a four-day week adopted by a textile factory in Tampere on January 26 affected almost 2,500 workers.[15]

Temporary insolvency caused periods of lawlessness in 1957, when the state was unable to fulfill all its fiscal obligations due on time. By the end of 1957 all the regular payments had been taken care of, but on January 10, 1958, the Ministry of Finance again ordered the fiscal offices to stop some payments. Because of the devaluation, the budget proposal was not submitted to Parliament until the beginning of October, and the 1958 budget was not completed by Parliament until January 22. The Cabinet had also prepared in January a program to cut down state expenditures. Only a small part of this was accepted by Parliament. On January 21, it was voted to hold the bills included in the government program until after the election, and Parliament recessed for vacation on January 23.

As mentioned above, the history of the Cabinet coalitions entered upon a new era in 1957. After the postwar cooperation of the three large parties in 1944–48 and the period of minority cabinets until 1951, Cabinet coalition had been based on the cooperation of the Agrarian Union and the Social Democratic Party. To this period also belonged the second Cabinet of Prime Minister K.-A. Fagerholm, which was in power during the first fifteen months of President Urho Kekkonen's term. The appointment of

13. Erkki Laatto, "Suomen taloudellinen kehitys 1.7.1956–30.6.1957" (The Development of Finland's Economy between July 1, 1956, and June 30, 1957), *Mitä Missä Milloin 1958* (Helsinki, Otava, 1957), pp. 220–27, and Laatto, "Suomen taloudellinen kehitys 1.1.1957–30.6.1958," *Mitä Missä Milloin 1959* (Helsinki, Otava, 1958), pp. 205–12.

14. *Tilastokatsauksia* (Statistical Review), XXXIII (1958), Nos. 7 and 8, Table 41.

15. *Kansan Uutiset,* Jan. 14, 1958, p. 12.

the first Cabinet of Dr. V. J. Sukselainen on May 27, 1957, was the beginning of the next period, which has been called the era of Agrarian leadership.[16]

In the first part of September 1957, the President replaced six resigned ministers; certain other ministers changed portfolios as well. An interpellation signed by 31 Social Democrats, which criticized the manner of the formation of the Cabinet and its "groping work," brought about on October 12 a vote of lack of confidence in the Sukselainen Cabinet, then already in its third form. The Social Democrats were irritated because five party members had joined the Cabinet against party rules. These had belonged to the minority of the 1957 party convention. After a long Cabinet crisis an expert Cabinet, selected from outside Parliament and headed by Rainer von Fieandt, was appointed on November 29. After this had failed as a result of the interpellations of the Social Democrats and the Agrarians—which dealt with the decision of the Cabinet to cancel the two-price system of cereal—on April 26, 1958, the President appointed the political or election time expert Cabinet of Reino Kuuskoski.

The approaching election began to overshadow political discussion during this spring term. The interpellation by the Communists in February was still considered by others as a propaganda move, but the discussion in Parliament—which led to the lack of confidence vote in April and in which 89 members participated—was already specifically called a "flow of election speeches."

The nomination process showed an unusual lack of inner cohesion in party organizations. This was especially true of the Social Democratic Party. For instance, the results of its primary membership vote, its district meetings, the activity of its opposition, and the decisions of party leadership created a situation in which the opposition founded first a separate parliamentary group and then an electoral alliance of its own in four constituencies. The member of Parliament of the Finnish People's Party from Tampere decided in January to join the Conservative Party. In Jyväskylä, on April 20, a rural union was founded to compete in two constituencies with the Agrarian Union, and in Lapland, on April 12, an Agrarian member of Parliament switched to another electoral alliance.

Simultaneously, a cleavage in organized labor developed, which can also be considered one result of the general strike of March 1956. A com-

16. Report of the Commission for the History of the Council of Ministers, Mar. 11, 1960.

mittee for the unification of organized labor decided on January 19,
1958, to begin preparing the rules which would be needed when a new
labor organization was founded. The Cooperation Organization of Labor
Unions started its activity in October 1958, and the Finnish Labor Union
was founded in November 1960 to compete with the earlier established
Finnish Federation of Labor.[17]

Economic difficulties and political cleavages were referred to by both
the Speaker of the Parliament and the President of the Republic on
June 6, 1958, during the closing ceremonies of the 1957 session of Parliament. The former complained that "general goodwill and mutual understanding among the parties had deteriorated while difficulties had been
growing," and the latter stated that "the most important national question for weeks after the election will be a reconstruction of the bridges
over which negotiators may reach each other to create preconditions for
formation of a cabinet which is based on a unitary majority."[18]

Even though the composition of the new Parliament and even the
flavor of the 1958 campaign seems to have had specific importance, the
voting decisions of many enfranchised citizens seem to have been made
in a political situation which looked exceptionally confusing.

17. Good background in the Finnish labor movement is in Carl Erik Knoellinger, *Labor in Finland* (Cambridge, Harvard University Press, 1960).

18. *Valtiopäivät 1957* (Minutes of the 1957 legislative session of Parliament), pp. 4999, 5001.

2. Design of the Study

ELECTIONS IN THE POLITICAL SYSTEM

No member of society can attain all his wants, whether they be his hopes for material goods, freedom of action, or increased possibilities for leisure. Therefore aspirations and possibilities always clash in society. Many of these controversies are settled within the family or in the economic system.

The political system, too, adjusts conflicting aspirations by creating official decisions which bind all groups and individuals that belong to the system. In current political science, the system analysis approach seems to compare a political system to the functioning of a production plant. The raw material consists of contradictory aspirations which have not been adjusted on the unofficial level, or in other social systems, while the output amounts to a flow of official decisions, especially legislation.[1]

The magnitude of political decisions varies with the magnitude of opposing interests. One adjustment of the controversy between employers and employees in Finland was a decision by Parliament requiring employers to give their employees full pay for a three-week vacation, a decision which can be enforced if necessary. Drivers may feel that a city imposes on them with a speed limit of 35 miles per hour, while pedestrians feel that such a speed is too high in the city. The conflict between jewelers' right to property and burglars' freedom of action has been decided in favor of the former.

The use of political power in a constitutional state follows legal procedures. There are, in other words, systems of norms and expectations, which are stated by efficient legislation and approved by custom, regulating how authoritative political decisions are made. These political decisions include laws and appropriations. Their exact content seems to depend more and more on the decisions of the so-called executive branch. Public administration in its wider meaning may also include the independent

---

1. David Easton, "An Approach to the Analysis of Political Systems," *World Politics,* 9 (1956–57), 383–400; Easton, *A Framework for Political Analysis* (Englewood Cliffs, Prentice-Hall, 1965), p. 50. See also Karl W. Deutsch, *The Nerves of Government* (New York, Free Press, 1963), Chapter 7.

legal courts, but their decisions are considered by many to be outside the field of political decision making.[2]

Attempts to gain power and the use of power are intertwined. One motive of the representatives' legislative behavior is probably the desire to be re-elected,[3] and political parties often aim at cabinet posts. The content of decisions made by the political system depends on who makes the decisions.

There are, of course, political systems in which the governed, or the majority of them, are unable to influence the choosing of power holders. It is a characteristic of so-called democratic systems that the behavior of enfranchised citizens settles the competition for power, at least for parliamentary membership. In other words, the formal political decision makers are changed or remain with the approval or upon the wish of the governed citizens. Obviously, even in democratic societies, no collective decisions are made on a broader basis than the elections—with the possible exception of the sale of some consumer goods.

The basis of political power in a democracy is the people, more specifically, the enfranchised citizens. One model of political decision making would be the following. First, when transferring their power for a certain time period to the representatives, the citizens make the basic decisions on who gets the opportunity to make individual official decisions. Then the elected power holders appoint additional people to participate in the decision making. Some decisions, which the system creates, may specifically concern the elected or appointed power holders (for instance, decisions on authority and compensation), but most decisions complete a circle by giving general orders back to the people from whom the power derives.

The described judicial model of official decision making is clear and consistent. But, in reality, the political system may create decisions totally outside the sequence of official power relations, as when the leaders of political parties act in response to the views presented by interested pressure groups. Finnish legislation pays very little attention to the unofficial power centers of the system, the parties and the pressure groups. The press, or more generally the mass communication media, is considered by many to be the third focal power factor. The roles of these three fac-

2. On the other hand, a very comprehensive idea of the seven stages in political decision making is expressed by Harold D. Lasswell in *The Future of Political Science* (New York, Atherton Press, 1963), pp. 14–26.

3. John C. Wahlke, Heinz Eulau, William Buchanan, and Leroy C. Ferguson, *The Legislative System* (New York, John Wiley & Sons, 1962), pp. 121–26, 291–94.

tors are distinctive, although they sometimes cooperate; for instance, many Finnish newspapers are quite close to certain parties.

Figure 2.A depicts the decision making process which takes place in a political system. The official power relations are arranged along the edges of the figure and the three unofficial powers are located in the middle. The decisions made by the system affect all parts of it.

This figure attempts to underline especially the importance of various communication channels. Of course, a precondition for influencing de-

FIGURE 2.A. A Model of Decision Making and Communication Channels in a Democratic Political System*

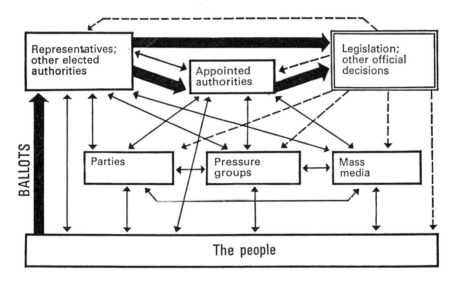

- ➤ Official power relations
- → Communication channels
- --→ Direction of the effect of decisions

* This presentation has been developed from a drawing by Lester W. Milbrath during a speech at the University of Turku on November 1, 1961; see also Milbrath, *The Washington Lobbyists* (Chicago, Rand McNally, 1963), pp. 180–82. He presented—besides parties, pressure groups, and mass media—opinion leaders as a fourth "equal" power and communication factor, in order to emphasize the research which has noted their importance. However, in this oversimplified model, comparison of opinion leaders with the three political powers might be misleading, because the people have not been classified (for instance, as to their participation in communication) and because it might be more reasonable to picture the opinion leaders as a mediating factor linking the people with all other communicating factors.

cisions is some access to the decision makers. The channels of communication may only mediate information, but they can also serve as channels of unofficial influence. For instance, parties have connections to both the elected and the appointed makers of official decisions, to the pressure groups and mass communication media, and, of course, to the citizens in general. But all these channels have two directions; the other five factors in turn may originate communication toward parties and thereby may influence party decisions. The political parties are cited to show just one example of the possibility of connecting any one part of the political system with the other parts by communication channels, as well as of the actual or potential opportunities for unofficial influence. All these channels mediate communication in two directions. Moreover, communication need not proceed directly; the alternative possibilities are numerous.

Where the components of a political system attempt to influence each other and, ultimately, the official decision making, the shortest communication channels in Figure 2.A may be inefficient or even blocked. However, optional indirect channels are usually available. The relative importance of the channels, or even of the components themselves, varies in different political systems. Even in the same system their utility and actual use vary at different times and in different situations.

During the normal political process, attempts to influence are directed mainly at the elected power holders and the appointed civil servants who make important decisions. Parties and pressure groups may be so concerned with the official political decisions that the use of channels toward the people remains relatively small. Yet the people are not quite outside or without influence. The parties are mindful of ensuring their popularity. And many channels from the people to the decision makers are efficient even if they are only imagined. For example, members of the United States House of Representatives really heed what they perceive to be the opinion of their constituents. This occurs even when the voters actually do not know whether or not a specific matter is being dealt with in Congress.[4]

The usual direction of the communication channels, however, will change as the time approaches when the citizens assume their official role in decision making. The power centers of the political system direct more and more communication toward the enfranchised population, and

4. Warren E. Miller and Donald E. Stokes, "Constituency Influence in Congress," *American Political Science Review*, 57 (March 1963), 47, 53–54.

there are more and more attempts to influence their opinions. The candidates and the parties especially operate efficiently. They not only send communications through the mass media but also utilize all other means of communication as much as possible.

All channels toward the people take on a special election character: the speeches by representatives, party posters, public appearances of officials to stress the importance of participation, the support given by pressure groups to representatives, and the campaign material of newspapers and of radio programs. Of course, official political decisions may also concern elections (for instance, election legislation or a decision by the President to dissolve Parliament). The government's decision on the distribution of parliamentary seats among the constituencies no longer belongs to this class, because the government has no alternatives in that decision.

The starting point of this study is the idea that the political powers attempt to direct their main attention to those parts of the system which are making the most important decisions. The enfranchised citizens use their power seldom. But when their turn arrives, their word also carries importance. Therefore, the nature of communication within the political system changes enough before elections to make the campaign a special phase, separate from the normal political process. Parties consider this so important that their activity includes a period of internal campaign preparations before they direct it at the people.

THE PRESENT RESEARCH PROBLEM

In drawing a general picture of a parliamentary election in Finland, an attempt will be made to analyze the behavior of enfranchised citizens who are performing their official task in political decision making in order to transfer their political power to the 200 members of Parliament. Particular attention will be paid to those factors which affect the decision making of the citizens and especially to the importance of the election campaign. The data used are from 1958, when a parliamentary election took place on July 6 and 7. The study is limited in locale to Tampere, but more general conclusions are attempted. For instance, the city will be compared to Korpilahti, a rural commune in a far corner of the same constituency.

Two basic concepts—the election campaign and voting behavior—must be explained before listing the more specific topics of the study.

1. The 1958 campaign can be defined as that communication directed

by the political powers toward the citizens which specifically aimed at influencing the voting decisions realized in July 1958. This study describes the election activities of party organizations and the campaign material of newspapers, which, of course, are intertwined. In order to define the approximate duration of an election campaign, when the party organizations completed their preparations and moved to open campaign activities will be noted. Also, changes in the volume of campaign material and other political material in the newspapers will be studied. The content of the campaign will be analyzed mainly through newspaper coverage. In order to note its specific character, earlier political material of the newspapers must also be analyzed. On the other hand, a description of the campaign will require information on local party organizations in the city as well.

2. Voting decisions include a decision to participate and the choice of one of the competing parties. The latter decision is completed by a selection between the candidates. These decisions are put into effect on polling days, but they may be made much earlier. Therefore, in this study the concept voting behavior will refer to the formation of voting decision without regard to the time of the decision.[5] Consequently, the aims of the study demand information on the time of and the possible changes in the voting decisions of the citizens.

3. When universal suffrage was granted to the Finns in 1906, it was considered quite desirable that the voters carry out an independent judgment, "weighing reasons and counter-reasons."[6] But empirical voting studies have emphasized how often many people choose their party before the political situation and the campaign can have any influence on their choice. In addition, the importance of various group memberships in the political behavior of individuals has been stressed.

To find out factors which influenced the 1958 voting behavior, three time periods will be studied. The object is: (a) to classify the population just before the campaign according to political interest and attitude toward parties; (b) to observe the influence of earlier experiences on that

5. Rune Sjödén writes about "election behavior" in his book *Sveriges första TV-val* (The First TV Election in Sweden) (Stockholm, Sveriges Radio, 1962), p. 25. He means, in part, exposure to election propaganda, and partly "going to the polling place to cast a vote for a certain party." This concept is clear, but it limits the observation to the actual election campaign, and it analyzes the concept according to a chronological, not a systematic, principle, all of which handicaps the study of creating a voting decision.

6. *Eduskunnan uudistuskomitean mietintö* (Report of the Parliament Reform Commission) (Helsinki, 1906), pp. 64, 118, 125

interest and party affiliation; and (c) to study how precampaign differences in activity and voting expectation in turn predict exposure to the election campaign and possibly participation in the election. The social groups which will be mainly dealt with are small groups and the supporters of a given party.

4. It is possible to summarize earlier research findings on the political behavior of small groups with two statements. (a) Small groups tend to create uniform attitudes toward politics. Thus they often have a focal importance when party affiliation is first assumed and, correspondingly, many changes in party position may be explained by the mobility of new small groups.[7] (b) Discussions in small groups supplement mass political communication. The communication advances in two steps so that opinion leaders mediate the content of mass media to other members of their small groups.[8]

5. It is also possible to define a social group so broadly that one considers as a group all the people who have a shared attitude toward some question.[9] Therefore, the predisposition to vote for the same party makes the supporters of a party a large social group.[10] Of course, the intensity of party identification may differ widely; the followers of the party include both its most eager members and persons who vote for it only because they feel nothing better exists. According to research findings: (a) there is a general tendency to adopt the position of the party in individual program matters, too;[11] but (b) the more closely citizens identify with the party the more intensely they want to be informed of

7. Bernard R. Berelson, Paul F. Lazarsfeld, and William N. McPhee, *Voting* (Chicago, The University of Chicago Press, 1954), pp. 94–98, 148–49; Herbert McClosky and Harold E. Dahlgren, "Primary Group Influence on Party Loyalty," *American Political Science Review, 53* (September 1959), 757–76; Sidney Verba, *Small Groups and Political Behavior* (Princeton, Princeton University Press, 1961), pp. 22–27.

8. Erik Allardt and Yrjö Littunen, *Sosiologia* (Porvoo—Helsinki, WSOY, 1961), pp. 46–49; Elihu Katz, "The Two-Step Flow of Communications," *Public Opinion Quarterly, 21* (1957), 61–78.

9. When a group is defined in this way many members have only a potentiality for interaction, as David B. Truman indicates when writing about interest groups, *The Governmental Process* (New York, Alfred A. Knopf, 1951), pp. 34–35, 114, 502–24.

10. See Miller, "Party Identification and Partisan Attitudes," in Raymond E. Wolfinger; ed., *Readings in American Political Behavior* (Englewood Cliffs, Prentice-Hall, 1966), pp. 248–49.

11. Mark Benney, A. P. Gray, and R. H. Pear, *How People Vote* (London, Routledge & Kegan Paul, 1956), pp. 139–45; Angus Campbell and Henry Valen, "Party Identification in Norway and the United States," *Public Opinion Quarterly, 25* (Winter 1961), pp. 516–21; Bo Särlvik, "Party Politics and Electoral Opinion Formation," *Scandinavian Political Studies, 2* (1967, in press).

the stands taken by their party,[12] and the more nearly their opinions conform to the opinions of their party.[13]

6. In an earlier Finnish study, which dealt with the 1956 presidential election, the general conclusion was reached that basic findings of panel interviews with American and British voters were also applicable to a group of young Finnish voters.[14] When the present study was begun, it was reasonable to presume that once again many findings would not differ from the earlier ones. Comparison with other voting studies is, therefore, one of the objects of this study. The work does not begin with a systematic summary of earlier election studies, but they are referred to in dealing with various details, as well as in making the general conclusions.

7. An attempt has been made to devote special attention to the correlation of party identification and political activity[15] and to the so-called cross-pressure hypothesis.[16] Cross pressures can also be presumed to correlate with a loose party identification. Furthermore, it seems consistent that when one finds that party affiliation and voting decision correlate with certain factors, these factors will be more clearly distinguishable among strong than among weak identifiers of the parties.

Consequently, those persons who identify closely with a party have an exceptionally good opportunity to participate actively in the campaign work of their party. They can make known the values adopted or spread by the party—for instance its program and other aims. But this, in turn, presupposes the role of an opinion leader in a small group. Particular attention is given to whether the behavior of party identifiers intensified

12. Paul F. Lazarsfeld, Bernard Berelson, and Hazel Gaudet, *The People's Choice* (New York, Columbia University Press, 1948), pp. 95, 167; Sheldon Jerome Korchin, "Psychological Variables in the Behavior of Voters" (Harvard University, unpublished dissertation, 1946), p. 160; R. S. Milne and H. C. Mackenzie, *Straight Fight* (London, Hansard Society, 1954), p. 98.

13. Angus Campbell, Philip E. Converse, Warren E. Miller, and Donald E. Stokes, *The American Voter* (New York, John Wiley & Sons, 1960), pp. 128–33; Campbell and Valen, *Public Opinion Quarterly, 25*, 519–20.

14. Pertti Pesonen, *Valitsijamiesvaalien ylioppilasäänestäjät* (Student Voters in the Election of the College of Presidential Electors) (Helsinki, Tammi, 1958).

15. Benney, Gray, and Pear, *How People Vote*, pp. 47, 130, 134; Berelson, Lazarsfeld, and McPhee, *Voting*, pp. 25–26; Campbell, "Voters and Elections: Past and Present," *Journal of Politics, 26* (1964); Pesonen, *Student Voters*, pp. 83–84, 142.

16. Allardt, *Social struktur och politisk aktivitet* (Helsingfors, Söderström & Co., 1956); Campbell, Gerald Gurin, and Miller, *The Voter Decides* (Evanston, Row, Peterson & Co., 1954), pp. 130–32, 158–59; Lazarsfeld, Berelson, and Gaudet, *The People's Choice*, p. 62; Pesonen, *Student Voters*, p. 192.

the campaign, and especially to whether the voting decisions of weak identifiers were influenced also by such strong party identifiers as did not participate in the party's organizational activity.

8. In addition to these objectives, it may be possible to present specific aspects of the 1958 election which can be interpreted as the effect of the political situation on voting behavior and on the result of the election.

The Method of the Study

The objectives of the study presuppose interview data. In principle, it would have been possible to interview a sample either of the whole population or of a limited area. Practical reasons necessitated confining the interviews and observations to a small area. However, this had certain advantages—for instance, detailed descriptions of party activity were more accessible. The best possible decision probably would have been to use a sample of a whole constituency. However, this study deals only with the city of Tampere and its comparison with one rural commune, Korpilahti.

Tampere's considerable distance from Helsinki was considered an advantage in its selection as the area to be studied. It was interesting also because of the fairly even competition of the Communists and Social Democrats, and the appearance there earlier in the year of the Independent Social Democrats as a third leftist party. It was also possible to obtain experienced interviewers there. The desired comparison area needed to be a rural community in the same constituency, ruled by a non-socialist majority, where the Agrarians and the Communists were the most popular parties. Of the three communes which fulfilled these expectations, Korpilahti, the largest and most distant from Tampere, was selected.

The time of voting decision and the possible changes in voting intentions were so important for the study that the memory of the interviewees was not considered to be sufficient. Therefore the material was gathered through a panel interview. Voting intentions were measured before the campaign period, and the same persons were asked soon after the election how they behaved in the election. The first interview was performed May 15-25, 1958.

Of course, both interviews had to collect some information based on the memory of the interviewees: for instance, about earlier experiences in the first interview and about the exposure to the campaign and the attitudes toward it in the second. The panel-interview method—in a

study concerning students—had been employed during only one previous election in Finland. Therefore, in the 1958 interviews special attention was paid to the desire of the interviewees to respond. The interviewees were not informed in May about the proposed second interview,
because it was feared that an expected re-interviw would have an influence
on the development of their opinions. The questionnaire is presented in
Appendix 1.

The random sample interviewed in Tampere in May consisted of 501
persons, or 87 per cent of the total sample. Refusals represent 6 per cent
of the sample. The re-interview reached 476 persons, or 84 per cent of the
original sample. The comparison sample of Korpilahti consisted of 97
persons. Appendix 2 presents information on sampling, interviews, and
representativeness of the samples.

The analysis of the interview material was carried out mainly in the
Institute of Political Science at the University of Helsinki. Some of the
scales and classifications are explained in Appendix 3. The statistical
significance of the conclusions of the Tampere material has been tested
mainly by means of the chi square and t-test; some conclusions are based
only on the consistency of the correlations in the sample.

The information gathered through interviews was supplemented by
material from two other sources: a statement of the taxable income of
the interviewees and their spouses in 1957 and 1958 was released by the
assessment boards; and information on electoral participation was checked
by means of the voting registers. Later, the latter source also provided
information on participation of the sample in the 1962 election.

In order to supplement the conclusions based on interviews, simultaneous observations were made by using such other means as the registers
of voters, the documents of the central electoral board, and the register
of civic societies of the Ministry of Justice. To get a general picture of
political organizations in Tampere, the announcements to the official
register of societies were used. Also, the objectives of the study demanded
observation of the campaign activity, interviews of some party functionaries, and acquaintance with newspaper material about the election.

The following newspaper content analyses were made: (1) a study of
seven newspapers in Tampere during twelve weeks, April 14 to July 6,
both for the volume of material on parties and the election, and for their
election advertisements; (2) a pro and con classification of statements
on parties and some program details between April 14 and May 11; (3)
a repeated classification of these attitudes from June 9 to July 6; (4) the

presentation of individual candidates in the newspapers during the latter four-week period; and (5) the volume of political material and the attitude toward political parties of two newspapers read in Korpilahti (the political issues which were studied allowed a comparison between the content of newspapers and the opinions of interviewees); (6) a corresponding comparison was one of the reasons why statements about the papers' own party were coded for April 14 to May 11, and June 9 to July 6; and (7) as background study of the trends in the volume of election material between January 6 and July 6, using whole news items as rough units of measurement.

3. An Industrial City
and a Rural Commune

Typical Finnish constituencies have both rural and urban populations, and the district organizations of most political parties have to take into account the variety of local conditions within their areas of activity.

In Tampere, large-scale industry has existed since the early part of the nineteenth century. Its population—only 36,000 in 1900—was 140,000 in 1965. During the 1950s industrial activity apparently did not develop as fast here as in Helsinki or Turku, but Tampere still remains the most typical large industrial city in Finland. It is also the urban center of the large economic area which surrounds it. Since the 1930s at least, one of its aims has been to become the site of the district governor's offices.

Tampere is the only city located in the Northern Häme constituency. It alone had over two fifths of the constituency's population at the end of the 1950s (Table 3.1). But only about half of the population of this relatively industrialized constituency lived in its only city and its two boroughs. The percentage of adults living in the 28 rural communes fell below 50 for the first time in 1958. Of course, part of that population, too, has become urbanized: in the neighboring communes of Tampere and in smaller industrial centers, for instance. However, the constituency contains many typical agricultural communes. But, by 1958, the major economic activity of every corner of the area was not directed into the center of the constituency, and this was taken into consideration when the new administrative province, Central Finland, was created in 1960. Although this study concentrates mainly on Tampere, comparisons with Korpilahti are attempted. This rural commune, divided into two halves by Lake Päijänne, was still located in 1958 in the northeastern corner of the Northern Häme constituency. The redistricting of 1960 cut this connection.

PARTY SUPPORT IN TAMPERE

Tampere is known both as "the beautiful city of factories" and as "the city of workers." It has been a traditional center of labor movements. Its local Workers' Association was founded in 1887 and gradually became

34

TABLE 3.1. Number and Population of Local Governmental Units in Finland and in Northern Häme Constituency in 1958

	Cities	Boroughs	Rural communes	Total
Number of units for local self-government				
Whole country	35	32	482	549
Northern Häme	1	2	28	31
Number of voting districts				
Whole country	430	134	4,419	4,983
Northern Häme	55	14	208	277
Resident population in 1,000s				
Whole country	1,286.4	340.8	2,767.5	4,394.7
Northern Häme	121.4	24.3	148.1	293.8
Enfranchised population in 1,000s				
Whole country	802.0	205.9	1,598.3	2,606.3
Northern Häme	76.8	14.7	89.3	180.8
Resident population in per cent				
Whole country	29.3	7.7	63.0	100.0
Northern Häme	41.3	8.3	50.4	100.0
Enfranchised population in per cent				
Whole country	30.8	7.9	61.3	100.0
Northern Häme	42.5	8.1	49.4	100.0

DATA SOURCE: *Statistical Yearbook of Finland, Year 1959* (Helsinki, 1960), pp. 3, 6, 16–17; *Official Statistics of Finland XXIX* A:27 (General Election in Finland 1958), pp. 5, 16, 30–33.

very active in politics. For example, it played a considerable role in Finland's anti-Czar General Strike of 1905. Russian revolutionaries held some secret meetings there in order to avoid espionage by the Czarist regime; thus in 1905 V. I. Lenin and J. V. Stalin met for the first time in the house of the Tampere Workers' Association. Finland's Federation of Labor was founded in Tampere in 1907. The most decisive battle of the civil war of 1918 took place in that city, when 25,000 Red Guard members defended it against the advancing governmental army.

On polling days the majority of the inhabitants of Tampere has voted for socialist parties. Within the left, however, the Communist movement was relatively unsuccessful in the 1920s. But the FPDU came to the fore in 1945, almost equaled the SDP in the parliamentary election, and received even more votes in the municipal election of the same year. Of Finnish cities, Tampere is second only to Kemi in total amount of socialist support. In the parliamentary election of March 7–8, 1954, there were in Tampere:

	Number of persons	Percentage
SDP voters	19,383	27.6
Communist (FPDU) voters	18,175	26.0
Conservative voters	12,772	18.2
Voters for the FPP	5,873	8.4
Voters for the Agrarian Union	242	0.3
Others and disqualified ballots	200	0.3
Additional absentee ballots	1,051	1.5
Nonvoters	12,399	17.7
Total Electorate	70,115	100.0[1]

1. *SVT* (Official Statistics of Finland), *XXIX* A:24 (Helsinki, 1954), pp. 26–27.

This distribution of votes, like the results of other elections as well, illustrates the three partitions of political affiliation characteristic of Tampere since 1945. The two leftist parties have run a fairly even competition, although the support of the Social Democrats has been regularly slightly larger. The voters for the Conservatives and the Finnish People's Party together have been the third group. This three-way partitioning of political power has been especially crucial in the municipal elections. Repeated contests have centered on obtaining a quota of over one third in the municipal council, which is enough to block important economic decisions such as the sale and purchase of land. In 1956 the municipal council was composed of 19 Social Democrats, 18 so-called bourgeois deputies, and 16 representatives of the Finnish People's Democratic Union. Finally, in 1960, the last group elected 18 deputies for one four-year period. The bourgeois group, in turn, was then left at 17, or without the desired one-third quota. The Agrarian Union, the biggest non-socialist party in Finland, which gets almost all its support in rural areas, has been insignificant in Tampere. In the 1956 presidential election the Agrarian candidate did receive 1,421 votes in that city, but most of these votes would not have gone to his party in a parliamentary election. The Swedish People's Party received 439 votes in the municipal election and elected one deputy in 1936, but it did not put up a separate slate of candidates in the subsequent 1945 municipal election.[2] And it has never run slates in national elections in the Northern Häme constituency.

During the four years following the 1954 election, significant changes occurred in the party system and in party support in Finland. The presidential candidate nominated by the Finnish People's Party did not receive

2. *Tampereen kaupungin tilastollinen vuosikirja 1958* (Tampere: Department of Statistics of the City, 1959), Tables 156 and 157.

many votes in January 1956, and the municipal election in the fall of the same year indicated a declining trend of the FPP itself. The Social Democratic Party was about to split. For instance, a declaration published in Tampere's SDP newspaper, *Kansan Lehti,* on May 15, 1958, gave final proof that the opposition within the party had decided to enter the campaign as independent Social Democrats not in cooperation with the party.[3] And the Northern Häme constituency was not the only place; the minority wing of the 1957 party convention participated in this election with their own candidates in three other constituencies as well. No factual knowledge was available concerning the respective support of the two wings.

TABLE 3.2. Party Preference, by Sex, of the Adult Population of Tampere in May 1958

Parties	Men	Women (per cent)	Total Sample	Men	Women (number)	Total*
Finnish People's Democratic Union	31	15	22	9,950	6,700	16,650
Social Democratic Opposition	4	5	5	1,400	2,450	3,850
Social Democratic Party	31	34	33	9,800	15,300	25,100
Agrarian Union	1	3	2	300	1,200	1,500
Finnish People's Party	5	7	6	1,550	3,050	4,600
Conservative	18	19	18	5,750	8,500	14,250
Swedish People's Party	1	1	1	150	300	450
"Some labor party"	2	1	1	650	450	1,100
Nonpartisan	3	12	8	1,100	5,300	6,400
No answer	4	3	4	1,250	1,650	2,900
Total	100	100	100	31,900	44,900	76,800
Number of cases	*205*	*296*	*501*	*205*	*296*	*501*

* The number of male respondents multiplied by 155.6 and that of female respondents by 151.7.

The number of inhabitants entitled to vote in Tampere had increased in these four years by 6,678 persons, or 10 per cent. The corresponding increase in the whole country had been only 3 per cent. Table 3.2 classifies the 76,800 enfranchised inhabitants of Tampere according to their party preference in May 1958. A comparison of the table with the result of the

3. *Kansan Lehti,* May 15, 1958, p. 5.

1954 election shows that (a) the number of nonpartisans was smaller than that of nonvoters in the previous elections; (b) the Finnish People's Party had, perhaps, lost support to the Conservatives; (c) the number of supporters of the Social Democrats was now larger than the number of votes cast for that party in the previous election; and (d) the Communist support had decreased. At least the last conclusion does not appear to be correct. Obviously, survey studies have to cope with the general tendency of some Communists to say that they support the Social Democrats.[4] In addition, 5 per cent of the interviewees refused to express a party affiliation or said only that they support "some labor party."

The official election statistics indicate the number of votes each party received in each municipality or commune, but only for Helsinki are the votes further broken down into four smaller local units. However, in most places differences exist between the various sections of that unit; information on this is obtainable, although not published in official statistics. Also, people living in different parts of Tampere tend to vote differently. Support for the Communists is strongest in certain suburbs, while that for the Conservatives is concentrated in the central areas of the city. Even there, Communists dominate some voting districts, which would also substantiate the general notion that the supporters of these two parties do not feel at home together. On the other hand, supporters of the Social Democrats are more equally distributed over the city and do not form a majority in any voting district.

Among the supporters of most parties one recognizes the general rule of Tampere's population: there are three women to two men (Table 3.2). However, there were two significant exceptions. Among the Communist supporters there were three men to two women in 1958. An exception in the other direction concerns the nonpartisans, almost all of whom were women. Among the men 97 per cent favored one party more than others, while 88 per cent of the women had a party preference.[5] Yet in Finland women have been enfranchised as long as men.

Because women are the majority, Tampere has more unmarried women

4. Allardt, *International Journal of Comparative Sociology*, 5 (1964) 51–52; and communication with Mr. Tauno Hellevuo of the Finnish Gallup Institute. The tendency to Communist under-representation is common in sample surveys. A Norwegian example is in Valen and Daniel Katz, *Political Parties in Norway* (Oslo, Universitetsförlaget, 1964), pp. 344–45.

5. The percentage of men among FPDU supporters was 59 ($n = 108$) and among other interviewees 36 ($n = 393$), $t = 4.34$, $p < 0.001$. The difference between nonpartisans and others was equally significant.

and widows than men in these marital statuses. The interviewed sample contained 26 per cent single women, but only 6 per cent single men. There were 33 per cent married women and 35 per cent married men. The latter difference of two percentage units is a reminder of the approximateness of information achieved with a sample.

Figure 3.A summarizes the data of Table 3.2 and shows, in addition,

FIGURE 3.A. Party Preference by Sex and Marital Status in Tampere, May 1958 (in percentages)

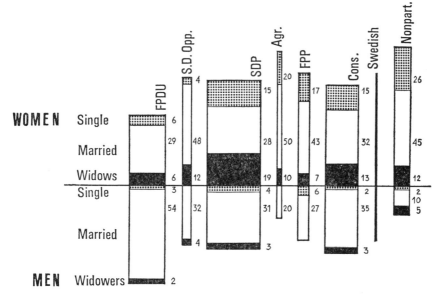

the distribution of both sexes according to marital status. Although Communist support was exceptionally small among women, the proportion of married women in the Communist group was about equal to that among the Social Democrats. On the other hand, the support of Communists was lower than average among unmarried women and widows, who were an exceptionally large portion (34 per cent) of the Social Democrats. Widows especially were prone to support the sDP.[6] Also, widows did not share the tendency of other women to have no

6. In the comparison FPDU/others $t = 3.29$, $p < 0.001$ and $t = 2.78$, $p < 0.01$; in the comparison SDP/others $t = 2.26$, $p < 0.05$. Here widows and divorced women have been classified in the same group. It is possible that the proportion of divorced women was above average among the female supporters of the FPDU (12 per cent, $n = 44$, of others 4 per cent, $n = 252$), but this is not statistically significant.

party preference.[7] Moreover, Figure 3.A leads to the supposition that if the two spouses favored different parties, the husband was apt to be a Communist; and the wife might be either nonpartisan or a supporter of the independent Social Democrats, the Agrarians or, perhaps, the Finnish People's Party.

It is not surprising that Communism was more popular among men than among women in Tampere. The same condition has been found elsewhere;[8] generally women have been more conservative than men.[9] In many countries one finds not only more nonvoting but also more nonpartisanship among women than among men.[10]

TABLE 3.3. The Relationship between Party Preference and Age: May 1958 (in percentages)

Age (and year of birth)	Total sample	FPDU	SDP and Opp.	Non-soc.	SDP	S.D. Opp.	Agr.	FPP	Cons.	Non-partisan
21–24 (1933–1936)	8	12	6	5	6	8	30	13	–	12
25–42 (1915–1932)	37	40	38	37	35	52	10	47	35	28
43–64 (1893–1914)	47	46	45	47	47	36	40	33	52	55
65 and over (before 1892)	8	2	11	11	12	4	10	7	13	5
Total	100	100	100	100	100	100	100	100	100	100
Number of cases	*501*	*108*	*189*	*136*	*164*	*25*	*10*	*30*	*93*	*42*

The age distribution of party supporters is given in Table 3.3. The sample was classified in four parts. A total of 55 per cent of the sample had been entitled to vote in the 1930s, whereas 45 per cent had first been

7. However, there were more single women among nonpartisan women than among other women, $t = 2.06$, $p < 0.05$.

8. Elis Håstad, et al., *"Gallup" och den svenska väljarkåren* (Gallup and the Swedish Electorate) (Uppsala, Hugo Gebers Förlag, 1950), pp. 146–47.

9. Benney, Gray, and Pear, *How People Vote,* pp. 47, 107; Angus Campbell and Robert L. Kahn, *The People Elect a President,* Survey Research Center Monograph Series, 9 (Ann Arbor, 1952), pp. 34–35; Lazarsfeld, Berelson, and Gaudet, *The People's Choice,* p. 25; Seymour Martin Lipset, *Political Man* (Garden City, Doubleday & Company, 1960), pp. 156, 165, 221; Pesonen, *Student Voters,* p. 104; Joseph Trenaman and Denis McQuail, *Television and the Political Image* (London, Methuen and Co, 1961), p. 140.

10. R. S. Milne and H. C. Mackenzie, *Marginal Seat* (London, The Hansard Society for Parliamentary Government, 1958), p. 37.

able to vote in 1945 or after. The proportion of interviewees enfranchised before Finnish independence was 8 per cent, while the four youngest age groups, who voted for the first time in the 1958 parliamentary election, were also 8 per cent of the sample.

Those interviewees who had been entitled to vote during the Grand Duchy of Finland concentrated their support mainly on the Social Democrats and the Conservatives. The FPDU did not have many supporters in this age group. On the other hand, the youngest age group had an above average representation among the supporters of the FPDU, the FPP and the Agrarian Union. A random error may have kept the youngest Conservative supporters out of the sample. The Communists appeared relatively younger than both the Social Democrats and the supporters of the four nonsocialist parties.

Some comparisons of age groups in two-party systems have revealed a tendency of young persons to support a radical party and of older people to support a conservative party.[11] This was also the case in Tampere in May 1958. A classification of the population according to the tripartite division of political opinions shows the relatively younger age of Communists than of the other two groups. A closer look within the left and the right, however, leads to one qualification. In order to interpret Table 3.3 in this connection, one needs to differentiate between leftist radicalism and nonsocialist radicalism.

It is not difficult to discover a basic reason why the popularity of the left was so high in Tampere that it controlled two thirds of the municipal council, received 67 per cent of the votes cast in 1954, and counted as supporters 69 per cent of the persons who mentioned a party preference in 1958. According to the 1950 census, the percentage of wage workers among the total gainfully employed males was 42 in the whole country, but 71 per cent in Tampere. Private enterprise, management, and white collar groups accounted for 28 per cent in Tampere, while only 1 per cent were engaged in agriculture.[12]

Of course, the similarity of the proportion of wage workers and the

11. Benney, Gray, and Pear, *How People Vote*, pp. 46, 105–06; Berelson, Lazarsfeld, and McPhee, *Voting*, pp. 60–61; Campbell and Homer C. Cooper, *Group Differences in Attitudes and Votes*, SRC Monograph Series, 15 (Ann Arbor, 1956), pp. 20–22; Korchin, *Psychological Variables* (1946), pp. 93, 99–107. Lipset, *Political Man*, p. 270, mentions also four multi-party countries in which relatively many old persons are Conservative. Cf. Pesonen, *Student Voters*, pp. 106–08.

12. *SVT* (Official Statistics of Finland), *VI C:102* (Census of 1950), *4*, Table 1; *Tampereen kaupungin tilastollinen vuosikirja 1958*, Table 33.

TABLE 3.4. The Relationship between Party Preference and Occupation: May 1958 (in percentages)

Occupational class	Total sample	FPDU	SDP and Opp.	Non-soc.	SDP	S.D. Opp.	Agr.	FPP	Cons.	Non-partisan
Farmers	1	–	1	2	1	–	–	–	2	2
Agrarian labor	2	2	2	1	3	–	10	–	–	–
Labor and services	69	94	78	35	77	80	80	40	30	79
Lower white collar	15	2	12	34	11	16	–	33	39	2
Top-ranking position	13	2	7	28	8	4	10	27	29	17
Total	100	100	100	100	100	100	100	100	100	100
Number of cases	*501*	*108*	*189*	*136*	*164*	*25*	*10*	*30*	*93*	*42*

support of labor parties does not give evidence that all workers were left politically and all the others nonsocialist. Occupations are compared with expressed party preferences in Table 3.4. The classification of occupations into five groups is similar to that used by the Finnish Gallup Institute.[13] Each individual has been classified according to the occupation of the family's main supporter. Labor and services, including agricultural labor, were 71 per cent of the total sample. Labor was represented more among the leftist groups and less among the nonsocialist groups, with the possible exception of the Agrarian Union. But only one in five Social Democrats was not a wage worker and one out of three Conservative and FPP supporters was a worker. A reexamination of Table 3.4 indicates that among the three occupational groups the left as a whole was supported by the following percentages:[14]

Labor and services	84($n = 310$)
Lower white collar work	35($n = 78$)
Top-ranking position	30($n = 54$)

Occupation is an obvious reason for a political preference, and the occupational structure of the population of Tampere is an important explanation for its political color.[15] But occupation alone does not explain

13. Suomen Gallup Oy, *Ammattiryhmitys* (Occupational Grouping) (Helsinki, 1958).

14. The percentages concern only persons with a party preference.

15. Data on the correlation of occupation and party support, which have been collected by the Gallup Institute about the whole Finnish population, have been published in such works as Onni Rantala, *Konservatiivinen puolueyhteisö* (The Conservative Party Com-

the division of citizens into leftist and nonsocialist supporters. Only the FPDU had a socially homogenous group of supporters in Tampere. It was supported by every third wage worker. On the other hand, the Social Democrats and the nonsocialists competed for the support of various occupational groups. The SDP was more successful among the white collar groups than the nonsocialists were among labor. But, in a city with such a heavy labor majority, even a small portion of labor support was relatively significant in the total support of the nonsocialist parties.

POLITICAL ORGANIZATIONS IN TAMPERE

Soon after the founding of the SDP its organizational activity covered the whole country. More precisely, the SDP

> formed a clear-cut mass party attempting to make the greatest possible proportion of its voters regular members; its aim was to practice political education among the working class and to finance the activities from the proceeds of membership fees. It should be borne in mind that the party was not established primarily as an electoral organization. As the working class was not in possession of suffrage until 1906, the original object of the party was to awaken the workers and to increase their class consciousness.[16]

Two aspects might be emphasized in the above quotation. (1) The described attempt of the SDP was followed later by other Finnish parties as well. Especially after World War II they, too, have established comprehensive mass organizations. In the late 1940s and 1950s, the Agrarian Union and to a smaller degree the Swedish People's Party, the FPDU and the Conservatives actually recruited as members a larger proportion of their voters than the SDP did. (2) Electioneering still is not the only nor even the main purpose of party organizations. In this respect Finnish parties resemble those of many other European democracies but are largely unlike political parties in the U.S.A. The organizations function permanently, not temporarily; they educate their members and other people and also play a considerable role of their own in political decision making.

We do not intend to analyze the structure of Finnish political parties

---

munity) (Vammala, 1956), p. 24; Allardt and Pesonen, "Structural and Non-structural Cleavages in Finnish Politics" (Institute of Sociology, University of Helsinki, mimeo. 1961), p. 22; and Allardt, *International Journal of Comparative Sociology,* 5, p. 51.

16. Nousiainen, *Democracy in Finland,* p. 29.

in this connection. Let us simply note what kind of local party units existed in Tampere in 1958. There was at that time one registered political club or association for every 300 enfranchised persons in the city. Because political associations and clubs can also function without formal registration, the number obtained from the register of associations of the Ministry of Justice might be smaller than the actual number of active political units. But generally clubs are registered in order to become legal entities. It is also possible that the Register of Associations leads to an overestimation of the real number, because not all the registered but discontinued associations formally notify the Ministry of the end of their activity.

The registered political associations with units in Tampere can be classified into three groups, about equal in size, which, however, do not correspond to the distribution of popular support among the parties. One such group consists of the local units of the Communist Party, and another includes local units of the Finnish People's Democratic Union and associations closely related to it. A third group represents the aggregate of all other political associations, which are mainly Social Democratic. The classification is as follows:

Units of the Finnish Communist Party (SKP)	88
Other member associations of the FPDU	44
Local units of the Democratic Youth League	16
Pioneers of Democracy	11
Local associations of the Social Democrats	65
District organization of "The Young Eagles"	1
Agrarian associations	4
Associations of the Finnish People's Party	7
Associations of the National Coalition	11
Association of the Swedish People's Party	1
Total	248

This includes organizations of district (constituency) and ward (voting district) level active in Tampere. Seventeen registered political associations and those founded after 1958 are not included.[17]

The notifications to the Register of Associations also make it possible to study the principles according to which the leftist organizations have been developed (for the FPDU see Appendix Table 1).

17. The figures include all political associations in Tampere, which were announced to the Register of Associations of the Ministry of Justice, with the exception of 17 political associations. Some of these are difficult to classify by party, and some have obviously ceased their activity without notifying the Register of Associations.

After the legalization of Communist activity in 1944, a citywide Communist association, a citywide association of the FPDU and the Democratic Youth League, and three other democratic youth organizations were at once established.[18]

Various principles have been followed in developing the Communist (SKP) organization. In 1945, five local units started to work on an area basis, and five others—those of shoe, municipal, textile, metal, and construction industry workers—were for persons employed in a specific field.[19] In 1946-48, sixteen units were established in various plants, while only four other occupational fields and three sections of the city got a registered Communist association.[20] After the electoral defeat of the FPDU in 1948, the Communists concentrated on improving their activity in various parts of the city, and the party seems to have aimed at establishing as many registered local units as there were voting districts (wards) of the city. In 1949, 25 such units were announced to the Register; in 1950-57, 15 new ones working in certain sections of the city were established. In 1958, the total number was 48, which almost equaled the recently increased number of voting districts (55). Some new plants also got their own Communist organizations: eight in 1949-51 and three in 1952-57, while the idea of interplant Communist organizations covering specific occupational fields had been abandoned by the end of the 1940s.[21]

The Finnish People's Democratic Union had no active plant organizations of its own. Its local organization comprised in 1958 the associations of workers in five different fields;[22] and ten ward associations scattered throughout the city, three of which dated back to 1945. And there was one Social Democratic unit which had at that time entered the FPDU.[23] In the same year three local associations were founded for women, and later seventeen other women's democratic organizations were started at

18. Register Nos. 36646, 36809, 45250, 59795, 36724 and 36857.

19. Register Nos. 39720, 39124, 37487, 37740, 36960, 37739, 39268, 39123, 45481 and 37100.

20. The fields are: car mechanics and workers in the food, transportation, and clothing industries (register nos. 47729, 47727, 47726 and 40996).

21. See Appendix Table 1. The last report to the Register concerning an association of a certain occupational field dealt with authorizing new persons to sign the name of the Communist Construction Workers' Unit in 1949.

22. Food workers, office workers, construction workers, railroad workers and civil servants (register nos. 65575, 47804, 59668, 43387 and 47769). The FPDU reported in 1961 that it had 22 units within local unions or in work plants in the whole country.

23. Register nos. 37131, 37101 and 37760. In 1945 the Democratic Association of Evacuated Karelians was also started, register no. 37968.

the ward level in Tampere. The Democratic Youth League of Finland had a total of fourteen associations, whose activity was likewise concentrated in their local sections of the city. The Register of Associations also included eleven associations of the Pioneers of Democracy, the youngest of which was the district organization for Tampere, founded as early as 1947.[24]

The activity of the Social Democratic Party had much longer traditions in Tampere. In 1944 the Register included sixteen associations of the SDP. Six of them had an unlimited sphere of activity.[25] The others were organized in two suburbs, in four fields of work (shoe, textile, metal, and construction workers), and among four other groups (vocational, Christian, working-class students, and sportsmen). In addition, the Register noted three women's and eight youth organizations. By 1958 the Tampere organization of the SDP covered sixteen occupational fields—more than similar Communist or FPDU organizations. On the other hand, only three plants had a Social Democratic organization, and there were only eight organizations at the ward level in the city. The three women's organizations continued their existence and the number of youth organizations had increased to twelve. There were also eight local units of the party which were called Workers' Societies.[26]

The local organizations of the nonsocialist parties do not look impressive, at least if comparison with the leftist organizations is based only on the number of registered associations, without attention to their size or activity. The National Coalition (Conservatives) had five registered local associations, two started in the 1920s, one in 1951, and two very recent ones. In addition, the Conservatives had one women's and two youth organizations. The Finnish People's Party had two local and two youth associations, while its only women's organization registered in Tampere comprised the whole constituency. The Agrarian Union and the Swedish People's Party were represented by one organization each for both Tampere and its surroundings.[27]

24. Register no. 47592. New associations of the Pioneers of Democracy were founded in 1958 after a pause of ten years.

25. These included the Social Democratic City Organization and the Socialist Discussion Society (register nos. 24721 and 24640).

26. According to information from the district secretary of the Party, 14 registered Social Democratic associations were inactive in 1958, while the local Christian Social Democratic unit was not yet registered. In 1959, the new Social Democratic League founded three associations in Tampere, and five local party units switched to the League.

27. The Agrarian Club of Tampere Area was founded in 1939 and the Swedish one in 1922 (register nos. 31616 and 7872).

Vertically, the Communists, the FPDU, and the SDP had city level organizations between the ward and the district level. The center of the constituency, Tampere, is the home of the district organizations. In 1958, registered associations at this level included, in addition to the party organizations proper, district organizations for the Democratic Union of Finnish Women, the Social Democratic Temperance League and women's organizations, the Agrarian Youth organization, and the Conservative Women's organization. On the other hand, the Communists had a district organization for Tampere, but the northeastern corner of the constituency was already included in the neighboring district organization which in 1960 began to cover the newly created Central Finland constituency.

Permanent district headquarters functioned in Tampere for the SKP, the FPDU, the SDP, the Agrarian Union, the FPP, and the Conservatives. These offices cooperated directly with the city- and ward-level local associations. City organizations of the left and Conservatives also employed full-time party functionaries for the city area only.

According to the May 1958 interviews, 18 per cent of the men, but only 6 per cent of the women belonged to a political organization. Thus, the membership of political organizations comprised about 5,600 adult men and 2,900 women, a total of about 8,500. It is quite possible that the membership files contained more names, because this approximate number includes only those enfranchised members who also said that they were strong supporters of their party.[28]

The percentages of all party supporters who had organization membership were the following:

28. First the interviewees ranked one party first. An additional question concerned the certainty of party preference. Persons who considered themselves sure supporters of a party were further asked whether they were members in a party organization (QQ. 20–21). However, Rantala found that, in the case of the Satakunta district organization of Conservatives, joining the organization was not sufficient evidence for a sure party affiliation. Many members were only slightly informed about parties and, some had even joined two different parties simultaneously. Rantala, *Conservative Party,* pp. 133–34. In Norway, 62 per cent of dues-paying members were classified as strong identifiers, Valen and Katz, *Political Parties,* p. 189. It may also be mentioned that the Conservative organizations in northern Häme included, in 1956, 5,442 members who paid their membership fees, in other words 21 per cent of the votes cast for the party in 1954; Rantala, *Konservatismi ja sen kannattajat* (Conservatism and Its Supporters) (Helsinki, Tammi, 1960), p. 201. The percentage based on the present sample, 10 per cent, is smaller because it is based on both voters and nonvoters, and because youth members and weak identifiers are excluded. The difference may also be caused by the standard error of the information and by the possible higher level of organization of rural supporters.

FPDU	$21(n = 108)$
Social Democrats	$13(n = 164)$
Finnish People's Party	$3(n = 30)$
Conservatives	$10(n = 93)$

The percentage for the FPDU was higher than for any other party.[29] The Social Democrats, in turn, were probably more organized than the Conservatives. This order of the parties could be expected on the basis of the number of registered associations. On the other hand, the difference in the number of associations was larger than that in the percentages. Therefore, the average membership of the conservative associations was the largest and that of the FPDU the smallest. A low level of participation in the organizational activity of the Finnish People's Party has been reported earlier[30] and seems to have been the case in Tampere in 1958 as well.

THE PRESS IN TAMPERE

In early elections, the editorial staffs of provincial party papers often took care of the practical campaign arrangements. Such functions were soon to be assumed by the developing party organizations, but the more basic roles of a party press have remained prominent in Finland as in many other European countries. However, there has been a decreasing trend in the number of newspapers in general, and especially of party papers. Local competition left most provinces with only one newspaper in a clearly leading position, with most of the advertising and the widest circulation.[31] Often this development has borne no obvious relationship to party support in the area of circulation.

Tampere is a good example of such a disproportion. Although the nonsocialist parties received only one third of the popular support in Tampere and had a proportionally even smaller local party organization, the second largest (later largest) organ of the National Coalition, the *Aamulehti,* was nevertheless the main local newspaper. In the spring of 1958, the total circulation of daily newspapers in Tampere was about 53,000. The circulation of *Aamulehti* alone represented about three fifths

29. $t = 2.60, p < 0.01$.

30. For example Nousiainen, *Suomen poliittinen järjestelmä* (The Finnish Political System) (Porvoo-Helsinki, WSOY, 1963), pp. 63–64; Pesonen, *Student Voters,* pp. 54–55, 83.

31. In 1930, there were 123 daily newspapers in Finland. This included 99 party papers. In 1963, the corresponding figures were only 94 and 59. Compare Rantala, "Suomen puoluelehdistö" (The Finnish Party Press), *Politiikka* 1964, 14–16; and Torsten Steinby, *Suomen sanomalehdistö* (The Daily Press in Finland) (Porvoo, WSOY, 1963), pp. 110, 119.

TABLE 3.5. Circulation and Estimated Number of Regular Adult Readers of Daily Newspapers in Tampere: May 1958

Newspapers (party and place of publication)	Circulation[a]	Regular readers[b]	Readers per copy
Hämeen Yhteistyö (FPDU, Tampere)	3,630	4,300	1.2
Kansan Uutiset (FPDU, Helsinki)	2,353	5,200	2.2
Kansan Lehti (SDP, Tampere)	4,200	10,400	2.5
Suomen Sosialidemokraatti (SDP, Helsinki)	750	1,400	1.8
Aamulehti (Conservative, Tampere)	33,200	71,150	2.1
Uusi Suomi (Conservative, Helsinki)	2,193	4,000	1.8
Helsingin Sanomat (Independent, Helsinki)	5,842	19,450	3.3
Other newspapers	..	2,450	..
Total	52,168	118,350	(~2.2)

a. Information through circulation managers or an independent circulation inspecting agency.

b. Each respondent representing 153.3 persons (n = 501).

of that total; all the other newspapers together comprised the remaining two fifths (Table 3.5).

Aamulehti really provided information for almost every inhabitant of Tampere. According to the May 1958 interviews, 93 per cent of the persons entitled to vote read it regularly. In addition to the 2 per cent who read no newspaper, only 5 per cent did not read this predominant paper of the city. The next in popularity was the *Helsingin Sanomat*, the largest paper nationally. It was read regularly by every fourth inhabitant, while every seventh read the local organ of the Social Democratic Party, the *Kansan Lehti*. Moreover, generally the inhabitants of Tampere read no other paper than the *Aamulehti*. This was true of 51 per cent of the sample. Only 4 per cent read either the *Helsingin Sanomat,* the *Kansan Lehti* or one of the Communist papers, the national *Kansan Uutiset* or the local *Hämeen Yhteistyö,* as their only newspaper. The average number of newspapers read regularly was 1.6.[32]

The number of newspapers read correlates with party affiliation. People supporting nonsocialist parties read on the average more newspapers (1.7) than those supporting the FPDU (1.6) and the SDP (1.5), while the nonpartisans read the fewest papers (1.3). It is in line with these differences that *Aamulehti* was the only newspaper of a majority of the nonpartisans (64 per cent), of every second Social Democrat and Communist

32. This does not include periodicals or so-called communal papers.

(53 and 50 per cent) and of a smaller proportion of the Conservatives and FPP supporters (41 and 30 per cent). The small percentage of the Finnish People's Party readers is a result of their special interest in the

TABLE 3.6. Relationship of Party Preference to Regular Reading of the Newspapers: May 1958 (in percentages)

Newspapers	Total sample	FPDU	SDP and S.D. Opp.	Non-soc.	SDP	S.D. Opp.	Agr.	FPP	Cons.	Non-partisan
Hämeen Yhteistyö	6	21	1	1	1	–	–	–	2	2
Kansan Uutiset	7	27	1	1	1	–	–	–	1	7
Kansan Lehti	14	6	25	8	28	8	20	10	6	2
Suomen Sosialidemokraatti	2	–	3	3	3	–	10	3	2	–
Aamulehti	93	87	93	94	92	96	80	87	98	98
Uusi Suomi	5	–	1	17	1	–	–	3	24	2
Helsingin Sanomat	25	12	24	41	23	28	10	63	38	19
Päivän Sanomat	1	2	1	–	1	–	–	–	–	–
Others	3	–	2	6	2	–	–	6	6	–
No newspaper	2	3	3	1	2	4	10	3	–	2
Total*	158	158	154	172	154	136	130	175	177	132
Number of cases	501	108	189	136	164	25	10	30	93	42

* Some respondents read two or more papers.

Helsingin Sanomat, previously the main organ of the Progressive Party.

Nevertheless, regular reading of the predominant local paper still correlated with party affiliation. According to Table 3.6, the Conservatives read the paper of their own party more than the Communists or Social Democrats did, perhaps also more than the people in favor of the FPP.[33] However, readers of the two other local newspapers were politically much more homogeneous. The *Hämeen Yhteistyö* was read by hardly anyone but some of the Communists, and an approximately equal proportion of Social Democrats read the *Kansan Lehti.* The larger local circulation of the latter paper was partly because of its additional readers with a different political affiliation. The independent Social Democrats seemed to be far less interested in this paper than were the supporters of the party proper.

Two Helsinki papers, *Kansan Uutiset* and *Uusi Suomi,* did not have

33. $t = 3.03$, $p < 0.01$; $t = 3.00$, $p < 0.01$; $t = 1.76$, $p < 0.10$.

many readers outside the sphere of their respective party supporters. The former was read regularly by about every fourth Communist, the latter by about every fourth Conservative. The *Helsingin Sanomat* had more regular readers, but even this correlated with party affiliation. The Communists read it least, and the nonsocialists read it most. About two thirds of the people supporting the Finnish People's Party were among the regular readers of this paper. *Suomen Sosialidemokraatti* was not particularly popular in Tampere, but it did have a few readers among the Social Democrats and the nonsocialists. The new trade union paper, *Päivän Sanomat,* had even fewer readers. Consequently, the Communists seemed to be more exposed to their own party communication than the Social Democrats to theirs. Ten per cent of the Communists read both of the party papers mentioned above, and a total of 38 per cent read at least one.

Tampere, and Finland in general, is but one example of the fact that the circulation of the leftist press does not match the popular support of these parties.[34] According to some speculations, this might be compensated in part by an above average number of readers per copy. But apparently this was not true in Tampere. One might estimate that every *Kansan Lehti* circulated in the city had on the average more adult readers (2.6) than one copy of *Aamulehti* (2.1). But the independent *Helsingin Sanomat* was the only paper with an even higher average number of readers per copy (3.3).

Attempts to circulate politically unbiased material are made in Finland, especially by the state-owned Finnish Broadcasting Corporation. The year 1958 was still part of the era of more than three decades when the press and the radio were the chief mass communication media. Television became common in Finland soon thereafter and played a role in the campaign preceding the 1960 municipal elections. For three decades the number of radio licenses had increased every year; in 1955 their number exceeded one million.[35] In Tampere 94 per cent of the interviewees had a radio receiver in their homes.[36] Obviously, even many of the 6 per cent without a radio had access to the programs.

---

34. For similar information on Sweden and Norway, see Jörgen Westerståhl and C. G. Janson, *Politisk press. Studier till belysning av dagspressens politiska roll i Sverige* (Göteborg, 1958), p. 15, and Stein Rokkan and Per Torsvik, "Presse, velgere og lesere" (chapter 19 of the forthcoming book Valg i Norge, mimeo.), Table 1.1.

35. *Mitä Missä Milloin 1958*, p. 327. Annual radio and TV license payments provide the major income of the Finnish Broadcasting Corporation, which operates on a noncommercial basis.

36. Of the nonpartisans only 83 per cent ($n = 42$).

KORPILAHTI, THE COMPARISON GROUP

It is more difficult to make a living in Korpilahti than in Tampere, and, especially during situations of expanding economy, its inhabitants tend to migrate elsewhere. In 1958 the commune had 4,276 enfranchised inhabitants, or 343 (7 per cent) less than in 1954. The major occupation in the commune was agriculture, with a pattern of small farming strongly supplemented by sales of timber and by forest work. Industry was represented by a dairy and by two sawmills, only one of which was active in 1958 after the Rauma-Repola Corporation had moved its machinery to a more profitable place. According to the 1950 census, 69.1 per cent of the 7,779 inhabitants of Korpilahti depended for a living on agriculture and forestry, fishing, etc. The corresponding percentage in all rural communes in the country was 60.[37]

It is a remarkable feature of Finnish party history that the Social Democrats received a heavy rural vote as soon as universal suffrage had been introduced. The SDP and Christian Labor party gained 39.0 per cent of all rural votes in 1907, and this proportion rose to 49.7 per cent in nine years. But the present study deals with an even more leftist region. The Socialist vote increased from 62 to 67 per cent in all rural communes of northern Häme constituency between 1907 and 1916, and in Korpilahti it rose from 68 to 79 per cent. The socialist tradition has been preserved, although the Communist movement was relatively unsuccessful in the 1920s in this constituency and especially in Korpilahti. Moreover, Korpilahti was politically more similar to Tampere than to other rural communes in the country until the election of 1945 divided the leftist vote differently in the two places. In Tampere the SDP proved to be somewhat stronger than the newly founded FPDU, but in Korpilahti the SDP won only 21 per cent and the FPDU 42 per cent of the votes. Increasing Agrarian support enlarged the total nonsocialist vote from 34 per cent in 1945 to 49 per cent in 1954.

There were 4,619 inhabitants entitled to vote in Korpilahti in 1954, and of these 1,101 (23.8 per cent) were FPDU, 605 (13.1 per cent) SDP, 1,339 (29.0 per cent) Agrarian, 108 (2.3 per cent) FPP, and 191 (4.1 per cent) Conservative voters; 36 (0.8 per cent) votes were cast for other parties. Absentee ballots that had not yet been included amounted to 126 (2.8 per cent), and 1,088 (23.6 per cent) persons refrained from voting.

Such a distribution of political opinion was almost like that in those

37. OSF VI C 102 (1950 Population Census), 2, 38–39.

northern communes in Finland where politics becomes crystallized as the dual fight of the Agrarian Union and the FPDU. In Korpilahti, Agrarian Union support was about twice as high as it was in all other rural communes of this constituency. Korpilahti also had heavier Communist support than the other rural communes of the constituency. On the other hand, the most popular party of the constituency, the SDP, was considerably less supported there than it is on the average in this constituency.

The commune was divided into eleven voting districts. In five of these a single party had majority support, namely, the Agrarian Union in four, and the FPDU in one. The latter had two thirds of the votes in Vitikkala, where the radical traditions of the now inactive sawmill had developed among workers as early as the 1920s. The Communists had the smallest support in those three districts which had largest SDP support. Two of these three were characterized by an Agrarian majority. More than half of the FPP and Conservative voters lived in the central "church village," the biggest voting district of the commune.[38]

In the May 1958 sample, support of the various parties was distributed as follows:

	Men	Women	Total
FPDU	20	17	19
Social Democratic Opposition	2	2	2
Social Democratic Party	24	28	26
Agrarian Union	36	21	29
Finnish People's Party	2	4	3
Conservatives	4	7	5
No answer	2	2	2
Nonpartisan	10	19	14
	100	100	100
Number of cases	*50*	*47*	*97*

Social Democratic affiliation is obviously overrepresented in the sample. Even if the mean error is taken into account, the Social Democratic support is measured as at least 21 per cent. This exceeds considerably the actual SDP vote (13.1 per cent) in the preceding election, which, however, does not include Social Democratic nonvoters.

A comparison of men and women shows two similarities with Tampere: (1) more women than men were nonpartisan; and (2) the Com-

38. *Eduskuntavaalien tulokset Hämeen läänin pohjoisessa vaalipiirissä 7.–8.3.1954 pidetyissä vaaleissa* (Results of the 1954 Election in the Northern Häme Constituency) (published by the Conservative district organization, Tampere, 1954), p. 4.

munists appealed more to men, the SDP to women. Of the nonsocialist parties, the Agrarian Union was more popular among men, the Conservatives and the FPP probably among women.

TABLE 3.7. Relationship of Party Preference to (a) Age and (b) Occupation in Korpilahti: May 1958 (in percentages)

	FPDU	SDP	Agr.	FPP and Cons.	Non-partisan	Total sample
(a) Age						
21–24	17	4	4	–	7	6
25–42	44	36	57	38	22	43
43–64	33	32	39	50	57	40
65–	6	28	–	12	14	11
(b) Occupation						
Farmers	27	40	96	38	43	55
Agrarian Labor	6	16	–	12	21	10
Labor and services	61	36	–	–	29	26
Lower white collar	6	8	4	38	–	7
Top-ranking position	–	–	–	12	7	2
Total	100	100	100	100	100	100
Number of cases	*18*	*25*	*28*	*8*	*14*	*97*

The age distribution of the population in Tampere and Korpilahti (Tables 3.3 and 3.7a) looks similar. A comparison of the party groups also shows differences similar to those in Tampere. In Korpilahti, too, the supporters of the FPDU were on the average younger than those of the SDP or of the two nonsocialist parties. Agrarian supporters were as young as those of the FPDU, although the former did not have many first-time voters. The young were more radical than the old, again within both the leftist and the nonsocialist groups. To interpret these age differences, one might now assume that the first voting decisions remain relatively static, and that changing political situations may create different political generations.

In the days of the Grand Duchy of Finland, three out of four inhabitants of Korpilahti voted for the SDP and actually no other party was locally active. Almost all persons who had been enfranchised then were Social Democrats four decades later. The Communists were most popular among those age groups during whose first voting experience the party was legalized. Also, most supporters of the Agrarian Union were those who had been entitled to vote for the first time just after World

War II, when the Agrarian Union rose to the position of the foremost party of the commune.

A majority of the inhabitants of Korpilahti worked in agriculture, and 50 per cent of these supported the Agrarian Union. This socially homogeneous party had hardly any other support. Other parties received some support from the farmers. Farmers, too, comprised more than half of the interviewed Conservatives and seemingly more of them were Social Democrats than Communists. The Social Democratic support also came from workers, especially agricultural workers, while a majority of the FPDU support was among workers. All the parties had some support among the few white collar interviewees, but proportionally most of their support went to the Conservatives and the Finnish People's Party.

Four parties had established organizational activity in Korpilahti, and a fifth one, the FPP, started its first association during the 1958 campaign. The Conservative club met mainly in the center of the commune. It had also an independent youth club. The Agrarian organization comprised one commune association and eight ward-level associations, two of them in the church village and six in other voting districts of the commune; only four voting districts were without a local Agrarian club; their youth club was not active in 1958. The SDP had three associations, the one in the church village being the most active. The organization of the FPDU, directed from Jyväskylä instead of Tampere, was based on small discussion groups or cells in various parts of the commune.[39]

On the basis of the interviewed sample, one might estimate that these associations totaled about 530 members who were entitled to vote and were sure identifiers with their party.[40] Party membership among the men was 22 per cent, and among women only 2 per cent. The small size of the sample hardly allows a comparison of the various parties. But at least the findings of both samples showed similarity: because in Korpilahti 21 per cent of the Communists, 12 per cent of the Social Democrats, but none of the FPP were members of their party; among the interviewed supporters of the Agrarian Union 11 per cent claimed to be party members; the Conservatives seemed relatively most organized.

39. Paavo Hoikka, "Vaalitaistelu maalaiskunnassa" (An Election Campaign in a Rural Commune) (Master's thesis in Political Science, University of Helsinki, 1958), pp. 42–48.
40. Each respondent represents 44.1 persons.

The local newspapers of Korpilahti were published in Jyväskylä. In Korpilahti, as in Tampere, one newspaper had gained unquestionable predominancy. This was the *Keskisuomalainen,* a Central Finland organ of the Agrarian Union, which in 1958 had a total daily circulation of 45,363 copies. In Korpilahti it sold about 1,200 copies and was read by 92 per cent of the sample. Other newspapers read were the Social Democratic *Työn Voima* (110 copies); the Conservative *Jyväskylän Sanomat* (about 100); the nonpartisan local paper for six rural communes *Koillis-Häme* (90 copies); the *Helsingin Sanomat* (86); the *Kansan Uutiset* (66); the *Uusi Suomi* (57); the national Agrarian paper *Maakansa;* and the *Hämeen Yhteistyö.* The local *Koillis-Häme* and the Communist *Kansan Uutiset* were read by 8 per cent of the sample, the independent *Helsingin Sanomat* and the Agrarian *Maakansa* by 4 per cent.

On the average, each person in Korpilahti read 1.3 newspapers. This included no professional or other periodicals, nor, for instance, the *Maaseudun Tulevaisuus* of the agricultural producers. Only 26 per cent read regularly any newspaper other than the *Keskisuomalainen,* which was read by all the Agrarian supporters, 92 per cent of the Social Democrats, 83 per cent of the Communists and 75 per cent of the supporters of the two other nonsocialist parties. The reading of other newspapers correlated more clearly with party affiliation. In addition to the *Keskisuomalainen,* only the nonpolitical *Koillis-Häme* had readers in all different party groups.

One might estimate that the *Keskisuomalainen* had about 3,925 regular adult readers. Consequently, this paper had an average of 3.3 readers per copy. It was found that only 2.1 adult persons read each copy of the *Aamulehti* in Tampere. It is possible that generally each newspaper copy serves more persons in a rural commune than in a city.

The radio was about equally common in both places. In Korpilahti, 92 per cent of the sample had a receiver at home.

SUMMARY

More than 70 per cent of the population of the city examined is composed of wage workers and those in service occupations. Politically, its enfranchised inhabitants are oriented toward the left to the extent that the supporters of the Communists, the Social Democrats, and the nonsocialist parties form three almost equally large groups. Yet the leading provincial newspaper, read regularly by almost everyone in Tampere, openly supports the National Coalition (the Conservatives).

The surrounding rural areas of this city are also exceptionally leftist. In 1954, the two leftist parties received 56.9 per cent of the votes cast in the rural communes in the Northern Häme constituency (compared with only 43.5 per cent in the rural communes of the whole country). The SDP was especially popular in this constituency. In Finland, as a whole, one finds—broadly speaking—four political regions: namely, the Swedish-speaking coast; the economically developed Southern areas with many Social Democratic and Conservative voters; the rather well-to-do agricultural regions in the west with strong nonsocialist traditions; and the wide northern and eastern areas where the Agrarians and the FPDU dominate.[41] Northern Häme constituency is a typical part of the second-mentioned SDP stronghold.

The comparison locality of this study, Korpilahti, which belonged to the same constituency in 1958, is a politically exceptional community. Although it shares the constituency's socialist traditions, it is more Agrarian and more Communist than the constituency in general. It is also situated far from its center and is a part of the economic area of Jyväskylä. For example, the inhabitants of Korpilahti read the Jyväskylä and not the Tampere newspapers. Actually the socialist leaning before World War I and the post-World War II history of this commune remind one of northern Finland. Erik Allardt has found in his ecological comparisons of rural south and rural north that only in northern Finland was the "factor of socialist traditions" related to Communist strength in 1954, on the one hand, and to the decreasing tendency of Communism since 1948, on the other.[42] By the 1962 election, Korpilahti would have been on the northern side of Allardt's dividing line.

The Agrarian Union received no particular support in Tampere, nor in other cities of the country. This is easy to explain. In the comparison group the Agrarian Union was supported by people engaged in agriculture, who are nonexistent in Tampere. The social structure of the Communists was similarly homogeneous in Tampere. Most rural Communists were also wage workers. Nonsocialist support was found in all occupational groups, but mainly among the middle classes and the persons in leading positions. In both places the supporters of the Social Democrats were, so to say, mediators between the other two major groups. In Tampere they were not only wage workers, but also white

41. See Onni Rantala, "The Political Regions of Finland," in *Scandinavian Political Studies*, 2 (1967, in press).
42. Allardt, *International Journal of Comparative Sociology, 5*, p. 68.

collar people, while in Korpilahti they were in between the FPDU and Agrarian supporters.

The above summarizes only some of the differences between the two localities. One might also emphasize the population changes. In four years, the adult population had increased 10 per cent in Tampere, but decreased 7 per cent in Korpilahti. Thus, the number of inhabitants entitled to vote was 15 times larger in Tampere than in Korpilahti in 1954, but 18 times larger in 1958. A comprehensive ecological analysis by Olavi Riihinen provides an additional opportunity to compare the two communities. In this study, which used the 548 communes as units of analysis, several basic dimensions were found. If such factors are converted to factor scores for the individual communes, we find that Tampere and Korpilahti differed greatly from each other as regards their "expansiveness" (Tampere high, Korpilahti low), "division of labor" (Tampere very high, Korpilahti moderately low), and "centrality" (Tampere high, Korpilahti moderately low). On the other hand, an above average "pressure toward conformity" was characteristic of both places, and both were rather close to the national average in their "narrowing of differences in per capita income," "propensity for economic disturbance," and "changes in per capita income." [43]

Some observations of similarities have been presented too. Let us repeat the male majority of the FPDU supporters and the female tendency to nonpartisanship—both to be expected on the basis of previous studies. Moreover, the Communists were exceptionally young, and age differences also existed between the nonsocialist groups. About every ninth person who was entitled to vote and had a sure party preference claimed to belong to a political organization—a bigger proportion of the Communists than of the Social Democrats, but a bigger proportion of the latter than of the FPP supporters. Similarities in newspaper readership were also mentioned. One out of fifty read no newspaper; in addition, one out of twenty did not read the predominant newspaper of his own locality. In general, the choice of newspaper correlated with party affiliation. In both places people had easy access to radio programs.

Only one industrial city is the subject of this study, but the political behavior of its people is hardly unique. Obviously, the comparison group supports many of the findings presented in this chapter for knowledge of the locale.

43. Olavi Riihinen, *Teollistuvan yhteiskunnan alueellinen erilaistuneisuus* (Regional Differentiation of Industrial Society) (Porvoo-Helsinki, WSOY, 1965), especially pp. 236–39.

4. Interested and Indifferent Citizens

A summary by Frederick H. Harris of his study of political participation in a North Carolina county seems to offer a perspicacious "cumulative scale" of political activity:

> Some voters, but hardly any nonvoters belong to politically oriented associations;
> some members of such associations also contact public officials and political leaders;
> some individuals, who contact officials and leaders, attend party meetings;
> some attendants of party meetings also electioneer before elections.[1]

Following this sequence one sorts out more and more individuals but hardly adds new ones to the group of politically active citizens. Lester W. Milbrath illustrated the same idea more recently, when he pictured a "hierarchical ranking of behaviors," ranging from the "apathetics" through "spectator" and "transitional" activities to the "gladiatorial activities" of political behavior.[2]

Such behaviors might rank differently in another political system. But similar scalcability exists generally. Obviously, it is only a matter of agreement as to which criterion makes a person politically active if the electorate is to be dichotomized into active and inactive persons. The sheer act of casting a ballot may be considered too demanding a qualification. For instance, in the words of Angus Campbell, "the truly passive citizen is a non-voter who does not vote because of lack of motivation."[3] But one might also think of criteria which fall outside the other end of the Harris scale. One might consider as political activity, for instance, a gladiatorial attempt to gain a political office, in which case all those citizens who are not interested at least in getting nominated would be called passive or inactive.

1. Frederick H. Harris, Jr., "A Study of Political Participation in Two North Carolina Counties," Research Previews 3 (Institute for Research in Social Science, University of North Carolina, mimeo. 1955), pp. 1–7. The paper is summarized by Robert E. Lane, *Political Life* (Glencoe, The Free Press, 1959), pp. 93–94.

2. Lester W. Milbrath, *Political Participation* (Chicago, Rand McNally & Company, 1965), pp. 17–18.

3. Angus Campbell, "The Passive Citizen," *Acta Sociologica, 6* (1962), 9.

Casting a ballot is of basic significance to the theory of representative democracy, and it is easier to obtain information on voting participation than on most other political behavior. In many studies, conclusions about political activity have been based on voting participation.[4] Sometimes participation in elections and political interest are even considered to be the same. In that case it is unnecessary to pay attention to the degree of interest that differentiates those people who do go to vote. But comparisons between voters are especially necessary to understand voting behavior, including nonvoting. And differences in interest are not restricted to the ballot days or to the campaign period. Political participation is a fruitful object of study even when a campaign does not interrupt the normal political process.

Manifestations of Interest

Very few persons can take direct part in official political decision making. For instance, in the spring of 1958 the following number of inhabitants of Tampere held a position of state or municipal trust:

In the Cabinet of Finland there was one minister, or 0.1 persons per 10,000 inhabitants of the city.[5]

In the Parliament there were seven persons,[6] or 1 per 10,000 inhabitants.

The city government had 9 trustee members (1.2 per 10,000) and 3 ex officio city manager members.

The city council elected in October 1956 had 53 members (7 per 10,000), and it had the same number of vice-members.

The number of other municipal trusteeships filled by the city council, which were mainly memberships in various boards, was 480 (62.5 per 10,000), but to some extent they were held by the same inhabitants of the city.[7] These boards also had vice-members.

4. For instance, Herbert Tingsten, *Political Behavior* (London, P. S. King, 1937); and Erik Allardt, *Social Struktur och politisk aktivitet* (Helsingfors, Söderström & Co., 1956).

5. The industrialist Lauri Kivekäs was Minister of Commerce and Industry in the Cabinet of Rainer von Ficandt, and in that of Reino Kuuskoski appointed on April 26, 1958; in the former, the city manager Erkki Lindfors also was Second Minister of Social Affairs.

6. Kustaa Alanko, Anna Flinck, Väinö Hakkila, and Kaisa Hiilelä (sdp), Elli Stenberg and Leo Suonpää (fpdu), and Artturi Tienari (Conservative).

7. Election boards (170 persons), boards of assessors (45), 29 other boards (204), the parents' councils of high schools (55) and other positions of trust (41). *Tampereen kaupungin kunnalliset hallintokunnat, virastot ja laitokset v. 1958* (The municipal gov-

Although most citizens belong—after the election is over—to the governed and not to the governing, the electorate does not necessarily withdraw from taking an active part in the political process. As mentioned above, 11 per cent of the inhabitants of Tampere had a strong party affiliation and also had joined the party organization. Many other associations had political importance. At home, almost all people had a chance to be exposed to political information via newspapers and radio, and presumably persons with an interest in politics also discussed politics.

In the study of student voters, enfranchised Finnish students gave an estimate of their interest in politics in December 1955, and their specific interest in the presidential election six weeks later was measured with an index of voting participation and exposure to the campaign. The very significant correlation of these two measures justified the conclusion that the precampaign self-estimate of political interest was a useful method of predicting active voting behavior.[8]

When the Tampere sample was asked in May 1958: "How interested are you generally in politics and governmental affairs—very, rather, little, or not at all?", the distribution of the answers was as follows:

| | Percentage of: | | |
	Men	Women	Total
Not interested	12	25	20
A little interested	42	57	51
Rather interested	30	14	21
Very interested	15	4	8
Don't know	1	–	–
	100	100	100

Thus the inhabitants of Tampere tended to estimate their interest as lower than the adult students had estimated theirs in December 1955 (very interested was also 8 per cent, but rather interested was 43 per cent). In both groups men were more interested than women.[9]

Table 4.1 gives the percentage of persons who often read newspaper articles in certain fields and often listened to certain radio programs (QQ. 5.B & 6). The table also shows the correlation of exposure to

---

erning bodies, offices and establishments of the city of Tampere in 1958, Tampere, 1958), pp. 23–140. In addition to these, the city government elects trustee members to various committees.

8. Pesonen, *Student Voters*, pp. 146–47.
9. Ibid., p. 73. In this comparison $\chi^2 = 44.49$, $v = 3$, $p < 0.001$.

TABLE 4.1. (a) The Percentage of Persons Exposed Frequently to Selected Topics in Newspapers and Certain Radio Programs, May 1958; and (b) the Correlation of Exposure with Self-estimated Interest in Politics†

Communication Media and Selected Topics	Men ($n = 205$)		Women ($n = 296$)		Total sample ($n = 501$)	
	(s)	(b)	(a)	(b)	(a)	(b)
Newspapers						
Government and Parliament	66	.43***	28	.38***	44	.53***
Economy	50	.48***	23	.29***	34	.49***
Sports	57	.09	16	.07	33	.25***
Movies	24	.19***	34	.12**	30	.11**
Literature	22	.21***	24	.28***	23	.26***
Public speeches	14	.22***	22	.31***	19	.25***
Radio						
News broadcasts	87	.22***	83	.17***	85	.21***
Radio theatre	56	−.15**	66	.07	63	−.03
Talks about parliament	61	.24***	50	.21***	55	.25***
Press review	56	.14**	51	.21***	53	.18***
"In the focus" (current events)	53	.34***	47	.18***	49	.23***
"The Social Mail Box"	44	.02	46	.03	45	.07
Sports reports	62	−.09°	32	.04	44	.10**
Religious services	21	.01	50	−.02	38	−.12***
Agricultural lectures	7	−.06	6	−.07°	7	−.07*

† Biserial correlation coefficients; Toivo Vahervuo, *Psykometriikan metodeja I* (Porvoo, WSOY, 1952), pp. 156–58. Level of statistical significance indicated in the table is determined by the *t*-test. The levels of significance are indicated and denoted as follows: ° symptomatic, $p < 0.10$; * almost significant, $p < 0.05$; ** significant, $p < 0.01$; *** very significant, $p < 0.001$.

each kind of communication and the self-estimated political interest.

In the newspaper content, the government and the parliament were the most interesting topic, while coverages of meetings and public speeches were the least interesting. Men were especially prone to read about government, economics, and sports, while movies were the most popular topic among women. Coverage of festivals and public speeches also seemed to interest more women than men.

Radio programs were defined more distinctly than the fields of newspaper content in the questionnaire. Partly because of this technical reason, listening to the radio seemed more selective than newspaper reading. The nine programs were on three levels of popularity. News broadcasts were often listened to by 85 per cent (often or sometimes by a total of 94 per cent), while agricultural talks on Sunday morning were heard by only 6 per cent (often or sometimes by 19 per cent) of the city sample. The popularity of the other seven programs was in between the two extremes. They were often listened to by 38–63 per cent of the adults in Tampere. Many programs appealed about equally to both sexes. However, sports comments and talks about the parliament interested men more, while religious services and the radio theater interested women. Females, who stay more at home, seem to have been a slight majority of the radio audience as a whole.

Exposure to many kinds of mass communication correlated with the estimate of one's interest in politics. But to detect correlations we have to control for sex. A good example is sports commentary on the radio. According to Table 4.1, listening to it correlates with political interest, but only because men were more interested in sports than women. On the other hand, if women were more exposed than men, the total sample may show only apparent negative correlation. Thus the negative correlation of political interest and listening to religious services on the radio was caused only by the greater exposure of women to these programs. It is also possible that the total sample conceals a correlation in an opposite direction among men and women. Such is the case in Table 4.1 concerning the audiences of the radio theater.

However, with these reservations, we do find in the table a genuine positive correlation between self-estimated political interest and reported exposure to precampaign mass communication.

1. A negative correlation was uncommon, but not nonexistent. The more interest the inhabitants of this industrial city had in politics, the less they listened to the radio's agricultural program.

2. The "Social Mail Box" was heard equally often by men and women. Exposure to this program did not correlate with political interest.

3. Significant positive correlation existed between readership of movie topics and political interest. Among men, political interest and listening to the press reviews also correlated significantly.

4. There are seven further positive correlations in Table 4.1 that are consistently very significant. The greater the self-estimated political interest: the more exposure to newspaper articles on the government, the Parliament and the economy, literary reviews, and commentaries on speeches; and to talks on Parliament, reviews of current affairs, and news broadcasts on the radio.

Exposure to normal or precampaign political mass communication is measured by a scale which considers three such topics in the newspapers and two radio programs (Appendix Table 3). Only the literary articles and news broadcasts of point 4 are excluded. The correlation of this scale with the self-estimated political interest is already obvious from Table 4.1.[10]

Political interest may also be displayed in private discussions. The second interview included questions on how people participate in political discussions, and to what extent their friends inquired about their opinions (QQ. 61, 62). The responses were used to classify the sample into opinion leaders, ordinary participants in discussions, and outsiders. Table 4.2 gives data on the political interests of these three groups of citizens.

TABLE 4.2. Relationship of Self-estimated Interest in Politics, by Sex, to Kind of Participation in Political Discussions (QQ. 14, 61, and 62) (in percentages)

	Men					Women				
	Degree of Interest					Degree of Interest				
	None	Little	Some	High	Total	None	Little	Some	High	Total
Outsiders	46	34	8	10	24	55	38	29	10	40
Participants	42	44	46	37	43	41	51	45	20	46
Opinion leaders	12	22	46	53	33	4	11	26	70	14
Total	100	100	100	100	100	100	100	100	100	100
Number of cases	24	85	59	30	198	69	157	42	10	278

It seems as though more men than women discuss politics. But, if sex is controlled, the expected correlation between political interest and kind of participation in discussions is also noticeable. About one half of the noninterested were complete outsiders, while a majority of the very interested not only took part in discussions; but also belonged to the group of opinion leaders. The higher the self-estimated interest was in May, the more active was the participation in discussions in July.

This correlation reminds us of three earlier research findings: (1) interviewees are able to express a realiable estimate of their own interest in politics; (2) political interest may be shown in various ways— but those who reveal one kind of interest are likely to be more interested

10. Among men, the difference is $\chi^2 = 38.70$, $v = 3$, $p < 0.001$ and among women $\chi^2 = 43.81$, $v = 4$, $p < 0.001$.

in general; and (3) the existence of a strong correlation, despite the two month's interval, makes political interest, or the lack of interest, seem somewhat consistent.

If the active remain active and the passive remain passive, even during years and decades, one might expect the noninterested to remain nonvoters. The first interview did include a question (Q. 29) on previous participation or eventual nonvoting. The answers themselves may lead to an overestimation of activity, but apparently they do suggest classes whose previous voting frequency has been different. It was possible to obtain reliable information about participation in July 1958 through the voting register. In 1958 the turnout of six groups, classified according to reported earlier participation, was the following:

	Percentage
Persons who had always voted	89(n = 373)
Once nonvoters	78(n = 36)
Twice nonvoters	77(n = 22)
Often nonvoters	65(n = 37)
Continual nonvoters	30(n = 10)
Two youngest generations	74(n = 19)

Consequently, the highest turnout in July 1958 was characteristic of those people who said in May that they had participated in all previous elections. And the more nonvoting there had been previously, the more likely that it re-occurred. It would seem that both the participation of a majority of the electorate and the nonvoting of the minority tend toward permanency.

If participation in an election is considered as one evidence of political—even other than electoral—interest, the above conclusion supports the earlier finding about a general tendency of citizens to maintain their political interest and activity at a constant level. Actually, the interviewees themselves seemed to link the casting of a ballot with general political interest: a total of 10 per cent of the May sample reported previous nonvoting because of lack of interest and did not differentiate in their answers between current elections and a general interest in politics. To illustrate this, we might quote the statements of five females:

> I do not care about politics. As long as I get food I feel good. I'd rather sleep that time. (Wife of shoeworker, 31)

> I don't want to be a partisan. (Pensioner, 57)

Because politics does not interest me. (Industrial worker, 29)

When I was younger, I did go to vote. Now I don't have the strength, nor the interest. (Widow of industrial worker, 81)

I am disgusted by it all. (Cashier, 64)

On the other hand, a large proportion of the Tampere electorate have always gone to the polls. Their interest is evidenced in normal times between elections by their exposure to political communication and participation in private discussions. We shall turn again in Chapter 9 to the campaign and electoral behavior of the indifferent and the interested citizens.

INTEREST AND FIRMNESS OF AFFILIATION

Not all people who cast a ballot are equally active; nor are all the choices made with an equally firm political preference. Correspondingly, during the normal periods between elections, political interest has many degrees and may have continuous unidimensionality, while party affiliation is also perceived differently. When the electorate is grouped into party members, other party supporters, or nonpartisans, one difference of degree is already taken into consideration. But the difference in identification of those party supporters who remain outside the membership files is still not accounted for.

In some connections attention has been paid to the approximate unidimensionality from nonpartisanship or independence to increasingly firm party affiliation and, finally, to party membership.[11] This dimension was presumed when the interviewees were asked whether they had a strong party preference, and the announced strong supporters of parties were further asked about party membership (Q. 21). The distribution of the answers was as follows:

| | Percentage of: | | |
	Men	Women	Total
Nonpartisan	5	13	10
Week preference	29	29	29
Strong preference	42	45	44
Party members	18	6	11
No information	6	7	6
	100	100	100

11. Stein Rokkan and Angus Campbell, "Norway and the United States of America, Citizen Participation in Political Life," *International Social Science Journal, 12* (1960), 72–74.

Women were more often nonpartisan and men had more often joined the parties, but the total percentage of party members and others with a sure preference did not differ much.[12]

The firmness of party affiliation will be measured for many conclusions in this study by means of a simple dichotomy of the sample. The 55 per cent called strong party identifiers comprises those individuals who said they have a strong party preference. Party members are included. The other 45 per cent, whom we shall call weak identifiers, consists of: (1) persons who said the party of their preference is merely closest to what they would desire; (2) the nonpartisans, and (3) persons who refused to state a party preference. The above division of party supporters into strong and weak identifiers, and the inclusion of the "no information" group with the weak identifiers (including nonpartisans), obviously needs to be supported by specific evidence.

Earlier studies have revealed that the more strongly people identify with their party, the more interested they are in politics in general. Let us, therefore, examine what differences in interest existed between people who perceived their party affiliation with a different intensity. The focal correlation is shown in Figure 4.A, where the inhabitants of Tampere are classified according to their self-estimated political interest. The distribution of the strength of party preferences shows again the increase in party identification as interest in politics increases. Among the noninterested only 35 per cent were strong identifiers, as compared to 88 per cent of the very interested. One half of the latter had even joined the party. Even the two middle columns are different, although not quite convincingly so. And Figure 4.A seems to support the combining of the no information group with the weak party identifiers and the nonpartisans.

Let us next look at the variations in activity revealed by reported behavior. One such behavior is newspaper readership. The average number of newspapers read regularly by the various groups was the following:

Nonpartisans	1.31 newspapers
Weak party preference	1.54 newspapers
Strong party preference	1.64 newspapers
Party members	2.31 newspapers
No information	1.44 newspapers

12. 60 per cent and 51 per cent, $t = 1.95$, $p < 0.05$. A corresponding observation has been made in Norway. More men than women were strong party identifiers, but the difference between the two sexes was small. Campbell and Valen, *Public Opinion Quarterly*, 25 (1961), 511.

FIGURE 4.A. Political Interest by Firmness of Party Affiliation in Tampere, May 1958 (in percentages)

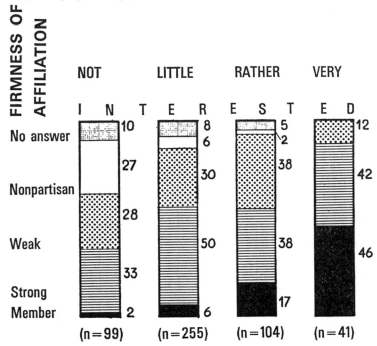

Again the nonpartisans were the least active, and the party members the most active. Those party supporters who remained outside the membership files also showed differences in degree. The weak supporters were more like nonpartisans, the strong supporters more reminiscent of party members. Also it seems again justified to combine those respondents whose party preference is not known with the weak identifiers.

Table 4.3.a repeats the above information in a slightly different form and presents additional data:

1. Party members are the most politically active group. In addition to what has been mentioned already, there is evidence for this in their exposure to political mass communication and their lively participation in political discussions. Yet the activity of party members and other persons presumably does not differ as much as their own estimate of interest in politics. Nonpolitical matters do not create any more activity

TABLE 4.3. Relationship of (a) Firmness of Party Affiliation and (b) Sex and Party Identification to Participation Characteristics: May 1958 (in percentages)

| | (a) | | | | | | (b) | | | |
	Total sample	Non-partisan	Uncertain preference	Sure preference	Party members	No information	Men Weak	Men Strong	Women Weak	Women Strong
Self-estimate:										
Very or rather interested in politics	29	6	30	26	78	16	35	59	16	21
Communication media:										
Read regularly two or more newspapers	48	35	44	51	67	34	48	51	38	57
Read regularly three or more periodicals	32	24	41	27	38	25	24	27	41	32
Had a radio receiver at home	94	84	97	96	98	78	93	95	91	97
Political mass communication:										
Scale values 2 to 5	67	49	64	70	89	56	73	85	53	64
Other communication:										
Listened often to religious services	38	39	39	40	22	41	17	24	52	47
Listened often to sports reports	44	31	50	46	45	22	65	59	29	35
Other political activity:										
Discussed politics*	67	55	67	68	83	45	75	76	58	67
Number of cases	501	49	145	220	55	32	82	123	144	152

* Includes opinion leaders and ordinary participants, 2nd interview; see Table 4.2.

among party members than among others; members listened even less than others to the religious services on the radio.[18]

2. Nonpartisans are the most passive citizens. They also tend to remain outside activities other than political participation as well; for instance, every sixth had no radio receiver.

3. The other politically passive group was those persons who refused to name their party preference. One reason for this unwillingness to respond may have been an actual lack of political opinion. And they were passive in other respects too. They listened less to sports commentators and read few periodicals. Table 4.3.a seems to provide consistent evidence for combining these interviewees with weak identifiers.

4. The activity of the majority of the Tampere inhabitants (73 per cent) ranged between that of party members and nonpartisans. It does not seem to make much difference whether these interviewees reported a weak or a firm party preference. However, by all measures with the exception of self-estimated political interest, the persons with sure party affiliation were the most active group, especially when politics was concerned—that is, in terms of newspaper reading, exposure to political communication, and probably political discussions.

The one consistent conclusion about Table 4.3.a is, therefore, the expected one: the stronger the party identification, the more active the interest in politics. The most active persons tended to join the organization of the party of their preference, and the presumed unidimensionality from nonpartisanship to party membership may have existed. But obviously the 44 per cent who reported a sure affiliation, and did not belong to party organizations, still identified quite differently with their party. Thus the present classification of strong and weak identifiers seems appropriate but unclear.

Table 4.3.b presents the stated dichotomy of weak and strong identifiers separately for men and women. Within both sexes the strong identifiers were more active in politics. However, let us point out some differences. Whatever the strength of their party identification, women seemed to estimate their own interest lower than the men. On the other hand, the number of newspapers read by the men, or the way they discussed politics, apparently did not correlate with the strength of

13. 22 per cent ($n = 55$) and 40 per cent ($n = 446$), $t = 2.87$, $p < 0.005$. This comparison is handicapped by the fact that men were more numerous among members, but fewer among listeners of the said program, but there seems to have been a difference within the two sexes separately. Males, 17 per cent ($n = 36$) and 22 per cent ($n = 169$), females 32 per cent ($n = 19$) and 51 per cent ($n = 275$).

their party identification. It was only among women that political discussions and number of newspapers read increased with increasing sureness of party affiliation. With some exaggeration we might conclude that a classification of Tampere inhabitants into weak and strong party identifiers revealed men whose idea of their own interest differed, but women whose behavior indicated a different level of political activity.

The Centripetal Tendency of Strong Identifiers

A comparison of parties revealed that their supporters had joined the party organizations in different proportions (p. 48). Let us continue the comparison by determining how many additional strong identifiers remained outside the membership files. According to the May interview, the following proportions were either members or otherwise sure of their affiliation:

Parties	Members		Percentage of: Other sure supporters		Total strong identifiers
Finnish People's Democratic Union	21	+	48	=	69 ($n = 108$)
Swedish People's Party	–		67		67 ($n = 3$)
Social Democrats	12		51		64 ($n = 164$)
Conservatives	10		54		64 ($n = 93$)
Finnish People's Party	3		43		47 ($n = 30$)
Social Democratic Opposition	4		28		32 ($n = 25$)
Agrarian Union	–		30		30 ($n = 10$)
Aggregate	12	+	48	=	60 ($n = 433$)

It seems as if there were three types of parties. Most strong identifiers supported the Communists, the Social Democrats, or the Conservatives. Secondly, the Finnish People's Party probably had both a small membership and few strong identifiers. At the third level were the Social Democratic Opposition, just beginning to take independent steps, and the Agrarian Union. The first three parties were the most institutionalized and also had the strongest local organizations. The Finnish People's Party was much newer, and the last two parties had not yet become locally established.

We have found some correlation between party affiliation and the choice of newspaper (Table 3.5). For a deeper comparison, the different intensities of party identification now need to be taken into consideration. Table 4.4 leads to the following conclusions:

1. Possibly the weak supporters had a greater tendency than the strong

TABLE 4.4. Relationship of Party Preference and Party Identification to Choice of Newspaper: May 1958 (in percentages)†

Newspapers	FPDU Weak	FPDU Strong	SDP Weak	SDP Strong	FPP Weak	FPP Strong	Cons. Weak	Cons. Strong
FPDU								
Hämeen Yhteistyö	15	24	–	2	–	–	3	2
Kansan Uutiset	9	35***	–	2	–	–	3	–
SDP								
Kansan Lehti	9	5	17	35**	13	–	6	7
Suomen Sosiali-demokraatti	–	–	–	5*	6	–	3	2
Cons.								
Aamulehti	91	85	83	97**	88	86	100	97
Uusi Suomi	–	–	2	1	–	7	12	31*
Nonpartisan FPP								
Helsingin Sanomat	12	12	18	26	50	79°	41	36
S.D. Opp.								
Päivän Sanomat	3	1	–	2	–	–	–	–
Nonpartisan business								
Kauppalehti	–	–	–	–	–	7	–	3
No newspaper	3	3	7	–*	–	7	–	–
Number of cases	33	75	60	104	16	14	34	59

† Within each party group, the significance of the difference between each percentage pair is determined by the *t*-test. If the number of cases is too small, the test of exact probability is used (cf. Sidney Siegel, *Non-parametric Statistics* (New York, McGraw-Hill, 1956), pp. 96–104. The levels of significance are denoted as in Table 4.1.

ones to read newspapers of other parties. This is suggested, for example, by the greater interest of weak members of the FPDU in *Kansan Lehti* and *Aamulehti,* and the corresponding difference in the FPP supporters' attitude toward *Kansan Lehti.* But the table contains no statistically significant differences to support this point.

2. The readers of the local Communist and Social Democratic newspapers apparently tended to be sure, rather than uncertain, supporters of their respective parties.

3. However, strong party identifiers had a very clear tendency to read the Helsinki organ of their party. Thus sure FPDU members read *Kansan Uutiset* significantly more than the uncertain members; and *Suomen Sosialidemokraatti* had no Social Democratic readers other than strong identifiers of the party. Correspondingly, *Helsingin Sanomat* had more

sure than uncertain FPP supporting readers, and *Uusi Suomi* was read more by sure Conservatives.

4. The weak supporters of the Social Democratic Party read exceptionally few newspapers; for example, they read the locally predominant Conservative newspaper less often than the sure Social Democrats.

Let us particularly stress the tendency of strong party identifiers to read their party's central organ published in Helsinki. The supporters of each party form a wide and, to a great extent, unorganized social group, whose members share party choice. The closer the persons belonging to such a group identified with the group, the more they aimed toward contact with the group's focal source of norms and values through the direct communication published in the capital city.

Who Was Interested in Politics?

It has been pointed out above that: (1) men were more interested in politics than women; (2) "a certain law of positive correlations" [14] seems to be true of political participation, as it also prevails in many other areas of society; and (3) party members and, to some extent, other strong party identifiers were more interested in politics than were the weak identifiers. Table 4.5 presents supplementary data about the (a) interests, (b) demographic characteristics, and (c) earlier experiences of the politically interested persons. The measure of political interest is a scale of exposure to political mass communication, and the data is controlled for sex.

a. According to many empirical findings, the law of positive correlations tends not to recognize the conceptual borders which separate political interests from other social participation. A general isolation from society usually includes lack of political interest. The individual outsiders do not care much about politics; and political inactivity has also been found in entire groups, whose members have exceptionally few possibilities for social participation. [15]

The measure of nonpolitical social participation used in Table 4.5.a is the number of associations in which the interviewees reported membership (Q. 38). Political associations are not included. Men tended to

14. Allardt and Littunen, *Sosiologia* (Porvoo-Helsinki, WSOY, 1958), p. 173.
15. Campbell, *Acta Sociologica, 6,* p. 13; Allardt, "Community Activity, Leisure Use and Social Structure," *Acta Sociologica, 6* (1962), 67–82.

TABLE 4.5. Relationship of Exposure to Political Mass Communication, by Sex, to (a) Interests, (b) Demographic Characteristics, and (c) Certain Previous Experiences: May 1958 (in percentages)

	Men				Women			
	0–1 Low	2–3	4–5 High	All	0–1 Low	2–3	4–5 High	All
(a) Interests								
Members in two or more associations	22	34	42	35	11	12	30	16
Went to movies during preceding month	37	45	34	39	32	26	23	28
Read regularly three or more periodicals	22	22	31	26	29	32	55	36
Listened often to religious services	17	23	21	21	38	58	58	50
Listened often to sports reports	59	62	63	62	23	40	37	32
(b) Demographic Characteristics								
Married	68	84	93	85	57	56	55	56
21–24 years	15	11	3	8	12	6	3	8
25–42 years	37	36	38	37	43	37	25	37
43–64 years	41	49	51	48	33	51	61	46
65 and over	7	4	8	7	12	6	11	9
Labor and services	78	81	69	76	69	71	63	68
Tax rate below 4,000	46	51	37	44	59	60	61	59
Rented home	78	62	54	62	65	64	49	61
(c) Experiences								
Secondary or vocational school education	44	47	59	48	51	43	56	50
More education than father had	68	58	78	69	65	66	68	66
Knew father's party preference	68	52	80	72	55	68	76	68
Lived always in Tampere	32	27	20	25	23	21	34	25
Number of cases	*41*	*73*	*91*	*205*	*123*	*102*	*71*	*296*

participate more than women in associations, which can be seen from the distributions on page 75.[16] For example, 39 per cent of the men but only 21 per cent of the women reported membership in a trade union. But both sexes experienced more exposure to political mass communica-

16. $\chi^2 = 40.20$, $v = 3$, $p < 0.001$.

	Percentage of:		
	Men	Women	Total
Belonged to no association	26	53	42
Belonged to one association	39	31	34
Belonged to two associations	24	11	16
Three or more associations	11	5	8
	100	100	100

tion with more association membership.[17] Consequently, in Tampere, too, a low interest in politics characterized those persons who had remained outside associations.

For the sake of comparisons, Table 4.5.a includes additional data on other kinds of nonpolitical interests. The law of positive correlations prevailed when the exposure of women to political mass communication correlated highly with magazine reading. On the other hand, interest in religious services or sports commentators on the radio had little to do with political interest. The correlation of movie interest with political interest might have been negative.

b. The casting of a ballot is the most usual measure of political activity, and the typical independent variables chosen are such demographic characteristics as are obtainable from election statistics or from voting registers. Individuals who tend to be politically inactive are: (1) women; (2) single persons, especially unmarried men; (3) the young and, to some extent, the old; (4) workers, especially unskilled workers; and (5) persons with low income and without property. Thus a high turnout is typical of: (1) men; (2) married persons; (3) the middle-aged; (4) people in a top-ranking position, in white collar and professional jobs; and (5) individuals with a high income or with more property.[18]

Table 4.5.b provides no data on participation in elections. But we can observe the impact of the above characteristics on the normal, or precampaign, interest in political mass communication.

1. The lesser interest of women than men in politics has been indicated already.

17. Males: $\chi^2 = 5.36$, $v = 2$, $p < 0.10$; Females: $\chi^2 = 12.32$, $v = 2$, $p < 0.001$; the whole sample: $\chi^2 = 27.69$, $v = 5$, $p < 0.001$.

18. A pioneering statistical study was Tingsten, *Political Behavior*. Findings mentioned in the summary have been published in Finland in Allardt and Kettil Bruun, "Characteristics of the Finnish Non-Voter," *Transactions of the Westermarck Society*, III. A corresponding summary of interviews is given by Lane, *Political Life*, pp. 48–49.

2. Single men paid less attention than married men to political mass communication.[19] No corresponding difference existed between women.

3. The young had the least interest and the middle-aged the most interest in political mass communication. Women's interest seemed to begin later in life than did that of men. And in the oldest age group there were both very interested persons and persons who had lost interest.

4. There was a smaller than average proportion of workers in the group most interested in political communication.[20]

5. Women's political interest did not correlate with their own or their spouse's income. But in the group of uninterested men there was an above average proportion of individuals with a taxable income less than 400,000 old marks ($1,250.). Furthermore, persons who lived in their own house or apartment were more interested in political mass communication than were the ones who rented their homes.[21]

The five comparisons appear to provide consistent evidence for the same conclusion. Those demographic characteristics that are known to be typical of people with a high voting frequency were, in Tampere, also typical of those persons whose exposure to political communication exceeded the average before the election campaign had started.

c. Socioeconomic indexes often include information on education, in addition to data on occupation and income. And the higher the education, the more active the political participation.[22] In Table 4.5.c, persons with secondary or vocational schooling are compared with those who have only elementary school education. There may have been a slight difference among men in Tampere: as expected, the group with lower education seemed less interested in political mass communication.[23] But the question remains largely unanswered, because our sample contained too few intrviewees with higher education to permit an analysis of their political interest. However, the schooling of most inhabitants of Tampere exceeded that of their fathers. And especially those men who were very interested in politics were more educated than their fathers.[24] Yet political

19. $\chi^2 = 14.00$, $v = 2$, $p < 0.001$.
20. M $t = 1.87$, $p < 0.05$; F $t = 0.96$.
21. $t = 1.97$, $p < 0.025$. In the comparison of persons living in own and rented home, M $\chi^2 = 6.99$, $v = 2$, $p < 0.05$ and F $\chi^2 = 5.26$, $v = 2$, $p < 0.10$.
22. Campbell, Converse, Miller, and Stokes, *The American Voter*, pp. 476–77; Milbrath, *Political Participation*, pp. 122–24.
23. $\chi^2 = 3.92$, $v = 2$, $p < 0.20$ and $\chi^2 = 3.48$, $v = 2$, $p < 0.20$.
24. $t = 2.67$, $p < 0.005$.

interest did not correlate strongly with the fact that persons had studied more than their fathers. And observations on geographic mobility lead to opposing conclusions for men and women. Men who had migrated to Tampere had an interest in politics, whereas it was the women who had always lived in Tampere who were more interested.[25]

According to Table 4.5.c, political interest correlates more with knowledge of father's party preference than with education or mobility. This is similar to some American and Norwegian findings, but at the same time it is in contrast to what is known about the French electorate.[26] The most natural interpretation of the Tampere difference is the possibility that politics had not been discussed in the homes of those who were unable to mention their father's party, while the knowledge of father's party preference may be an indirect indication of the parents' interest in political matters. Therefore, an individual's interest in politics might have been awakened in his parents' home. In the same way, the roots of indifference might be traced to families in which the parents had no interest in politics, or at least did not discuss it in the presence of their children.

CONSEQUENCES OF POLITICAL INTEREST

Political interest seems to develop gradually, although the strength of its growth depends on stimuli received at a young age. A person's degree of interest then reveals itself in many kinds of active or inactive behavior. Consequently, it becomes difficult, if not impossible, to say in a correlation of the two factors whether political interest is a cause or a consequence. In this section, let us see how, the (a) knowledge of politics, (b) the number of opinions, and (c) the attitude on the approaching election correlate with normal, or precampaign, political interest. These are called consequences of interest. However, this is not meant to exclude the possibilities that these factors might also be considered either as stimuli of interest, or simply as different sides of the same phenomenon.

a. Knowledge of politics in Tampere was measured by two questions. The first concerned the parties represented in the parliament and their

25. When persons much exposed to mass communication are compared to others: Males, $t = 1.54$, $p < 0.10$ and Female, $t = 1.80$, $p < 0.05$.

26. Rokkan and Campbell, *International Social Science Journal*, 12, 85; communication with Philip E. Converse. See also Converse and Georges Dupeux, "Politicization of the Electorate in France and the United States," *Public Opinion Quarterly*, 26 (1962), pp. 1–23.

order in terms of size (Q. 18). Of course, the more accuracy expected in the answers, the fewer the experts. The other question touched upon alertness in observing the political situation: "Do you happen to remember when the next Parliament will be elected?" (Q. 28) With increasing accuracy expected, the percentages of knowledgeable persons decreased as follows:

In 1958	82
In the summer of 1958	79
In July 1958	63
In the beginning of July	17
July 5–8, 1958	13

A majority (69 per cent) of the Tampere inhabitants were aware of the names of at least five parties and did also expect the election. But every third person did not realize in May that the election would take place in July, and every sixth person was not even aware that it was an election year.

FIGURE 4.B. Interest in Politics by Political Knowledge in Tampere, May 1958 (in percentages)

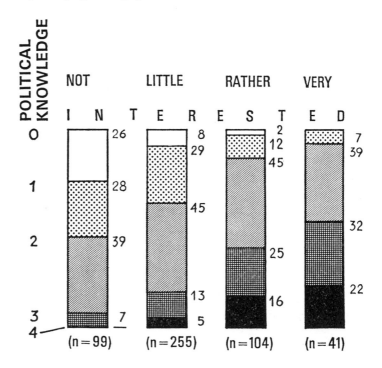

A scale which combines these answers measures political knowledge. Figure 4.B indicates the very significant correlation between interest and knowledge.[27] The higher the persons estimated their interest, the more they knew about politics.

It seems logical to presume that those persons who tended to lack interest were relatively uninformed as well. Appendix Table 2 offers two examples to prove this point: (1) The expected sex difference is evident especially when comparing married persons. There were not many expert wives nor politically ignorant husbands. Widows were also politically uninformed, but the political knowledge of unmarried women did not differ from that of the average inhabitant of the city. (2) The intensity of party identification was an important psychological measure related to political interest (Figure 4.A). And Appendix Table 2 shows a similar correlation between political knowledge and party identification. Party members were the political experts, and nonpartisans were the least knowledgeable.

Political interest revealed itself also in exposure to political mass communication. Presumably, the origin of a considerable part of political knowledge was newspaper reading and radio listening. To verify this presumption, political knowledge is compared, in Table 4.6, with the amount of exposure to political mass communication. Because sex and party identification are here controlled, as their effect has been indicated already, there are four separate cross tabulations. All of them indicate that people's political knowledge was better, when they paid more attention to political mass communication.

Therefore, a good knowledge of politics can be considered as one consequence of political interest. But men who did not identify with their party appeared to be more knowledgeable than women, to some extent even without regard to exposure to communication. Table 4.6 also indicates that the citizens' knowledge about politics was not derived from newspapers and radio alone. Some were exposed to communication but did not become experts, while others were rather well informed without paying attention to mass communication. These deviant cases bring to mind two additional facts: (1) the content of mass communication will be remembered differently by different persons; and (2) the mass communication media are not the only sources of political information.

b. According to some studies, the number of opinions increases if inter-

27. $\chi^2 = 73.90, v = 6, p > 0.001$.

TABLE 4.6. Relationship of Sex, Strength of Party Identification, and Exposure to Political Communication to Political Knowledge: May 1958 (in percentages)

	Men						Women					
	Weak identifiers			Strong identifiers			Weak identifiers			Strong identifiers		
Political communication	0-1 (low)	2-3	4-5 (high)	0-1 (low)	2-3	4-5 (high)	0-1 (low)	2-3	4-5 (high)	0-1 (low)	2-3	4-5 (high)
Political knowledge												
0 (low)	18	6	4	16	-	3	28	15	-	7	9	2
1	23	15	19	32	18	5	40	29	17	41	19	15
2	41	49	37	32	45	41	28	42	66	39	58	51
3	18	18	33	15	27	28	4	7	10	11	7	22
4 (high)	-	12	7	5	10	23	-	7	7	2	7	10
Total	100	100	100	100	100	100	100	100	100	100	100	100
Number of cases	22	33	27	19	40	64	69	45	30	54	57	41

TABLE 4.7. Relationship of Number of Economic-political Opinions, by Sex, to Interest in Politics, Party Identification, and Knowledge of Politics: May 1958 (in percentages)

	Men				Women			
	0 (low)	1	2 (high)	Total	0 (low)	1	2 (high)	Total
Percentage who:								
Estimated themselves very or rather interested in politics	17	47	50	45	11	17	25	18
Were highly exposed (scale values 4–5) to political mass communication	13	47	56	44	19	20	30	24
Were party members	13	11	22	18	9	6	5	6
Had strong party preference	50	56	64	60	42	55	57	51
Had good knowledge of politics (scale values 3–4)	30	36	40	38	13	11	17	14
Number of cases	*30*	*55*	*120*	*205*	*93*	*88*	*115*	*296*

est increases.[28] To measure the number of opinions, a sum scale was used in this study, which takes into account the response or lack of response to questions about five debated items, dealing mainly with economic policy. According to Table 4.7, the earlier conclusion was again valid in Tampere in May 1958: an increasing interest in politics brought about an increasing number of opinions, and this holds whether the number of opinions is judged by means of self-estimated interest or exposure to political mass communication. Moreover, strong party identifiers had more opinions than weak identifiers. On the other hand, party members had scarcely more opinions on economic policy than others did; there was a difference among men,[29] but no such correlation was found among women.

An abundance of opinions thus proved to be one consequence of political interest. This included the readiness of the interested and partisan per-

28. Campbell, Gurin, and Miller, *The Voter Decides*, pp. 107–110; Antti Eskola, "Mielipiteiden määrä ja aktiivisuus" (The amount of opinions and activity), *Politiikka* 1961, 55–66; Lazarsfeld, Berelson, and Gaudet, *The People's Choice*, pp. 41–42; Pesonen, *Student Voters*, pp. 86–89.

29. $t = 1.95, p < 0.05$.

sons to give reasons for their opinions (data not shown). But it did not
seem to be related to any special knowledge of politics.

c. Before the actual election campaign began, most of the Tampere
inhabitants already knew what they would do in the election, to be held
in two months. Six per cent did not intend to participate, while a ma-

TABLE 4.8. Relationship of Precampaign Intention to Vote, by Sex, to (a) Previous Election Participation; (b) Self-estimated Interest in Politics; (c) Exposure
to Mass Communication; and (d) Party Identification (in percentages)

	Men					Women				
	Will not vote	No deci- sion	Sure deci- sion	Total Per cent	Num- ber of cases	Will not vote	No deci- sion	Sure deci- sion	Total Per cent	Num- ber of cases
(a) Previous par- ticipation										
Often a non- voter	15	31	54	100	13	44	24	32	100	34
Once or twice a nonvoter	5	–	95	100	22	–	17	83	100	36
Always voted	2	6	92	100	162	3	10	87	100	210
(b) Interest										
Not interested	12	16	72	100	25	19	20	61	100	74
Little or rather interested	3	6	91	100	148	5	10	85	100	211
Very interested	–	3	97	100	30	–	18	82	100	11
(c) Mass commu- nication										
Scale values 0–1 (low)	10	13	77	100	40	11	16	72	100	123
Scale values 2–3	1	8	91	100	74	7	7	86	100	102
Scale values 4–5 (high)	2	4	93	100	91	4	16	80	100	71
(d) Party Identi- fication										
Nonpartisan, don't know	4	39	57	100	23	21	38	41	100	58
Uncertain preference	7	7	86	100	59	8	14	78	100	86
Sure preference	2	2	96	100	87	3	3	94	100	133
Party members	–	–	100	100	36	5	–	95	100	19
Total sample	4	7	89	100	205	8	13	79	100	296

jority (83 per cent) knew which party they were going to vote for. Only
11 per cent of the respondents were indecisive at that moment. Of these,
4 per cent did not know whether they would participate, and 7 per cent
intended to vote but did not know for which party.[30]

These attitudes toward the next election also varied according to political interest. Especially the interested persons knew in May which party
they would support in the election of July (Table 4.8). Furthermore, the
more strongly these persons identified with their party the firmer was
their voting intention. The other seemingly final decision, the decision
to abstain, had been made especially often by those who were not interested in politics. The most clearcut reluctance was found in the group
of previous nonvoters.

Both indecisiveness about choice and unwillingness to vote were found
in the very same groups. In Table 4.8 the only exceptions to this are the
women grouped according to the scale of political mass communication;
here women at both ends of the scale often lacked a decision. A general
consequence of high interest was an above average tendency to make an
early voting decision, whereas the politically indifferent citizens were less
willing either to decide between parties or to take part in the election at
all.

Going to the polls presupposes a motive that is at least strong enough
to overcome the resentment caused by the interruption of other affairs.
One might think that one motive is the belief that the election in question has political significance and that the ballot of an individual voter
has some desirable effect on the outcome of the election. The interviewees
were asked to choose one out of three different views on the importance
of the approaching election (Q. 34). The alternatives and the distributions of the opinions were these:

The outcome of this election has a decisive effect on the future conduct of the country's affairs	39
Apparently the election will somehow clarify the political situation	41
Elections are useless, because it does not seem to make any difference who is sitting in Parliament	13
Don't know	7
	100

30. It may be stressed that a sure voting intention was sometimes based only on the
interviewee's knowledge of the time of election, which he was told by the interviewer.
Among persons with a sure decision, 15 per cent had not remembered a while ago that
this was an election year; among the nondeciders there were 32 per cent, and among
those who did not intend to vote, 35 per cent.

Two out of five inhabitants of Tampere considered the election to be very important, and a total of four out of five thought that the election had some importance for the conduct of governmental affairs.

Appendix Table 3 indicates a correlation between political interest and the evaluation of the election. Therefore, another consequence of political interest seems to be a tendency to stress the importance of an election. However, this correlation was not quite linear, as, even in the group of the most interested citizens, some tended to belittle the importance of the election.[31]

A comparison of the voting intentions of persons who evaluated differently the importance of the election reveals additional significant differences. Among those who considered the election useless 18 per cent ($n =$ 66) had decided not to vote, while only 3 per cent of those who considered the election to be of great importance had made the same decision.[32] Consequently, the belief that the election was of importance created additional impetus to participate, and believing it to be of little significance decreased this intention. But one must also remember the possibility that the expression of the latter view could be a means of rationalizing an unwillingness to vote, which was actually based on some other reason.

Most inhabitants of Tampere did intend to participate in the election coming up in two months. Even a majority (62 per cent) of those persons who considered the election to be useless intended to go to the polls and knew which party they would vote for.

THE COMPARISON GROUP

In Korpilahti, the interview revealed the following self-estimates of political interest:

| | Percentage of: | | |
	Men	Women	Total
Not interested	30	30	30
A little interested	44	57	51
Rather interested	20	13	16
Very interested	6	–	3
	100	100	100
Number of cases	50	47	97

31. If one compares the rather and very interested as to percentage of persons who considered the election useless, $t = 1.64$, $p < 0.10$ and percentage of scale values 4 and 5 $t = 1.89$, $p < 0.05$. Thus the direction of the series may change at this point.
32. $t = 3.22$, $p < 0.002$.

Compared with the responses of the Tampere inhabitants, these distributions indicate less interest in Korpilahti. Table 4.9 presents additional

TABLE 4.9. Political Interest in Korpilahti in May 1958, and Comparison with the Tampere Sample (in percentages)

	Men	Women	All	More (+) or less (−) than in Tampere		
				Men	Women	All
Very or rather interested in politics	26	13	19	−19	−5	−10
Read regularly two or more newspapers	42	30	36	−7	−17	−12
Had a radio receiver at home	90	94	92	−5	0	−2
Political mass communication Exposure						
scale values 4–5	42	6	25	−2	−18	−7
scale values 2–5	64	47	56	−16	−11	−11
Strong party identification	50	34	42	−10	−17	−13
Discussed politics	54	47	51	−22	−13	−16
Membership in an association	62	51	56	−12	+4	−2
Knew the election will be in July	56	57	57	−16	0	−6
Remembered correctly the three largest and 3–4 other parliament groups	26	11	19	−19	−4	−9
Good knowledge of politics (scale values 3–4)	18	11	14	−20	−3	−10
Many opinions	14	19	17	−45	−22	−30
High willingness to give reasons	34	28	31	−7	+8	+2
Sure decision to vote	92	62	77	+3	−17	−6
Considered the election decisively important	50	30	40	+7	−7	+1
Number of cases	*50*	*47*	*97*			

data on political interest and related factors and also makes comparisons with the urban sample. Apparently the level of interest did not differ greatly in the two places, although the inhabitants of Korpilahti were consistently somewhat less interested in politics than were the inhabitants of Tampere. In addition to the self-estimate, this showed in the number of opinions on economic policy; the exposure to political mass communication; participation in political discussions; and the knowledge of politics. On the other hand, people belonged to associations and were sure of their party affiliation and voting intention about equally often in each place. In addition, both willingness to give reasons for opinions, and views on the importance of the election reached a higher percentage in the comparison group, but these differences are not statistically significant.

Appendix Table 4 presents data for supplementary comparisons concerning political mass communication. Inhabitants had equally easy access to radio and newspapers in both places, although the newspapers sold fewer copies in Korpilahti. On the whole, exposure to communication seemed about equally frequent. At least newspaper content dealing with the economy and with sports, as well as news, press reviews, and sport comments on the radio caught the people's attention just as much in Korpilahti as in Tampere. However, there was some tendency toward a different choice of material. Political topics and programs were less popular in the rural commune, and there were other even greater differences. The country people read little about movies, and they listened much more than city people to religious services and agricultural lectures on Sunday mornings.

However, such a comparison of various percentages in the two places is not so significant as a test in the comparison group of the correlations which prevailed in Tampere.

In the case of mass communication, for example, we find that the higher the rural inhabitants estimated their interest in politics, (a) the more carefully they read their newspapers, and (b) the more often they listened to radio talks about Parliament and to programs on current affairs. The latter are the very programs which are included in the scale of political mass communication exposure. The reported behavior of the comparison group thus seems to support the estimate they gave of their own political interest.

Many other examples could be cited of the cumulative character of political participation in Korpilahti as well as in Tampere. For instance, in Korpilahti politics was discussed by 58 per cent ($n = 19$) of the rather or very interested persons, but only by 34 per cent ($n = 29$) of the non-interested. Twenty-six per cent of the former, but only 3 per cent of the latter had joined political parties. Strong party identifiers included 54 per cent ($n = 24$) of the persons highly exposed to political mass communication, but only 36 per cent ($n = 42$) among those little exposed. Previous non-voting was reported by 16 per cent of the very and rather interested persons, but by 45 per cent of the noninterested.

The rural sample is too small to make any conclusions about the differences between weak and strong identifiers. It might be mentioned, however, that the Agrarian *Maakansa* was read more by the sure than by the uncertain supporters of the Agrarian Union. A weak identifier read on the average 1.2 newspapers and a strong identifier 1.3 newspapers. The proportion of sure party supporters in the sample happened to be largest among the Conservatives (80 per cent) and the Agrarians (61 per cent); the proportions were smaller among the Social Democrats (52 per cent), People's Democrats (42 per cent), and supporters of the Finnish People's Party (33 per cent).

Some parallel answers can be given to the question: "Who were the interested people?" According to Table 4.9, men were more interested than women. One might, however, presume that the political roles of women and men were not differentiated in the same way in this rural commune as in the industrial city. For example, uncertainty about party preference and voting intention was even more common among women in Korpilahti than in Tampere. Their tendency to stress the importance of the election was smaller, and they read fewer newspapers. But, in general, women and men differed less from each other in Korpilahti than in Tampere as far as political discussions, political knowledge, number of opinions, and willingness to give reasons were concerned. This lower level of political interest in Korpilahti was notable especially in contrast to the high level of interest of the city men.

In Korpilahti, too, people with higher incomes were more interested in politics. For instance, the percentage of persons who paid no communal tax was 52 among the noninterested, but only 29 among the little interested, and 16 among the rather or very interested. Of the different occupational groups, farmers seemed to be most interested in politics. At the other extreme were the interviewees classified as agricultural laborers, among whom 60 per cent ($n = 10$) considered themselves entirely uninterested.

In Tampere the young people were not interested, but this was not the case in Korpilahti. Here the correlation among men was slightly opposite, and women had less interest as they grew older.[33] Among different marital statuses, the unmarried persons were the most and the widows the least interested.

According to Table 4.10, participation in associations was equally com-

33. Among women entitled to vote in the 1930s there were 86 per cent ($n = 14$) of the noninterested, 44 per cent ($n = 27$) of the little interested and 17 per cent ($n = 6$) of the very interested.

mon in both places. The more the inhabitants of Korpilahti participated, the more interested they were in politics. Membership in at least one association was reported by 34 per cent of the noninterested, 55 per cent of the little interested, and 95 per cent of the rather and very interested. Periodicals were also read more in the country by the interested than by the uninterested, and Appendix Table 4 shows the almost significant positive correlation between political interest and exposure to religious services and sports commentators on the radio.

A comparison of previous experiences to current political interest gives further support to the findings in Tampere. For instance, the interviewees who were more aware of their father's party affiliation were more interested in politics. At least one year of education beyond elementary school had been acquired by 21 per cent of the rather and very interested, by 16 per cent of the little interested, but by none of the noninterested persons.

Among the consequences of political interest let us mention that: (a) there was better knowledge of politics among those persons with higher interest;[34] (b) men seemed to have more opinions on economic policy along with more exposure to political communication, while the number of women's opinions did not correlate in a similar way with exposure to mass communication media; (c) the willingness to give reasons for opinions seems to increase with increasing political interest and exposure to political communication; and (d) no more than 23 per cent ($n = 13$) of the noninterested women had a sure voting intention. A typical characteristic of the noninterested inhabitants of Korpilahti was a lack of decisiveness about the approaching election. To quote one unskilled worker (age 52): "I figure they never brought any advantage, but let's see again in July what happens." The 40-year-old widow of a farmer had gone to the polling place in 1939, before she had reached voting age. And "because they did not let me vote then," she has not wanted to try in any later election.

But, in fact, only 4 per cent of the interviewees in Korpilahti had decided to abstain from voting in the election. The number of uncertain persons (19 per cent) was greater than in Tampere. But already in May the rest of the sample had a clear intention to vote.

34. The two highest scale values of political knowledge were not obtained by any noninterested person, ($n = 29$), but by 14 per cent ($n = 49$) of the little interested and 37 per cent ($n = 19$) of the very interested.

Summary

Conclusions about political activity based on the act of casting or not casting a ballot actually deal with only one kind of political participation. However, it might be possible to define other dimensions of political activity that so far have not been clearly differentiated. On the other hand, it is known that political interest is to a large extent unidimensional. Voting is one of the possible evidences of active political behavior. It divides the electorate roughly into the passive quarter and the active three quarters. However, the same dimension of interest vis-à-vis indifference is evident when the political process operates normally without the temporary additional excitement caused by campaign activities.

Before the start of the 1958 campaign, the respondents estimated how interested they were in politics. They classified themselves into groups whose behavior actually proved to be different. The interested people especially liked to choose political topics from newspapers and radio programs, and persons who considered themselves interested in May revealed in the later interview as well a particular tendency to discuss politics.

The citizens were also classified into weak and strong party identifiers. The nonpartisans belonged to the former group and party members to the latter, but there was, apparently, more classification error in the middle of this dimension. Here, as in other studies, strong identification and political interest were correlating characteristics. When people reported a sure party affiliation, they revealed an above average identification with the group consisting of the party's supporters. Their great desire to read the central organ of the party can be interpreted as an attempt to gain access to the center that creates norms for this group.

In order to describe those who were interested in politics, we observed their other interests, their demographic characteristics, and earlier experiences. The interested were socially active in other ways, too. For instance, they participated more than the average person in associations, and they read an above average number of periodicals. On the other hand, movies were a more typical interest of the politically uninterested persons. The demographic characteristics of the interested persons were similar to those of persons with a high voting frequency described in earlier studies. An above average interest existed among men, especially married men, the middle-aged, the wealthy, and persons with high income. And as for the earlier experiences of the interested citizens, politics had been a topic of frequent discussion in the homes of their parents.

One consequence of political interest, involving frequent exposure to political mass communication, was an increasing knowledge about politics. Interested people also had more opinions on economic policy, although an abundance of opinions did not seem to be based particularly on political knowledge. Corresponding observations were made about the willingness of persons to give reasons for their political viewpoints.

Although this work, for conceptual reasons, attempts to separate the precampaign or normal political participation from that taking place during a campaign, the relationship between the two has been evident even in this chapter. For example, the interested persons especially were regular voters. Also they were in May the most certain of their participation in the next election and of the party they would vote for. Moreover, the more interested they were in politics, the more they tended to consider the election important.

People who lived in Korpilahti made a lower estimate of their interest than did people in Tampere. The corresponding difference was also evident in a somewhat lower level of exposure to political topics in newspapers and radio. This comparison between Tampere and Korpilahti reminds one of the correlation of political participation with the central-peripheral dimension. According to Norwegian studies, peripheral communes have been characterized by low politicization and low voting turnout, and in the U.S.A. the farming population has shown less interest in politics than have the urban people.[35] When applied to the social positions of individuals and defined in terms of communication, the central-peripheral dimension seems to incorporate many variables which are individually related to political participation.[36] On the other hand, the comparison group gave rather consistent support for the viewpoint that correlations of certain variables in Tampere are by no means restricted to that place. The findings also concur with research findings in other Western countries.

The politically indifferent and the politically interested citizens differ from each other in many respects. How large a proportion of the electorate should be included in each concept and how many persons should be left in between the two as ordinary citizens is merely a matter of agreement on definition.

35. Rokkan and Valen, "The Mobilization of the Periphery: Data on Turnout, Party Membership and Candidate Recruitment in Norway," *Acta Sociologica, 6,* 111–58.
36. Milbrath, *Political Participation,* pp. 110–12. Lane, *Political Life,* p. 196.

5. Party Identification

When interviewees were asked what they considered to be the best thing about the party of their choice, some of them did not describe their party at all. In spite of the wording of the question, many described their own experiences. Here are some typical answers given by three female supporters of the Social Democratic Party. In the opinion of a 71-year-old former industrial worker, the best thing about the party was "because I have belonged to it from the beginning and it is somewhat more moderate." A 52-year-old industrial worker said, "I have always voted for it and I feel like belonging to them; my husband was also one of them"; and a 24-year-old industrial dressmaker mentioned that "from my very childhood I've heard my parents support it; that's all I know about."

The oldest of these citizens had decided on her party affiliation for Spring 1958 no more recently than half a century ago. Likewise, the other two women did not weigh political reasons and counter-reasons independently. Their party preference in May 1958 was based on a viewpoint which they had learned earlier from other members of their family.

In this chapter, observations will be made on the connections between party preference and certain experiences outside the sphere of party activity, especially economic circumstances, the way of thinking in family circles, and geographic and social mobility. Some general data on the permanence of party affiliation are included.

According to the hypothesis of this study, we expect to find that (1) small groups tend to create uniform ways of thought among their members; and (2) persons who are subjected to conflicting political norm pressures perceive their party identification to be weaker than do persons who are subjected to uniform pressures; (3) a further objective of the study is to test the assumption that when party preference correlates with economic and other corresponding characteristics, the strong party identifiers differ more than do the weak identifiers of the same party (pp. 29–30, points 4, 7).

PARTY PREFERENCE AND THE STANDARD OF LIVING

In Tampere the party preference of voters was influenced greatly by their occupations. The FPDU was supported almost entirely by wage workers, while most white collar workers supported nonsocialist parties (p. 42). Occupation was naturally both a consequence of education and a determinant of income.

TABLE 5.1. Relationship of Party Preference to (a) Respondent's Education and (b) the Education of the Respondent or the More Educated Spouse: May 1958 (in percentages)

	Total sample	FPDU	SDP and S.D. Opp.	Non-soc.	SDP	S.D. Opp.	Agr.	FPP	Cons.	Non-part.
(a) Own education										
Grammar school	49	58	60	21	62	52	60	27	14	62
Vocational training of 2 months to one year	15	20	17	13	17	16	30	10	13	2
One year or more in vocational, secondary, or adult educational school	23	20	18	33	16	28	10	30	38	29
Secondary school	8	1	3	18	3	4	–	23	18	5
Gymnasium	5	1	2	15	2	–	–	10	17	2
(b) Education of self or spouse										
Grammar school	41	47	52	13	52	48	50	13	10	57
Vocational training of 2 months to one year	14	20	17	11	17	20	20	10	10	2
One year or more in vocational, secondary, or adult educational school	28	30	25	32	24	28	30	34	32	31
Secondary school	10	2	4	24	4	4	–	23	27	5
Gymnasium	7	1	2	20	3	–	–	20	21	5
Total	100	100	100	100	100	100	100	100	100	100
Number of cases	*501*	*108*	*189*	*136*	*164*	*25*	*10*	*30*	*93*	*42*

Elementary school (now eight years) was the only formal education of every second person (Table 5.1.a). This includes the 4 per cent who had attended only a circuit school. But when the education of the married persons in the sample was counted as that of the more educated of the two partners (Table 5.1.b), it was found that three fifths had received vocational or other education supplementing the elementary school.

These two ways of measuring education lead to similar observations on the correlation between party affiliation and education. The leftist supporters did not differ greatly from party to party, although the Social Democratic parties may have included a few more people with a secondary education, as they did more white collar workers; while among the Communist supporters there were seemingly more persons with vocational schooling. In general, the leftist supporters had a lower level of education than the nonsocialists.[1] Almost one half of FPP or Conservative supporters either had completed secondary school or were married to someone who had. Among all those who had received secondary school at all and their spouses, only about 4 per cent supported the Communists and 14 per cent the Social Democrats. In the sample the Conservatives had slightly more education than the supporters of the Finnish People's Party, which corresponds to their probable occupational differences.

The income tax rate allocated for 1957 is used here to measure the level of income. In the case of married persons, it had to be decided whether the best indicator would be that of the respondent, that of the respondent and spouse together, an average of the two, or perhaps the income of the spouse who earned more. The last alternative seemed to indicate best the level of income, and it was also the one easiest to compare with that of single persons. Appendix Table 5 shows that the way of measuring income really affects conclusions. More supporters of the nonsocialist parties than of the left had no income of their own, but when the measure is either the income of the interviewee or his spouse, the difference caused by proportion of nonsocialist wives, who do not work, disappears.

The data shown in Appendix Table 5.b on the income tax rate of the different party supporters or their spouses is also presented in Table 5.2. For each party the table shows the medium tax rates and the lower and upper quartiles. From this it can be seen that:

1. The supporters of the Social Democratic Party and the nonpartisans had the lowest incomes, and the supporters of nonsocialist parties earned

1. See, for instance, Campbell, Converse, Miller, and Stokes, *The American Voter,* pp. 207–09; Campbell and Robert L. Kahn, *The People Elect a President* (Ann Arbor, The University of Michigan, 1952), pp. 31–32, 38; Wolfgang Hirsch-Weber and Klaus Schütz, *Wähler and Gewählte* (Berlin, Verlag Franz Vahlen, 1957), pp. 255–63; Herbert Hyman, *Political Socialization* (Glencoe, The Free Press, 1959), pp. 36–37.

TABLE 5.2.   Relationship of Party Preference in May 1958 to 1957 Taxable Income
of Respondent or Spouse (in new marks)

Party Preference	Lower Quartile	Median	Higher Quartile	Number of cases
FPDU	2,770	3,870	5,110	108
SDP and S.D. Opp.	2,180	3,530	4,990	189
Nonsocialist	2,980	4,890	7,230	136
SDP	2,060	3,430	4,950	164
S.D. Opp.	3,730	4,180	5,180	25
Agrarian	1,480	3,320	3,750	10
FPP	3,740	4,980	6,660	30
Cons.	2,990	5,160	8,110	93
Swedish	3,000	4,260	9,130	3
Nonpartisan	1,860	2,400	4,100	42
Total sample	2,700	3,880	5,530	501

a. One dollar was the equivalent of 231 marks before September 15, 1957; it became the
equivalent of 320 marks in 1957 and 3.20 new marks in 1963.

b. Total includes 24 interviewees who refused to reveal party affiliation.

the highest. The Communists may have earned more than the Social
Democrats, but they earned less than the Conservatives and FPP supporters.

2. The deviations were different. The most uniform were the earnings
of the members of the FPDU, whose quartile deviation was 117,000 old
marks. The corresponding figure for the Social Democratic supporters
was 145,000; for the supporters of the Finnish People's Party, 146,000; and
for the Conservatives, the remarkably higher amount of 256,000 marks.

We can now hypothesize that the more educated persons among leftist
supporters had less firm party affiliations than did persons with only an
elementary school education. In addition, we can presume that white
collar workers are apt to be weaker identifiers than wage workers, and
that persons with high income weaker than those with a low income. On
the other hand, the hypothesis presumes that strong identifiers with the
nonsocialist parties often had higher education, top-ranking positions, and
above average earnings.

According to Table 5.3, these presumptions are best supported in the
case of the Conservatives. Among them, the strong identifiers seem to
have had more education and to hold higher positions than the weak

TABLE 5.3.   Relationship of Party Preference and Party Identification to Economic
Characteristics: May 1958 (in percentages)†

	FPDU		SDP		FPP		Cons.	
	Weak	Strong	Weak	Strong	Weak	Strong	Weak	Strong
One year or more post—grammar school training								
Self	15	25	30	16*	56	71	65	78
Self or spouse	33	32	40	26°	75	79	76	83
Completed secondary school								
Self	3	1	7	5	31	35	32	37
Self or spouse	6	1	7	7	38	50	44	51
Total in white collar occupations	3	4	18	19	63	74	71	66
Of these in a top-ranking position	–	3	2	12**	31	21	26	30
Income over 200,000 in 1957								
Self	82	67°	67	65	69	71	62	62
Self or spouse	91	88	75	77	88	79	76	85
Income over 600,000 in 1957								
Self	12	5	7	10	19	23	27	17
Self or spouse	12	9	10	12	32	28	36	34
Resided in own house or apartment	36	33	38	44	44	50	62	47
Telephone	–	1	10	11	38	21	41	44
Radio receiver	97	97	88	96*	100	100	97	98
Number of cases	33	75	60	104	16	14	34	59

† Significance of the differences by the *t*-test, as denoted in Table 4.1.

identifiers. In the Finnish People's Party, there are two expected differences. The strong identifiers had more education than the weak ones,
and the FPP supporters in less important white collar positions especially
tended to identify strongly with the party. Among the People's Democrats
the weak supporters seemed to earn more than the strong identifiers, but
those with secondary school training tended toward weak identification.

But, contrary to the hypothesis, a top-ranking position was held by
only a few strong Communist identifiers, and a similar statistically significant difference prevailed among the Social Democrats. The introduction
of the additional variable, party identification, in Table 5.3, together with
Tables 5.1 and 5.2, obviously leads to the conclusion that occupation,

education, and income have only a slight, if any, impact on the strength of party identification in Tampere.

Table 5.3 also provides data describing the standard of living of the interviewees. Again no notable differences were found between the weak and strong identifiers. For instance, although the amount of home ownership and private telephone service varied from one party to another, the data do not indicate that these things relate to intragroup differences between weak and strong identifiers.

Angus Campbell and Henry Valen have made a comparison between the party identification of Norwegians and of Americans. They also assumed that social differences would be larger among strong identifiers than among the independent supporters of the same parties. This turned out to be true of the supporters of the Norwegian nonsocialist parties, but in Norway the party identification of labor supporters did not correlate consistently with the characteristics used in the study. The Communists were too few to be analyzed. And in the United States, the expected differences were in fact small, but they were larger among the Republicans than among the Democrats.[2] It can be seen that Table 5.3 has features in common with the Norwegian observations. Possibly the smaller consistency in the Finnish data is caused by the study's concentrating on only one city. But more than that, the measure used in Norway was "purer," as it classified only 25 per cent of the interviewees into the group of strong identifiers.[3]

It is also necessary to remember that not all large differences between weak and strong identifiers have to be consistent with the hypothesis, because the social structure and standard of living of the supporters of the various parties also differed little in Tampere. Moreover, objective measures may describe poorly how people themselves perceive their subsistence. S. Martin Lipset describes three basic needs which, if not satisfied, radicalize political attitudes independently of level of income or class structure. These needs are a secure livelihood, satisfying work, and social status.[4]

SUBSISTENCE AND PARTY PREFERENCE

We will consider two such psychological variables, related to subsistence, that can be presumed to have an independent impact on party preference.

2. Campbell and Valen, *Public Opinion Quarterly*, 25 (1961), 513–16.
3. Ibid., pp. 509–10.
4. Lipset, *Political Man*, pp. 232–48.

In order to determine the distance between real possibilities and economic aspirations, the interviewees were asked to evaluate whether their living was satisfactory or whether additional income would be necessary (Q. 9); and, in order to identify the insecurity of subsistence, they were asked about their unemployment experiences (Q. 12).

Their answers reveal the citizens' wide diversity of attitudes toward their livelihoods. A construction worker (age 44), who was a strong Communist supporter, was taxed for 370,000 old marks in 1957 and for 690,000 old marks in 1958. But he felt he could manage satisfactorily only if he were to receive an additional 50,000 marks per month. Without personal experience of unemployment, he considered it indispensable that the state "will create jobs and jobs better paid than those in unemployment relief works." He was not at all satisfied with the conduct of governmental affairs. On the other hand, a widow, who was a horticultural worker and a strong identifier with the Social Democrats, felt her subsistence was satisfactory, although her annual taxable income was below 200,000 marks in 1957, and even smaller the following year. She believed that "people in charge of our country's affairs have done their best" and she did not want to "demand anything from the state because the state also has many difficulties."

Ten per cent of the respondents felt it necessary to get at least 20,000 marks more per month, and 26 per cent of the sample estimated they would need an additional 10,000 marks or more per month to get along satisfactorily. But a three-fifths' majority was relatively satisfied with their income. Classification according to the respondent's or the spouse's income tax rate results in the following distribution of answers to Q. 9:

	Percentage:		
	Below 4,000 a year	Above 4,000 a year	Total
Got along satisfactorily	50	72	60
Income perhaps too small	28	20	24
Income definitely too small	19	8	14
Don't know	3	0	2
Total	100	100	100
Number of cases	*266*	*235*	*501*

As expected, satisfaction with subsistence tended to increase as income increased.[5] However, one half of the low income group considered their

5. $\chi^2 = 5.30$, $v = 2$, $p < 0.01$.

subsistence satisfactory, while some dissatisfaction existed in the high income group. And among the dissatisfied, the higher the real income was, the more additional income was felt to be necessary.[6]

Obviously, the number of dissatisfied persons would have been smaller if unemployment had not been exceptionally high during the spring of 1958. At the time of the May interview about 1,600 names were filed in the city's municipal unemployment register. This was three times higher than it had been at the same time in the previous year. It is true that all but a hundred of the registered unemployed actually were occupied in employment works of the municipality or the state,[7] but it is likely that working in employment camps is generally perceived as unemployment, for such reasons as the limits it places on normal social participation.[8]

In the sample for this study, 4 per cent of the respondents were unemployed, in employment works, or married to such a person. The group of partially unemployed and their spouses, which is not included in the official statistics, amounted to 7 per cent of the sample.

The figures below show the correlation of unemployment with dissatisfaction. Previous unemployment was also taken into consideration. The percentage of satisfied persons was the following:

	Income below 4,000	Income above 4,000
No unemployment experience	55($n = 185$)	78($n = 196$)
Persons with unemployment experience	40($n = 81$)	42($n = 40$)

Only two fifths of the persons who had experienced unemployment were satisfied with their subsistence, and the size of their incomes did not seem to have any effect on that proportion. On the other hand, a majority of the persons who had never experienced unemployment were satisfied with their income. Their satisfaction increased with increasing income.

Party preference was related to both satisfaction and unemployment experiences (Appendix Table 6). Only two fifths of the People's Demo-

6. Needing at least 15,000 marks per month was expressed by 26 per cent ($n = 132$) of the dissatisfied with small income, but by 48 per cent ($n = 67$) of the dissatisfied with high income; $t = 3.06$, $p < 0.01$.

7. *Tampereen kaupungin tilastollinen vuosikirja* (The Statistical Yearbook of the City of Tampere), 1958, Table 138.

8. Allardt, "Social Factors Affecting Left Voting in Developed and Backward Areas" (paper delivered at Paris, International Political Science Association, Sept. 1961), p. 9.

crats, but four fifths of the nonsocialist supporters said that they got along satisfactorily. And almost every second People's Democrat had been unemployed or was married to someone who had. On the other hand, unemployment experiences had remained quite unknown to the supporters of nonsocialist parties (maybe not to the Agrarians of Tampere). As for the Social Democrats, the proportion of presently and formerly unemployed persons was the same as that of the whole city. They were also more satisfied with their incomes than were the People's Democrats, but less satisfied than the nonsocialists.

When it is seen that, even when their incomes were higher, the People's Democrats were less satisfied than the Social Democrats, it becomes apparent that difference in income alone does not explain the correlation of party preference with subsistence satisfaction. Figure 5.A presents this correlation, controlled for income. We find that (1) within each party group satisfaction increased with higher incomes, but at the same time

FIGURE 5.A. Party Preference by Satisfaction with Subsistence, of Low and High Income Groups, in Tampere, May 1958 (in percentages)*

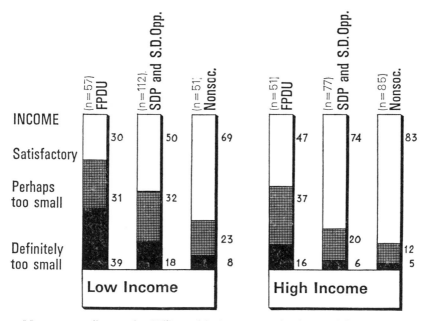

* Income according to the 1957 municipal tax rate, whereby married persons have been classified by either own income or that of the better earning spouse. High income = 400,000 old marks or more. Satisfaction according to question 9, including the "don't know" group (2%) in the alternative "perhaps too small."

(2) independent of their actual incomes, Communist supporters were the least satisfied with their incomes, and nonsocialist supporters the most satisfied. And Social Democrats in both income groups rated their satisfaction close to the average of all city inhabitants.

Figure 5.B shows the corresponding information about unemployment.

FIGURE 5.B. Party Preference by Unemployment Experiences, of Low and High Income Groups, in Tampere, May 1958 (in percentages)*

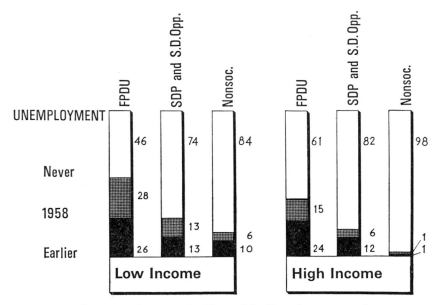

*Income and party preference as in Figure 5.A. Unemployment experiences concern both the interviewees and their spouses. The "presently unemployed" include fully unemployed persons (4%) and those partially unemployed due to shorter work weeks (7%).

We find that (1) unemployment experiences like dissatisfaction, were more common in the lower than in the higher income groups, and (2) unemployment experiences had also been more frequent among Communist supporters. This is true of current as well as of former unemployment. Insecurity of subsistence proved to be a radicalizing factor in Tampere, as elsewhere. Even the recollection of unemployment had the same effect.[9]

9. This finding about individuals might be compared with the factor analysis of aggregate data, which was performed separately for five groups of Finland's communes. The relative support of the FPDU was not related to the factor of insecurity within the group of cities and towns. Within another group of special interest here, that of the rural com-

TABLE 5.4.   Relationship of Annual Income Tax Rate (1957) and Party Preference to Unemployment Experiences: May 1958* (in percentages)

	Below 4,000				Above 4,000			
	FPDU	SDP and S.D. Opp.	Non-soc.	Total sample	FPDU	SDP and S.D. Opp.	Non-soc.	Total sample
No unemployment (respondent) or spouse	44	71	71	63	60	76	89	73
Present unemployment	15	5	5	9	6	4	–	4
Partial unemployment	16	10	5	11	11	6	5	7
Earlier unemployment	25	14	19	17	23	14	6	16
Total	100	100	100	100	100	100	100	100
Number of cases	52	83	21	187	48	51	18	132

* Table includes agricultural laborers and workers not in service occupations.

It is necessary to control three factors before returning to the comparison of weak and strong party identifiers. First, it is obvious that the various occupational groups had been subjected differently to unemployment. The percentages without any unemployment experience were as follows:

Manual workers	67($n = 319$)
Service workers	84($n = 37$)
Lower white collar employees	93($n = 138$)[10]

Consequently, if one wants to know about that part of the sample, fairly uniform as to occupation, which had suffered the most unemployment, one has to concentrate on manual workers. This has been done in Table 5.4, and the conclusions remain unaltered. We find that, among the Tampere manual workers of all income levels, the People's Democrats

munes of southern and western Finland, such communes which were characterized by insecurity tended to have both a below-average proportion of Communist voters in 1954, and an above average increase in Communist vote from 1948 to 1958. Allardt, *International Journal of Comparative Sociology, 5* (1964), 68.

10. $\chi^2 = 6.42$, $v = 2$, $p < 0.001$. The manual workers' class (64 per cent of the sample) includes here those persons who are classified in Table 3.3 as agricultural laborers or workers, excluding, however, the service occupations (7 per cent of the sample). Correspondingly, unemployment correlates with education: no unemployment was experienced by 73 per cent with an elementary education, but 95 per cent with a secondary school education.

had had the most unemployment experiences,[11] and the nonsocialists, whose income was above the average, had the least.

Another possible source of error may lie in the use of the 1957 income tax rate for correlation with interview data gathered in May 1958. Even though a part (3 per cent) of the sample did not pay Tampere communal taxes in 1958, the conclusions have been rechecked by using the 1958 tax rate.[12] In Appendix Table 7, satisfaction and unemployment are compared with party preference and with the 1958 income. Again the conclusion based on Figures 5.A and 5.B is supported. Party preference was related to dissatisfaction and unemployment, independent of size of income.

Finally, we have to remember that so far the observations have been made on two mutually correlating variables (p. 98). On the basis of Table 5.5, it is now possible to make observations on both variables simultaneously. In the table individuals are classified into four types,

TABLE 5.5. Relationship of Taxable Income, Satisfaction with Subsistence, and Unemployment Experiences to Party Preference: May 1958 (in percentages)

Party Preference	Below 4,000			
	Satisfied, employed	Dissatisfied, employed	Satisfied, unemployed	Dissatisfied, unemployed
FPDU	9	20	25	47
SDP and S.D. Opp.	43	47	38	35
Nonsocialist	29	16	16	6
Nonpartisan	14	11	12	6
No information	5	6	9	6
Total	100	100	100	100
Number of cases	*102*	*83*	*32*	*49*
	Above 4,000			
FDPU	12	30	35	61
SDP and S.D. Opp.	33	32	47	26
Nonsocialist	47	27	–	9
Nonpartisan	5	4	6	4
No information	3	7	12	–
Total	100	100	100	100
Number of cases	*151*	*44*	*17*	*23*

11. In the lower income class $t = 3.15$, $p < 0.01$, in the higher $t = 2.33$, $p < 0.02$.
12. Information obtained through the board of assessors in 1959.

according to whether they had both, either, or none of the two radicalizing characteristics.

Within the two extreme classifications, the relative popularity of the People's Democrats and the nonsocialist parties varied greatly. For example, in the above average earnings category one half of the satisfied and never unemployed persons supported a nonsocialist party, whereas a majority of the dissatisfied and unemployed preferred the FPDU. And again we find that the relative support of the Social Democrats did not correlate noticeably with either satisfaction or unemployment. However, the focal aspect of Table 5.5 is that the citizens' party preferences correlated separately with their satisfaction and with their unemployment experiences. The more leftist the chosen party was, the wider the gap between economic aspirations and current possibilities, and the less secure the perceived subsistence. The FPDU may have been favored even more by the insecure than by the dissatisfied. Furthermore, one finds the most nonpartisanship among those persons who had small earnings but were satisfied with their living security.

According to Table 5.3, strength of party identification did not correlate highly with the amount of annual income. In the whole sample as well, it seemed that party identification did not correlate either with satisfaction with subsistence or with work security: the percentage of satisfied persons was 60 among both weak and strong identifiers, and an even larger percentage (76) of both weak and strong identifiers had never experienced unemployment. But, in order to avoid wrong conclusions, party preference must be controlled. This is required also by the previously mentioned hypothesis (p. 91).

In Table 5.6 the size of income is also controlled. In this case, the sample has been classified into such small subgroups that many differences between the percentages lack statistical significance. Nevertheless, some conclusions can be pointed out, at least about the sample itself.

1. Despite the correlation of party preference with income satisfaction, strength of party identification and satisfaction of persons whose income was low did not correlate.

2. An increase in income gave much more satisfaction to the weak than to the strong Communist supporters. Most strong Communist identifiers were dissatisfied even with above average earnings.

3. An opposite change occurred among Social Democrats and nonsocialists. Their strong party identifiers were more satisfied than the weak supporters were, as the annual tax rate rose above the average.

TABLE 5.6. Relationship of Party Preference, Party Identification, and Income Tax Rate to (a) Satisfaction with Subsistence and (b) Unemployment Experiences: May 1958

	(a) Per cent satisfied	(b) Per cent never unemployed	Number of cases
Below 4,000			
Weak FPDU	32	53	19
Strong FPDU	29	45	38
Weak SDP and S.D. Opp.	52	68	44
Strong SDP and S.D. Opp.	49	78	68
Weak nonsocialist	68	73	22
Strong nonsocialist	69	93	29
Total Weak Identifiers	52	68	123
Total Strong Identifiers	49	71	143
Above 4,000			
Weak FPDU	64	79	14
Strong FPDU	38	54	37
Weak SDP and S.D. Opp.	64	76	33
Strong SDP and S.D. Opp.	84	86	44
Weak nonsocialist	75	100	36
Strong nonsocialist	90	96	49
Total Weak Identifiers	70	85	103
Total Strong Identifiers	73	81	132

4. Unemployment experiences strengthened Communist affiliation. This was especially true of cases with above average earnings.

5. Unemployment experiences had an opposite influence on Social Democrats. In both high and low level income categories, there was less unemployment among strong than among weak Social Democratic supporters.

6. A similar correlation can be seen among the nonsocialists with low earnings. Unemployment weakened their identification with the party.

We can conclude that those persons who identified strongly either with the People's Democrats or with the nonsocialist parties were the most obvious representatives of the special character of their respective groups. These two were the most widely separated as far as both satisfaction and unemployment were concerned; the weak identifiers in both groups were less different. This is in accordance with our expectations.

Because in neither satisfaction nor unemployment were the Social Democrats much different from the average Tampere inhabitants, it was not consistent with the hypothesis to expect differences between weak and strong Social Democratic identifiers. Yet there was a difference, which might be explained by the competition for popular support between the Social Democrats and the FPDU, which was keener than that with the non-socialist parties. One might in this connection also mention the possibility of changing values within this party. In 1958 the Social Democrats were no longer the radical party that appealed especially to the dissatisfied and unemployed citizens. A certain "three-step" radicalization process seems to have been occurring within the sphere of leftist supporters. It was evidenced first by a weakening identification with the Social Democratic Party, then by conversion to the FPDU, and finally by a strengthening identification with the People's Democrats. A corresponding three-step moderation of attitudes in the opposite direction was of course also possible.

Apparently unemployment both increased radical leftist support and created dissatisfaction with earnings. But dissatisfaction was also a separate radicalizing factor.[13] Actually, in this relationship we can not be sure which variable was the dependent one. A Communist affiliation may have brought about dissatisfaction, if the readers of Communist newspapers were reminded most often about their present miseries. According to a qualitative observation, this was actually true, but for this comparison newspapers were not analyzed quantitatively. Furthermore, while strong Communist identifiers were most exposed to the press of their party (Table 4.4), dissatisfaction seemed to be even more typical of them than did unemployment.[14] Better earnings seemed to increase the satisfaction of the weak supporters, but decrease that of the strong Communist identifiers.[15]

13. In this work dissatisfaction with subsistence is used as an indication of a distant level of aspiration. Distant aspirations and a choice of a better situated reference group presumably are closely interlinked. About the effect of the latter as a radicalizing factor see, for instance, Allardt, *Social Struktur,* pp. 73–74.

14. Let us mention the percentage of strong FPDU identifiers in the four groups of Table 5.5. These were 56 per cent ($n = 18$) of satisfied not unemployed, 77 per cent ($n = 13$) of dissatisfied, 67 per cent ($n = 6$) of unemployed, and 93 per cent ($n = 14$) of dissatisfied and unemployed.

15. A comparison of the taxable incomes for 1957 and 1958 gives us a three-fold classification. Among the Communist supporters the percentage of satisfied persons was the following:

	Weak	Strong
Annual income decreased	33 ($n = 15$)	29 ($n = 34$)
No more than 10% increase	60 ($n = 5$)	53 ($n = 19$)
Annual income increased more	67 ($n = 12$)	21 ($n = 19$)

The findings are similar in both income classes. The most satisfied persons had stable or only slightly increasing incomes, while among the strong identifiers increasing income

Let us repeat that security of subsistence and a wide distance between level of aspiration and actual standard of living are only examples of the kind of economic factors which may affect party affiliation. Other determinants of party preference are the many social factors which belong neither to the sphere of economic behavior nor to the direct mass communication from political powers. Lack of channels of communication in the group, a belief in the possibility of individual social rise, and conservative local traditions are, according to Lipset, three factors that tend to weaken political radicalism.[16] In the introduction to this study, attention was paid also to political socialization and to the general tendency of small groups to create uniform political attitudes among their members (p. 29).

UNIFORMITY OF FAMILY CIRCLES

The present work contains very little data on small groups. However, something can be said of the interviewees' spouses and parents (Q. 33). We assume that children often inherit their parents' party preference and that the political opinions of spouses tend also toward uniformity. A third hypothesis is that the party identification of citizens who share the party preference of their family tends to be stronger than that of those who disagree with their parents or spouse.

Two thirds of the respondents were aware of the present or previous party affiliation of their fathers and mothers (Table 4.5.c). As expected, most of them reported the same party for both their parents. Only 7 per cent claimed that their parents had different party affiliations.

According to the responses of married interviewees, the next generation of married couples also usually agreed politically. A comparison of the answers with the respondents' own party preference gives the distribution on page 107.

In two respects husbands and wives said the same thing: (1) they usually agreed politically with the spouse, and (2) if there was a disagreement, the husband was generally more to the left and the wife to the right. It was noted earlier that women tended toward conservatism (p. 40). (3) Moreover, the distributions suggest the possibility that some

---

brought dissatisfaction. These statistically insignificant observations are reminiscent of the view that both a decrease and a rapid rise in the standard of living move the level of aspiration farther away.

16. Lipset, *Political Man, pp.* 248–61. About local tradition, see also Rantala, "Poliittisen regionalismin syntyselityksiä" (Explanations for the Beginning of Political Regionalism), *Politiikka* (1962), pp. 158–65.

	Percentage of:	
	Husbands	Wives
Spouse supported the same party	70	64
Spouse was more "to the left"	1	6
Spouse was more "to the right"	5	2
Did not know spouse's party	21	25
Spouse was nonpartisan	3	3
	100	100
Number of cases	*159*	*146*

husbands overestimated the agreement of their wives. Perhaps some wives, who were thought to agree with the husband, actually disagreed or did not even know what party the husband supported. The greater influence exerted by husbands than wives on the spouses' party preference may be manifested by those cases in which the interviewee was unaware of the spouse's party. In these situations men obviously had a party affiliation more often than women.[17]

A comparison between respondents and their parents is not concerned with existing small groups. It deals rather with the political socialization that took place in the parents' home during the interviewees' youth. Inheritance of party preference and constancy of the inherited position was not as common as the similarity between married couples (Appendix Table 8). However, people agreed with their fathers considerably more often than would have happened at random in a multiparty system. Every second person who knew his father's party preference shared it. Consequently, one third of the total sample mentioned that their party was the same as their fathers'. There was hardly any difference between men and women, yet men who had given up their fathers' party may have moved more to the left. Women tended to remain more nonpartisan or to shift to the right.

The percentage distribution on page 108 indicates the party preferences of the respondents and of their fathers. It includes only those persons who knew their father's party.

A Social Democratic home was the origin of most Social Democratic supporters in Tampere (73 per cent), and of one half of the supporters of the FPDU; only every third Communist supporter's father had the same party preference. The change of generation had brought about in the city a weakening of Social Democratic and Agrarian affiliations, but an increase in Communist and FPP support. Figure 5.C shows the May 1958

17. 88 per cent ($n = 34$) and 70 per cent ($n = 37$), $t = 1.90$, $p < 0.10$.

| | Percentage of: | |
	Fathers	Respondents
FPDU	10	24
Soc. Dem. Opposition	3	6
Social Democrats	53	35
The Agrarian Union	14	2
The Finnish People's Party	2	6
The National Coalition	16	19
The Swedish People's Party	1	1
The Young Finnish Party	1	.
The Old Finnish Party	1	.
Nonpartisan	.	7
	100	100
Number of cases	*324*	*324*

party preference of the offspring of fathers with four different party affiliations. Children of Communists had generally remained Communists and never stepped outside the leftist parties. Next in permanence was the Conservative support. Every fourth child of Social Democratic supporters had become a Communist, and some were supporting nonsocialist parties. But Social Democratic opinion had been inherited much more

FIGURE 5.C. Percentage Distribution of the Interviewees' Party Preference, Classified according to Father's Party Preference

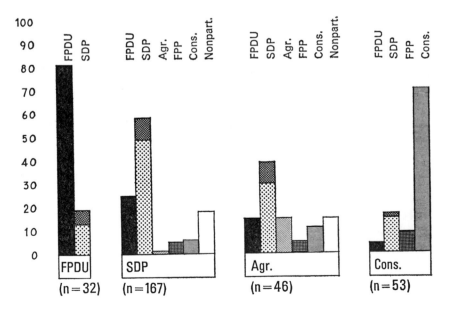

FPDU (n=32)   SDP (n=167)   Agr. (n=46)   Cons. (n=53)

often than an affiliation with the Agrarian Union. Only 15 per cent of those children of Agrarian fathers who now lived in the city agreed with the father. An equal proportion had become People's Democrats or other bourgeois supporters. For those from an Agrarian home, the most typical change was to become a supporter of the Social Democrats.

The main conclusion reached thus far is that there is a uniformity between their parents' party preference and those of the enfranchised population of Tampere in May 1958. On the other hand, two obvious reasons for giving up the father's party have been mentioned: geographic mobility (see pp. 117–20 below) and the changing party system. The latter was evidenced by the support given the post-World War II parties, the FPDU and the Finnish People's Party, by the inhabitants of Tampere. Relatively most changes to the left from the father's party had occurred among those men who were born between 1915 and 1926.[18] Their first opportunity to vote had been in 1945 or 1948, when Communist activity had recently become legalized after a pause of a decade and a half.

Two other aspects of the comparison of age groups throw light upon early political socialization. First, the youngest of those born from 1927 to 1936 agreed the most with their fathers.[19] Obviously, they had acquired the least independence from the influence of the home. In the afore-mentioned student study, it was also found that parents' influence on party affiliation decreases with increasing age, although it does not dis-continue altogether.[20] Moreover, it is notable that the father's party was least known by two groups, those born before 1893 and between 1921 and 1923.[21] Suffrage had not been extended to the parents of many of the former group, while the special character of the latter may have been a product of the disturbance which wartime military service caused in the normal political socialization of that age group.

Table 5.7 can be used to test the hypothesis concerning party identifica-tion. However, we must stress again that some of the observations are based on too few cases to be reliably generalized. There are three findings:

1. Among persons who did not know, agreed, or disagreed with their father's party affiliation, the first tended least toward strong party identifi-cation. This is to be expected, because knowledge of father's party added

18. 37 per cent of the men in this age group, 25 per cent of older ($t = 1.43$, $p < 0.20$) and 10 per cent of younger ($t = 2.96$, $p < 0.01$).

19. 42 per cent, of the others 30 per cent ($t = 2.43$, $p < 0.002$).

20. Pesonen, *Student Voters*, p. 99.

21. In the given age groups 43 per cent and 41 per cent were unaware, of the others only 25 per cent ($t = 2.11$, $p < 0.005$ and $t = 2.03$, $p < 0.005$).

TABLE 5.7. Percentage of Strong Party Identifiers in the Sample, Classified according to Agreement with Father's Party Preference, Sex, Marital Status, and Agreement with Spouse's Party Preference: May 1958

	Agreed with father		Disagreed with father		Father's party not known		Total sample*	
	M	W	M	W	M	W	M	W
				(per cent)				
Married, agreed with spouse	70	44	69	78	54	55	65	57
Married, disagreed with spouse	50	..	44	17	67	..	50	44
Married, total	68	45	65	70	55	58	63	59
Single	78	77	20	61	70	51	67	64
Total sample	69	59	61	67	57	54	63	59
				(number of cases)				
Married, agreed	*59*	*55*	*48*	*37*	*41*	*38*	*148*	*130*
Married, disagreed	*4*	*1*	*9*	*6*	*3*	*2*	*16*	*9*
Single	*9*	*44*	*5*	*23*	*10*	*43*	*24*	*110*
Total sample	*72*	*100*	*62*	*66*	*54*	*83*	*188*	*249*

* Nonpartisan respondents are excluded here, as elsewhere in the table.

to political interest (p. 77), and because political interest, in turn, correlates with the strength of party identification (Figure 4.A).

2. The degree of party identification of persons agreeing or disagreeing with the father was seemingly similar. Of the former, 63 per cent, and of the latter, 64 per cent were among the strong identifiers. In reality, the correlation among men and women was in an opposite direction. Abandoning the father's political position decreased the identification of men but increased that of women. The former does, but the latter does not concur with the hypothesis. If the effect of marital status is also controlled, the group contradicting the hypothesis seems to be that of married women, and the differences among married men are too small to support the hypothesis.

3. Persons agreeing with their spouse were stronger identifiers than those who disagreed. This is also expected.

The hypothesis that membership in uniform small groups tends to strengthen party identification was thus supported, especially by findings about married couples and about groups consisting of unmarried persons and their parents. But women who live continuously in a uniform family group—who first learn to support their father's party and then marry a man of the same opinion—obviously do not become strong identifiers with that party. A presupposition of a strengthening party identification among women would be based on a political awakening, created either by the independence of a single woman or by the adoption of a new party affiliation from the husband.

PERMANENCE OF PARTY AFFILIATION

The above remarks about political socialization indicate that changes in adopted party preference are exceptional and slow. This is evidenced also by the relative consistency of the aggregate distribution of votes cast in different parliamentary elections. Let us now present interview data on changes in party choice. Later on, attention will be paid to those changes which occurred during the 1958 campaign. Here we will observe the frequency of earlier changes and compare persons who have remained constant with those who have changed their preference. According to the hypothesis, persons who have adopted a new party preference identify less strongly with their party than do those who remain constant.

Obviously, the frequency of changes is not reliably revealed by the recollection of the respondents.[22] A classification of the sample into changers and constants probably makes the latter group too large. Yet the two classes are different enough to make their comparison useful. One might also think that actual voting experiences are recalled better than those changes of party which are independent of elections.

In Table 5.8, party preference in May 1958 is compared with recalled behavior in the 1954 parliamentary election. Only two thirds of the sample reveals constancy or change in party choice. The others either did not vote in 1954, had not yet come to voting age, or did not provide the information.

Among the two thirds on whom information was obtained, changes had not been numerous. Only 17 per cent ($n = 331$) had abandoned the party they voted for in March 1954 and had begun to support another party. Perhaps the supporters of the independent Social Democrats should be included in this percentage, inasmuch as that wing had been separated from the mother party after the 1954 election. If those changes are eliminated, the percentage of the changers is 11, and of the constants 89. Being based on memory, the latter figure may, of course, be too large. A comparison of Table 5.8 with the previously made assumptions (p. 38) shows

22. According to a discussion with Miller, this has been proved, for instance, by interviews in Detroit. Of a national sample in 1956, 59 per cent reported voting for Truman in 1948 and 64 for Eisenhower in 1952 (actual percentages of two-party vote were 52 and 56); Survey Research Center, The University of Michigan, Study No. 417.

TABLE 5.8. Relationship of Party Preference in May 1958 to Recalled Voting Behavior in the 1954 Election (in percentages)

	FPDU	S.D. Opp.	SDP	Agr.	FPP	Cons.	No information	Non-part.	Total sample
Same party in 1954	67	.	73	40	44	69	21	.	56
Voted in 1954 for									
FPDU	.	4	1	–	–	1	–	5	1
SDP	6	72	.	10	13	4	–	7	7
Agr.	1	–	3	.	–	1	–	2	1
FPP	–	–	1	–	.	7	–	–	2
Cons.	–	–	1	10	3	.	–	–	1
Swedish	–	–	–	–	–	1	–	–	0
Did not vote	5	12	12	–	7	9	21	38	12
21–24 years of age	12	8	6	30	13	–	21	12	8
No information	9	4	3	10	20	8	37	36	12
Total	100	100	100	100	100	100	100	100	100
Number of cases	*108*	*25*	*164*	*10*	*30*	*95*	*19*	*42*	*501*

that: (a) there were more nonpartisans than 1954 nonvoters in the sample; (b) the Finnish People's Party had lost more support to the Conservatives than it had gained from them, but it had won support from the Social Democrats; (c) an exceptionally high number of Social Democratic supporters had been nonvoters in the previous election, but this party had also lost more support to other parties than it gained from them; and (d) the number of Communist supporters had increased, which had not been assumed.

Party identification did differ. The following percentages of respondents perceived in May 1958 a strong party preference:

Constants in party choice　　　76($n = 275$)
Changers of party choice　　　37($n = \ \ 56$)
Nonvoters of 1954　　　　　　34($n = \ \ 38$)
Persons aged 21 to 24 years　　29($n = \ \ 31$)

If the support of the independent Social Democrats by former Social Democratic voters is not considered a change in party preference, the percentage of strong identifiers among the constants was 74 ($n = 293$), and among the changers 37 ($n = 38$). These comparisons show that persons who had not changed parties during the last four years identified more strongly with their party than did those persons who had adopted

a new party affiliation after the last election.[23] This finding is consistent
with our hypothesis.

Table 5.9 extends the observation to earlier years. It provides informa-

TABLE 5.9. Relationship of Party Preference in May 1958 to Recalled Stability
of Party Choice (in percentages)

	FPDU	S.D. Opp.	SDP	Agr.	FPP	Cons.	No Infor- mation	Total sample
Always the same party	56	40	75	50	30	63	32	60
Different up to 1939,								
same 1945 on	18	4	4	–	7	2	–	7
Different, 1945 on	8	52	8	20	40	19	–	15
21–22 years of age	6	–	3	20	7	–	5	4
No information	12	4	10	10	16	16	63	14
Total	100	100	100	100	100	100	100	100
Number of cases	*108*	*25*	*164*	*10*	*30*	*95*	*19*	*459*

tion, based on the interviewees' recollection, on the consistency of party
choice during the entire period of voting age.

Now 18 per cent of the sample cannot be included in the observation:
namely, persons born in 1935–36 (age 21 and 22), who were not entitled to
vote in the presidential and municipal elections of 1956; and those whose
earlier party choice was unknown because of nonvoting, lack of recollection, or unwillingness to answer. The political preference of the others
had not shifted easily. Only 27 per cent mentioned ever voting for other
than the present party. In the more recent elections since World War II,
another party had been voted for often by 13 per cent, only once by 6 per
cent, and never by 81 per cent of the city sample.

Of course, these answers may exaggerate the constancy. In addition to
possibly forgetting changes, some citizens do not even notice that they
have changed their party preference. This is evident in Table 5.9 in the
answers given by independent Social Democrats: only one half of the
former Social Democratic supporters now said they supported another
party.[24] If these persons are included in the group of changers, the percentage of all changers rises above 30. Two electoral terms earlier, some
former voters of the Progressive Party had become supporters of the new

23. In the latter comparison, $t = 4.48$, $p < 0.001$.
24. In Table 5.8 and Figure 5.D, the said persons are considered former Social Democratic voters.

Finnish People's Party without perceiving any change in party preference.[25] We might mention one supporter of the Swedish People's Party,
who had long lived in Tampere and thought he still voted for the party
of his choice when he had apparently been voting for such candidates of
another party as were recommended by the Swedes' local association.

Consequently, the two basic types of party change are not quite comparable. The continuous competition for popular support results in gains
and losses for the parties. But a large proportion of changes can be
explained as well by breaks in the party system or by certain characteristics
of the election procedure. In Figure 5.D, which shows the changes that
had occurred prior to May 1958, we find both kinds of currents. The following are examples of the second type.

1. Some citizens can no longer vote for their party if they should move
to a constituency where their own party does not nominate candidates.
Tampere still had Swedes who might have voted consistently for the
Swedish People's Party in certain other constituencies, or in Tampere, if
the whole country constituted one large constituency.

2. Those persons whose party discontinues must also change their
preference. Figure 5.D includes former voters of the People's Patriotic
Movement, the Progressive Party, and the Christian Labor Party.

3. New parties have to convert voters, other than the youngest ones,
from established parties. Thus two "lettings of Social Democratic blood"
had weakened that party's support in Tampere: the founding of the
FPDU in 1944, and the secession of the Opposition during the spring of
1958. The Finnish People's Party had not only inherited Progressive voters,
but had also converted support from the Social Democrats and the Conservatives. Another opportunity for the new parties is to activate previous
nonvoters.[26] But even this is not comparable to the exchange of supporters
between older parties.

The appearance of new parties after the war is also evident in the responses summarized in Table 5.9. For example, many FPDU supporters
recalled voting for another party during the 1930s, but not any more after
1945. Correspondingly, we find the supporters of the Finnish People's
Party and the independent Social Democrats to be more recent changers.

25. The sample included six respondents who reported regular participation and a
consistent vote for the Finnish People's Party although they had been entitled to vote
before 1951. Some conversions from the Progressive Party to the Finnish People's Party
via the Conservatives are no more shown in Figure 5.D.
26. This was likely to have happened, for instance, after the founding of the FPDU.

FIGURE 5.D. Voting Intentions in Tampere in May 1958, Earlier Voting Decisions, and Consequent Precampaign Changes in Party Preference*

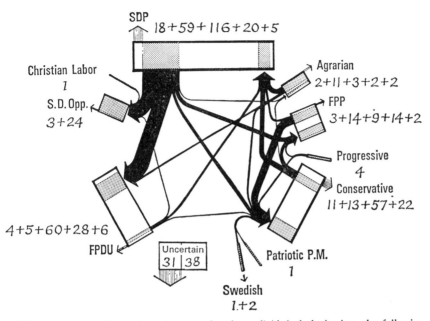

* The bar representing each party group has been divided clockwise into the following zones:
(1) Supporters who were uncertain about participation in the July election,
(2) (shaded) Former voters who now supported another party,
(3) Permanent supporters who had decided to vote for this party,
(4) (shaded) Supporters who had previously also voted for another party, and
(5) Supporters born in 1935 and 1936.

The width of the arrows relates to the number of changes in the direction in question. If more conversion, only the latest change is taken into account. The uncertain class describes those persons who reported at least two instances of nonvoting. That bar is divided into persons who were uncertain about voting in 1958 and persons who had made a voting decision.

The FPDU had gained Social Democratic supporters after 1945, but during these years the Social Democrats had been able to make compensating gains from the People's Democrats. Figure 5.D is a reminder of the fact that changes often compensate each other. Conclusions about the total number of changers are not possible if only net gains or losses are studied. Even the Agrarian Union, whose relative losses were the heaviest in the city, had gained supporters from other parties.

Let us, however, repeat the major finding presented in Table 5.9 and

Figure 5.D: that citizens have a general tendency toward permanency of party preference; and also that many changes have been caused basically by a change in the party system itself.

A comparison of the respective party identification of persons who had always voted for the same party and the changers is still in order (Table 5.10). This supplements the above finding on the correlation between

TABLE 5.10. Relationship of Party Preference and Party Identification to Recalled Stability of Party Choice: May 1958 (in percentages)

Stability of Party Choice	FPDU		SDP		FPP		Cons.	
	Weak	Strong	Weak	Strong	Weak	Strong	Weak	Strong
Always the same party	56	67	69	91	33	50	56	86
Different up to 1939, same 1945 on	8	25	6	3	8	8	4	2
Different, 1945 on	24	4	17	5	59	34	40	12
Total	100	100	100	100	100	100	100	100
Number of cases	*25*	*70*	*52*	*96*	*12*	*12*	*25*	*52*

one term permanence of party preference and strength of party identification. The hypothesis now gets additional support because the more strongly persons identified with their party in May 1958, the more likely it was that they had always voted for the same party. Even a shift to support the Social Democrats or the Conservatives as long ago as before World War II still labeled party affiliation with uncertainty. The one exception is that more sure than uncertain Communists had supported another party during the 1930s. But this is not contrary to the other findings. The strong identifiers were known to be older than the weak supporters, and it was also to be expected that sure Communists were so interested in politics already in the 1930s that they did not become nonvoters while their preferred party was illegal. It is also known that among the Communists few later converts were strong identifiers.

It has been reported about two other political systems that older persons tend toward stronger partisanship than younger,[27] and this is more likely because of their long affiliation with a party than because of age itself.[28] This was also supported by the Finnish data. Of additional interest in the

27. Campbell and Valen, *Public Opinion Quarterly*, 25, 511; Valen and Katz, *Political Parties*, pp. 211–12.

28. Campbell, Converse, Miller, and Stokes, *The American Voter*, p. 164.

Finnish case was the corresponding difficulty, experienced by new parties, in acquiring strongly identifying supporters.

MOBILITY

Inheriting the father's party affiliation is easy to understand when people settle in the father's occupation and do not change their environment. But in times of social mobility, this tendency to constant party preference runs counter to those factors which accommodate the party affiliation of mobile persons to new circumstances. This may cause a typical cross pressure situation, and we may assume that such a conflict causes uncertainty about the adopted party preference. The variety of impressions may even handicap the party identification of geographically mobile persons, who do not necessarily change occupation or social status.

Of course, geographic mobility often means more than just a move to the same circumstances in a new place. Geographic and social mobility often go hand in hand. An industrializing society tends to experience a continuous flow from rural to urban areas (see p. 58). On the other hand, in certain economically advanced societies, significant political importance is attached to the simultaneous "flight from cities," especially the movement of a relatively wealthy segment of the population to suburbs arising on the outskirts of great cities.[29]

The growth of Tampere, also, has been caused more by such mobility than by natural population increase. In 1950, only 40 per cent of the inhabitants of the city had been born there.[30] One quarter of the sample of May 1958, which represents only adults, were born in Tampere and had always lived there. One half had settled in Tampere after their twenty-first birthday, 31 per cent migrated there during 1945–56.

The party support of this quarter of permanent Tampere residents did not differ from that of the whole population, with the possible exception of a smaller amount of Agrarian support among the native born (Table 5.11). However, party preference did correlate with geographic mobility: the supporters of other nonsocialist parties had changed their place of residence more often than the leftist supporters. Supporters of the left had lived more frequently than the nonsocialists only in their place of birth, and in Tampere. More nonsocialists than Communists had lived in

29. See, for instance, Campbell, Converse, Miller, and Stokes, *The American Voter*, pp. 453–72.

30. *Tampereen kaupungin tilastollinen vuosikirja 1958,* Tables 43, 44, and 37.

TABLE 5.11. Relationship of Party Preference to Number of Places of Residence: May 1958 (in percentages)

Number of residences	Total sample	FPDU	SDP and S.D. Opp.	Non-soc.	SDP	S.D. Opp.	Agr.	FPP	Cons.	Non-part.
Always in Tampere*	25	25	22	26	21	24	10	27	28	29
One other place	31	35	38	19	38	40	20	10	19	24
Two other places	17	19	13	21	14	8	40	23	20	21
Three or more places	27	21	27	34	27	28	30	40	33	26
Total	100	100	100	100	100	100	100	100	100	100
Number of cases	*501*	*108*	*189*	*136*	*164*	*25*	*10*	*30*	*93*	*42*

* Includes the areas later incorporated into the city.

at least three places before moving to Tampere.[31] The frequent migrants also tended to have the highest incomes, although the differences were small.[32]

Seven per cent of the sample had originally lived in the area ceded to the Soviet Union.[33] The matter of evacuation—or prewar voting habits—must have had an impact on reported party preference because the FPDU was less popular among the evacuated persons than among other inhabitants of the city. These Karelians may have supported the Agrarian Union more than others did.[34]

As expected, party identification was to some extent related to the number of places of residence. The geographically stable leftist supporters tended to identify more strongly with their party than did the mobile ones. We find in Table 5.12 that more strong than weak Social Democratic

31. $t = 3.97$, $p < 0.001$ and $t = 2.22$, $p < 0.05$.

32. 4 per cent of assessed income over 800,000 old marks, if there had been no previous residence, or just one, but 14 per cent if previous residences had been three or more.

33. That area of Finland (mostly in Karelia), which was in 1944 ceded to the Soviet Union, had a population of 420,000. They moved voluntarily within Finland's new boundaries. See Wuorinen, *A History of Finland,* pp. 392–97.

34. The percentage of evacuated persons was 4 per cent among the FPDU, 9 per cent of the others, $t = 2.11$, $p < 0.05$. 30 per cent of the interviewed Agrarians belonged to the evacuated. Ten years earlier similar difference was found in Valkeakoski between the evacuated persons and other inhabitants of the town; Heikki Waris, Vieno Jyrkilä, Kyllikki Raitasuo, and Jouko Siipi, *Siirtoväen sopeutuminen* (The Adjustment of the Evacuated Population) (Helsinki, Otava, 1952), pp. 285–86.

TABLE 5.12. Relationship of Party Preference and Strength of Party Identification to Number of Places of Residence: May 1958 (in percentages)

Number of Residences	FPDU Weak	FPDU Strong	SDP Weak	SDP Strong	FPP Weak	FPP Strong	Cons. Weak	Cons. Strong
Always in Tampere	15	29	22	21	25	29	26	29
One other place	40	34	26	44	19	–	21	18
Two other places	21	17	20	11	25	21	12	24
Three or more places	24	20	–	24	31	50	41	29
Total	100	100	100	100	100	100	100	100
Number of cases	*33*	*75*	*60*	*104*	*16*	*14*	*34*	*59*

supporters had made only one move. A corresponding symptomatic difference was found among those Communists who had lived in Tampere all their lives.[35] Even such weak evidence for supporting the hypothesis was not found among the identifiers with the FPP and the Conservatives. However, it is not easy to apply the hypothesis to these nonsocialists because geographically mobile persons showed a particular tendency to support a nonsocialist party.

Although it showed a net gain, the city lost many persons too. The interviewees were asked whether they wanted to live in Tampere permanently or whether they would like to move away (Q. 2.B). Generally the respondents felt at home in Tampere, as 83 per cent were unwilling to move elsewhere. Among the supporters of the four parties, dichotomized according to party identification, the percentage of satisfied persons was the following:

	Weak	Strong
FPDU	82	91
Social Democratic Party	80	87
Finnish People's Party	75	79
National Coalition	73	86

In addition to their above average mobility, the supporters of the nonsocialist parties proved to be more willing to leave Tampere than were the leftist supporters. Still, unwillingness to leave the city characterized all groups. The individuals' thriving also correlates with their party identification. The strong identifiers felt more at home than the weak,[36]

35. $t = 2.34$, $p \sim 0.02$ and $t = 1.73$, $p < 0.10$.
36. 87 per cent and 77 per cent, $t = 2.76$, $p < 0.01$.

which is indicated above separately for each party. This finding supports the hypothesis about party identification, if even planned migration causes such conflicting impressions as were presumed to accompany geographic mobility. However, another interpretation might be that a strongly perceived party affiliation is one of the numerous factors that make a citizen feel at home in his place of residence.

Social mobility can be observed here only indirectly by using the information on occupation and education. A comparison of the occupations of Tampere inhabitants with those of their fathers shows first of all a disappearance of those in agriculture. Twenty-one per cent of the fathers were farmers and 9 per cent were agricultural laborers, but only 2 per cent of the respondents were engaged in agriculture (Table 3.3). A detailed comparison of the occupational structure of these two generations is given in Appendix Table 9 and summarized in the following percentages:

Father	Supporter of family	
Farmer	Labor	23
Labor	Labor	36
White collar	Labor	5
Farmer	White collar	5
Labor	White collar	12
White collar	White collar	10
No information, etc.		9
		100

One half of the city inhabitants belonged to their fathers' occupational class. Upward social mobility is represented most nearly by those white collar employees whose fathers were laborers, and downward mobility by those wage workers whose fathers were in the white collar class. In the following pages the offspring of farmers will be called urbanized, the offspring of wage workers either occupationally stable or upward mobile, and those of white collar employees either occupationally stable or downward mobile.

The following observations are based on Table 5.13:

1. Few urbanized persons were born in Tampere, while the occupational stability or upward mobility of persons with labor background was not related to geographic mobility. Apparently some differences existed among the children of white collar employees, because the socially stable had moved more often than the representatives of downward occupational

TABLE 5.13. Relationship of Occupational Mobility to (a) Number of Places of Residence, (b) Party Preference, (c) Agreement with Father's Party, (d) Stability of Party Choice, and (e) Party Identification (in percentages)

Respondent:	Labor			White collar		
Father:	Agri-culture	Labor	White collar	Agri-culture	Labor	White collar
(a) Places of Residence						
Always in Tampere	6	33	35	11	36	25
One other place	43	29	34	30	23	19
Two other places	22	13	23	11	20	11
Three other places	29	25	8	48	21	45
(b) Party Preference						
FPDU	27	31	42	7	2	2
SDP and S.D. Opp.	44	47	29	33	36	15
Nonsocialist	18	12	21	56	53	78
(c) Agreement with Father						
Same party preference	24	41	33	42	36	48
(d) Stability of Choice						
Always the same party	69	72	60	65	79	69
(e) Identification						
Strong party identifiers	51	58	54	67	52	52
Number of cases	*115*	*180*	*26*	*27*	*60*	*46*

mobility. Moreover, of the two urbanized groups white collar employees had been more mobile geographically than blue collar workers.[37]

2. Party preference, too, correlates not only with occupation (see Table 3.3), but with occupational mobility as well. Because the nonsocialist parties were supported most by the stable white collar groups, and least by the stable wage workers,[38] one could trace the party choice of occupationally mobile persons back to that of their father's occupational class. Moreover, the downward mobile workers appeared to have the greatest tendency to support Communism, but this again may be an evidence of political radicalization caused by distant aspirations.

3. The one statistically significant finding about the correlation between inherited party preference and occupational mobility is that urbanized wage workers more frequently abandoned their father's party than did other workers.[39] In addition, it is likely that there were fewer representa-

37. In the group "3 or more places" $t = 4.13$, $p < 0.001$ and $t = 1.94$, $p < 0.10$.
38. The workers: 12 per cent and 19 per cent, $t = 1.56$, $0.10 < p < 0.20$; white collar persons: 78 per cent and 54 per cent, $t = 3.00$, $p < 0.01$.
39. $t = 2.996$, $p < 0.01$.

tives of occupational mobility than representatives of stability who agreed with their father's party preference, and this also parallels our expectations.[40]

4. The downward mobile persons may have had the greatest tendency to party change, but the most lasting party preferences were not among the stable, but among the occupationally upward mobile persons.

5. The observations on strength of party identification also lack statistical significance. One does find within the sample that stable wage workers were stronger identifiers than were other labor or occupationally upward mobile white collar employees. But as far as white collar groups are concerned, the urbanized seemed to be the most likely to identify strongly with their party.

Thus the expectations were generally supported by those observations concerning the impact of occupational mobility on party preference and its inheritance or constancy. But, contrary to the hypothesis, the stable white collar employees did not identify strongly with their party. This was mainly because of the weak identification of the FPP supporters in this occupational group. And there were more strong identifiers among the stable white collar employees than there were among those who had risen from labor homes to lower white collar occupations.[41]

One explanation of the relationship between party identification and geographic and occupational mobility, might lie in referring again to the cross pressure hypothesis. Obviously, mobile persons are more likely than stable persons to be subjected to conflicting group norms. The decreasing effect of cross pressures on political interest has been demonstrated in many studies. The correlation of interest and partisanship makes it equally natural to link cross pressures with the strength of party identification.

The Comparison Group

Many of the above findings about party preference and party identification were also true in Korpilahti, or were easy to apply to the local circumstances. The following section deals first with party preference (Table 5.14), and then with party identification.

1. It is more common in Korpilahti than in Tampere to live in one's

---

40. Comparing these two $t = 1.63$, $0.10 < p < 0.20$.

41. The percentage of strong identifiers was 41 per cent ($n = 32$) of those rising to lower white collar work, 64 per cent ($n = 28$) of those rising to leading position, $t = 1.89$, $p < 0.10$.

TABLE 5.14. Relationship of Party Preference in Korpilahti to (a) Standard of Living, (b) Subsistence, (c) Political Unity of Family, (d) Stability of Party Choice, and (e) Mobility (in percentages)

	FPDU	SDP	Agr.	FPP and Cons.	Non-part.	Total sample
(a) Standard of Living						
Education beyond grammar school	17	6	36	50	43	26
Taxable income over 200,000	22	20	25	50	29	27
Home owners	72	68	100	87	71	81
Telephone	6	12	25	37	21	19
Radio receiver	94	88	86	100	93	91
(b) Subsistence						
Satisfied	22	48	50	37	36	41
Never unemployed	44	60	89	87	86	73
(c) Political unity						
Agreed with the father's party preference[a]	30	94	86	42	.	66
(d) Stability of choice						
Always the same party[b]	64	83	86	57	.	78
(e) Mobility						
Always in Korpilahti	50	56	54	37	29	47
Two or more other places	22	24	11	25	36	23
Unwilling to move elsewhere	67	88	89	75	57	76
Belonged to father's occupational group[c]	50	48	84	57	62	63
Number of cases	*18*	*25*	*28*	*8*	*14*	*97*

a. In per cent of those aware of father's party.
b. In per cent of those reporting earlier voting decisions.
c. In per cent of those reporting father's occupation.

own house (or apartment). Radio and telephone are equally common. The lower standard of living in the rural communes, however, is indicated by its lower taxes. Thirty-three per cent of the sample or their spouses paid no income tax for 1957, and only 7 per cent paid on more than 400,000 old marks. Only 26 per cent had gone to secondary school or even briefly to a vocational school.

The supporters of the Finnish People's Party and the Conservatives had an above average education. Within the left, the FPDU supporters may have gone more to vocational courses, the Social Democrats, in turn, more to secondary school. The FPP and Conservative supporters also paid the highest taxes and the Social Democrats probably the lowest. Moreover, party affiliation seems to correlate in Korpilahti, just as in Tampere, with the frequency of telephone and even radio ownership. The supporters of the Agrarian Union were in between the left and the nonsocialists as far as education and taxation were concerned, although in Korpilahti 52 per cent of the Social Democrats, 39 per cent of the Communists, 25 per cent of the FPP and Conservative supporters, but only 18 per cent of the Agrarians were quite without taxable income. Home ownership was especially typical of Agrarian supporters.

2. Although unemployment had been more rare in Korpilahti than in Tampere, dissatisfaction with subsistence was more common. As in the city, the supporters of the FPDU were the most dissatisfied group as well as that with most unemployment experiences.[42] The Social Democrats, in turn, had experienced more unemployment than had the supporters of the FPP and the Conservatives. However, in May 1958 the only unemployed in the sample were 12 per cent of the Social Democrats, while the unemployment experiences of the Communists included either current partial unemployment or earlier unemployment. The Agrarian supporters had been no more unemployed than the supporters of other nonsocialist parties. Unlike their counterparts in Tampere, the interviewed supporters of the Finnish People's Party and the Conservatives were also dissatisfied with their earnings in this rural commune.

3. Most married couples agreed politically in Korpilahti, as in Tampere. Married persons and widows or widowers had the following ideas of their spouse's party affiliation:

| | Percentage of: | | |
	Men	Women	Total
Spouse agreed	79	51	64
Spouse disagreed	3	20	12
Spouse's party unknown	18	29	24
	100	100	100
Number of cases	*34*	*41*	*75*

Again it seems that men were often too confident that their wives agreed or at least were aware of their party affiliation. A 37-year-old Communist supporter called his wife "a tag-along," and an 84-year-old man, who did not support any party in May, believed that "my wife will sure vote the way I do."

42. $t = 2.32$, $p < 0.05$ and $t = 3.46$, $p < 0.01$.

The distribution of the respondents' and their fathers' party support is as follows:

	Percentage of:	
	Fathers	Respondents
FPDU	3	19
S.D. Opp.	1	2
SDP	28	26
Agrarian	26	29
FPP	2	3
National Coalition	4	5
Nonpartisan, no information	32	14
No answer	4	2
	100	100

Obviously, Communist support especially had increased among the new generation. More of the Communist supporters in Korpilahti, as in Tampere, had been brought up in Social Democratic than in Communist homes. Some even came from Agrarian homes, and a great many were unaware of their father's party. The inhabitants of Korpilahti supported the Agrarian Union as often as their fathers had. On the whole, the inhabitants of this commune agreed more often with their father's party preference than did the city people. Of all persons who knew their father's party, 66 per cent ($n = 62$) agreed with it, 14 per cent were more to the left, 10 per cent more to the right, and 10 per cent nonpartisan. In the total sample, including those unaware of their father's party, those who knowingly supported their father's party comprised 44 per cent (in Tampere, 36 per cent).

In some respects the comparison of the age groups was also similar to the findings in Tampere. For example, of the youngest interviewees, born between 1930–36 (age 21 to 26), none supported other than the father's party. Among those born between 1915–20 were 14 per cent of those who were aware of their father's party, but 21 per cent of those who were not aware of it. The latter difference may indicate the disturbance of political socialization caused by military service, which was observed in Tampere too. The oldest interviewees in Korpilahti did not know what party their fathers had supported. If other than the father's party affiliation had been adopted, the direction to the Left had been favored by the young persons especially. Among those entitled to vote as early as the 1930s there were 83 per cent of the changers to the Right, but only 44 per cent of the changers to the Left.

4. The control group also had a tendency to stick to their adopted party preference. Three quarters of the sample responded to this question, and 78 per cent ($n = 68$) of these said that they had always voted for the same party. For example, 36 per cent of the FPDU supporters in May 1958 had at some time cast a vote for the Social Democratic Party or the Agrarian Union. Among the Social Democrats 17 per cent had voted for either the FPDU, the Agrarians or the Finnish People's Party. Apparently, the Agrarian Union (14 per cent), the Conservatives and the FPP had also gained former Social Democratic voters, and the Conservatives had made some gains from the FPP.

5. People who lived in Korpilahti were not as geographically mobile as those in Tampere. One half of the sample had always lived in Korpilahti, and only 10 per cent had lived in three or more places before settling there. Here too, as in the industrial city, the most geographically mobile seemed to have been the supporters of the Finnish People's Party and the Conservatives. The Social Democratic and Agrarian supporters were the most stable and also felt most at home. They had also most often inherited their father's party preference. The Agrarian supporters were most often in the occupational class of their father. Within the small sample, the occupational class of the father was shared by about as many politically agreeing persons (60 per cent, $n = 24$) as by disagreeing persons (67 per cent, $n = 15$). But it was typical of the occupationally mobile persons not to know their father's party nor to have any party preference.

According to Table 4.10, relatively fewer inhabitants of Korpilahti than of Tampere were strong party identifiers. This is reminiscent of the American situation, where the urban population tends to be more partisan than the rural.[43] A seemingly contradictory Norwegian finding was the tendency of farmers to be strong partisans.[44] However, the Finnish data support both findings simultaneously. The former difference might be traced back to the center-periphery dimension (p. 90), whereas the intracommunal comparison showed that within Korpilahti the Agrarian Union had the most partisan group of supporters. In the intracommunal comparison we found that the strength of party identification correlates with many similar factors in both Tampere and Korpilahti.

The correlation of party identification with the standard of living may have been more in accordance with the hypothesis in Korpilahti than in

43. Campbell, Converse, Miller, and Stokes, *The American Voter*, p. 163.
44. Valen and Katz, *Political Parties*, p. 213.

Tampere. For instance, the percentage of persons who were taxed for an annual income of above 200,000 old marks was the following:

	Weak	Strong
FPDU	28	14
Social Democrats	17	27
Agrarians	9	33
FPP and Conservatives	25	75

Higher income seems to have weakened Communist party identification, but increased that of nonsocialist supporters. However, it was not expected that Social Democratic affiliations would become more certain as income increased. In many other respects, strong party identifiers were more typical representatives of their party than the weak identifiers. Sure FPP and Conservative supporters had higher education than the uncertain ones, but sure Social Democrats less than the uncertain supporters of this party. All sure Agrarians were farmers, but the group of uncertain Agrarians included white collar persons. A Conservative in a leading position was a strong identifier, but an agricultural laborer who supported the FPP was a weak identifier, etc. Yet home ownership was more common among strong identifiers than among weak identifiers, irrespective of their choice of party.

The impact of satisfaction or unemployment on party identification did not support the findings in the city. The nonsocialist supporters with a strong identification did express more satisfaction with their subsistence than did the weak supporters, but this was also true of the Communist supporters. Especially many weak Communist identifiers said their income was "maybe too small." It also seems that partial or earlier experience of unemployment had been more common among uncertain than among sure People's Democrats.

The relationship of party identification with family uniformity supported the hypothesis. For instance, married persons gave the following information about the party of their spouse:

	Percentage of:	
	Weak	Strong
Spouse agreed	49	84
Spouse disagreed	19	3
Spouse's party not known	32	13
	100	100
Number of cases	*43*	*32*

According to the figures above, party identification was weakened by both political disagreement and ignorance of the spouse's affiliation. The percentage of strong identifiers was higher among persons agreeing with their father's party (59 per cent, $n = 41$) than among those who had abandoned (33 per cent, $n = 15$)[45] or did not know it (50 per cent, $n = 24$). Observations on occupational mobility were also in line with expectations. The number of strong identifiers included only 20 per cent ($n = 15$) of those who had risen to being a farmer from the home of an agricultural laborer or to a white collar position from the ranks of labor. Among persons who had moved from agriculture to labor, 29 per cent ($n = 21$) were strong identifiers, but, among those who were engaged in their fathers' occupation, 49 per cent ($n = 55$) fell in this category.

SUMMARY

Most citizens live in a politically uniform family. They are married to a person with the same party affiliation, their parents have also been of the same opinion, and few differences exist between the two generations. However, in the above passages, as in many other studies, the uniformity of small groups may have been overestimated. The interviews only measured what the respondents think that other persons feel. Of course, these others could give more reliable information about themselves. On the other hand, many persons in the sample were unwilling to tell the interviewer about their parents' or spouse's party if they were not sure about it.

Party preference once adopted seems to remain quite permanent. The general rule is to learn of party affiliation in the parents' home and then to hold on to it without change. However, the youngest citizens had the greatest tendency to agree with their father. Such was the case in both Tampere and Korpilahti, and a similar finding has been made about Finnish students. Upon acquiring independence, citizens become subject to new factors that influence their party choice.

Two main causes of party change have been noted above. (1) A change of social environment separates persons from the father's party affiliation. We found some influence of both the new occupation and the father. The likelihood of inheriting the father's party was greatest if a person had remained in the father's occupational class. Because of the less mobility in rural groups, change of party and abandonment of the father's affiliation were less frequent in the comparison group than in the city. (2) The founding of new parties left many persons estranged from the father's

---

45. $t = 1.75, p < 0.10$.

affiliation. Old persons seem to be less able to adopt a new party than were young persons.

Because of the latter finding, we have to return to the interpretation of Table 3.3, which showed that young persons had an exceptional tendency toward political radicalism, and also, separately, to a leftist or bourgeois' radicalism (p. 41). Perhaps this is only because the two new parties had succeeded in gaining more popularity among the young persons than among those with longer established opinions, which could have happened as easily if a new Conservative party had been started. Therefore it seems more reasonable to speak about the political differences between generations than the influence of age on political attitude.[46] An earlier conclusion about the comparison group was that even the stage of local party organizational activity was indicated by certain permanent characteristics of the age groups (p. 54).

The general correlations between party preference, for example, and an objectively measurable standard of living or a subjectively perceived subsistence might, in the case of individual citizens, either coincide or conflict with other factors influencing party choice. The uniformity of impressions has been described above through the use of uniform families as stability. According to expectations, conflicting impressions brought about weaker party identification. The converters also had difficulty identifying with a new party. A party affiliation perceived as sure was to some extent caused by a party choice made easy by an unconflicting environment and the consistency of a person's development.

In the foregoing chapter attention has been paid especially to what increases and what decreases the strength of party identification. The most significant conclusion is that the correlations concur, in general, with findings on two other western political systems. This is even more noteworthy, when one realizes that the heavily labor-dominated city of Tampere is in many respects a unique locality, even in Finland.

Later in this study, party identification will be again considered, as an independent variable, for example, in observing its impact on exposure to normal and campaign communication, or on the formation of voting decisions. This chapter has already shown that in many respects the strong party identifiers are the most typical representatives of their party. The persons who are uncertain of their party preference are thereby narrowing the cleavages which separate the supporting groups of the parties.

46. See also Lipset, *Political Man,* p. 267.

6. Newspaper Content and
Citizens' Opinions

References to future elections can be found in newspapers even in times when there is no election campaigning. But, in the beginning of May 1958, the political content of Finnish newspapers was dominated by the coming election in an abnormal way. It was often mentioned in the interpellation debate, which led to the Parliament's vote of lack of confidence for the Rainer von Fieandt cabinet on April 18, 1958. It was also referred to in the speeches during leftist May Day celebrations. This was transferred to the newspapers, which reported and commented on these topics. The editorials and political columns dealing with other topics had advised the readers about the election too. Some election advertisements had been published already, and many newspapers were running regular columns devoted to the approaching election.

Yet two months before the election the parties were just beginning their campaign, and preparations for campaign activity were by no means finished. It is not possible to include the four weeks, April 14 to May 11, 1958, in the actual election campaign period (see Chapter 7). Therefore, in this chapter, analysis of the political content of newspapers is undertaken with the presumption that the political editors still had not begun to pay major attention to the election at that time. Correspondingly, one can presume that the 1958 campaign, as such, had not influenced the citizens prior to the time of the first interviews of this study.

ATTITUDES TOWARD OWN PARTIES

The Finnish political newspapers are not usually critical of their own party, but they present mainly negative aspects of the other parties.[1] Such an attitude certainly colored the statements about parties published between April 14 and May 11 by the seven newspapers most widely read in Tampere. In the present study a statement means each independent entity of thought which usually takes about a paragraph, but may be

1. For election campaign, see Nousiainen, *Tutkimus eräiden sanomalehtien vaalipropagandasta vuoden 1956 presidentinvaaleissa* (A Study of the 1956 Election Propaganda in Certain Newspapers) (Acta politica, edidit Institutum Politicum Universitatis Helsingiensis, Fasc. 1), pp. 18–24.

shorter. The six organs of three parties contained during the four weeks a total of 2,536 statements about some Finnish party. 751 were classified as praising a newspaper's own party, and 1,339 as criticizing another party. Only 149 statements on the newspaper's own party and 262 statements about other parties could be classified as neutral. The Social Democratic press was almost the only one which contained any amount of self-criticism. The seventh newspaper, *Helsingin Sanomat,* had been the main organ of the discontinued Progressive Party, but it had become independent politically in 1936, and after that it did not praise any party consistently in its editorials. In the selection of news material, in 1958, it did favor the Finnish People's Party enough to be considered inclined to its support.

According to Table 6.1, the FPDU papers wrote the most about their party. The local *Hämeen Yhteistyö* averaged ten statements about the FPDU in each issue. Among these, only 10 per cent left the party unpraised. In *Kansan Uutiset,* among corresponding statements, neutral ones amounted to 12 per cent. The Conservatives were mentioned by *Aamulehti* and by *Uusi Suomi* only half as often as was the FPDU by its press. Among statements of the *Uusi Suomi* 31 per cent were neutral; in the local *Aamulehti* letters to the editor even included a small negative article, condemning the lack of Conservative representation in a local rural political debate arranged by the Agrarians and the Social Democrats.[2] The Social Democratic Party was mentioned less often by *Kansan Lehti* and *Suomen Sosialidemokraatti* than the FPDU by its press, but more often than the National Coalition was mentioned by *Aamulehti* and *Uusi Suomi*. The SDP press on the whole wrote positively about its party, but such things as "quarrels which had been public for more than a year"[3] caused criticism in certain speeches and declarations published by these papers. The *Helsingin Sanomat* printed negative statements about the Finnish People's Party when reporting speeches by representatives of other parties as, for example, during the interpellation debate in Parliament.

The *Hämeen Yhteistyö* was fond of describing Communist activities in Parliament. According to this paper the FPDU was a party which had been in opposition not only to the Government but to all other groups as well: "Only the People's Democrats opposed the present plans . . .

2. *Aamulehti (AL)*, April 22, 1958, p. 3.
3. A statement by the Social Democratic city organization to the party council, *Kansan Lehti (KL)*, May 10, 1958.

TABLE 6.1. Classification of Statements in Seven Newspapers about Their Affiliated Party between April 14 and May 11, 1958

Central idea	Hämeen Yhteistyö (FPDU)	Kansan Uutiset	Kansan Lehti	Suomen Sosiali- demokr. (SDP)	Aamu- lehti (Cons.)	Uusi Suomi	Helsingin Sanomat (Indep.)
Prolabor activity	29	26	23	14	–	–	–
Support of middle class interests	–	–	–	1	4	–	5
Fair-minded, middle of the road	4	2	1	6	3	3	4
Fatherland, interest of the whole	4	10	3	8	11	16	2
Foreign policy of party	11	12	1	9	12	6	–
Social policy of party	6	18	7	5	–	2	–
Reduction of unemployment	13	17	6	13	2	6	–
Other economic policy	13	22	10	13	6	8	9
Party conduct	42	17	29	16	10	4	8
Ability, party leaders	14	8	11	6	7	2	–
Unity, clarity of party	14	41	18	20	8	12	8
Other positive statements	15	27	13	18	6	6	3
Number of:							
Positive statements	165	200	122	129	70	65	39
Neutral statements	18	28	21	24	29	29	21
Negative statements	–	–	6	4	1	–	6
Total	183	228	149	157	100	94	66
Statements per issue	10.2	8.4	5.5	5.8	3.7	3.5	2.4
Positive statements per issue	9.2	7.4	4.5	4.8	2.6	2.4	1.4

but others were unwilling to listen to our warnings." In this newspaper
and in *Kansan Uutiset* it was difficult to make a distinction between
political and other content. Even straight news articles were usually supplemented by appeals favoring the party: "no wonder small farmers all
over have joined the demand of the People's Democrats to change the

law on agricultural income." The Social Democratic newspapers liked to mention their party's previous action: "the Social Democratic Party was the only one to throw a life preserver when the cries of distress of tenant farmers rose from the depths." They also stressed the unity of their party and explained its program: "This party of ours is tenacious . . . and its feeling of solidarity is great and strong . . . only the Social Democrats are a party seriously willing and also able to help the under-privileged segments of the country." The Conservative press published especially many positive articles about the party, when reporting on the spring meeting of the party council. They also stressed the opposition position of the party: "The line of Conservative economic policy in this campaign is, on the one hand . . . a merciless criticism of the recent economic policy, and on the other hand, a presentation of the basic prin-ciples of our own economic policy." And they explained the party pro-gram: "A social market economy and the people's capitalism combining to effect economic democracy are the means of steering our society from continuous economic crisis to welfare and security." [4]

Table 6.1 offers one possible classification, of the kind needed for quantitative observations of such statements. According to the table, only the leftist press praised its party's social policy and activities on behalf of the workers, whereas the interests of the middle class were sometimes mentioned by *Helsingin Sanomat* as well as by *Aamulehti*. The Con-servative papers wrote the most about the interests of the whole and of the fatherland, while the Communist *Kansan Uutiset* praised especially the unity of its party and the clarity of its goals.

Certain kinds of statements were more common in the Helsinki, and others in the Tampere, press. The national newspapers praised their own party's activity to eliminate unemployment, their economic policy in gen-eral, and their activity for the fatherland and the welfare of the whole, while the Tampere newspapers mentioned more often the methods and the leaders of the party. The leftist press in Tampere also cited general concern for the interest of the workers. The *Kansan Lehti* did not publish statements about the fair-mindedness of the party as often as did the main organ of the Social Democrats.

After the four weeks period described above, persons who were inter-viewed in Tampere were asked to tell what is "best about the party which

4. *Hämeen Yhteistyö* (HY), April 11, 1958, p. 2; *Kansan Uutiset* (KU), May 10, 1958, p. 9; *KL* May 8, 1958, p. 3; *Suomen Sosialidemokraatti* (SS, by Väinö Tanner), May 11, 1958, p. 5; *Uusi Suomi* (US, by Tuure Junnila), April 21, 1958, p. 4; *AL* April 21, 1958, p. 10.

TABLE 6.2. Party Preference and Expressed View about Most Positive Aspect of Supported Party: May 1958 (in percentages)

	Total sample	FPDU	SDP and S.D. Opp.	Non-soc.	SDP	S.D. Opp.	Agr.	FPP	Cons.
Most positive aspect									
Prolabor activity	32	68	37	–	37	32	–	–	–
Favors some other group	4	–	2	9	2	4	30	17	4
Fair-minded, middle of the road	8	–	11	9	12	5	–	27	2
Social policy	6	9	8	2	8	9	–	–	4
Fatherland, interest of the whole	8	1	4	19	5	–	10	10	23
Economic policy	2	–	–	6	–	–	–	–	8
Accomplishments	3	2	4	2	5	–	–	3	2
Party conduct	13	10	13	17	11	23	–	13	21
Ability, leaders	3	–	1	7	1	–	–	–	11
Size and power	1	–	3	–	3	5	–	–	–
Inherited preference	4	1	6	5	5	9	30	–	4
Other views	7	8	3	10	3	4	–	13	9
No answer	9	1	8	14	8	9	30	17	12
Total	100	100	100	100	100	100	100	100	100
Number of cases	*395*	*93*	*174*	*128*	*152*	*22*	*10*	*30*	*85*

you ranked first" (Q. 20.B). Table 6.2 compares the answers, classified only according to the leading, or first mentioned, idea.

The answers by People's Democrats were more uniform than those of the supporters of any other party. A majority liked the party because it "votes for matters concerning workers" (wife of machine driller, 32). Among others, these three men expressed the same idea:

> That party favors the cause of the people, at least promises good, others don't even promise. (Construction worker, 40)
>
> It has, in Parliament, tried to favor the working men. (Janitor, 47)
>
> Mainly the workers' party, and the most abused. You must be enough of a Communist to know how to ask for your pay. (Bus-driver, 35)

In addition to the focal merit of the party, that of favoring labor, some supporters of the FPDU also mentioned its internal policies, its methods, and, to a lesser extent, other reasons. For example:

It is absolutely democratic. The leaders are unable to do anything without permission from local units. (Stone worker, 40)

It has favored the people's cause most sincerely. (Shoe worker, female, 24)

They have kept their promises; children's allowances were their accomplishment. (Unskilled worker, 42)

The only party of ours which creates progress. (Unskilled worker, 51)

Nothing but their arousing of persons, they make you think. They don't think themselves, though; they exaggerate. (Watchman, 56)

The supporters of the Social Democratic Party, too, felt that their party favored the interests of the workers, and they also praised the party's social policies and its methods:

Usually it is the one that fixes things for working people. (Kitchen assistant, female, 55)

An old workingman's party which favors the people's cause. (Electrician, male, 64)

Its program includes activities for the underprivileged persons. (Treasurer of a hospital, male, 41)

It favors social security, especially for children and old people. (Barber, female, 45)

They do not exaggerate; in my opinion, they at least try to do constructive work. (Dressmaker, female, 49)

It is not fanatic, but presents ordinary matters. (Office employee, female, 22)

In addition, however, the supporters of the Social Democratic Party mentioned the fair-mindedness of their party, its accomplishments, and its power:

Its politics are fair, and it favors others, too. (Seamstress, female, 48)

During the decades since I remember, the workers' living has been developed to the present satisfactory circumstances. (Widow of agricultural worker, 71)

It is the biggest party and has the most to say and states they favor the cause of the poor. (Businesswoman, 32)

The answers by supporters of Independent Social Democrats were mainly a repetition of the above-mentioned ideas:

> I think that it might be favoring the cause of the poorer and the working people. (Cabinetmaker, male, 25)
>
> Among other things, they have favored the interests of the old, and children's allowances are their merit, and they supported the workers even before any People's Democrats existed. (Crane operator, female, 32)[5]
>
> It does not sway in any direction. (Shoe worker, female, 45)
>
> Fair and not too extreme. (Industrial worker, male, 36)

The persons who supported the Agrarian Union in Tampere mentioned the interests of another occupational group, the farmers. They also considered concern for the interests of the whole and their long-standing attachment to this party as its most positive side:

> I'm a farmer from Karelia. (Unskilled worker, male, 54)
>
> It has organized life in the country well. (Wife of bicycle mechanic, 21)
>
> They don't always think of their own interest. (Restaurant assistant, female, 22)
>
> I'm born in the country, my roots are in the country although I now live in a city. (Industrial worker, female, 47)
>
> The spirit of my father obliges me to support it. (Wife of construction worker, 30)
>
> Previously I have been a farmer, and I still feel I need to support it. (Warehouse employee, male, 47)

The supporters of the Finnish People's Party thought that the best aspect of the party was its interest in the middle classes and in the welfare of the whole. They mentioned especially often the impartial character of the party, and they also praised its methods:

> Generally working for the middle classes and the wage earners. (Former train conductor, 65)
>
> Because for an ordinary person it is the most suitable and a peaceful party. (Saleswoman, 47)

5. The respondent is one of those who thought they supported the SDP but because of candidate selection (Q. 37) were classified as Opposition supporters.

It attempts to favor interests fairly; for instance, interests of office workers. They follow the rule of the golden mean. (Student, male, 21)

It is patriotic, it represents the wage-earning civil servant. (Wife of a headmaster, 35)

It is the party that looks out for everybody's needs, and it is not too extreme. (Clerk, female, 25)

Its activity is more restrained and pertinent. (Office employee, female, 34)

It aims at keeping the unbiased constitution effective. (Chemist, male, 35)

The reasons given by the Conservative supporters were concentrated in two classes. They praised concern for the interest of the whole and the methods of the party:

They are patriotic, and they keep the well-being of the nation in the foreground. (Technician, male, 53)

It wants to keep the country united, and the borders protected. It has more brainpower behind it. (Foreman, 48)

They try to work earnestly for the good of the people, they don't rank their own interest first. (Wife of manager, 58)

They have tried in a most upright way to manage the fatherland's affairs. (Building contractor, male, 50)

They don't agitate and they include most economists. (Telephone operator, female, 54)

Additional answers by the Conservatives were spread over many other classes. They praised especially the abilities of party leaders and the economic policies of the party:

It includes most Christian members, for instance, clergymen. (Midwife, 51)

Because the top needs educated citizens. (Wife of bureau employee, 56)

It is no class party, any group of people can join it. (Civil engineer, male, 47)

The Swedish People's Party also had supporters in Tampere. They liked their party because it "favors the interests of the Swedish segment of the population" (saleswoman, 50), and "attempts to be unbiased" (B.A. in business administration, male, 47).

The percentage distribution in Table 6.2 shows that the activities of leftist parties on behalf of workers are highly praised in this industrial city. There were many ways of expressing the concept: "workers," "laborers," "the people," or "the working people," but very few used the term "working class." No difference in the choice of words existed between the two leftist parties.

In order to summarize the quantitative observations of the most typical statements in each party group, it could be said that, according to the inhabitants of Tampere, the best aspects of each party were the following:

FPDU: a workers' party;

SDP: a workers' party, also unbiased, with accomplishments and power;

All leftist parties: the social policy;

Agrarian Union: the interests of the farmers and the tradition of this affiliation;

Finnish People's Party: the interests of the middle class and fair-mindedness;

National Coalition: patriotism and the interests of the whole, party conduct, able leaders, and economic policy.[6]

It is noteworthy that more supporters of the FPDU than of other parties were able to respond to the question about the best aspect of the party.[7]

The statements of newspapers and the answers given by the interviewees are somewhat similar. Activities on behalf of the workers and social policies were praised by both leftist newspapers and leftist supporters; the interests of the fatherland and of the whole were referred to chiefly by Conservative newspapers and Conservative supporters. The supporters of the Finnish People's Party praised their party for the very same things as the *Helsingin Sanomat* did. The comparability of Tables 6.1 and 6.2 is, however, weakened by the fact that Table 6.1 includes all the statements in the newspapers, whereas in Table 6.2 each response is classified in only one class. Partly for this reason, the citizens appeared to have more polarized party images. Yet it might be justified to say

6. Some t-tests to compare percentages: Working for labor FPDU/SDP $t = 4.84$, $p < 0.001$; interest of another own group Agrarian + FPP/Cons. $t = 2.49$, $p < 0.02$; fair-mindedness SDP/FPP $t = 1.67$, $p < 0.10$ and FPP/Cons. $t = 3.25$, $p \sim 0.001$; the party conduct Cons./Others $t = 2.05$, $p < 0.05$.

7. $t = 4.71$, $p < 0.001$.

that the newspapers had more diversified ways of praising the party, as they referred regularly to topics that were hardly ever mentioned by the respondents. For instance, they mentioned the foreign policy of their party, but in the minds of the citizens this seemed of only slight importance in May 1958.

The persons who intended to vote were asked: "Are you satisfied with the activities of the party?" One interviewee out of seven was unable to express satisfaction or dissatisfaction with the party, for such reasons as: "it has operated for such a short time" (charwoman, 63, S.D. Opp.); "I vote for a person and not for the party" (midwife, 51, Conservative); "nothing is perfect" (ex-conductor, 65, FPP); "difficult to say, because I'm a Finn, after all" (industrial worker, male, 41, FPDU). A majority of the respondents, to be sure, were satisfied. But the people's satisfaction did not match the lack of criticism in party press: one quarter did express dissatisfaction with the activity of their own party. And even some satisfied persons did not seem very delighted with their party:

> Maybe the FPDU pushes things too hard, but I think that is necessary in politics. (Sheet metal worker, male, 36)
>
> I am not always quite satisfied, but I have always been supporting the Social Democrats. (Bricklayer, male, 52)
>
> Party leadership is too weak now. (Commercial agent, male, 50, Conservative)
>
> They don't get their business through easily. (Wife of railroad worker, 49, Conservative)

According to Table 6.3 the supporters of the FPDU, the Conservatives, and perhaps also the Independent Social Democrats were the most satis-

TABLE 6.3. Relationship of Party Preference to Satisfaction with the Activity of Supported Party: May 1958 (in percentages)

Satisfaction	Total sample	FPDU	SDP and S.D. Opp.	Non-soc.	SDP	S.D. Opp.	Agr.	FPP	Cons.
Satisfied	60	73	51	60	48	68	71	41	65
Dissatisfied	27	13	43	19	48	9	–	30	17
Don't know	13	14	6	21	4	23	29	29	18
Total	100	100	100	100	100	100	100	100	100
Number of cases	*389*	*104*	*167*	*118*	*145*	*22*	*7*	*27*	*84*

fied with their party. On the other hand, one half of the persons who intended to vote for the Social Democrats criticized the party. Perhaps the FPP supporters, too, were less satisfied than the Conservatives.[8] Let us remember that the Social Democratic press had criticized its own party, and *Helsingin Sanomat* had criticized the Finnish People's Party.

There is not enough interview material to permit conclusions about causes of dissatisfaction. As far as the Social Democrats are concerned, the reason was obvious: many supporters of the party disliked the fact that the "Social Democratic affairs have become so much a matter of quarreling among themselves" (horticultural worker, female, 56). We might also quote other kinds of reasons given by supporters of different parties:

> FPDU:
> The FPDU is somewhat too extreme (carpenter, male, 49); I would expect more real good activity (pensionee, female, 58); The leadership is wrong (painter, male, 35).
>
> Social Democrats:
> It has given up too much in compromises (judge, 47); Even they make mistakes; you cannot demand all, as all has not been given (carpenter, male, 36); Older persons ought to leave room for the young (shoe worker, female, 57).
>
> Conservatives:
> You find in the National Coalition also some attempts for personal gain (student, female, 26); It lacks a social way of thinking (pastor, 46).

The reasons given for satisfaction with the party were generally similar to the praises of the party described above. But, on the basis of question 32.A, it is also possible to conclude that citizens found it easier to give reasons for dissatisfaction than for satisfaction. A reason was given by only 38 per cent ($n = 232$) of those persons who were satisfied with the activities of the party, but by 74 per cent ($n = 107$) of the dissatisfied persons.[9]

RANK ORDER OF PARTIES

"The list is very good," responded an interviewed Communist, upon receiving the card which listed the seven parties in their seating order

---

8. FPDU/SDP $t = 4.11$, $p < 0.001$; FPP/Conservative $t = 2.29$, $p < 0.05$.
9. $t = 6.78$, $p < 0.001$.

from left to right in parliament. He had been asked to rank the parties in such an order that the most appealing one was first and the most disagreeable was last. After some consideration of the list, he finally decided to place the Conservatives last.

A comparison of the second and the last parties in the ranking order by party preference is given in Table 6.4. A majority of People's Demo-

TABLE 6.4. Relationship of Party Preference to (a) Second and (b) Last Ranking Party: May 1958 (in percentages)

Parties	FPDU	S.D. Opp.	SDP	Agr.	FPP	Cons.	Swed-ish	Non-part.	Total sample
(a) Second									
FPDU	.	8	11	–	3	–	–	.	4
S.D. Opp.	27	.	38	10	–	2	–	.	19
SDP	30	56	.	60	43	26	–	.	18
Agr.	14	4	10	.	3	4	–	.	7
FPP	3	8	13	–	.	50	33	.	15
Cons.	5	4	9	10	43	.	33	.	7
Swedish	1	–	–	10	–	5	.	.	1
Don't know	20	20	19	10	7	13	34	100	29
(b) Last									
FPDU	.	16	38	60	87	79	67	5	35
S.D. Opp.	6	.	4	–	–	2	–	–	3
SDP	8	–	.	10	–	–	–	–	2
SDP or S.D. Opp.	4	.	.	–	–	1	–	–	1
Agr.	3	20	13	.	7	3	–	–	7
FPP	4	4	2	–	.	–	–	–	2
Cons.	33	12	9	20	–	.	–	–	11
Swedish	19	32	16	10	3	5	.	2	12
Don't know	23	16	18	–	3	10	33	93	27
Total	100	100	100	100	100	100	100	100	100
Number of cases	*108*	*25*	*164*	*10*	*30*	*93*	*3*	*41*	*474*

crats ranked as second best one of the Social Democratic wings, perhaps more often the party than the Opposition. Only 14 per cent ranked the Agrarian Union second, and five per cent chose the Conservatives. On the other hand, the latter was the least agreeable party to 33 per cent of the People's Democrats.

The other inhabitants of Tampere obviously rejected the FPDU. Only one out of ten Social Democrats ranked it second, and most nonsocialists ranked it last. Even among the Social Democrats, it seems to have been

the least popular party. However, they did not place it last as often as the
nonsocialist supporters did,[10] because many of them also turned their
backs to the entire right: the Swedes, the Agrarians, and the Conservatives. The Opposition supporters differed from other Social Democrats
tending to rank the FPDU less often, but perhaps the Swedes more often,
in last place.[11]

The closeness of the supporters of the two Social Democratic wings was
quite natural, although more noticeable among the Opposition than the
party proper. Therefore, Table 6.4.a does not show Social Democratic
sympathies in a way comparable to the others. In the following distribution, the second choice of those Social Democrats, who mentioned the
other wing of the party, has been replaced by their actual third choice:

	Percentage of:		
	Opposition	Party	Total Social Democrats
FPDU	28	20	21
Agrarian	8	18	17
Finnish People's Party	28	28	28
Conservative	8	13	12
Swedish People's Party	–	1	1
Don't know	28	20	21
	100	100	100
Number of cases	*25*	*164*	*189*

This also indicates the Social Democrats' closer attachment to nonsocialist
parties than to the extreme left. Only one out of five chose the FPDU, and
another one out of five was unable to answer. The most popular other
party was obviously the Finnish People's Party. Perhaps nonsocialist parties were more popular among the supporters of the party proper than
among the Social Democratic Opposition.[12]

The supporters of nonsocialist parties hardly ever ranked the Social
Democrats last, but possibly more than one half of the Agrarians in
Tampere ranked it second. The supporters of the FPP divided their preference evenly among Social Democrats and Conservatives, and one quarter
of the Conservatives ranked the Social Democrats second. One half of

10. $t = 7.74, p < 0.001$.
11. $t = 2.71, p < 0.01$ and $t = 1.66, p < 0.10$.
12. 60 per cent and 44 per cent, $t = 1.48, p < 0.20$.

them considered the Finnish People's Party to be next to the best choice. Consequently, the political cleavage which cut most sharply into the Tampere electorate was that between Communists and non-Communists.[13] Philip E. Converse has analyzed these preference orders further and also has shown considerable similarity to data from France, another country with a large Communist following. He calculated the average distances between each pair of parties, as perceived by the supporters of each party, and, furthermore, expressed the party positions on a single continuum. Converse concluded that "in both cases, the gulf between the two main parties of the Left (Communists and Socialists) is very nearly as large as the length of the segment occupied by all the non-Communist parties together." [14]

The newspapers read in Tampere contained more criticism of other parties than presentation of positive aspects of their own parties (p. 131). Table 6.5 shows which parties were criticized by each newspaper during a period from twelve to eight weeks before the election. These figures, again, include the textual content of the newspapers: for instance, editorials, political columns, reports on Parliament, and summaries of public speeches.

The newspapers did not attempt to criticize especially those parties which were unpopular among the supporters of their parties. For instance, the major criticism of the Social Democratic and Conservative newspapers and the *Helsingin Sanomat* was directed at the Agrarian Union, which was ranked last by relatively few persons. Even the Social Democrats were criticized more than the FPDU by *Uusi Suomi* and *Helsingin Sanomat,* although the latter party was undeniably the least popular among their readers. Over 40 per cent of the critical statements in *Hämeen Yhteistyö* and *Kansan Uutiset* dealt with the Social Democrats, by whom their readers were more attracted than repelled. The Swedish People's Party was not criticized by the leftist press, although many of the leftist supporters found that the least agreeable party.

Some difference can be seen between the papers published in Tampere

13. Let us add that male and female supporters of the various parties agreed on the least popular party, whereas the female tendency to Conservatism was apparent in the choice of the "next best" party. Among the FPDU supporters, men liked the Independent Social Democrats more, but women liked the Agrarians; and, among the Conservatives, men apparently preferred the SDP, women the FPP.

14. Converse, "The Problem of Party Distances in Models of Voting Change," in M. Kent Jennings and L. Harmon Zeigler, eds., *The Electoral Process* (Englewood Cliffs, Prentice-Hall, 1966), p. 191.

TABLE 6.5. Classification of Negative Statements about Other Parties in Seven Newspapers between April 14 and May 11, 1958

Number of Statements

Parties	Hämeen Yhteistyö (FPDU)	Kansan Uutiset	Kansan Lehti	Suomen Sosiali-demokr. (SDP)	Aamu-lehti (Cons.)	Uusi Suomi (Cons.)	Helsingin Sanomat (Indep.)	Total sample
FPDU	.	.	54	40	49	23	28	194
S.D. Opp.	14	24	10	52	18	21	19	158
SDP	84	80	.	.	25	35	47	271
Agr.	58	45	98	134	104	138	135	712
FPP	11	3	5	7	13	14	.	53
Cons.	41	66	14	5	.	.	30	156
Swedish	3	1	6	1	1	9	5	26
Right wing	13	20	–	–	–	–	–	33
Total	224	239	187	239	210	240	264	1,603
Number of statements per issue	12.4	8.9	6.9	8.9	7.8	8.9	9.8	8.9

Per cent

Parties	Hämeen Yhteistyö (FPDU)	Kansan Uutiset	Kansan Lehti	Suomen Sosiali-demokr. (SDP)	Aamu-lehti (Cons.)	Uusi Suomi (Cons.)	Helsingin Sanomat (Indep.)	Total sample
FPDU	.	.	30	17	23	10	11	12
S.D. Opp.	6	10	5	22	9	9	7	10
SDP	38	34	.	.	12	14	18	17
Agr.	26	19	52	56	50	57	51	44
FPP	5	1	3	3	6	6	.	3
Cons.	18	28	7	2	.	.	11	10
Swedish	1	0	3	0	0	4	2	2
Right wing	6	8	–	–	–	–	–	2
Total	100	100	100	100	100	100	100	100

and in the capital city. In Tampere, the Social Democratic and Conservative papers published more anti-Communist writings, while the Helsinki papers tended to criticize the Agrarians. Only the main organ of the SDP paid attention at this stage to the Opposition within its party. *Kansan Uutiset* criticized the Conservatives more often than *Hämeen Yhteistyö,* whereas the latter included more criticism of the Agrarian Union.

No studies have been made in Finland of the editorial staffs of newspapers with the purpose of revealing the influence of various individuals and factors on the obtaining, selection, and coloring of political material.

One might think that the political content is determined by the opinions of the readers (or actually the editors' image of the opinions of the readers), by the stands taken by the editors, and finally by party platforms and the opinions of party leaders. The role of the editorial staff is finally decisive, but it might correlate to varying degrees with the first and last mentioned factors.

Furthermore, we might think that the editorial staff's image of the opinions of the readers can influence the choice of material in three ways: (a) Newspapers tend to please their readers, and thus mirror their opinions. (b) The news value of the story may be considered. (c) It also serves a political purpose to clarify the differences between one's own party and one close to it, in order to make it more difficult for supporters to change to another party, and perhaps to get new supporters from where they are most to be hoped for. An example of the first factor may be the anti-Conservative writing of *Kansan Uutiset* and the anti-Agrarian content of *Helsingin Sanomat*. The general attention paid to the Agrarian Union may have been caused partly by the focal position of this party at the time and the consequent news value of many statements about the party. The last factor is represented by the anti-Social Democratic writings of the Communist press.

In addition, (d) newspaper connections with party leadership may have created some criticism of the Agrarians in a situation where all other parties considered themselves in an opposition position, outside government responsibility. (e) Helsinki newspapers possibly had more direct connections to party leadership than local newspapers. At any rate, *Suomen Sosialidemokraatti* criticized the party's opposition on an average of twice a day, but *Kansan Lehti* only two or three times a week. (f) The tactical requirements of the choice of material may have been influenced also by local circumstances. It seems that anti-Communist writing was more important as viewed from Tampere than from the capital city.

THE NEGATIVE ASPECTS OF OTHER PARTIES

A few examples might portray somewhat the content and flavor of the writings which various newspapers published during April and May 1958 in criticism of other parties. The quantities of statements are given in Appendix Table 10, grouped into 15 classes according to their content. The table is somewhat inaccurate because of the difficulty of classifying certain individual statements.

All six non-Communist newspapers criticized the FPDU especially for its lack of patriotism, for its activities favoring the interests of a foreign country, and also for its militaristic, rigid, and revolutionary character. "The Communist leaders declare even openly that they aim at derailing this country on the Czechoslovakian and Hungarian road. . . . The Communist Party and the FPDU . . . are actually the most dangerous enemies of the working class and of all labor organizations." Moreover, one could read in newspapers that the activities of the FPDU did not really interest the public: "Mrs. Hertta screaming from a truck seemed to amuse more than interest the curious public who gathered around." And they reminded the readers of the abandonment of the party by some leaders: "When Communist bosses accuse the Right of publishing books which are distasteful to them and their revolutionary goals, why don't they publish memoirs of right wing politicians who have jumped over to the Communist camp?" [15]

The Independent Social Democrats were considered by their opponents as a weak and disintegrating group which had been "supported and touchingly pushed ahead by the Agrarian Union." Especially the Communist press reminded readers of the internal struggles of the Social Democrats and of the unreliability of the Opposition, while the Social Democratic papers criticized more the Opposition leaders. A description of unreliability was, for example: "An advertised collection of contributions has been arranged in the name of the Labor Information Center. I do not believe that any considerable amounts have been collected . . . But it is one possible explanation of . . . how the active leadership of the Opposition is financed." [16]

Only the Communist press said that the Social Democratic Party discriminated against workers: "Is it for reasons of national health, so that the poor won't gain too much weight, that the Social Democratic bourgeoisie lift the bread basket higher and higher?" They also directed their words at leaders of the party in particular: "Leskinen and other Social Democrats who depend on the Conservatives cannot aim at upsetting the present cabinet . . . because the current policy is quite parallel to their policy." The internal controversy of the Social Democratic Party was criticized by all newspapers. To a great extent the criticism from the right differed from that of the left, for example: "Industrialization is

15. *KL*, May 3, 1958, p. 5 (Arvo Tuominen); *AL*, April 27, 1958, p. 6 (reference is made to Hertta Kuusinen) and April 19, 1958, p. 6.

16. *Helsingin Sanomat*, April 26, 1958, p. 4; *SS* May 2, 1958 (Kaarlo Pitsinki).

not at all advanced by the Social Democratic policy of heavy taxation." [17]

The Agrarian Union was criticized by all, but less by the Communist press than by the others. It was considered a selfish, class party and a party which discriminated against wage workers: "It is contrary to the ideas of the Agrarians that the poor with their numerous offspring would learn to live in so much joy and glow that something would even accompany the pieces of bread." Criticism of the Agrarians was directed especially at agricultural policy, and the party was described as an untrustworthy tactician. "The purpose now is . . . to utilize the question of the Saimaa Canal for an Agrarian election trump by means of the visit of the President and his company to the Soviet Union." Internal struggles also were described: "Within the Agrarian Union, too, obviously serious disagreements exist, because Korsimo's party terror is no longer able to quiet them down." [18]

The Finnish People's Party was very little criticized. It was, however, described as weak and inefficient, especially by the Conservative press. This, in turn, gave the FPP reason to criticize the National Coalition for misinterpretations: "There is reason to warn the citizens against the inappropriate propaganda which again began to be used by the National Coalition when it desperately tries to maintain that votes cast for the Finnish People's Party would be lost." Most of the criticism of the Conservatives, however, was voiced by the Communist press, which considered it an especially antilabor, class party. Sometimes the FPDU newspapers pointed hazily at the right without mentioning clearly which party they referred to: "The FPDU members have fought many victorious battles, while the reactionaries have attempted to capture the last bite of bread even from the mouths of children and old people." [19]

The interviewees were also asked to tell, "What irritates you most about the party which you ranked last?" Some general conclusions can be drawn by comparing their answers (Appendix Table 11) with the critique of newspapers: (a) on the whole, interviewees' criticism contained approximately the same ideas as were published in newspapers; (b) yet the image of the membership of the party they opposed tended to be more clearly crystallized into a few principal thoughts; and (c) the

17. HY, April 22, 1958 (Leo Suonpää); KU, April 18, 1958; HS, May 5, 1958, p. 2 (Esa Kaitila).
18. SS, April 15, 1958, p. 3; HY, April 18, 1958, p. 3; US, April 17, 1958, p. 6.
19. HS, May 5, 1958, p. 2 (Esa Kaitila); HY, April 15, 1958, p. 6.

citizens also tended to speak in more general terms, for example, about ideologies and principles of party goals, whereas the criticism of newspapers was more current, dealing with political tactics, the details of parliamentary work, etc.

The party most commonly ranked as the least desirable was the FPDU (p. 141). This party was considered by its opponents primarily as too strict, divisive and revolutionary, or unpatriotic:

> They are too arrogant, quite out of their minds. (Carpenter, male, 58, SDP)
>
> I don't like their awful wildness and negative attitude toward the fatherland. (Cook, female, 53, Conservative)
>
> It is not a Finnish party, it depends on foreign factors, it is not nationally reliable. (Teacher, male, 31, SDP)
>
> They aim at a revolution, they are unpatriotic and create disorder. (Civil Engineer, female, 35, FPP)
>
> The Communists are miserable folks, because, among others, they have tried to liquidate me. (Pensioner, male, 65, Conservative)
>
> Too insane, they only praise the Soviet Union, and would like the same system here. (Wife of metal worker, 23, FPP)

The content of criticism did not seem to correlate much with the party affiliation of the respondent. However, between the Social Democrats and the Conservatives there was a difference, insofar as the Conservatives criticized more the unpatriotic character of the FPDU, while the Social Democrats concentrated more on the rigid and violent character of the party.[20]

Persons who disliked the Independent Social Democrats the most criticized this party especially for breaking up the unity of the workers:

> Because it split; why in hell did they split, why did they not stick together? (Wife of paper worker, 50, FPDU)
>
> This messing of one's own nest annoys me. (Wife of pulp worker, 74, SDP)

The Social Democratic Party was criticized for its inner struggles, and also for taking poor care of the workers:

20. Lack of patriotism; SDP 13 per cent ($n = 69$) and Cons. 31 per cent ($n = 70$), $t = 2.68$, $p < 0.01$; rigidity: SDP 39 per cent and Cons. 26 per cent, $t = 2.02$, $p < 0.05$.

> They don't serve the workers' interests; they only quarrel. (Machinist, male, 22, FPDU)

> They rise against the working men; the workers' life and circumstances are not improved. (Car mechanic, male, 31, FPDU)

About one tenth of the respondents ranked the Agrarian Union last. In their criticism they mentioned especially the state support of agriculture and, in connection with this, discrimination against workers and class party character:

> Misfortunes in any other occupation are not compensated for, but the farmer gets all kinds of state aid and compensation for frost damages. (Janitor, 30, S.D. Opp.)

> They always quarrel about the price of cereal and fertilizer, and persons like me soon do not even see butter. If they dig a bit of ditch others pay for it, although they did it for themselves. (Custom employee, female, 30 SDP)

> They keep filling their own bag. (Wife of warehouse worker, 50, SDP)

> The eternal cry about poor living and helping peasants with the means of us common people. Supporting a large family with the small pay of one man makes you extremely sparing, and in comparison, the endless cry of farmers and their support is irritating because I imagine they can provide themselves with almost everything they need for everyday living. (Carpenter, 31, SDP)

These examples also illustrate that many city opponents of the Agrarian Union did not differentiate between the party and persons engaged in farming in general.

The Finnish People's Party was least popular among only a few leftist supporters. Criticism centered on its being small, weak, and antilabor:

> Too small a party and too close to the Nazis. (Watchman, 56, FPDU)

> A weak party without any clear goals. (Lathe operator, male, 46, FPDU)

> Because we are workers; that party serves least the interests of workers. (Unskilled worker, 45, SDP)

The National Coalition, which was least popular among 16 per cent of the respondents, was not called weak. But this party was considered especially antilabor. Some persons also called it a militaristic party, or the extreme opponent of their own party:

> They try to take the workers' pay away. (Weaver, female, 51, SDP)
>
> It is the main opponent of the workers and the biggest enemy of People's Democrats. (Construction worker, 57, FPDU)
>
> It does not especially irritate me, but it is the party of the owning class, therefore, its maneuvers don't please me. (Sheet smith, male, 36, FPDU)
>
> They all represent the big shots, and exploit workers. (Wife of industrial worker, 30, FPDU)
>
> So that war won't come but peace would remain. (Former dairy maid, 70, Agrarian)

The inhabitants of Tampere ranked the Swedish People's Party last more often than they did the Conservatives, even though it had not taken part in the elections there since the 1930s, and was not subjected to noticeable criticism in the press. Sometimes it was a question of "a matter of feeling that is difficult to define" (teacher, male, 30, FPP), but most opponents of this party referred to its Swedish character:

> The Swedes irritate me generally. (Nurse, female, 37, S. D. Opp.)
>
> They are too few and don't have much to say, and don't need to either with their strange language. (Wife of fireman, 32, SDP)
>
> Compared to the Finns they are like foreigners, and don't stick to the common good, but to their own interests. (Carpenter, 45, S. D. Opp.)
>
> Because this is Finland, we don't need any foreigners, although certainly they are Finns, too. (Truck driver, 33, FPDU)

SOME SELECTED ITEMS OF POLITICAL DEBATE

When newspapers wrote about parties and about politics in general, they paid attention mainly to current or past events. Discussion of precise goals and future plans was rare. Moreover, the newspapers seldom expressed their own opinions on many of the platform details under study here.

The selected platform issues deal with the socialization and the regulation of economy, industrialization, opinions on the conflict about the number and the size of farms, and the opinions of newspapers on taxation and increases in the state's social expenditures. The seventh point of political dispute, the attitude toward the possibility of Communist participation in the government, was less pertinent to the content of political decisions. Of course, political discussion went on about many goals left outside this study, such as the possible increase in the number of places of employment, unemployment insurance, number of hours in the work week, means of helping capital formation, and stabilization of monetary value.

Table 6.6 summarizes the number and content of statements on these seven points published by the seven newspapers. It suggests three different groupings of the newspapers as either advocates or opponents of certain goals.

1. All newspapers agreed on the necessity of industrialization. The Social Democratic press referred to this more often than any other paper; *Suomen Sosialidemokraatti* averaged as much as two statements per issue.

2. The Communist press often wrote about their party's participation in the Cabinet. They demanded, although generally without precise wording, the establishment of "a coalition government representing all working groups of the nation,"[21] whereas all other newspapers opposed Communist participation in the government.

3. The attitude toward the other issues under study, especially socialization, regulation of economy, and increased social expenditures, was either leftist or rightist. The two extremes were represented by *Hämeen Yhteistyö* and *Helsingin Sanomat,* neither of which ever contained neutral statements; but the actual line of cleavage came between the Communist and Social Democratic papers on one side and the Conservative papers and the independent *Helsingin Sanomat* on the other.

Aamulehti wrote almost daily about "larger and economically stronger farming units," but this topic was dealt with very little in *Uusi Suomi.* The least obvious leftist and rightist differentiation, however, appeared in writings about taxation. Only *Hämeen Yhteistyö* consistently demanded additional taxes, but not for everybody. And *Kansan Uutiset* also stressed the lowering of certain taxes: "The taxation burden of the less privileged must be relieved in municipalities by legislation that makes local taxes graduated."[22] The paper demanded more taxes, especially for corporations and "capitalists with high incomes."

21. *HY,* April 20, 1958, p. 1 (the FPDU parliament group).
22. *KU,* April 14, 1958, p. 4.

TABLE 6.6. Attitude of Seven Newspapers toward Selected Platform Items: Number of Statements Pro and Con between April 14 and May 11, 1958

	Hämeen Yhteistyö (FPDU)	Kansan Uutiset (FPDU)	Kansan Lehti (SDP)	Suomen Sosiali- demokraatti (SDP)	Aamu- lehti (Cons.)	Uusi Suomi (Cons.)	Helsingin Sanomat (Indep.)
(a) Socialization							
Pro	1	6	5	8	–	–	–
Neutral	–	1	3	5	–	1	–
Con	–	–	–	–	5	5	3
(b) Government regulation of economy							
Pro	1	3	4	4	–	–	–
Neutral	–	–	2	1	2	4	–
Con	–	–	–	–	6	6	6
(c) Industrialization							
Pro	16	19	37	54	15	27	28
Neutral	–	3	3	8	8	4	–
Con	–	–	–	–	–	–	–
(d) Size of farms							
Many small ones	1	6	4	5	–	–	–
Neutral	–	5	6	2	4	3	–
Larger ones	–	–	–	–	18	–	9
(e) Lower taxes							
Pro	–	11	3	1	18	16	24
Neutral	–	4	6	1	5	6	–
Con	5	12	–	1	–	–	–
(f) Increased social support							
Pro	4	10	1	3	–	–	–
Neutral	–	4	2	1	3	1	–
Con	–	–	–	–	2	8	12
(g) Communist participation in government							
Pro	11	22	–	–	–	–	–
Neutral	–	3	–	–	–	–	–
Con	–	–	2	4	5	4	6

The interviewed inhabitants of Tampere expressed their opinions on the same questions. They gave their answers just after the four-week period of the newspaper analysis. Their opinions, classified according to party, can be seen in Table 6.7.

One of the questions combined two of the topics described above. The

TABLE 6.7. Relationship of Party Preference to Opinion on Selected Items of Political Debate: May 1958 (in percentages)

Items and Opinions	Total Sample	FPDU	SDP and S.D. Opp.	Non-soc.	SDP	S.D. Opp.	Agr.	FPP	Cons.	Non-part.
(a) Socialization (Q. 24)										
Socialize	26	62	27	4	24	40	10	3	4	12
Present ownership	25	17	34	25	34	36	20	24	26	12
Desocialize	30	10	22	62	23	16	70	70	59	19
Don't know	19	11	17	9	19	8	10	3	11	59
(b) Regulation of Economy (Q. 27)										
Too much freedom	15	37	15	3	14	28	–	3	3	19
Present situation	17	11	26	14	26	20	20	17	11	7
Too much regulation	33	19	27	60	27	24	40	70	60	17
Don't know	35	33	32	23	33	28	40	10	26	67
(c) Industrialization (Q. 23)										
New plants	62	74	60	62	62	52	40	77	61	45
Industry is sufficient	31	24	36	31	36	36	60	23	29	24
Don't know	7	2	4	7	2	12	–	–	10	31
(d) Size of farms (Q. 25)										
Many farms	40	43	50	26	49	52	20	27	27	40
Fewer and larger farms	41	38	36	60	36	40	60	60	60	17
Don't know	19	19	14	14	15	8	20	13	13	43
(e) Lower taxation or increased social support (Q. 26)										
Lower taxes	79	76	81	89	80	84	90	90	88	62
Increased state support	11	20	15	8	16	8	10	10	8	9
Don't know	10	4	4	3	4	8	–	–	4	29
(f) Communist participation in government (Q. 35)										
FPDU or a coalition including the FPDU	21	65	16	3	15	24	10	3	2	3
All parties	25	20	32	18	33	28	20	33	14	26
No Communist participation	34	3	39	65	39	40	50	54	69	5
Expert cabinet	1	1	1	2	1	–	–	–	3	2
Don't know	19	11	12	12	12	8	20	10	12	64
Total	100	100	100	100	100	100	100	100	100	100
Number of cases	*501*	*108*	*189*	*136*	*164*	*25*	*10*	*30*	*93*	*42*

interviewees were asked: "Which do you now consider more important: lower taxes or increased state support to the needy?" A large majority, about four out of five, considered lower taxation more important. Otherwise the points in Tables 6.6 and 6.7 correspond to each other.

Before comparing the newspapers with the opinions of the citizens, a few general observations can be made about the responses. (a) In Tampere it was easiest apparently to answer those two questions—industrialization and lower taxation—about which opinions were parallel and not in conflict. The "don't know" group was smallest in these. (b) The nonpartisans had exceptional difficulties in expressing political opinions, because the "don't know" group was always largest among them. (c) A party preference shared between two persons was not at all a guarantee that they would agree on individual political matters. Actually, there was no unanimity on any point among any group of party supporters. It was possible for a given newspaper to represent an exact preference, but concerning the groups of party supporters one can at best speak of a majority opinion and a greater or smaller consistency of all opinions.

A comparison of Table 6.7 with Table 6.6 on newspaper writing leads to the following observations:

1. Industrialization was hoped for by a considerable majority of the supporters of each party. All seven newspapers had also agreed on this point. It might be that the Agrarians in Tampere were more in favor of the opposing alternative, but this finding lacks statistical significance, and besides no Agrarian newspapers were analyzed.

2. The attitude of the Communists and nonsocialist supporters differed on other points. Here again, the disagreement followed the differences in the respective newspapers. The People's Democrats were especially fond of socialization and Communist participation in the government, while the supporters of nonsocialist parties especially liked desocialization or people's capitalism, less government regulation, larger farms, and the elimination of Communists from the government.

3. The attitude of Social Democrats allowed only one possibility for separating clearly the opinions of the left from those of the right. This was the size of farms, a fairly out-of-the-way problem for city people. Even here the grouping into left and right did not mean unanimous opinions in either group.[23] More than a third of the leftist supporters

23. The opinion "as many farms as possible" was supported by significantly more leftist than nonsocialist supporters, $t = 3.49$, $p < 0.001$.

agreed with the opinion of *Aamulehti,* and one fourth of the non-socialists held an opposing view.

4. Otherwise the SDP supporters seemingly mediated between the two extremes.[24] The watershed of opinion was on neither side of the Social Democrats, but put them in the difficult position of the middleman. The Social Democratic inhabitants of Tampere showed no tendency to follow their party press when it joined the left against the nonsocialists. Neither did they agree with the press when it joined the right and opposed Communists. It seems that the Social Democrats had an above average tendency to be satisfied with the present circumstances: for example, with the current ownership of the economy or regulation of business life.

Of additional interest are the internal comparisons of the two Social Democratic wings and of the supporters of the nonsocialist parties:

5. The sample contained so few supporters of the Independent Social Democrats that it is impossible to conclude which wing of the divided party was more to the Left in May 1958. It may be that the Opposition supported socialization and regulation more strongly, and the party proper approved of increased social support.[25] But the data might also give evidence for the assumption that the opinions of these two groups did not differ considerably.

6. The opinions of the FPP supporters and the Conservatives were also distributed in about the same way. In the sample one finds only two slight differences, and they were not statistically significant: the Conservatives opposed more rigidly any Communist participation in the government,[26] whereas the FPP supporters were more to the right in their antisocialization and antiregulation opinions, that is, on those points on which *Helsingin Sanomat* did not publish neutral statements.

WEAK AND STRONG PARTY IDENTIFIERS

Despite the mutual correlation of political opinions and party affiliation, a shared favorable attitude toward a party was still far from unifying the political thinking of the party's supporters. Even the common party

24. Testing differences between FPDU and Social Democrats one gets, for instance: (a) $\chi^2 = 34.79$, $p < 0.001$ and (b) $\chi^2 = 24.24$, $p < 0.001$; and differences between SDP and nonsocialists (a) $\chi^2 = 46.27$, $p < 0.001$, (b) $\chi^2 = 32.88$, $p < 0.001$ and (f) "no Communists in government" $t = 4.59$, $p < 0.001$.

25. (a) $t = 1.46$, $0.10 < p < 0.20$, (b) $t = 1.56$, $0.10 < p < 0.20$ and (e) $t = 1.38$, $p < 0.20$.

26. Comparing Agrarians and FPP (53 per cent) with Conservatives and Swedes $t = 1.88$, $p < 0.10$.

affiliation was felt with different intensities. We could expect the strong party identifiers to have specific opinions close to the official points of view of their party. We have already found that the strong identifiers were the most willing to be exposed to their party's newspapers, especially to its main organ published in the capital city (p. 73).

The measure of party identification in Table 6.8 is again a dichotomy

TABLE 6.8. Relationship of Party Preference and Party Identification to Opinions on Selected Items of Political Debate: May 1958 (in percentages)

Items and Opinions	FPDU Weak	Strong	SDP Weak	Strong	FPP Weak	Strong	Cons. Weak	Strong
(a) Socialization (Q. 24)								
Socialize	55	65	18	28	6	–	9	2
Present ownership	15	18	49	26	19	29	41	17
Desocialize	12	9	13	29	69	71	38	71
Don't know	18	8	20	17	6	–	12	10
(b) Regulation of economy (Q. 27)								
Too much freedom	12	43	13	13	6	–	3	3
Present situation	15	9	27	26	19	14	18	7
Too much regulation	5	24	25	29	62	79	50	66
Don't know	55	24	35	32	13	7	29	24
(c) Industrialization (Q. 23)								
New plants	70	76	55	65	75	79	56	64
Industry is sufficient	30	21	43	32	25	21	29	29
Don't know	–	3	2	3	–	–	15	7
(d) Size of farms (Q. 25)								
Many farms	36	45	52	48	38	14	29	25
Fewer and larger farms	46	35	42	33	56	64	68	56
Don't know	18	20	6	19	6	22	3	19
(e) Lower taxation or increased social support (Q. 26)								
Lower taxes	76	71	73	81	94	86	85	86
Increased state support	15	19	20	11	6	14	12	2
Don't know	9	10	7	8	–	–	3	12
(f) Communist participation in government (Q. 35)								
FPDU or a coalition including the FPDU	55	70	20	12	6	–	3	2
All parties	18	21	30	35	32	36	20	10
No Communist participation	9	–	35	41	50	57	53	78
Expert Cabinet	–	1	–	1	–	–	9	–
Don't know	18	8	15	11	12	7	15	10
Total	100	100	100	100	100	100	100	100
Number of cases	*33*	*75*	*60*	*104*	*16*	*14*	*34*	*59*

of uncertain and sure supporters of the parties. The opinions are the same as those presented in Table 6.7. Some subgroups contain very few cases; the two subgroups supporting the Finnish People's Party especially are too small for statistically significant conclusions. Yet Table 6.8 may show more about the population of this study than is proved by the sheer test results, because many results are mutually consistent. Four findings are especially obvious:

1. The opinions of strong identifiers were, as expected, more in agreement with the statements of the party press than were the opinions of weak identifiers. The sure People's Democrats hoped for socialization, many small farms, additional state expenditures for social purposes and, remarkably, also for Communist participation in the government. Strong FPP supporters criticized the regulation of the economy more than did the weak, while they supported more large farming units and the exclusion of the FPDU from government responsibility. Among the Conservatives, the sure ones especially favored desocialization and less regulation and opposed Communist participation in the government.

2. Similarly, weak identifiers had a tendency to support opinions which disagreed with the official position of the party, although they also avoided choices and gave many "don't know" answers. For example, among the interviewed FPDU supporters, weak identifiers tended slightly to agree with the ideas of desocialization, the settlement policy advocated by *Aamulehti,* and lower taxation, as well as with the idea that the FPDU should not participate in the government. Among uncertain FPP followers, there was support for socialization, regulation, smaller farms, and Communist participation in the government; and the weak Conservative identifiers favored socialization and additional state support more than did the strong supporters.

Rather similar findings have been obtained in a recent study of Norwegian political parties. In that study, the two levels of party support—weak and strong identifiers—were also compared with a higher, or more official, level in the party, which in the Norwegian case was the local party leadership. Notable differences were found between the political opinions of leaders and those of their followers; the strong identifiers showed a tendency to differ from other party supporters, leaning toward the opinions expressed by the leaders.[27] Two additional conclusions about Table 6.8 concern the special case of Social Democrats in Tampere and such differences as suggest the diffusion of new ideas:

27. Valen and Katz, *Political Parties,* pp. 252–59.

3. The weak and strong SDP identifiers were not consistently different from each other in the same way as the Communists, FPP supporters, and Conservatives. In considering the ownership of the economy, the weak Social Democrats came often to the conclusion that the present circumstances were better than either more or less socialization.

4. In interpreting certain details of Table 6.8, one might conclude further that the strong party identifiers adopted new ideas more quickly than did the weak supporters. For example, many circles had begun to demand new, effective action to hasten the industrialization of the country, and, during April and May 1958, all seven newspapers were favorable to this idea. In May 1958 this was agreed upon by a larger proportion of the strong than of the weak identifiers of each party.[28] Opposition to socialism had been for a long time a focal point of the Conservative program, but the idea of active desocialization, represented by the public sale of stocks in the so-called state corporations, was a new one. It was a current issue, for example, because of the motion by Tuure Junnila in parliament in February 1957.[29] The strong Conservative identifiers had generally adopted the idea, but a considerable number of the weak identifiers still favored the traditional goal of simply opposing further socialization.

One question was answered by the weak identifiers more often than by the strong. It dealt with the size and number of farms (Table 6.8.d). In this case, perhaps the weak Conservatives followed the official position of their party more often than did the strong supporters. It is difficult to say why this occurred. One possible explanation might be the weak identifiers' habit of reading mainly the local newspaper. And this settlement policy had been touched upon a great deal by the local Conservative and, to some extent, the Social Democratic newspapers.

In any case, the focal finding of Table 6.8 is that the stronger the party identification, the less the opinions deviated from the ideas presented by the party press. And when newspapers mentioned the name of their own party, it was almost always done with a positive tone. However, the supporters of each party differed in their satisfaction with the party, just as they differed in their detailed opinions (Table 6.3).

Strong identifiers were more satisfied with their party than weak supporters were. Table 6.9 indicates this separately for each party group.

28. Even in the total sample, the difference between weak and strong identifiers was only symptomatic ($\chi^2 = 2.84$, $v = 1$, $p < 0.10$), but the conclusion is supported by the consistency of the differences in each party.

29. *Valtiopäivät 1957* (Legislative session of 1957, private member's motion no. 39).

TABLE 6.9. Relationship of Party Preference and Party Identification to Satisfaction with the Activity of Supported Party: May 1958 (in percentages)

Satisfaction	FPDU		SDP		FPP		Cons.	
	Weak	Strong	Weak	Strong	Weak	Strong	Weak	Strong
Satisfied	57	78	40	53	23	57	48	72
Dissatisfied	20	11	58	42	46	14	24	14
Don't know	23	11	2	5	31	29	28	14
Total	100	100	100	100	100	100	100	100
Number of cases	*30*	*74*	*48*	*97*	*13*	*14*	*25*	*57*

Because weak identifiers did not otherwise express special dissatisfaction —for example, they criticized the general conduct of the country's affairs no more than did the strong identifiers[30]—the weakness of party identification obviously decreased satisfaction with the activities of the party, or vice versa, dissatisfaction weakened party identification. Perhaps this correlation is because of the greater exposure of strong identifiers to communication favoring the party. Furthermore, within the sample, the difference between weak and strong identifiers was greatest among the supporters of the Finnish People's Party, and smallest among the Social Democratic group.

Table 6.2 summarized the best aspects of each party as expressed by its supporters. Corresponding data for the weak and the strong identifiers of four parties separately indicate again differences which lack statistical significance. It seems, however, that the sure identifiers gave more reasons that were typical of the supporters of that party. They praised the FPDU and the SDP for favoring the interests of the workers; the Finnish People's Party for advancing the interests of white collar employees; and the Conservatives for working on behalf of the good of the whole. The weak identifiers seemed to mention more the social policy of the FPDU, the power of the SDP, the methods of the FPP, and the leaders of the Conservatives. On the other hand, only strong People's Democrats praised the methods of their own party, which were subject to special criticism by the party's opponents. The persons who said they had inherited their party affiliation were usually strong identifiers.

The other parties were ranked by the weak and strong identifiers in

30. The satisfaction of whole groups of party supporters was different, but there was no difference within each party between the weak and strong identifiers. This is shown by the following percentages of dissatisfied supporters: FPDU weak 85 per cent and sure 89 per cent; SDP weak 70 per cent and sure 71 per cent; Cons. weak 77 per cent and sure 81 per cent.

an almost similar way (data not shown). One common aspect in choosing the least desirable party was the ranking of the Swedish People's Party as last by the weak identifiers, while the strong identifiers gave the rank of last to a more natural opponent of the party. Strong Communist identifiers gave that ranking to the Conservatives; the Social Democrats ranked the FPDU, Agrarians, Conservatives and their own Opposition last; and finally the FPP supporters and the Conservatives found the FPDU the least desirable. The second place was often given by sure Communists to the Agrarian Union, which was less criticized by the Helsinki paper of the party than by its local paper. Among the Conservative supporters, the weak identifiers may have tended to support Social Democrats more, the sure the FPP more.

The above comparison again supports the conclusion that weak identifiers were outside the current mainstream of politics (p. 158). This is a possible interpretation of their negative attitude toward the party that for some time had not appeared on the local political platform and was seldom mentioned by the newspapers. But what was observed about the citizens' praising of their own parties and their attitudes toward other parties did not reveal any connections between their opinions and the material of newspapers. However, the expected closeness of the strong identifiers to the official view of the party was evident both in the opinions on selected points of political discussion and in the satisfaction with their own party. Consistently strong identifiers also gave more opinions and were more ready with an answer than were the weak identifiers.

THE COMPARISON GROUP

In Korpilahti, the supporters of the three most popular parties expressed gratitude for the parties' concern for their interests. The FPDU was considered a party "which takes the best care of workers' affairs," takes care of the small farmers, or simply "tries to side with him who has nothing." According to the view of a small farmer, "they try to build up cooperation between city labor and rural farm labor," and one unskilled worker praised the FPDU as follows: "I don't know anything else, but in the winter they quarreled about the children's allowances and it was probably because of them they remained unchanged; I don't know otherwise whether they succeeded."

The supporters of the Social Democrats, almost without exception, labeled their party as one forwarding the interests of labor: "Because that is my field, it is my own party. Only a silly man does not look out for his own advantage." The reason given by a small farmer was simply that "people say that it is supposed to be the best." Likewise, the Agrarian Union was considered a party singularly devoted to advancing the interests of farmers: "They work mainly for the good of the farmers, whose livelihood depends on the soil," and "to some extent they care for the interest of the small farmer." In the opinion of one farmer "that party is usually supported here in the country," and a small farmer mentioned: "I got used to it, and also my father was eager. The country spirit is influential even under strained circumstances."

A foreman who supported the Finnish People's Party said, in turn, that his party "takes care of things in a way which is consistent with my own thoughts." In the opinion of one farmer the National Coalition "was a straightforward party, which has not been messing up things in the government." A teacher who supported it considered its "patriotism and legalism" the best aspects of his party.

In other words, the rural comparison group praised the parties in almost the same way as did the inhabitants of Tampere; among the deviations were some praises given by FPDU and SDP supporters for concern for small farmers' interests.

When the comparison group ranked parties in an order of preference, the four least liked parties were the same as in Tampere. Last place went most often to the Communists, then to the Swedish People's Party and the Conservatives, and, in the opinion of fewer respondents, to the Agrarian Union (Appendix Table 12). The criticism of the parties, too, was of somewhat the same character. "The Communist business is too glaring" (farmer, Agrarian), "Its program does not coincide with the vital conditions of the small farmers" (small farmer, Conservative), and "The Communists are like those having an imaginary illness, not satisfied with anything, only always against the government and the parliament" (forest foreman, Agrarian). The FPDU was also identified with the interests of a foreign country: for example, "The Russians chased me twice away from my home, and that really makes me mad" (farmer, Agrarian).

The Agrarian Union was also criticized in Korpilahti as in Tampere: "Many things annoy me—the state support, the cow support, and the party is never satisfied" (carpenter, FPDU); "The continuous rise of food prices" (foreman, FPP); "The price of cereal is only propaganda; they say it should be lowered, but still it is not lowered" (worker, FPDU).

The National Coalition was called "the party of the big shots" by both Communist and Agrarian supporters; "They look out more for the interests of industry than of agriculture" (farmer, Agrarian); and "It is the extreme right wing, and does not attend to the working man's interests" (electrician, SDP).

The Swedish People's Party was criticized in Korpilahti, too, for its "strange language"; "because it favors the Swedish cause and because Finland belongs to the Finnish" (farmer's wife, Agrarian); and "The Swedes look after their own interests; they have their own ways and means" (unskilled worker, SDP).

The Agrarian Union was ranked as the second most popular party more often in Korpilahti than in Tampere. It was especially favored by the Social Democratic supporters, while the Conservatives were less to the liking of the Social Democrats in Korpilahti than in Tampere. Agrarian supporters were divided between the SDP and the nonsocialist parties, and the rank orders by the People's Democrats were almost the same in both places (although no FPDU supporter placed the SDP last in Korpilahti). A disapproving attitude toward the People's Democrats was revealed by the fact that only one Social Democrat out of five gave the FPDU the second place of preference.

In comparing the weak and strong party identifiers, one has to remember the ever increasing risk of wrong conclusions. We might mention, however, that weak identifiers in Korpilahti had a general tendency not to answer questions. Among Communist supporters only the weak identifiers ranked the Agrarians, and only the strong identifiers the Social Democrats, as the second best party. The Conservatives were considered most unacceptable by only 8 per cent of the weak, but by 50 per cent of the strong Communist supporters. Among the Social Democrats, the weak identifiers liked the FPDU, but the strong identifiers preferred the Agrarians, and even the FPP. Weak Social Democrats often placed the Conservatives last, while the FPDU was ranked last by the strong identifiers. Weak Agrarian identifiers seemingly favored the Independent Social Democrats and the Swedes, but strong Agrarians favored the FPP and the Conservatives. Consequently, while the cleavage between the left and the bourgeois was more clear in the thinking of strong than of weak Communists, the situation was reversed among the Social Democrats. Weak Social Democrats divided the parties into the left and the bourgeois, but sure ones into Communists and non-Communists.

Opinions on the selected issues were more clearly divided into left and right in Korpilahti than in Tampere (see Table 6.10). The Social Democrats had a mediating position in the case of the return of Communists

TABLE 6.10. Relationship of Party Preference in Korpilahti to Opinions on Selected Items of Political Debate: May 1958 (in percentages)

Items and Opinions	FPDU	SDP	Agr.	Cons. and FPP	Non-partisan	Total sample
(a) Socialization (Q. 24)						
Socialize	28	28	14	–	14	19
Present ownership	11	12	25	38	–	15
Desocialize	22	16	43	37	36	30
Don't know	39	44	18	25	50	36
(b) Regulation of Economy (Q. 27)						
Too much freedom	17	12	11	12	7	11
Present situation	11	12	18	–	22	14
Too much regulation	28	12	28	25	21	23
Don't know	44	64	43	63	50	52
(c) Industrialization (Q. 23)						
New plants	50	56	61	63	43	54
Industry is sufficient	39	32	28	12	21	29
Don't know	11	12	11	25	36	17
(d) Size of farms (Q. 25)						
Many farms	56	52	39	37	43	44
Fewer and larger farms	33	40	57	63	43	49
Don't know	11	8	4	–	14	7
(e) Lower taxation or increased social support (Q. 26)						
Lower taxes	61	64	79	88	64	70
Increased state support	17	28	7	–	7	16
Don't know	22	8	14	12	29	14
(f) Communist participation in government (Q. 35)						
FPDU or a coalition including the FPDU	44	20	–	25	–	15
All parties	28	12	29	12	21	22
No Communist participation	6	44	64	63	–	36
Expert cabinet	–	–	–	–	7	1
Don't know	22	24	7	–	72	26
Total	100	100	100	100	100	100
Number of cases	*18*	*25*	*28*	*8*	*14*	*97*

to the Cabinet, but the distribution of Social Democratic and Communist opinions was similar when socialization, regulation of the economy, or the relationship of taxation and social expenditures were considered. But the similarity of Social Democrats and Communists in Korpilahti was caused mainly by the fact that the opinions of the rural Communist supporters were farther from the official party line than were those of the city Communists. The only case of more leftist opinions on the part of the rural Communists dealt with the number of farms. They wanted as many farms as possible, even if they were small.

More questions were unanswered in Korpilahti than in Tampere. It was in the case of the two alternatives given about the main principle of settlement policy that more rural people chose one or the other.

Here again, the weak identifiers had fewer opinions than the strong supporters. And, to some extent, the strong identifiers were closer to the opinions of their party proper. The strong FPDU supporters especially demanded more regulation of the economy, while the weak supporters thought business was too much controlled. Industrialization was demanded more by strong than by weak SDP supporters. Among the Agrarians the difference was in the opposite direction. Weak Social Democrats, who were more to the left in their attitudes toward other parties, also demanded more socialization than the sure Social Democrats.

All FPP and Conservative supporters interviewed in Korpilahti were satisfied with the activities of their party, but only one half of the People's Democrats were satisfied with their party. A difference between weak and strong identifiers could be observed among Social Democrats, and especially among the Agrarians. In that latter group, 81 per cent ($n = 16$) of the strong, but only 33 per cent ($n = 9$) of the weak, identifiers claimed to be satisfied with the earlier activities of the party.

SUMMARY

Each publication of the Finnish political press is accustomed to praise its own party and to criticize the others. The content of three Tampere papers and the Helsinki papers of the same parties in April and May 1958 provided no exception to this general rule. The independent *Helsingin Sanomat* was very nearly the voice of a fourth party. The content and tone of statements about a newspaper's own party did differ considerably. When writing about other parties, five newspapers were parallel in criticizing mainly the Agrarian Union. Only the Communist newspapers criticized the Social Democrats most.

The content of the statements published about other parties was repeated, in part, in the opinions expressed by the citizens concerning the parties of their first and last preference. The positive images of persons about their own parties, however, may have been crystallized into fewer basic ideas than were the many-sided praises in newspapers. The supporters of the FPDU and those of all the left tended especially to identify their occupational class with the party. The city inhabitants who criticized the Agrarian Union, in turn, generally identified that party with persons engaged in agriculture. We found also that in criticizing other parties the papers dealt with current topics, such as details of parliamentary work, while the citizens expressed more general criticisms of party principles. Some people were dissatisfied also with the activity of their own party; most of these supported those parties which had been to some extent criticized by their own press.

When the inhabitants of Tampere rank ordered the parties, the widest cleavage in the system proved to be that between the FPDU alone, on the one hand, and all the rest together, on the other. This was true of the press, too, when it took a stand on possible Communist participation in the government. However, the published critical statements about parties were directed only slightly toward those parties which the supporters of the newspapers' parties considered displeasing.

Opinions expressed on certain points of political dispute were also studied. Generally, the Communist and the Social Democratic newspapers represented the leftist standpoint, while the Conservative papers and the *Helsingin Sanomat* were of the opposite opinion. All seven newspapers agreed on the principal demands for extended industrialization of Finland.

The supporters of the parties, in turn, were not unanimous on any question. The majority of the People's Democrats took an opposite stand from that of the majority of the nonsocialist supporters, and this concurred with the stands taken by the press of these parties. If opinions are considered to represent a continuum, those of the SDP supporters were in between these two extreme groups. And, obviously, this was not influenced by the leftist or rightist statements made by the SDP press. Industrialization was considered necessary by city inhabitants in general, which was again in line with the content of the newspapers they read.

A comparison of the weak and the strong identifiers of each party led again to some conclusions about the differentiation of the supporters and about the diffusion of communication. The stronger the party identification, the closer were the political opinions to the standpoint of the party press, and the more satisfaction there was with the activities of the party. Because these strong identifiers were also much exposed to their own party press, especially to its main organ, the mass communication directed at them may have influenced the development of their opinions towards consistency with the party line. Of course, one might also argue that the party affiliation of some people tended to strengthen when the party press presented pleasing ideas, but the apparent tendency of strong identifiers to adopt new ideas first supports the conclusion that newspapers do play a role in preparing opinions, and that it is more effective for strong party identifiers.

The content analysis of newspapers had two main goals in this chapter: (1) The political content of newspapers was considered to represent or at least to be close to the party platform and the views of party leadership. Therefore, the content of newspapers has been interpreted as an indicator of the values and goals of parties. (2) On the other hand, attention has been paid to the role of newspapers as informers of news, preparers of opinions, and perhaps also mirrors of their readers' opinions. In handling their focal communication role, that of influencing the opinions of citizens, the party papers obviously work to a large extent with political purposes in mind. But some stands may reflect the thoughts of the editorial staff itself, the close connections between the editors and party leaders, or at least their uniform way of thinking, without any primary consideration of their propaganda value.

Some observations about the writings in the Helsinki and the Tampere papers could be interpreted in the light of the former's having more direct connections with the leadership of the party. Thus distance from the norms-creating center of the group—party leadership and the focal political events being reported—had an impact on the group's opinions at the highly organized level represented by its press.

Compared to Tampere, Korpilahti is a distant place. Even this geographic distance from the center of the party seemed to have an impact on the opinions of the party supporters. The rural sample seemed to have looser connections with the official standpoints of the party, and opinion formation also seemed slower in Korpilahti than in Tampere. On the other hand, many details of the findings about Tampere were repeated in the comparison group: for example, the rank order of the four least popular parties was the same, and similar ideas were presented on the good and the bad sides of the parties. Only very limited comparisons are possible since the content of newspapers read in Korpilahti was not analyzed for April and May, and most representatives of the nonsocialist viewpoint supported a different party in these places.

Let us stress again some special characteristics of the Social Democratic Party. Both at the left and at the right it was often considered next to the best party. The attitudes toward other parties by its own supporters revealed a possible movement to the right, because the leftist direction was least popular among the strong SDP identifiers in Tampere. But at the same time, even the strong identifiers of this party were disconnected from the opinions of their party press. Perhaps quite remarkable changes in values were taking place among the Social Democrats, while the simultaneous split of the party was disturbing its normal opinion formation.

7. The Framework of the Campaign

Although the importance of future elections is continuously felt in the political system, the election campaign is here defined as a period of limited duration, distinguishable from the normal political process. Yet it is impossible to understand voting behavior without a proper time perspective and background of normal politics. Therefore the preceding chapters described many aspects of the parties and the electorate which are not directly connected with the election.

The election campaign attempts to activate or alter the voting predispositions and therefore seems to provide another major explanation for voting behavior. In the following description of the campaign we will first observe who carried the campaign into effect and how. Thereafter, in Chaper 8, we will describe the content of the communication that filled the framework of the campaign.

In observing a certain election, one has to remember that the changing political situation gives each campaign a different character. Even the Finnish party system has not been constant in many successive elections. Although the frame of the campaigns obviously changes less than their content, the framework of each election campaign is developed by new methods, even new parties, and the liveliness of campaign activities also varies. On the other hand, the content of the campaigns is stabilized to some extent by those values which are continuously stressed by each party.

PREPARATIONS FOR THE CAMPAIGN

Because the President of the Republic did not dissolve Parliament, the 1958 elections had to take place "on the first Sunday in July and the day following that."[1] The number of representatives, to which each constituency was entitled, was known quite early, and the formal decision by the Council of Ministers in January 1958 transferred only one seat from the Western Kuopio constituency to the constituency surrounding Helsinki.[2] The Northern Häme constituency was entitled to thirteen parliamentary seats, as in 1951 and 1954.

The Department of Judicial Administration of the Ministry of Justice

1. Law on Parliamentary Elections (336/1955) § 43.
2. *Suomen asetuskokoelma* (Finland's Statute Book) No. 10/1958.

has national responsibility for conducting Finnish state elections.[3] On the local level, the official preparations for the elections require decisions by the municipal councils and the activity of census officials. One duty of the city magistrates is to act as specific election officials; the central electoral boards of the constituencies and the boards of voting districts are appointed for the sole purpose of organizing a certain election.[4]

The central electoral board of the Northern Häme constituency had not changed since the 1956 presidential election, and the city council had divided Tampere into 55 voting districts in June 1956 (increasing the previous number of districts by eleven). The districts averaged 1,400 persons entitled to vote; the register of the first district had 2,847 names and those of the others from 821 to 2,362. The bench of magistrates, the legally constituted election board for the city, also had to be divided into 55 separate units. In March the magistrate asked local party organizations to name their share of the necessary additional chairmen and members. The public announcement of the magistrate concerning voting districts and polling places was published on June 18, 1958.

Administrative preparations carried out by the local election board before it is divided include: (1) preparing the register of voters, (2) providing absentee ballots for those who request them, and (3) getting the facilities ready for actual polling.[5]

The preparation of the registers is probably the most interesting of the three, because the newspapers utilize that opportunity extensively to remind their readers of the approaching elections. The 1958 registers were based on the January 1957 census. The preliminary registers of the city totaled 79,046 names, or 2,253 more than the previous ones. The checking of the registers was made very easy by mailing to each enfranchised inhabitant of the city a so-called election card, which showed exactly how the addressee's name and personal information was printed in the register. The number of the appropriate voting district also was noted on the cards. They were mailed at the beginning of the week of March 15 to 22, during which time the registers were available for public inspection. Voters had to appeal for corrections before the meeting of the election board on April 5.

Among such official decisions as deal with the actual framework of the

3. By-laws of the Council of Ministers (995/1943) § 16 and the Statute on the Ministry of Justice (38/1933 and 333/1960) § 2.

4. Law on Parliamentary Elections, Articles 3–6.

5. Law on Parliamentary Elections, §§ 10–17, 20, 23, 43–47.

campaign, there is the decision of the city government concerning the period for free distribution of posters. Decisions by the state-owned broadcasting corporation about election programs on the radio are also a part of the official preparations for the election. In addition, in the 1958 election, the governing board of the radio denied its own employees the right to run as candidates.[6]

Certifying and publishing the final ballot of the constituency is the important task of the central election board. After the deadline for nominations, 40 days before the election, this board checks the lists of candidates and draws the order of the electoral alliances. This, of course, is instrumental for numbering each list of candidate. On May 28, the following order was drawn up in Tampere: the Agrarian Union (2–14); the Independent Social Democratic Electoral Alliance (15–27); the Finnish People's Party (28–40); the Electoral Alliance of the Popular Center (41–45); the National Coalition (46–58); the People's Democratic Electoral Alliance—FPDU (59–71); and the Social Democratic Electoral Alliance (72–84). The titles and numbers were officially certified on June 12.[7]

Campaigning is, of course, carried on mainly by the political parties. Even for many official preparations it is necessary that the parties cooperate with public authorities. This makes it possible to man the election boards so that the "various kinds of opinions are represented on them." However, the nomination of candidates demands no initiative at all on part of the central electoral board.

In preparing for a campaign, the focal activities of political parties include: (1) the nomination of candidates; (2) possible consultations with other parties about joint electoral alliances; (3) financing the election; (4) strengthening the campaign organization in other ways; (5) decisions concerning the platform and propaganda themes; (6) detailed planning of the campaign activities; and (7) practical preparations of the campaign material.

Nominations

Each electoral alliance was entitled to thirteen candidates in the Northern Häme constituency. In 1954, when the Small Farmers' Party no longer ran alone, this constituency had five electoral alliances. After the split of

6. The National Pension Institute informed five district agents that if they were elected to Parliament they could not remain employed by the institute, *HS*, March 26, 1958, p. 19.

7. On June 9 the original name suggested by the Social Democratic Opposition was not confirmed because it was considered too misleading, *AL*, June 10, 1958, p. 7.

the Social Democrats, six parties were again nominating a full number of candidates. And a new party, the Popular Center, also nominated six persons, five of whom were approved for the final list.[8] Consequently, the inhabitants of Tampere and the rest of the Northern Häme constituency had to write in the circle of the ballot any one number from 2 to 84. In the whole country, a total of 1,087 candidates were running for Parliament.

Because Finnish legislation does not mention political parties, the elimination of, or search for, candidates cannot be officially regulated. This task belongs usually to the leading bodies of the parties' district organizations. Even most party rules do not clearly determine the procedure. For instance, in the Conservative Party, national leadership, district trustees, and the executive councils of local clubs all have to "make preparations for and direct state and local election activities." According to the Social Democratic party rules, the "arrangement of lists of candidates" is the responsibility of the annual district conventions of the party.[9]

The preparations of the SDP have for a long time included a kind of closed primary. Local and municipal organizations have nominated candidates, and the party members have voted for them. Each member has been entitled to vote for two more persons than were last elected from Social Democratic lists in that constituency: a maximum of one quarter of the candidates could be changed later by joint action of national party leadership and the district trustees.

In the primary elections of February 16–17, 1958, the Opposition candidates gained about one quarter of the Social Democratic votes. Both the party itself and the *Päivän Sanomat,* a paper supporting the Opposition, were pleased with this outcome.[10] In Northern Häme about 3,500 members of the party voted, each for a maximum of seven persons.[11] In March the party district convention decided to follow the outcome of the vote with one exception: the Opposition leader, Aarre Simonen, ninth in the primary vote, was excluded.[12] Then when the Opposition announced its

8. One candidate's list was disqualified because of technical deficiencies.

9. *Kansallinen Kokoomus r.y:n säännöt* (Art. 11), *Kansallisliitto r.y:n säännöt* (Art. 9), and *Kansallisseuran säännöt* (Art. 8), (Rules of national, district, and local Conservative organization, Helsinki, 1950, 1954, and 1951). *Suomen Sosialidemokraattisen puolueen sääntökokoelma* (Collected rules of the Social Democratic Party of Finland, Helsinki/Pori, SDP, 1957), pp. 24, 30.

10. "The party people have turned their back on the undisciplined opposition which appeared among them," *SS,* March 18, 1958; "The Social Democratic Opposition went beyond its goals," *Päivän Sanomat,* February 20, 1958.

11. *KL,* February 20, 1958, p. 4.

12. *KL,* March 17, 1958, pp. 1–2. The Social Democratic Party Council had decided on

independent electoral alliance after the party trustees had met on May
10th, the district leadership made rapid replacements. Five candidates, who
had participated in the primary, now joined the Independent Social
Democratic Alliance. In addition, it was joined by three trade union
men, one small farmer, one technician representing white collar employees, and three persons employed by the Workers' Sport Federation.

Other parties arranged advisory polls among their members. The
local units of the FPDU nominated candidates in February and March 1958,
and they took an organizational vote during three weeks in April. Each
member of the party was allowed to vote for five persons in Northern
Häme. The final nomination was the responsibility of the district committee.[13] Conservative candidates were nominated in the spring conventions of the district organizations, after a national trial vote in 1957, and
some membership polling. The candidates, who were suggested by the
committee of the district organization, were nominated in an extraordinary district convention on January 19, but the names were first published
after the regular district convention in March.[14] The Finnish People's
Party asked the 20 local organizations to designate suitable national candidates or "power engines" as well as provincial, local, and Tampere candidates. The district organization then decided on February 23 to nominate
the three chairmen of the party and five other persons, and authorized its
committee to complete the list.[15]

The local units of the Agrarian Union had already discussed candidates
in the Fall of 1957. A few district organizations arranged primaries. In
the Northern Häme constituency, the preliminary nominations were decided by seven subgroups in January and February; the women's district
organization also nominated one candidate. The finally decisive district
convention, arranged in Tampere on March 4, belonged to the series of
party district conventions which were timed from March 2 to March 25
in such a sequence that the party secretary was able to attend them all.[16]

January 18 to advise the party's executive council and district organizations "to refuse to
nominate for candidacy the five members of the party who entered the government on
September 2, 1957, against party rules and party decisions, and who thereafter have
worked against the party," SS, January 19, 1958, p. 1.

13. Information from HY and KU.

14. AL and US.

15. Communication with the district organizer of the party.

16. The only exception was on March 17, when Mr. Arvo Korsimo attended two district
meetings and Mr. Matti Kekkonen replaced him at a third one during the same day. In
the Eastern Kuopio constituency the nomination was altered later. Information from
Maakansa (MK) and communication with the district organizer.

Tampere (*above*) and Korpilahti: an industrial city and a rural commune.

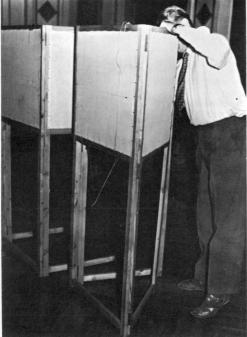

The local election board's administrative preparations for voting: *(top)* providing absentee ballots for use on voting day; *(left)* putting up the voting shelters; *(above)* ensuring just before voting begins that the ballot box is empty.

Kansallisen Kokoomuksen vaaliliitto

Kansandemokraattien vaaliliitto – SKDL

46	47
Asunta, Mikko, maanviljelijä, Ruovesi.	**Böök, Leo R.,** rovasti, Tampere.
48	**49**
Hietala, Toivo, pankinjohtaja, varatuomari, Tampere.	**Joutsen, Olavi,** metsäteknikko, Jämsä.
50	**51**
Kivelä, Eero, sosiaalijohtaja, Tampere.	**Nahkola, Matti,** varatuomari, Nokia.
52	**53**
Perttula, Leena, ylihoitaja, Tampere.	**Ratia, Yrjö,** dipl. insinööri, Korpilahti.
54	**55**
Santamäki, Lauri, kansakoulunopettaja, Tampere.	**Seppä, Hellin,** agronomi, Tampere.
56	**57**
Tienari, Artturi, sosiaalipäällikkö, fil. maisteri, Tampere.	**Tuurna, Arno,** varatuomari, kaupunginjohtaja, Helsinki.

58

Wiherheimo, Toivo, fil. maisteri, Helsinki.

59	60
Stenberg, Elli Aleksandra, vaatetustyöläinen, kansanedustaja, Tampere.	**Suonpää, Leo Evald,** toimitsija, kansanedustaja, Tampere.
61	**62**
Seppi, Usko Edvard, pienviljelijä, kansanedustaja, Ruovesi.	**Honkonen, Kuuno Ola,** voimistelunopettaja, Tampere.
63	**64**
Nieminen, Erkki Einar, opettaja, filosofian maisteri, Tampere.	**Virtanen, Väinö Rafael,** sosiaalisihteeri, Nokia.
65	**66**
Lehtinen, Aino Linnea, rouva, Tampere.	**Kanerva, Jalmari Arvid,** Nahka-, Jalkine- ja Kumityöväen Liiton piiriasiamies, Tampere.
67	**68**
Lepola, Jalo Aatos, toimitsija, Jyväskylä.	**Paasio, Erkki Olavi,** maalari, pääluottamusmies, Jämsänkoski.
69	**70**
Humalamäki, Väinö Olavi, viilaaja, Kangasala.	**Pettersson, Pauli Oskari,** metsätyömies, Kuhmoinen.

71

Niemi, Väinö Johan, metallityöntekijä, Lempäälä.

Portion of the final ballot of the constituency, with a number assigned to each candidate. These comprise the electoral lists and are used for candidate advertising at the constituency level *(see next page)*.

(*Above*) a joint poster of FPDU candidates; (*below*) a local Conservative party organizer instructing volunteers on the distribution of pamphlets.

The following page shows some samples of national posters used in the 1958 election. *In the top row from left to right:* "Who Is Responsible?" (FPDU); "Forward Strong People: Work, Peace, Security" (FPDU); "For Livelihood, Democracy, and Peace" (S. D. Opp.). *Middle row:* "Industrializing Country, Well-off Nation" (SDP); "From Forced Power to Parliamentarism" (SDP); "Construction—Not Destruction" (FPP). *Bottom row:* "The Agrarian Union Leans on These" (Agr.); "A Deserted Countryside?—NO, Says the Agrarian Union" (Agr.); "Mend the Affairs of the Country—The Decision Is Now in the Hands of the People" (Cons.).

(Left) a commercial advertising kiosk, available to all parties with no set time limit. *(Above)* in space rented out by the city on an eleven-day time limit, a "campaign discussion" in Tampere: the advertisement "People's Democracy Is the People's Only Security" had next to it the advertisement "This Is How the People's Democracy Is Secured." Answered the FPDU: "Mainstays of Bourgeois Power Are Rifles (Algeria, Cyprus) Electric Chairs (USA) Gas Chambers (Germany) . . . Workers Remember the Mass Executions in 1918 . . ." The advertisement to the right was supplemented by the arrow: "Did You Forget Hungary?"

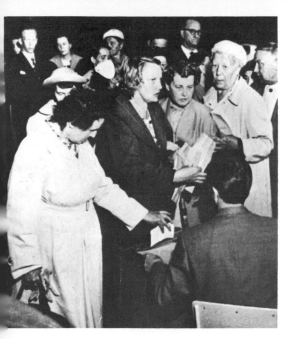

(*above, left*) first day of voting: vanguard, sure, and active voters; (*above, right*) second day of voting: an increase in the number of straggling, uncertain, and inactive voters. (*Right*) first count by the local boards. Then the ballots are sent, along with absentee ballots from other constituencies to the (*below, right*) constituency's central election board for the final count.

Opening Session of Finland's Parliament, the Eduskunta.

Obviously the party organizations wanted to provide as many members as possible with a feeling of participation in the nomination process. These actions also revealed the potential complications connected with early nominations and with attempts to follow strictly formal procedures. After the beginning of the election year, both the SDP and the FPP were faced with the fact that some members of their Parliament groups had entered the electoral alliances of other parties. Such rapid changes in the political situation demand that a fairly small group of party leaders be ready to change candidates, if necessary.

Attention was paid above to the nomination procedure, without mentioning the powers involved and their tactics. Let us only refer here to two points of view:

1. As Maurice Duverger has pointed out, some nominations, and campaign activities as a whole, may be mainly demonstrations serving other party goals than those actually connected with the outcome of the election.[17] This may sometimes be a factor in the seemingly useless attempts of parties to name a maximum number of candidates, or in their unwillingness to form electoral alliances with other parties.

2. One might imagine that three kinds of powers within a party conflict in the nomination process: (a) party leadership, which aims at the maximum total number of votes for the party and possibly considers the success of certain candidates very important; (b) subgroups in the party (women's, youth, and the occupational, local, and ideological interests), who usually want as few and as good candidates as possible; and (c) certain individual candidates and their personal supporters, who want as little competition as possible inside the electoral alliance, and who sometimes consider the total number of votes for the party less important than their own ranking within it.

Similar, but more rigid, conflicts may appear in bi- or multiparty electoral alliances, but there were none of these in the 1958 election in the Northern Häme constituency. However, the Finnish People's Party and the Conservatives formed a joint electoral alliance in four other constituences, and the FPP and the Agrarian Union in a fifth one.[18]

After nominations, the order of the lists of candidates still has to be

17. Maurice Duverger, *Political Parties* (second English edition, London, Methuen & Co. Ltd., 1959), p. 367. See also A. J. Allen, *The English Voter* (London, The English Universities Press, 1964), p. 194.

18. See Pesonen, "Vaaliliittoyhteistyön vaikutus eduskuntaryhmien voimasuhteisiin" (The Influence of Electoral Coalitions on the Distribution of Party Strength in Parliament), *Politiikka* (1965), 1–20.

arranged. The FPP and the Conservatives placed their thirteen names in alphabetical order; the Communist order ranged from the members of Parliament to the two next strongest names, two candidates from Tampere, and finally five candidates from various corners of the constituency. Their closed primary placed the first eleven Social Democrats in order as well as the first four in the lists of their Opposition.

In summary, 31 of the 83 candidates were from Tampere, where 42.5 per cent of the population of this constituency lived. They included six members of Parliament. There were eleven candidates from Helsinki (also with six members of Parliament); a total of eleven from the six communes surrounding Tampere; 28 candidates (one member) from other places in the constituency; and two candidates (one member) from smaller outside cities. None of the Agrarian candidates was from Tampere, while both the FPP and the Conservatives had seven candidates, and the Communists six from the city (and in addition four from the surrounding rural communes). The candidates of the Independent Social Democrats and of the SPP included five persons from Tampere; the former had nominated no less than four persons from Helsinki.

Initial Preparations and Aspirations

Certain other campaign preparations for 1958 had also begun in 1957. For instance, the headquarters of the Agrarian Union urged in January 1957 that the district secretaries "as their responsibility in election preparations check and complete in accordance with earlier plans the network of the so-called rear guard organization."[19] The local Conservative club of Tampere made reservations for the commercial advertisement kiosks in January 1957, and in August 1957 drew up the timetable for election preparations. The preparations continued for a long time. For instance, the Conservative Youth League arranged five election courses for May 1958, the last to be held on May 24 and 25.[20]

Although the financing of campaign and party activities will not be included in the study, we might mention a few pertinent observations. The parties themselves wanted to stress to outsiders the importance of membership fees and other subscriptions paid by their members. This was the theme in April 1958, when six party secretaries were asked by

19. The Agrarian Party files.
20. Information from the local Conservative party organizer and from pamphlets by the Conservative Youth League.

Päivän Sanomat, "Where do you get the funds for the campaign?"[21]
There were different ways of collecting money. The FPDU continued its
"one mark a day" collection and organized for the election two "savings
competitions." The Social Democratic Opposition started in January a
centralized collection "from people to people," the abundant advertising
of which did not mention the election. The SDP members paid their regular party taxes and sold special V-pins. In January members of the
Agrarian Union subscribed to the party a portion of their dairy incomes
from the fall of 1957. The Conservatives also taxed their members in
1958.[22] In general, parties began collecting their campaign funds in 1957
and continued these collections during the spring. The candidates themselves usually had to find their own campaign funds.

The thirteen available seats were too few to fulfil the hopes of each
party. The FPDU aimed now at five representatives; both the Social Democratic Party and its Opposition wanted four. The Finnish People's Party
wanted to regain the seat it had lost during the 1957 legislative session.
The national goal of the Agrarian Union was a 15 per cent increase in
the popular vote, in other words, 60 members in the new parliament.
This would have meant another seat in the Northern Häme constituency.
The Conservatives had more vague aspirations. The party spoke of 40
members of parliament, but did not analyze how these might be distributed among the different constituencies of the country.

THE CAMPAIGN ORGANIZATIONS

The postelection interview included the following question: "Did you
do actively anything in your family, among your friends, or perhaps
elsewhere for the electoral success of your party?" According to the
answers, 5 per cent of the Tampere inhabitants did some campaign work
outside their family (7 per cent of the men, 3 of the women); and an
additional 7 per cent (10 per cent of men, 5 per cent of women) within
their families. Thus only one out of nine adults recalled any campaign
activity for his party.

These active supporters can belong to the formal campaign organizations only if the parties have first recruited them as regular members.
Actually only 30 per cent ($n = 54$) of these active persons were party

21. *Päivän Sanomat,* April 12, 1958, pp. 1, 9. See also "Mistä rahat vaalitaisteluun"
(Where does the campaign money come from), *Uusi Kuvalehti,* 19/1958, pp. 9–11.
22. Information from newspapers and communication with party officials.

members. Thus voluntary propaganda work for the parties depended largely on other supporters than those belonging to the formal party organizations.

However, as expected, active campaign work was related to the degree of party identification. Attempts to further one's cause were made by the following percentage of the sample:

Nonpartisans	$2(n = 42)$
Those with uncertain preference	$7(n = 138)$
Those with a sure preference	$12(n = 214)$
Party members	$30(n = 53)$

The differences are statistically very significant,[23] and it must be stressed that these correlating responses were given at different interviews.

Consequently, the more supporters the parties recruit into their organizations, the more they should be able to increase the number of active campaign workers. Let us compare the distributions on pages 48 and 71 with the following data, which give the percentage of active campaign workers for five parties:

FPDU	18(men 21, $n = 63$; women 14, $n = 42$)
SDP	$12($ " 15, $n = 61$; " 10, $n = 98$)
Conservatives	$11($ " 19, $n = 37$; " 5, $n = 55$)
S. D. Opposition	$8($ " 13, $n = 8$; " 6, $n = 16$)
FPP	$4($ " 11, $n = 9$; " –, $n = 18$)

Quite in line with expectations, the above parallels the earlier finding concerning the degree of organization of the various party supporters.

The definition of a campaign organization is a subjective matter. Usually the concept refers only to those persons whose campaign work is directly connected with the party organization, either following party leadership, or at least operating with the complete knowledge of party functionaries.

Several principles are also useful when dividing the campaign organization into smaller structural units: (1) the main vertical levels, not unlike the normal party organizations, are the national leadership, the district level, and the local level; (2) at each level one finds the leaders and professionals on the one hand, and the voluntary campaign workers, so-called militants, on the other; (3) at each level one also finds auxiliary organizations, especially for youth and women; (4) furthermore, there are the campaign organization proper, the partly independent "electoral

23. $\chi^2 = 25.36$, $v = 2$, $p < 0.001$.

associations" of candidates and interest groups, and cooperating powers, such as the press. When the campaign organizations attempt to influence the electorate, they usually remain invisible. The direct contact of the public with campaign organizations is usually limited to using the election services and watching the actual distribution of some material.

It is an established custom of the party organizations to arrange for absentee ballots. In 1958, while less than 20 absentee ballots were ordered through the Agrarian organization in Tampere, the FPDU and FPP organizations handled about 200, the SDP district bureau 300, and the Conservative bureau about 900. Most ballots, however, were obtained directly from the magistrate's offices, because the total number of absentee ballots was 4,700 in Tampere. On polling days, parties are very willing to help the sick and the old to the polling places. In Tampere it was possible to order transportation from the Communists, the Social Democrats, and the local Conservative organization. The actual number of such services was in tens, not hundreds.[24]

In many cities, parties compete to get the best places for their posters. On the eve of June 28, there were unusually many pedestrians on the main street of Tampere, some of them obviously waiting for the campaign organizations due to appear at 9 p.m. When the trucks started, some were followed by so many persons that they did not even need to stop to distribute their loads. These trucks carried Communist propaganda. Certain others had only three, or even two unloaders. The public did not witness any hard competition, nor hear any arguments between the organizations. This street, of about half a mile in length, was just long enough for the 500 poster stands that were brought within one hour.

Getting the poster stands ready demanded volunteer work. People were also needed to mail letters and to distribute pamphlets. For instance, the office rented by the Independent Social Democrats from the beginning of May housed almost regularly more than one hundred persons doing volunteer campaign work.

The distribution of all kinds of material was the most noticeable, but hardly the most important, phase of the campaign. The propaganda material had been planned and prepared by the district organizations and individual candidates, and the most important material had been obtained for local use directly from the capital city. The national campaign plans and general outlines for the propaganda had been prepared by the national leadership and party headquarters.

24. Information from the district and city offices of parties.

The campaign has been defined as a period during which the parties change the focus of their attention from their normal activity to their attempts to influence voting decisions. This means that the leadership and functionaries of the party organizations proper become the core of the campaign organizations, too.

Some candidates, along with their supporters, then supplement the organization as if from the outside. Even inside the organization, it is not sufficient that the regular leadership concentrates on campaign work. They may be supplemented by volunteer and paid workers. The former are members of election and propaganda committees, the latter are temporary organizers and secretaries for some special areas. The planning of many details and the execution of many plans sometimes demand expert professional aid.

However, at the constituency and local level, only a few changes took place. The normal FPDU organization in Tampere was a suitable campaign organization; no election committees were established. The Social Democratic campaign work within the city was led by the city organization, and within the whole constituency by the district committee. The latter, however, had a special election division. The Opposition Social Democrats had to create a campaign organization. The minority of the district convention met twice to discuss the election, and the activities of the office were regularly led by four men whose personal friends around the constituency helped with the work locally. The Agrarians had a three member election committee, and the Finnish People's Party had more or less formally a nine member election committee and another employee hired for the campaign work. The Conservative associations in the city had a central group for making joint decisions. It had four special committees for preparing the campaign and a fifth one to carry out the plans.[25]

The change of the normal organization into a campaign organization might be most interesting at the local, "rank and file" level. We found that one third of the members recalled doing some campaign work. One result of recruiting members and arranging social programs for the normal organizations has been that the actual party activity, in the more limited meaning of the word, has remained alien to many who have joined the organization. As an efficient volunteer organization is necessary to the campaign, certain parties have nominated so-called rear guards to be responsible for campaign work. This has been done on the largest scale by the Agrarian Union. The party secretary, Arvo Korsimo, actually

25. Communication with the district offices.

mentioned in a speech in April 1958 that their rear guards, voting district leaders, and commune leaders numbered "34,741 men and women."[26] Of course, the members of such an organization were active in the other party organization, too, but what must be stressed is that their role as party members, or even their role as local party leaders, is not adequate as such in a campaign organization.[27]

If the party organization does not attract enough volunteers to the campaign organization, the leadership has to pay for the necessary routine functions. For instance, the Finnish People's Party's district organization hired three office employees to mail campaign letters, and the Conservative youth organization was paid for preparing the Conservative posters. Also the delivery organization of a local advertising paper distributed pamphlets. Yet all parties attempted to inspire their members with enthusiasm for voluntary campaign work and to educate them for this purpose. Useful means were membership publications and meetings, as well as specific courses and discussions. This was the flavor of the normal national and district meetings, and of other meetings, many of which were timed to suit election purposes. Typical of the special meetings for campaign workers was that of the Agrarian commune leaders in a movie theater in Helsinki at the opening of the campaign.[28]

THE PROPAGANDA MEDIA

Posters, letters, and pamphlets were the propaganda material distributed partly by the volunteer campaign workers.

There were three possibilities for outdoor advertising in Tampere. One company rented for one week at a time its 23 permanent advertising kiosks and four billboards. These were reserved in January 1957 by the Conservatives for the two last campaign weeks. The city rented advertising space from June 27 on. This was used by the Communists, Social Democrats, and the FPP. On the eve of June 28, free distribution of election posters was permitted on the sidewalks and in the parks. The parties were responsible for the maintenance of the posters and their removal on the evening of the second polling day.

26. *MK*, April 3, 1958, p. 1.

27. To illustrate the point, we might mention that the same person in Korpilahti was chairman of the municipal government, chairman of the commune-level organization of the Agrarian Union, and commune leader of the Agrarian rear guards. In other words, he had a leading role in official municipal government, in party organization proper, and in the campaign organization.

28. *MK* and *US*, April 1, 1958.

About 14,500 standard-sized posters were distributed in Tampere by parties and individual candidates, usually in little towers of two to eight posters. The Independent Social Democrats also had miniature posters no larger than a matchbox, and the Conservatives had largely oversized ones. Over twenty advertisements were painted for places rented from the city.

The interest of the public in this outdoor advertising was observed for this study. On the first day the posters appeared, the pedestrians did not seem to pay much attention to them. Actually, the only seemingly interested public were those who watched their distribution on the first night. Most citizens apparently paid no attention to the posters upon seeing them for the first time. Even on leaving their homes in the morning, people did not generally look at the posters that were visible near the bus stops.

After the election, the interviewees were shown pictures of nine different posters from which the names of the parties had been removed. All of these were party posters, not those of individual candidates. The distribution of responses concerning having seen and knowing the party the posters belonged to was as follows:

	Percentage who:	
	Recalled	Identified
One poster	84	78
Three posters	63	50
Five posters	39	22
Seven posters	21	6
Nine posters	11	0

Thus, on the average, four out of nine posters seemed familiar and the party represented by three of them was recognized or correctly guessed.

Campaign letters became common in Finland for the first time in 1958. Although this material is printed or mimeographed, the name and address on the envelope make it appear personal. For instance, the election office of the Independent Social Democrats mailed three different letters to 30,000 addressees. The individual candidates were especially fond of this means of campaign propaganda. Let us note, for the sake of comparison, that in Great Britain this kind of propaganda is officially recognized, and all candidates are allowed to mail free of postal charge one communication to each elector of the constituency.

The only letters sent by the FPDU were the presentations of individual candidates sent to their own occupational groups. But the Communists distributed abundant pamphlet material through mail boxes and also handed it out to the public attending their meetings. Other parties and candidates as well used this well-established propaganda media. It was complemented by the Social Democratic campaign magazine and by special, free deliveries of the local FPDU newspaper and the FPP and Conservative organization papers.

Fifty-nine per cent of the interviewees said that they had received a campaign letter, and 86 per cent remembered the delivery of other campaign material. But when asked, "What did you think of the pamphlets?" only 10 per cent found them in any way advantageous (Q. 66.C). In most families "they were right away thrown into the garbage."

The Finnish Broadcasting Corporation had eight election programs.[29] Five were nonpartisan, and the actual political communication consisted of two evenings of ten minute programs by six different parties, and on a third evening the big election debate among the representatives of the parties. On June 25, Eino Kilpi and Hertta Kuusinen of the People's Democrats spoke on the topic, "Why I am a member of the FPDU," and similar talks were given by two representatives of the Finnish People's Party and two of the Conservatives. Two days later the Swedish People's Party, the Agrarian Union, and the Social Democratic Party also presented talks. The two hour election debate took place on Friday evening, two days before the election. Six well-known candidates participated.

In a study of the exposure of the Swedish public to television and radio in 1960, the election debate was found to be more popular than the appearance of any single party.[30] This was the case in Tampere too, where the following percentages of the sample were exposed to the political programs:

	Whole program	Part, at least
Presentation of the FPDU, FPP and Conservatives	16	31
Presentation of the Swedes, Agrarians, and SDP	9	21
The great election debate	16	48

If the above is combined into a simple sum-scale, and even partial exposure is included, we get the following (cumulative percentage) distributions:

29. The three political programs are mentioned in the text; the nonpolitical ones dealt with electoral participation, the Finnish party system, and memories from elections of 50 years ago. See QQ. 45 and 47.

30. Sjödén, *First TV Election in Sweden*, pp. 57–58.

	Men	Women	Total
One program	59	62	61
Two programs	27	28	28
Three programs	11	13	12

The fact that about three out of five were reached by the radio programs corresponds to observations in England and Sweden before the breakthrough of television.[31] Let us also note that women again paid as much attention to radio programs as men did (see Table 4.1).

It is possible that exposure to election programs was superficial and that what was heard was easily forgotten. Although 48 per cent said they had listened to at least a part of the election debate, only 16 per cent remembered the name of any politician who had participated in the debate by the time of the postelection interview.

In the question on newspaper content, the interviewees were actually asked how carefully they read the material (Q. 64.B). "Careful attention" was paid by 11 per cent (17 of the men, 7 of the women), while 26 per cent paid no attention at all. It is likely that the persons who paid careful attention to campaign material also read it often. However, frequency of readership was queried only in the case of campaign advertisements (Q. 64.A). Appendix Table 13 shows the highly significant correlation of these two factors. Generally, the number of people who looked at advertisements about equaled the number of persons who listened to some radio program. The number of men looking at these advertisements was much smaller than the number who said in May that they often read the political content of their newspapers (Table 4.1). The interest of women remained almost unaltered.

Table 7.1 summarizes the quantity of campaign advertising published in the days immediately preceding the election. We find that the party commitment for advertising usually was that of the newspaper itself. Five papers carried paid propaganda of their own party only. The editors of *Kansan Lehti* actually completed with their own remarks many advertisements which the party opposition paid for, while *Aamulehti* had, in addition to Conservative material, some advertising of two other non-

---

31. At least one program was listened to by 69 per cent of the Greenwich sample in 1950 and by 68 per cent of the Bristol North-East sample in 1951; Benney, Gray, and Pear, *How People Vote*, pp. 160–61 and Milne and Mackenzie, *Straight Fight*, p. 93. The Swedish Radio broadcast in 1956 nine election programs; 86 per cent of men and 75 per cent of women heard at least one program, and the most popular one (debate of party leaders) was heard by 68 per cent of the total sample; Westerståhl and Särlvik, *Svensk Valrörelse, Arbetsrapport 1* (Statsvetenskapliga institutionen, Göteborgs Universitet, 1957), Tables 65 and 63.

TABLE 7.1. Column Inches of Advertising Space* Used by (a) Parties and (b) Individual Candidates of the Parties in Eight Newspapers between July 1 and July 6, 1958 (in column inches)

	Hämeen Yhteistyö (FPDU)	Kansan Uutiset (FPDU)	Kansan Lehti (SDP)	Suomen Sosiali-demokr. (SDP)	Aamu-lehti (Cons.)	Uusi Suomi (Cons.)	Helsingin Sa-nomat (Indep.)	Tampere-lainen (Indep.)
(a) Parties								
FPDU	187	570	–	–	–	–	29	18
S. D. Opp.	–	–	212	–	–	–	353	10
SDP	–	–	563	1027	–	–	267	88
Agr.	–	–	–	–	60	–	23	6
FPP	–	–	–	–	–	–	450	70
Cons.	–	–	–	–	562	971	724	12
Swedish	–	–	–	–	–	–	27	–
Others	–	–	–	–	12	108	288	24
(b) Candidates								
FPDU	164	435	–	–	–	–	19	–
S. D. Opp.	–	–	167	–	–	–	767	37
SDP	–	–	247	218	..	–	128	54
Agr.	–	–	–	–	127	–	–	–
FPP	–	–	–	–	256	–	1056	26
Cons.	–	–	–	–	590	784	321	34
Swedish	–	–	–	–	–	–	18	–
Others	–	–	–	–	–	48	99	46
Summary								
(a) Parties	187	570	775	1027	634	1079	2161	228
(b) Candidates	164	435	414	218	973	832	2408	197
Total	351	1005	1189	1245	1607	1911	4569	425

* Advertisements are here defined by appearance, not actual invoice. The *Tamperelainen* is only one issue, No. 26/July 3, 1958. The line "Others" in (a) includes two advertisements of the Taxpayers Union.

socialist parties. The parties advertised simultaneously only in independent newspapers.

It is also noteworthy that: (a) the main organs more consistently supported only their own party; (b) each party used, in addition to general advertising, that of individual candidates, the least for the SDP and most for its Opposition and the FPP; (c) even *Helsingin Sanomat* did not equalize the advantage which the leading local newspaper, *Aamulehti*, gave to Conservative propaganda, although this independent paper published many advertisements of the Independent Social Democrats and the Finnish People's Party—in addition to those of the Conservatives. Another leveler of local opportunity for propaganda was the weekly

advertising paper, *Tamperelainen*. The brand-new Popular Center Party
advertised in this paper only.

Although people looked at this campaign material, they generally disliked it. The evaluations (Q. 65) were distributed as follows:

	Percentage of:		
	Men	Women	Total
Positive evaluations	12	7	9
Negative evaluations	70	66	68
Did not read, don't know	18	27	23
	100	100	100

Thus it would seem that the campaign material in the newspapers was
no more highly regarded than were the party pamphlets.

The materials distributed by parties, the radio, and the newspapers
were the most important means of propaganda. Some magazines were
used for advertising. But no loudspeaker cars moved on the streets or in
the neighborhood of polling places in 1958, and no propaganda movies
were shown. The motion pictures, "Good News" of the Communists
and "Swamp" of the Agrarians, were shown only at rural meetings. And
the lists of candidates were signed by few people. The FPDU, for example,
tried to collect 60 signatures for each list; in other words, just the minimum number doubled.

CAMPAIGN MEETINGS

The postelection interview included the following question (58.A):
"Before the election there were meetings and festivals where the candidates made speeches. Did you attend any of them?" According to the
answers, about 6,000 adult inhabitants of Tampere went to some campaign meeting, and about 1,400 of these to two or more meetings. But
92 per cent did not listen to a single speech, and 84 per cent did not
remember hearing a friend tell about campaign speeches.

Different party meetings had been attended by the following percentages
of these 6,000 persons:

FPDU	66
S. D. Opposition	20
SDP	17
FPP	6
Cons.	9
The local debate	3
	121 ($n = 35$)

The percentages add up to more than 100 because some went to more than one party's meetings. The leftist cause mainly was forwarded by these meetings: two thirds of the people who went to such meetings heard Communist speeches, whereas very few listened to the FPP or Conservative candidates.

The numbers of meetings also differed, and again the Communists were the most active. During eight weeks they held 33 meetings intended for the general public and announced in the local newspaper. Almost all speakers were candidates living in Tampere: for example, Leo Suonpää spoke at eleven, Kuuno Honkonen at ten, and Elli Stenberg at nine different meetings. They were arranged formally by the democratic organizations in different parts of the city, but actually by the city offices of the FPDU and the Communist Party. One meeting, at the sport stadium on July 2, gathered more than 2,000 persons. Each of the six candidates from Tampere made a short speech, and five others joined them to form a football team, all wearing the number of their list of candidates on their backs. The chairman of the Communist Party, Aimo Aaltonen, visited Tampere in May. He made one speech at a meeting arranged by the metal workers, and another at an open-air gathering. And the FPDU held 182 public meetings elsewhere in the constituency during these eight weeks.[32] The activities inside the organization also continued.

On July 4, the Independent Social Democrats gathered 1,600 people in the sport stadium to see a Friday evening program, which included an oral examination of the candidates. The night before only 50 adults and 10 children were present at a dance hall to hear the welcoming speech for the election festival of the Social Democratic Party. The number of people sitting around the dance floor doubled during the two other speeches, but actually the majority of the people came, as they did to many other festivals, only when the dancing started. The biggest meeting of the SDP was held on June 3, when the party chairman, Väinö Tanner, and Vice Chairman Olavi Lindblom spoke to about 600 people.[33]

The Finnish People's Party held two meetings in Tampere, one in February, and another on May 4. Other nonsocialist meetings were the one arranged by the Agrarians for the evacuated people, and four held by

32. The figure is counted from issues of *Hämeen Yhteistyö* and thus excludes subsequent meetings not mentioned in the paper.

33. The meeting was organized by four local party units, reported in *Kansan Lehti*, June 4, 1958, pp. 1–2. During the eight weeks, the S. D. Opp. had four, and SDP nine campaign meetings in Tampere.

the Conservatives. The largest of these was to have been held in a park on June 5, but in the chilly weather only 50 persons attended.

Afterwards, certain general aspects of these meetings could be observed. At least in the summer this kind of campaigning obviously suits rural places better than it does the city. This was taken into account by each party, as they organized fewer meetings in the city than in the surrounding rural areas. Even within the city area the Communists especially arranged meetings in the suburbs rather than in the center. They had not only the most numerous, but also the best organized meetings. For example, when a Social Democratic meeting was held on July 3 in a suburban workers' hall, the place was still decorated by posters which had been placed there for the Communists' meeting on June 29. Very few meetings attracted more than a hundred people, including children. Charging an entrance fee seems to have increased rather than decreased attendance of these meetings. People did not pay keen attention to the speeches, and the public never asked questions or started arguments. The only debate took place on July 3 in the City Hall, when five candidates had been invited by the Taxpayers' Association for this purpose. Some joined them from the audience; even the Popular Center gained some publicity.

THE DURATION OF THE CAMPAIGN

Some newspapers still contained campaign advertising on the second polling day, but after the closing of the polling places voting decisions could no longer be influenced. The posters disappeared quickly and undelivered campaign material became useless.

Thus the ending of the campaign is much more specific than its beginning, and one can only hope for an approximate definition of its duration. A scholar's view might be based on (1) legislation and official decisions; (2) certain public pronouncements concerning the beginning of the campaign; (3) the campaign plans of the parties and observation of the actual transfer from preparations to open campaign work; or on (4) a study of the quantitative changes in campaign communication. However, none of these provides an exact definition.

1. If no surprise dissolution of Parliament occurs, parties can at least formally conduct their campaign for as long as they please. The candidates might be presented right after actual nominations. In practice, however, they are seldom advertised before the legal deadline for nominations. This is partly because of the impossibility of preparing all the district level

material before the lists of candidates have been numbered for the ballot. A suitable number can even suggest good slogans: for example, the Conservative member, T. A. Wiherheimo, was lucky to be able to advertise: "In '58 vote for list no. 58."

The sequence of the electoral alliances on the ballot is drawn 39 days before the election. However, according to law, these lists are on the agenda, for a second time, 36 days before the election, and in case of complaints the final ballot can still be changed by the central election board up to 24 days before the election. In Northern Häme a list of one candidate was disqualified on May 31, and thus the candidates got their final numbers 36 days before the election. The same day the Helsinki electoral board disqualified 15 lists.[34] The material carrying these numbers could not be prepared until the beginning of June. We might repeat that the Tampere city government permitted free distribution of posters for only ten days, and that while the radio carried its first nonpolitical election program 33 days before the election, its first political program was just 11 days before. And on other radio programs, the candidates were denied access to the air all during the two months before the election.[35]

Another precondition for a comprehensive campaign is that members of parliament be free to concentrate on their campaign work. In 1958, 183 of the 200 members ran for re-election. When the 1957 legislative session was closed, and the Speaker wished his colleagues "a happy summer and a successful election fight to those participating it," there were 30 days left until the elections.[36]

2. Qualitative statements about the beginning of the campaign give quite a conflicting picture of its duration. First it seems that other parties are told to start their campaigns early. The *Suomen Sosialidemokraatti* maintained in January that the Communist "*Kansan Uutiset* is already in full swing, trolling its election propaganda," and *Kansan Uutiset* considered that "the extreme Right" had in February "started the final spurt of the campaign fight with its newspapers"; the central committee of the Finnish Communist Party announced in the beginning of March that "the Conservative Party and other Rightist elements have already

34. The main reason for such numerous disqualifications was the fact that many candidates of new parties were, contrary to the law, simultaneously managers of other electors' associations, *HS*, May 29, 1958, p. 18, and June 1, 1958, p. 6.

35. The Board of the Radio Corporation decided in 1955 to deny access of candidates to its programs during one month, but in 1958, the ruling changed to two months (minutes of the Board meetings on February 11, 1955, and March 7, 1958).

36. Minutes of the 1957 legislative session, p. 5003.

started their election campaign for next summer, publishing lies about all kinds of back sliders, police spies, and shady characters." [37]

Then, of course, it follows that the campaign of one's own party begins much later. According to *Suomen Sosialidemokraatti* "the first step of the campaign can start" in the beginning of March; "the opening fanfares of the campaign have already been blown" in the middle of April; and the beginning of the actual campaign was at the end of the district conventions and on May Day. However, the chairman of the party still stressed on May 10 how important it is to "prepare for the campaign in an orderly manner." [38] After the district convention at the end of March, *Maakansa* wrote that the Agrarian Union can "in the coming weeks move trustfully to the campaign fields." According to *Kansan Uutiset,* the party members of "Nyland province were ready for their campaign" at the end of March, but one month later the FPDU still moved in its campaign preparations to a "new, more important period." The Conservative Women's League considered at the end of April that its most important task was "to take successful care of the campaign preparations." [39]

Obviously, any activity of the other parties is labeled election propaganda in order to undervalue and depreciate it, whereas late and repeated starting signals are fired for the campaign of one's own party to inspire its campaign organization with enthusiasm.

3. In practice, open election work mixes with other party activities quite some time before the elections. For instance, the 1958 New Year's proclamation of both the FPDU and the Conservatives did include some specific election communication. The so-called summer festival relay of the Agrarian Youth League started circling the country on February 16 as an election message relay. The district organization of the Finnish People's Party considered its meeting in Tampere on February 23 a definite election meeting, and the Conservatives distributed their oversized election posters at the end of April. Newspaper reporting on party preparations for the campaign had somewhat the character of campaign propaganda all through the spring.

Newspaper editors obviously are recognizing the approaching election when they start to place election news in a column reserved just for this purpose. As early as February 3, the *Helsingin Sanomat* had a general

37. *SS,* Jan. 23, 1958, p. 3; *KU,* Feb. 25, 1958, p. 4 and March 4, 1958, p. 5.

38. *SS,* March 2, 1958, p. 10, April 14, 1958, p. 5, March 10, 1958, p. 3 and May 11, 1958, p. 1 (Väinö Tanner); *KL,* May 17, 1958, p. 4.

39. *MK,* March 26, 1958, p. 3; *KU,* March 31, 1958, p. 3, April 28, 1958, p. 3, May 20, 1958, p. 5 and June 29, 1958, p. 3; *US,* April 20, 1959, p. 7.

column headlined "Toward the Election." For a long time, however, it appeared irregularly, and it usually covered only one column. A corresponding section in *Uusi Suomi,* entitled "On the Threshold of the Election," started on March 11. Parties announced their shift to specific campaign meetings, for instance, by advertising the discussions as election speeches. On April 10 *Maakansa* started to gather announcements of future campaign meetings in a series of large and uniform advertisements. On the same day, *Suomen Sosialidemokraatti* started its section, "The Election Approaches—Draw Up in Lines," which also carried notices of coming speeches.

The first election advertisements in newspapers—for example, in *Kansan Lehti* on March 4, and in *Aamulehti* on April 26—gave the impression of being accidental. The intensive propaganda in newspapers started much later. It is indicative that the advertising weekly, which all parties used, was given its first campaign advertisement on June 5 by the Popular Center. The SDP was the only new advertiser in its next issue on June 12. In the rural area, where no municipal regulations restricted the timing of outdoor advertising, the posters of the Agrarian Union were distributed only seventeen days before the election. This concerned not only the local, but also the much earlier prepared national posters. Many other parties and candidates decorated the walls of barns a full week later.

Consequently, open communication directed at the electorate takes place over many months simultaneously with the continuation of internal election preparations by the parties. During this period, the start of the campaign obviously depends on the central leadership and headquarters of the parties. Many individual candidates and their supporters get eagerly involved only shortly before the election, and many forms of the campaign are not utilized even as long as two weeks.

4. Campaign advertising was so abundant during the few days prior to the election that in just six days the leading Tampere paper published 1,600 column inches of these advertisements, and the largest newspaper of the country about 4,600 column inches (Table 7.1).

To provide a general picture of the time when the newspapers turn their major attention to the election, Table 7.2 summarizes the numbers of articles and advertisements mentioning the election during a half-year period (26 weeks). Because the actual length of the articles is not considered, the table can support only very general conclusions. For instance, it seems that *Helsingin Sanomat* had quite a bit of election coverage by the end of March and the beginning of April, whereas, although it did

TABLE 7.2. Two-Week Averages of Articles and Advertisements Mentioning the Election, Published in Seven Newspapers between January 6 and July 6, 1958

Time	Hämeen Yhteistyö	Kansan Uutiset	Kansan Lehti	Suomen Sosiali- demokraatti	Aamu- lehti	Uusi Suomi	Helsingin Sanomat
Jan. 6–19	0.2	0.6	0.1	0.5	0.2	1.1	2.1
Jan. 20–Feb. 2	0.3	0.8	0.3	1.0	0.4	0.7	2.1
Feb. 3–16	0.6	0.5	0.6	1.2	0.4	0.8	1.5
Feb. 17–Mar. 2	0.2	0.9	0.6	1.2	0.2	1.0	2.2
Mar. 3–16	1.2	1.4	0.5	0.4	0.4	0.6	1.4
Mar. 17–30	1.1	2.1	0.4	0.9	0.3	1.5	4.4
Mar. 31–Apr. 13	0.9	2.3	0.7	1.1	1.0	1.5	4.2
Apr. 14–27	0.3	1.2	0.5	1.9	0.9	1.2	4.6
Apr. 28–May 11	1.6	3.0	1.4	2.6	1.0	1.8	2.0
May 12–25	3.8	4.0	1.5	1.9	1.3	1.7	1.1
May 26–June 8	5.5	4.2	3.8	2.2	2.5	2.4	1.7
June 9–22	8.9	6.9	9.5	4.3	4.8	5.2	6.3
June 23–July 6	24.0	26.5	22.2	10.9	21.5	20.4	36.2

have many articles, they were very small reports on meetings and nominations.

Until the end of April, it was exceptional to see mention of the election even once a day in the three Tampere newspapers. It became more common only in May. About ten weeks before the election, the national FPDU paper, *Kansan Uutiset,* began to mention the election in at least three articles in each issue. This phase lasted no more than about four weeks in four newspapers. In every paper the election was dealt with much more often during the fourth and third weeks before the election than at any other time during that year. During the last two weeks before the election, this quantity again at least doubled in every paper, and even quadrupled in three newspapers.

When normal political writing was described in Chapter 6, the observation concerned newspapers published between April 14 and May 11. The newspapers dealt with the election at that time, but apparently not much more than is normal. According to Table 7.2, it became the current topic much later.

Table 7.3 provides additional information for the twelve weeks preceding the election. It includes all the political material of the newspapers, wherein the election or political parties were mentioned, but excludes certain political articles dealing, for example, with the government or Parliament, or political platform issues in general.

TABLE 7.3. The Distribution of Political Material in Seven Newspapers according to Articles concerning the Election and Parties, and Campaign Advertisements, (a) April 14 to May 11, (b) May 12 to June 8, and (c) June 9 to July 6, 1958* (in percentages)

	Hämeen Yhteistyö (FPDU)	Kansan Uutiset	Kansan Lehti	Suomen Sosiali-demokr. (SDP)	Aamu-lehti	Uusi Suomi (Cons.)	Helsingin Sanomat (Indep.)
(a) April 14–May 11							
Election	22	17	25	37	29	46	31
Parties	76	83	74	61	70	52	67
Advertisements	2	0	1	2	1	2	2
Total	100	100	100	100	100	100	100
Total column inches	*2,516*	*7,060*	*2,488*	*5,320*	*2,376*	*3,456*	*3,404*
(b) May 11–June 8							
Election	61	48	56	58	41	26	23
Parties	37	50	42	42	58	72	66
Advertisements	2	2	2	0	1	2	11
Total	100	100	100	100	100	100	100
Total column inches	*2,040*	*4,072*	*2,760*	*2,304*	*2,045*	*3,104*	*2,228*
(c) June 9–July 6							
Election	82	61	79	78	68	74	16
Parties	12	14	10	8	9	4	2
Advertisements	6	25	11	14	23	22	82
Total	100	100	100	100	100	100	100
Total column inches	*4,088*	*8,648*	*8,564*	*7,360*	*6,360*	*5,980*	*10,812*

* Only those articles and news stories are included that mentioned the election or parties. If both were mentioned, the entire article is classed as election. Titles and pictures are included. Advertisements are defined by appearance.

The volume of these materials reveals the total changes in the political content of newspapers. During the nine to twelve weeks before the election, the two main leftist organs wrote the most about politics. During the five to eight weeks before the election, the total political content of both papers was 3,000 column inches less, and it decreased in all other papers too. During the last period, one to four weeks prior to the election, the political content increased sharply: compared with the previous four weeks, it doubled in the Communist press and *Uusi Suomi*, tripled in the Social Democratic papers and in *Aamulehti*, and became five times as great in the *Helsingin Sanomat*.

Table 7.3 also classifies this political content into articles on the election, articles on parties, and campaign advertisements. The specific character of the campaign is easier to see from the changes in the proportion of these three kinds of material than from their total volume. As late as nine to twelve weeks prior to the election, newspapers wrote about the parties without hinting at the coming election. But, during the last four week period, parties were very seldom mentioned without referring also to the election. At that time campaign advertising made up about one quarter of the political content of *Kansan Uutiset* and of the Conservative press, and more than four fifths of the *Helsingin Sanomat*. The quiet period in between these two was obviously a transition period. The leftist papers began to pay more attention to the election than others did. Only *Helsingin Sanomat* had already begun to carry campaign advertising, which actually compensated for the simultaneous decrease in election articles.

Because the open campaign does not begin until eight weeks before the election, Figure 7.A is limited to this period of eight weeks. For each newspaper it shows the quartiles of the volume of text material concerning parties, elections, and campaign advertising. If each issue of the papers had contained an equal amount of the material, one half of the material would have been printed during the first four weeks, and each quarter would have been two weeks. However, we find that:

1. References of *Kansan Lehti* to political parties were the only example of equal distribution. Other newspapers decreased this type of material as the election approached. *Uusi Suomi* and *Helsingin Sanomat* actually published three quarters of this type of material during three weeks and the final one quarter during five weeks.

2. The election, in turn, was a postponed topic in each paper until the election was close; in other words, parties were written about, but with simultaneous references to the election. One half of all election articles in *Uusi Suomi* was published during one week only.

3. Campaign advertising was jammed in even closer to the election. The extreme example was *Aamulehti,* which published almost one half of all its campaign advertisements on the day before polling and on polling day.

How to define the start of the campaign remains a matter of agreement. If one would decide to call the open campaign that period during which three quarters of the election material for eight weeks were actually printed, an equal distribution of the material would stretch the campaign to last for six weeks. In reality, the campaign writing of the editorial

Figure 7.A. The Means and Quartiles of Text on Parties, the Election, and Campaign Advertising, Published by Seven Newspapers from May 12 to July 6, 1958 *

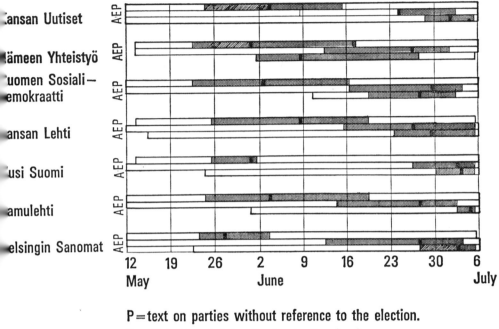

P = text on parties without reference to the election.
E = all text material referring to the election.
A = campaign advertisements.

* The total quantity of each class of material is represented by a bar, which is divided into four parts. The shaded areas represent the time before and after which one quarter was published. A line indicates the day dividing the material into two equal parts.

staffs increased so rapidly, when the campaign approached, that the Communist papers campaigned during four weeks only, the Social Democratic press and *Aamulehti* three weeks, and *Uusi Suomi* eleven days. The advertisers, in turn, woke up so late that this kind of campaigning lasted only two weeks in the Social Democratic papers, and in the Conservative papers less than one week.

Newspaper campaign propaganda and outdoor advertising in the rural areas were found to have two common features: (1) official decisions did not regulate the time of either media, but (2) the use of each was concentrated in those ten days which were considered to be a suitable duration for the election campaign by the city government of Tampere and the program council of the Finnish Broadcasting Corporation.

THE COMPARISON GROUP

Korpilahti was located too remotely in the Northern Häme constituency to provide its inhabitants with any chance of being elected to Parliament. During the whole era of the unicameral Parliament only one person from Korpilahti has been elected: the Social Democrat District Secretary, Kalle Lepola, in 1916 and 1917.[40] But at the same time, Korpilahti was the center of a corner in the constituency which was too important to be left without local candidates. In 1958 local candidates were nominated by four parties. The FPDU nominated Jalo Lepola, its functionary for the neighboring district and the son of Kalle Lepola, who had died in Russia. In the SDP primary, the vice chairman of the municipal council, Taito Vallenius ran but gained only 70 votes; in May he was nominated by the Social Democratic Opposition group. The Agrarian communal organization proposed the candidacy of the former police chief of Korpilahti, Arvi Salonen, who had moved to Helsinki. However, on January 26, an intercommune party meeting decided on the additional candidacy of the chairman of the Korpilahti municipal council, Veikko Laukkala, a farmer. The Conservative lists of candidates included the chairman of the Korpilahti temperance board, Yrjö Ratia, a civil engineer.

The technicalities of founding the so-called electors' associations of four candidates were handled locally. The managers for Laukkala, Ratia and Salonen were farmers from Korpilahti, and their lists were signed by 22 to 29 inhabitants of the commune; the rest of the signatures were collected mainly in the neighboring commune. Taito Vallenius' manager was a small farmer from Jämsänkoski, a nearby commune, and 27 out of his 39 signatures were also gathered in Korpilahti. No other papers were signed by people from Korpilahti. Jalo Lepola's manager was a Communist functionary from Tampere, and his signatures were also from the city. Of all the thirteen FPDU lists, only two were signed in places other than Tampere.[41]

Since 1954 the commune had been divided into 11 voting districts for the administration of the elections. In 1958 each district averaged 390 enfranchised persons, or less than one quarter of the Tampere average. The municipal council established an election board for each voting dis-

40. According to the biographical data collected by Martti Noponen.
41. Information from the archived petitions of candidates.

trict (the chairman, four members and vice-members) in the beginning of January. The population register was the basis of the voter's registers, which were publicly displayed in the assembly hall of the municipal council from March 15 to March 21, as required by law. The eventual requests for changes were on the agenda of the election boards on April 4; the final registers contained a total of 4,276 names.

In a wide and geographically broken up rural commune, campaign circumstances differ from those of a large city. Moreover, in Tampere, as in many other cities, local campaign work was undoubtedly helped by the location of party district offices in the same city. However, of the two places, Korpilahti was more typical of the country as a whole.

As a start in comparing Korpilahti campaign activity with that of Tampere, Table 7.4 summarizes the interview data that describe the reactions of the inhabitants of the commune. Other material about the campaign is based largely on the information gathered by a local observer.[42]

The relative size of campaign organizations was the same in both places (Table 7.4.a). However, there were differences in the behavior of women. They rarely worked for their party in Korpilahti (but 8 per cent did in Tampere). This is accounted for by the lack of women in party organizations in Korpilahti (p. 55). On the basis of the sample, we might estimate that although over 400 local adults attempted to further the success of their party in the commune, only about 200 of these were active outside the family. The observer, in turn, estimated that about 300 persons were active in the campaign. The two estimates do not differ much.

The Agrarian Union had the largest campaign organization, with about 160 so-called rear guards. Party headquarters provided them with seven issues of the paper published to educate the campaign organization. Each voting district (ward) had its chief, and another chief was responsible for the campaign activities in the whole commune. The Conservative campaign was directed by the ten-member board of the local association. Nine special campaign workers were also named, and the local candidate himself was the chief of the Conservative rear guards. Communication with Tampere was maintained; for example, the district party secretary paid five visits to Korpilahti. The Social Democratic organization nominated eight campaign workers, who felt that Korpilahti was left without much help from the Tampere district office. The Communist organization, which was divided into many small groups, was already working in con-

42. Hoikka, "Election Campaign in a Rural Commune," and discussions with him.

TABLE 7.4. Data on Campaign Activity in Korpilahti in 1958 and Comparison with the Corresponding Data from Tampere (in percentages)

	Men	Women	Total	Larger (+) or smaller (−) than in Tampere		
				Men	Women	Total
(a) Campaign work						
Worked for his party	17	2	10	+1	−6	−2
Knew a campaign worker	21	17	19	−7	+2	−2
(b) Normal mass media						
Listened to a campaign program on radio	62	50	56	+3	−12	−5
Listened to 2 or 3 campaign programs	31	24	28	+4	−4	0
Paid careful or some attention to election articles in newspapers	46	24	35	−3	−17	−9
Looked often or sometimes at campaign advertisements	77	61	69	+17	−6	+5
Evaluated favorably the propaganda in newspapers	17	4	11	+5	−3	+2
(c) Other campaign media						
Remembered three or more party posters	62	41	52	−17	−12	−12
Remembered one poster or more	79	83	81	−13	+5	−3
Identified one poster or more	69	72	70	−16	−1	−8
Received a campaign letter	31	33	32	−35	−21	−27
Received other campaign material	33	57	45	−50	−30	−44
Considered pamphlets useful	31	22	27	+22	+12	+17
(d) Campaign meetings						
Attended a campaign meeting	29	11	20	+19	+5	+12
Heard about campaign speeches	31	13	22	+8	+3	+6
Number of cases	*48*	*46*	*94*			

junction with Jyväskylä, the later capital of the new province. The local organization of the Finnish People's Party was founded on June 9, and its board of six members functioned first as a campaign committee.

At the level of a rural commune, campaign financing includes activity in three directions. Funds are collected for the upper levels of the organization and for local campaign work, and in return financial help is obtained from the district and national organizations. Ways of gathering funds included the sale of campaign buttons by the FPDU and the SDP, the saving campaign of the former, and the door-to-door collection of the latter. The organization of the Agrarian Union sold lots, and members donated to the party a part of their income from milk sent to the dairy in the fall of 1957. The donations were given mainly to the district organization, but 25 per cent was kept by the commune group to finance its own campaign. The local candidates of the parties had to finance their own speaking tours. Support given from other sources included outside speakers, ready-made posters, and other material for distribution in the commune. For example, the Social Democratic Opposition financed a large tour featuring both speakers and well-known popular entertainers.

Campaign meetings were a typically rural method of election campaign. According to Table 7.4.d, one third of the men in Korpilahti went to at least one such meeting (only one tenth in Tampere). Relatively more women, too, listened to campaign speeches in Korpilahti than in Tampere. On the basis of the sample, we might estimate that Korpilahti audiences totaled about 1,350 adult persons. Campaign speeches were also described to friends more often in the country than in the city.

The number of meetings and participants is given by party in the following:

	Meetings	Participants
FPDU	11	415
S. D. Opposition	5	210
SDP	8	140
Agr.	40	426
FPP	1	15
Cons.	11	380
	76	1,586

The above includes only meetings which were open to the general public, but here are also included meetings of three parties organized prior to the two months before the election. The first campaign meeting of the Conservatives had been held in 1957; the Agrarians started their meetings on April 17; and the biggest Communist meetings were the three May Day celebrations. More than 60 meetings, however, were held in June or July.

The Agrarian candidates had been advised by their party to make a minimum of thirty campaign speeches, and of these at least 20 should be given in their own commune. This party arranged more meetings in Korpilahti than all the other parties together. The speakers were the two local candidates, two candidates of the neighboring communes, and the one Agrarian member of Parliament from that constituency (Atte Pakkanen) whose residence is in Helsinki. And finally, the national leader of the campaign organization, Pekka Silvola, came to make a speech there. The three Communist May Day celebrations were organized in the three areas of strongest support. Altogether about 350 persons assembled at the meetings. The other FPDU meetings got only 65 participants. The only FPDU speaker was the local candidate, Jalo Lepola. A traditional midsummer celebration was also utilized for Communist election propaganda. The mobile unit of the Social Democratic Opposition visited Korpilahti during four days and arranged five meetings, three of them on Sunday, June 15. The speakers were the local candidate, Taito Vallenius, and Reino Joenpolvi, a Helsinki candidate nominated for the same constituency. The Social Democratic Party began with four meetings on June 29. One of the eight meetings held had not a single listener. The leading candidate of the Finnish People's Party from Tampere visited the only meeting of the party. The Conservatives arranged one meeting in each voting district with speeches by the local candidate, the three candidates representing agriculture, and a fifth candidate from Tampere. A joint rally was also arranged with a nearby borrough.

It was easier to get an audience at remote than at central meetings. The sample shows a slight tendency to attend meetings of one's own party rather than those of other parties, but Communists and Agrarian supporters went to each other's meetings, and Agrarians went to hear Conservative speeches.

The program of many a meeting consisted only of speeches and discussion. However, the Communists showed their own campaign movie and Russian news reels, and the Conservatives showed a movie about Korpilahti. All meetings, except those of the Social Democratic Opposition, provided a chance to discuss the speeches; and discussions really took place in Korpilahti. For example, an organized Communist debating group was present at many Agrarian meetings. The local observer described the beginning and final moments of an Agrarian meeting as follows:

> Especially on Sunday evenings, people from all close farms may have gathered in the yard of the house where the meeting was to be held, waiting for the campaign preachers. After the customary lengthy handshakes, they crowded into the living room to hear the election sermons and to debate them. The discussions started on general themes, but soon focused on local problems. . . . After more than four hours had passed, people began to hide behind the dusk, but the expressed opinions revealed their political position and where the group was seated. The wives threw in their own sharp comments on the Communist statements, while many farmers in the far corner agreed with the speakers. Finally, another fair handshake and the group separated.[43]

The Conservative campaign meetings closed with community singing, featuring "Those days on the shores of Lake Päijänne"; and the Social Democratic Opposition rallies were concluded by a xylophone artist, who performed "The Parade of Tin Soldiers Mounting a Guard."

The use of pamphlets and campaign letters was opposite in emphasis to campaign meetings; they were not sent to the rural population as much as to the city inhabitants. Almost every home in Tampere received campaign material, but only one half of the Korpilahti sample had received any. There was no such summary distribution to every mailbox in Korpilahti as was organized in Tampere. Pamphlets were handed out mainly in connection with meetings. Some printed material was simply thrown from cars driving through the commune.

However, some mail was sent to homes. For every Conservative meeting, fifteen personal letters of invitation were mailed, and the Conservative association sent out 550 letters, including the new party program and some other pamphlets. Of the 30,000 addresses of the Social Democratic Opposition, slightly more than 100 were from Korpilahti. Social Democratic material was also mailed to addresses recommended by the workers' associations. Upon local suggestion, some gratis issues of newspapers and party publications were mailed from the city. Letters sent by individual candidates should also be mentioned. For example, Arvi Salonen printed 2,000 letters, of which 500 were distributed through mail.

Posters were looked at in Korpilahti almost as much as in Tampere

43. Ibid., pp. 83–84.

(Table 7.4.c). Their total number, in relation to the population, was almost the same. Of the oversized Conservative posters, 50 were out already in April, and this was repeated during the last two weeks of the campaign, when all the posters were distributed. There were almost 1,000 Agrarian posters in the commune (five different kinds, 150–200 of each). The Communist and FPP posters were fewer, and the SDP distributed posters mainly for individual candidates. Other parties supplemented their own advertising with candidate posters. There were also the posters of the Conservative Youth League and those advertising Agrarian campaign meetings.

The distribution of posters actually began on June 19, when the trucks of Agrarians traveled the main highways on both sides of Lake Päijänne and delivered portions of their loads to the rear guards of each voting district. The posters were fastened on trees, barn walls, etc. Only the Conservative organization took care of their posters and kept them in good condition until polling day.

Election services by party organizations included in Korpilahti, as in Tampere, acting as agents for absentee ballots and arrangements for transportation on voting days. About 150 absentee ballots were issued in this commune. Two nonsocialist parties did not organize any other election service, but the Agrarians transported people to the polls with tractors, motorboats, and buses. On Sunday its rear guards observed who was left to be contacted on the second day and encouraged many of them to vote.

Campaign material presented in the normal mass media gained about equally large audiences in Korpilahti and in Tampere (Table 7.4.b). Perhaps the rural population had more interest in advertising than the Tampere readers, who were more interested in the news items in their papers. There was also greater difference between the sexes in the rural commune than in the city. In Korpilahti men seemed to be even more exposed to radio than women.

Men also had a more favorable attitude toward propaganda than women. However, people expressed mainly negative opinions about the campaign. Pamphlets were called "useless waste of paper" (farmer, 50, Agrarian), with "no effect on anybody" (small farmer, 65, Conservative), because "everybody keeps lying as much as they can" (carpenter, 35, FPDU). Let us point out, however, that the attitude toward pamphlets was less negative in the rural commune, where they were more rare than in the city. In the opinion of some people "they sure have some significance in a remote place" (farmer, 28, Agrarian). We might also label the attitude in Korpilahti toward the campaign as indifferent. When a group of observers followed the public conversation in a cafeteria before the election, they heard only one political debate. Much more was said about the prices of food, cigarettes, and alcohol. And when party posters were on display in the central village, only one out of eight passersby paid any attention to them.

SUMMARY

The Parliament of Finland was elected in 1958 for the first time after a four-year term. This took place on the ordinary election days, July 6 and 7. Out of the 200 members of Parliament, 187 sought re-election; ten out of the thirteen members of the Northern Häme constituency were running again. Four other members of Parliament were nominated there, but they were candidates in other constituencies as well. Six electoral alliances had the maximum number of candidates and one had five, the constituency thus totaling 83 candidates. The ballot included 31 persons from Tampere and 39 from elsewhere in the same constituency. Three were from the Korpilahti commune, and one candidate who had moved to Jyväskylä and another one who had moved to Helsinki were also locally considered to be their "own men."

The Northern Häme constituency was of special importance to the Social Democratic Opposition, because its leader, Aarre Simonen, had been elected there in 1951 and 1954. The Opposition announced in May that they would run their own slates in this, as well as in three other constituencies. Earlier Mr. Simonen, who ranked ninth in the party primary, had not been nominated by the party. The district board of the Social Democratic Party itself also picked some candidates in the new situation who had not entered the party primary. Even other parties organized some membership voting for advisory purposes. Their obvious purpose was to make as many voters as possible feel that they had played a role in the nomination of candidates.

The official preparations in Tampere had some new features, such as an increased number of voting districts (polling stations) and the so-called election cards, mailed to each person entitled to vote. The city government limited the time for free distribution of posters to ten days.

The larger the proportion of supporters who had joined party organizations, the more apt the parties were to have volunteer campaign workers. Only one third of the party members were active in campaign work, while one third of campaign workers were party members. The majority of campaign organizations thus functioned without personal connection to the leadership of the organization. When parties prepared their campaign organizations, they trained their members, established special trustees, and hired temporary labor. The existing Communist organization, however, was suitable for campaign work as such. For the whole constituency, each party employed functionaries and utilized at least some volunteer workers. Some had a city organization conducting the campaign in Tampere and a communal organization for Korpilahti. The role of campaign worker was considered different from that of party member or trustee, even when a person was functioning in both roles. This was markedly true of the Agrarian Union. Concerning campaign financing, parties gave outsiders the idea that it was based mainly on membership fees and contributions collected from members.

The forms of the campaign might be grouped into the use of normal mass media and the use of those propaganda media which are typical of an election campaign.

1. Newspapers commented on the election and published campaign advertising. In Tampere, 44 per cent of the inhabitants paid at least some attention to the campaign items and 64 per cent looked at campaign advertising. The corresponding percentages in Korpilahti were 35 and 69. Out of the eight campaign programs of the Finnish Broadcasting Corporation, three were political: on two evenings six parties spoke for themselves, and two days before the election a two hour campaign debate took place. In Tampere, 60 per cent and, in Korpilahti, 56 per cent were exposed to at least one such program.

2. Outdoor posters were to be seen in Tampere on advertising kiosks owned by a private company, on places rented from the city, and freely distributed on the sidewalks. After the election, an average of four out of nine such posters looked familiar to the interviewees, and they recognized three. In the rural commune posters were less dense, but in proportion to the population about as numerous as in the city. They were also remembered equally well. Pamphlets were mainly an urban campaign media. Campaign letters were mailed to inhabitants of both places. They were used especially by individual candidates. Election services (transportation, obtaining of absentee ballots) were not actually propaganda, but they certainly supported it.

3. Campaign meetings belong mainly to the class of actual campaign media, but in a way they are only a special form of the normal meetings

arranged for public audiences. About 8 per cent in Tampere, but 20 per cent in Korpilahti attended them. Even the number of such meetings was larger in the rural commune, where the Agrarian Union was the most frequent organizer. In the city most meetings were organized by the Communist FPDU. The speakers were mainly candidates and party functionaries. Discussion and debate took place in the rural commune, but not in the city.

In this study, the election campaign is considered a period of activity that is distinct from the normal political process. But, because it begins gradually while the parties are still engaged in campaign preparations, it is impossible to state exactly its duration. (1) From the official dates, let us mention that the number of the lists of candidates became certain 36 days before the election, and that the closing ceremonies of parliament took place 30 days before the election. Observations of the radio program and free delivery of posters show that the campaign lasted only ten to eleven days. (2) A qualitative analysis of public statements reveals that the activity of other parties is called campaign propaganda quite early, while the beginning of one's own campaign work is mentioned both late and repeatedly. (3) Two Helsinki newspapers adopted in March a special section for campaign items. Campaign advertising was heavy only in June. (4) The most reliable measure of the duration of the campaign might be an analysis of the trends in the volume of campaign material in newspapers, and of the relationship of campaign material to other political content. Obviously the editorial staffs campaigned for only two to four weeks, and the advertisers for one week or two. In addition to newspaper advertising, the free distribution of posters shows that the effective campaign lasted less than two weeks. This was the opinion of the officials too.

The citizens' attitude toward the campaign was indifferent and critical. Yet almost everyone obtained some information about the election. Only 7 per cent was not exposed at all to either newspapers and radio or to private discussions about the election. In Korpilahti the corresponding figure was 10 per cent. Should we consider also letters and pamphlets, which were given to the citizens even against their wishes, only 1 per cent of the inhabitants of Tampere and 5 per cent of those of Korpilahti remained entirely outside the campaign.

8. The Content of the Campaign

"Electioneering ought to be fair enough not to burn the bridges of co-operation after the campaign. Could not all the parties assemble before the actual campaign in a constructive consultation to limit the campaign to relevant facts?" This was the hope expressed by President Urho Kekkonen in the traditional presidential New Year's address on January 1, 1958, broadcast for the first time on radio and television simultaneously.

On January 4, the Finnish People's Party invited all parties to discuss moderation in the campaign. However, in the opinion of the Social Democrats it seemed "unlikely that during this decade Finnish parties would agree to the demands of fair play in the campaign," whereas "the People's Democrats no more fraternize in the election than between elections with those who oppose decisions in the interests of the working people." On May 19, the Chairmen and secretaries of the Agrarians, Conservatives, and both People's parties finally signed an agreement on "a decent campaign" to the effect that the "contracting parties shall not in their campaign spread information about each other which has been proved wrong, nor will they conduct a campaign which would offend and abuse the undersigned parties, their members, or their candidates," and "the foreign policy of no party to the agreement shall be labeled untrustworthy during the campaign."[1]

The fear of abusiveness, which was already apparent at the beginning of the election year, might have been caused by the experience that campaigns feature more attacks on competitors than presentations of one's own favorable goals. Possibly the particular aim of the parties, who initiated the campaign truce idea, was to weaken criticism likely to be directed at themselves. The press got topics for articles from the agreement itself. For example, other parties were accused of violating the agreed principles.[2]

In the following, we shall examine what content did fill the frame of the 1958 campaign. It is to be expected that the campaign material

1. *KL*, Jan. 1, 1958, p. 3, *KU*, June 9, 1958, p. 3 and *MK*, May 23, 1958, p. 2; Annual Report of the FPP of Its Activity in 1958 (Helsinki, 1959), p. 18.

2. However, the FPP considered that the agreement moderated the beginning of the campaign, ibid., p. 19. *Helsingin Sanomat* called the campaign feeble on June 26, 1958, p. 4.

differed from normal political material not only in quantity, but also in content.

CAMPAIGN PLATFORMS AND SLOGANS

Let us first look at the 1958 party campaign platforms—although it is difficult to define what a campaign platform means in Finland. For instance, the Coalition Party earlier labeled as campaign platform its basic party programs that were passed in party conventions; on the other hand, in 1958 parties designated as platforms even such declarations as were changed at different times of publishing. From the voters' point of view, it presumably has no significance who has written the platforms as long as they are published in the name of the party. They offer their readers a certain summary of the campaign debate, and perhaps also indicate the general desire of party leadership concerning what to say and how to say it during the party campaign. The primary purpose of the campaign platforms, like that of the campaign as a whole, is, of course, to influence the voters' decisions in a given election. Such a limited purpose was not true of actual party programs, not even of the new ones passed by the Communist Party and the Conservatives in their 1957 party conventions.

The most important platforms in 1958 were the actual platforms of the FPDU, Agrarians and Conservatives, and the so-called election declarations of other parties. Some parties had many of the latter kind—for example, separate declarations passed on the district level. Campaign platforms were further clarified in pamphlets, in press interviews of party leaders, and in such newspaper advertisements as had the nature of declarations.

The FPDU and the Conservatives were extremely critical of the power holders. The former concluded its program by demanding reforms that would be possible only if the FPDU won the election; and the latter advocated a basic change in the direction of the economic policies of the country. The Agrarian Union presented the political goals of agriculture. The Finnish People's Party emphasized harmony, and the Social Democratic Party stressed parliamentary practices, while the Independent Social Democratic electoral alliance simply quoted the campaign program of the Central Federation of Labor Unions.

The Rivals and the Intended Audience

A closer analysis of the campaign platforms might start with observing which parties they explicitly opposed. The FPDU criticized the right wing in general, but named specifically only "the present official leadership of the Social Democratic Party." The Independent Social Democratic electoral alliance, too, criticized only the executive units of the SDP, whereas in the April declaration of the Finnish People's Party the critique of the recent legislative term concentrated on the Social Democrats and the FPDU.[3] When these parties criticized the Social Democrats, they were focusing their campaign on a close rival. But, when the Conservatives demanded a change in the direction of policies, the reason they gave was a review of the entire postwar period. According to the Conservatives, all three—Social Democrats, Agrarians, and Communists—were jointly responsible for the mistakes. The platform of the Agrarians did not name specifically any party. The Agrarians only declared in a general way opposition to right wing policies and the revolutionary declarations of the left wing. The Social Democratic Party, in turn, criticized the "recent practices out of line with parliamentarism."

Secondly, let us observe what kind of voters the parties were most anxious to attract. Only the Conservative platform referred generally to the citizens, the whole nation, and "all of us." All other parties defined the voters they wanted by making references either to their characteristics or their thoughts.

1. The SDP appealed to "the wage-earning population of the country and the unprivileged homes of rural areas." Its Opposition, in turn, referred to labor and to members of organized groups: "the members and supporters of the Social Democratic Party, the labor unions, and sports associations," as well as to "women and the youth," which might have meant particularly members of the Social Democratic women and youth organizations.

2. The campaign declaration of the Finnish People's Party was most clearly of the other type, in appealing to "all those citizens who without reference to their economic and social status except a change in a new direction."

3. The FPDU and the Agrarian Union defined the object of their programs simultaneously in both ways. The objects of the former were "workers, small farmers and the intelligentsia," on the one hand, and "all progressive and peace loving citizens," on the other. The latter appealed to the "rural population," but at the same time invited all those,

---

3. For example, the pamphlet "Onko valtakuntamme suistunut raiteiltaan?" (Has our country been derailed?) (Tampere, FPP), p. 8, offers more detailed criticism but also includes a critique of the Conservatives, Agrarians, and Swedes.

"who in deeds and not only in words approve of the foreign policy consistent with the Paasikivi-Kekkonen line."

Policy Goals

Finally, we should note whether the different platforms offered alternative policy goals. The topics might be grouped here, as they were in the platforms of a few parties, to deal separately with foreign, internal, and economic policy.

No alternatives were offered for Finnish foreign policy: only three out of seven parties even mentioned this topic in their platforms. The Conservative pamphlet actually explained why it did not contain any section on foreign policy by stating that this election did not concern the foreign policy, which has to remain consistent with the line established by President J. K. Paasikivi, "on which our nation is unanimous." Correspondingly, the Finnish People's Party stated in its campaign declaration that "the foreign policy of our country must continue to follow the constructive national line of neutrality." Even the Agrarian Union supported "without qualifications the foreign policy of the Paasikivi-Kekkonen line," but it did not approve of the foreign policy of the right wing, whereas the platform of the FPDU was unevenly balanced: it pictured the Soviet Union as more able and more well-meaning than the Western powers and demanded more intercourse between Finland and the Soviet Union.

The internal political goals of the platforms dealt more with Cabinet coalition than with any other issue. The FPDU wanted to enter the Cabinet after having been an outsider for ten years, and it opposed "the taking of government policies into the hands of the Rightist elements." The Conservatives, in turn, suggested "a majority coalition on a wide parliamentary basis that would represent all democratic parties." This meant a coalition of all except the FPDU. The SDP demanded "responsible parliamentarism" and "an efficient cabinet leaning on the support of the Parliament," but its Opposition, which adopted the labor union platform, emphasized the cooperation of left wing members of parliament with the trade union movement. The Agrarian Union and the Finnish People's Party did not mention the composition of the government otherwise, but they demanded "harmonious center policies" (the Agrarians) and "increased constructive center thinking" (FPP). The latter, however, also advocated a general referendum practice "when great and important decisions are made." The FPDU wanted a broader democracy "through increased freedom of activity for the laboring masses."

Should one accept the position that the only purpose of an election is to decide who forms the Cabinet and how political decisions are made, the platforms did offer alternatives. Each party wanted not only many representatives, but also a significant role in the new Cabinet.

But the platforms emphasized mainly economic goals. Thus, the FPDU called all twelve of its demands economic ones, while the section of the Agrarian platform which dealt with fiscal policies was double in length to its other sections combined. According to the Conservative platform, the focus of this election was the decision whether the earlier economic policies would be continued or "a new road be entered."

In the economic policy sections, too, it was possible to avoid specific demands. This was done by the FPP, with the proposal that the solution of economic difficulties required increased center thinking, and by the SDP, in the statement that "the improvement of industrialization and rural economic life required an efficient parliamentarian Cabinet." The detailed economic demands either (1) set new goals, as in the case of the FPDU, Independent Social Democratic, Conservative, and Popular Center platforms; or (2) opposed the estimated economic development. Representative of the latter type was the invitation of the Agrarian Union "to a defensive fight against those powers which prepared a major attack to destroy the countryside." A corresponding theme had been used in 1954, when the Agrarian Union won two additional seats in Parliament.

It was generally agreed that a more vigorous economy was indispensable. But to achieve this, very different means were suggested. The FPDU proposed increased wages for workers and to other low salary earners; the trade unions requested easlier fiscal policies and a lower interest rate; the Agrarians proposed a flexible fiscal policy, soil and forest improvements, and development of traffic connections; the Conservatives wanted lower subsidies, lower taxation, and increased saving; and the new Popular Center advocated reduced state expenditures through the abolishment of all subsidies and simplification of public construction works. The demand for industrialization presented by the Social Democrats was joined by the Popular Center and by the FPDU as far as socialized industry was concerned, and by the Agrarians as far as the industrialization of rural areas.

In many details two parties were apt to mention the same goal. This is true especially of the overlapping social policy demands of the Communists and the Independent Social Democrats; in another connection the FPDU publicly declared support for the election program of the labor unions after the Independent Social Democrats had declared corresponding support.[4] The labor unions and the Agrarian Union demanded that the law on working hours should be extended to farm and forest labor; the Agrarians and the Conservatives requested the abolishment of support to wealthy persons; the Communists and Conservatives asked for improved possibilities for small enterprise; and the Finnish People's Party and the Conservatives demanded better balanced state budgets. An improved employment situation was generally considered necessary, although opinions differed concerning how this was to be realized. Unemployment insurance was an additional demand of the FPDU and the labor unions.

Opposing opinions concerned only two details. The FPDU wanted to socialize, but the Conservatives wanted to sell the stock of state-owned corporations to the public. The trade unions wanted to reform the law on agricultural income, but the Agrarian Union wanted to renew it.[5]

Differences in economic demands were not generally revealed in expressed disagreements. More pertinent were the goals emphasized or even mentioned in the platform. No party declared opposition to social reforms, but only two left wing parties displayed a detailed list of requested reforms. Neither did any party explicitly oppose benefits to agriculture and rural areas, but only the Agrarian Union listed detailed goals in this sphere. No party declared specific opposition to a balanced state budget and lower state expenditures, but only the Finnish People's Party, Conservatives, and Popular Center paid attention to this.

One should remember that in their campaigns parties attempt to gain votes from as many groups as possible. It is considered wise to avoid specific stands that might oppose someone's interests and possibly estrange potential voters. Rather unclear and emotional statements belong to this style of propaganda. And in order to emphasize their demands, the parties tended to designate opponents who had to be defeated, even if reasons for naming these opponents were only artificial. All parties except the Agrarian Union opened their 1958 platform with the idea that policies had failed since the previous election. Consequently, improve-

4. *KU*, May 24, 1958, p. 5. See also the *Kansan Uutiset* editorial, May 30, 1958, p. 4.

5. The party convention of the FPP, which gave the election proclamation, also decided on a separate declaration that urged "the Parliament group and Party Committee to advance attempts to get rid of the present law on agricultural income." *HS*, March 31, 1958, p. 8.

ments and "new roads" were promised, even though the promises lacked specificity and overlooked many relevant matters.

Slogans

The main ideas of the platforms were often given condensed expression in short slogans. They were repeated continuously. The FPDU and the Conservatives adopted slogans to emphasize their opposing attitudes. The general poster of the FPDU was titled, *Who Is Responsible?* And after their New Year declaration the Conservatives repeated the sentence, *It Is Time to Mend the Affairs of the Country.* The defensive attitude of the Agrarian Union in economic policies was, for example, expressed by the poster, *A Deserted Countryside?—No, Says the Agrarian Union.*

The only poster dealing with foreign policy in 1958 was: *The Safeguarding of the Finnish People Is Approved Foreign Policy—Vote for the Agrarian Union.* The internal policies of the platforms were sometimes emphasized: for example, by the FPDU, *The Danger Threatens from the Right*; the SDP, *From Forced Power to Parliamentarism*; and the FPP, *Construction—Not Destruction.*

The text of the other general poster of the FPDU, *Forward Strong People,* and its focal slogan, *Work—Peace—Security,* were published for the first time in the May Day declaration of the Central Committee of the Finnish Communist Party.[6] These key words crystallized the FPDU platform, and as the election came closer they characterized their entire party press. For instance, they were mentioned 24 times in six issues of *Hämeen Yhteistyö* from June 27 to July 4. Ideas reminiscent of the FPDU were the slogans of the Independent Social Democrats, *Livelihood—Democracy—Peace,* and *Assemble Powers, Labor.* For instance, they gave a uniform appearance to 83 different advertisements in the *Helsingin Sanomat* in ten issues (June 27 to July 6). The general poster of the Finnish People's Party also stated, *Work—Security.*

The campaign slogans of the Social Democratic Party were mainly deduced from the demand to industrialize. The headlines and advertisements of its press repeated, *Industry—Work—Future,* and the text of its posters was, *Industrializing Country—Well-off Nation,* which had in the rural poster an altered form, *Industrializing Country—Advancing Countryside.* Of local interest in Tampere were those comments which the editors of *Kansan Lehti* attached to the campaign advertising of the Opposition of their party, such as, *Votes Cast for the Dividers Will Support the Communists and the Bourgeois.*

6. *HY,* May 1, 1958, p. 3.

Conservative advertising gained additional uniformity from the re-peated label, *National Coalition to Election Victory*. The advertising of the Popular Center concentrated, for example, on the slogan, *Away with Subsidies and Fairness to Parliament*.

These were the central campaign slogans. The separate propaganda activities of women's and youth organizations employed slogans too, but not too many to confuse the public's idea of the main points of the platforms. Slogans, once invented, benefited the parties also, in that they helped to label the advertising with idealism and a programmatic nature. Individual sentences from the campaign platforms were utilized for the same purpose.

THE PRIMARY OPPONENTS OF THE PARTIES

The particular emphasis of the platforms was not the critique of other parties. On the other hand, the party newspaper normally published more criticism of other parties than positive presentations of their own party. In April and May 1958, *Suomen Sosialidemokraatti* and the Con-servative papers, as well, even criticized mere Agrarians more than they praised their own party, and no paper wrote as much about its own party as about other parties combined (Tables 6.1 and 6.5).

The comparison of the campaign with the normal content of the press presupposes here a continuation of the content analyses of Chapter 6. Table 8.1 and 8.3 represent this procedure regarding the three Tampere papers. The following list summarizes how many times per issue these papers printed a positive statement about their own party and a negative one about others. The figures are first for the twelfth to ninth, then for the fourth and third, and finally for the second and last weeks before the campaign:

April 14 to May 11	Hämeen Yhteistyö	Kansan Lehti	Aamulehti
Positive statements about own party	9.2	4.5	2.6
Negative statements about other parties	12.4	6.9	7.8
June 9 to June 22			
Positive statements about own party	7.9	7.2	5.6
Negative statements about other parties	14.8	8.8	9.7
June 23 to July 6			
Positive statements about own party	13.8	15.8	12.8
Negative statements about other parties	34.4	34.2	25.3

Even these figures show how the amount of political material increased as the election days approached. Although this measurement is not exact enough for detailed conclusions, we might point out that:

1. the papers did not praise their own party at any time as much as they criticized others;

2. *Kansan Lehti* and *Aamulehti* began their actual campaign with improved presentations of their own party and began to catch up with the *Hämeen Yhteistyö,* which had written even normally a great deal about its party, the FPDU (p. 131);

3. all papers doubled the material on their own party at the final stage of the campaign, but the critique of other parties increased much more during the hot era of the campaign so that it again characterized the political content of newspapers.

TABLE 8.1.   Percentage Distribution of Negative Statements about Other Parties in Three Tampere Newspapers (1) between June 9 and June 22, and (2) between June 23 and July 6, 1958

Parties	(1) June 9–June 22			(2) June 23–July 6			Total		
	HY	KL	AL	HY	KL	AL	HY	KL	AL
FPDU	.	30	36	.	34	36	.	33	36
S. D. Opp.	13	18	–	10	31	7	11	28	5
SDP	45	.	6	49	.	11	48	.	10
Agrarian	14	30	55	20	24	36	19	25	41
FPP	3	13	2	2	3	9	2	5	7
Conservative	10	7	.	11	8	.	10	8	.
Swedish	–	2	1	–	0	1	–	1	1
Right wing	15	–	–	8	–	–	10	–	–
Total	100	100	100	100	100	100	100	100	100
Number of statements	*118*	*105*	*116*	*344*	*444*	*354*	*462*	*549*	*470*
Number of statements per issue	*14.8*	*8.8*	*9.7*	*34.4*	*34.2*	*25.3*	*25.6*	*22.0*	*18.1*

HY = *Hämeen Yhteistyö* (FPDU).
KL = *Kansan Lehti* (SDP).
AL = *Aamulehti* (Conservative).

Each party fought against everyone else. Let us mention as an example a review, presented by the FPDU organization secretary to the Central Committee of the Communist Party of Finland, which was published under the headline, "Parties on the Scale." [7] But the fighting of the parties

7. *KU,* May 20, 1958, p. 4.

was not of equal magnitude in all directions. This is shown for Tampere in Table 8.1.

The main target of *Hämeen Yhteistyö* was the Social Democratic Party, which it criticized during the last weeks of the campaign an average of 17 times per issue. *Aamulehti* directed its critique at the Agrarian Union and the FPDU. *Kansan Lehti* divided its attention in three directions, and featured opposition to the FPDU, the Social Democratic Opposition, and the Agrarian Union. In this connection, however, we must remember that *Kansan Lehti* and *Aamulehti* accepted paid advertisements from some of their opponents (see pp. 182–83).

Changes in the Targets of the Critique

It has been presumed above that for tactical reasons the political press tends to criticize those other parties which—according to the perception of the editors and the party leadership—compete most vigorously for the support of persons close to its own party (p. 145). Because the specific aim of an election campaign is to influence the citizen's voting decisions (pp. 26–27), we might further assume that such tactical considerations are more apparent during the campaign than in normal times.

A comparison of Tables 6.5 and 8.1 supports this assumption. Although each party was more criticized during the campaign than in April and May, the rapidity of the increase in criticism seems to correlate with the stated reason of expediency. During the four campaign weeks, *Hämeen Yhteistyö* published 163 per cent more statements criticizing the SDP than it had published normally. Simultaneously, its critique of the Agrarians increased by 50 per cent and that of the Conservatives by only 20 per cent. In the content of *Kansan Lehti,* the center of gravity shifted even more. The critique directed at its normal main opponent, the Agrarian Union, increased by 40 per cent, but that directed at the FPDU by 235 per cent. During the last two weeks of the campaign, *Kansan Lehti* also criticized the Opposition of its own party more than the Agrarians. At this stage no less than 65 per cent of its negative statements were concerned with the left wing. Let us also mention that even the small normal critique of the Swedish People's Party was left out of the Tampere leftist papers during the campaign.

These changes in the content of the press concur with the presumption because the editorial staffs seem to have had a correct image of the attitude of their party supporters toward other parties (see Table 6.4). However, two exceptions must be mentioned. The Communist paper's critique of the Independent Social Democrats did not increase as much as might have been expected, considering that the supporters of the FPDU were almost as close to the Social Democratic Opposition as they were to the Social Democratic Party. And the SDP paper, *Kansan Lehti,* increased its critique of the Finnish People's Party in the beginning of the campaign, but paid relatively little attention to this party later in the campaign. Perhaps it was impossible to take every rival into account. On the other hand, both exceptions might also represent another tactic, a kind of principle of keeping silent, which was applied to a seemingly innocuous rival.

The Conservative *Aamulehti* supports in one respect our presumption about the campaign tactic. Although critique of the SDP and the FPP was almost absent in the beginning of the campaign, these parties (favored by the Conservatives) were attacked once again in the Conservative paper during the hot weeks. Perhaps the continuous critique of the Agrarian Union fit the presumption because of its importance among rural readers, but it was quite contrary to the presumption for the FPDU at that point to join the side of the Agrarians as the other main opponent of *Aamulehti*. A possible explanation was the special position of *Aamulehti* as the general newspaper in that local area. Dislike of the Communists was a common attitude of a majority of the readers of the paper. However, in such a situation, another tactic might be used, namely, criticizing a party generally discriminated against, in order to appeal to all other persons rather than just the supporters of this most distant (Communist) party. Another possibility is the attempt to aid some other party, and a likely aim is simply to activate the supporters of one's own party.

The Local and National Papers

Our view of the special local position of *Aamulehti* seems justified, when it is compared with the organization paper edited by the Conservative Party headquarters (Table 8.2). The latter, called *Nykypäivä,* stopped confining its criticism to the Agrarian Union, but its critique of the FPDU increased less, and that of the SDP and the FPP increased more than it did in *Aamulehti*. Despite this difference, the distributions in *Nykypäivä* did not differ much from the Conservative newspapers before and during the campaign. Furthermore, Appendix Table 14 reveals that, when the political content of the Conservative *Uusi Suomi* increased in June and July beyond that of May and June, this paper became especially critical of the Agrarian Union and the FPP. Such a trend was in line with our expectations concerning the main tactic of the campaign.

TABLE 8.2.   Percentage Distribution of Negative Statements about Other Parties in the Organization Periodicals of Three Parties before the 1958 Election

Parties	Tukimies (Agrarian) April	May	June	Suoma-lainen (FPP) Nos. 1 & 2*	Pirkanmaa (FPP) Apr. + May*	June	July	Nykypäivä (Cons.) April	May	June
FPDU	21	26	22	28	14	26	11	19	18	26
S. D. Opp.	2	–	3	9	3	5	2	5	4	6
SDP	34	32	33	34	24	36	26	13	7	15
Agr.	.	.	.	18	20	13	13	49	63	35
FPP	–	8	3	.	.	.	.	9	6	14
Cons.	27	21	31	11	39	20	48	.	.	.
Swedish	3	1	1	–	–	–	–	2	2	1
Left wing	–	–	–	–	–	–	–	3	–	3
Right wing	13	12	7	–	–	–	–	–	–	–
Total	100	100	100	100	100	100	100	100	100	100
Number of statements	*160*	*103*	*112*	*65*	*71*	*39*	*46*	*126*	*106*	*110*

* Double issues.

In Table 8.2, let us also note against which parties the Agrarian and FPP organization papers were writing. *Tukimies,* which was published for the Agrarian campaign organization, was very consistent; the distribution of its content remained almost unchanged during these three months. The three opponents were the Social Democratic Party, the Conservatives, and the FPDU. The only change from May to June worthy of mention seems to have been a decrease in statements about the FPP and the right wing in general, and a corresponding increase in specific statements about the National Coalition. The organization papers of the Finnish People's Party criticized in four directions. *Pirkanmaa,* distributed by the Northern Häme district organization of the party, wrote relatively little about the Agrarian Union; it campaigned first against the left wing, but later against the Conservatives.

Figure 8.A, too, presents information on the campaign rivals of newspapers. It thus depicts Appendix Table 14.b. Figure 8.A is not directly

FIGURE 8.A. Percentage Distribution of Articles Criticizing Other Parties in
Seven Newspapers from June 9 to July 6, 1958

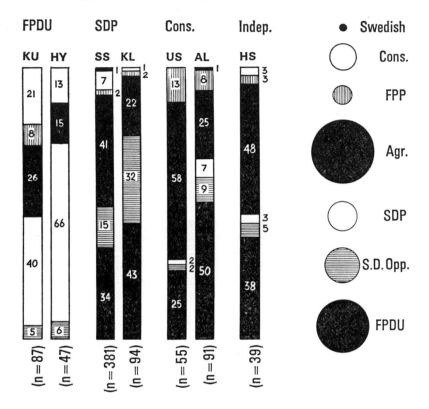

comparable with the above information, because the unit of quantifica-
tion is the whole article rather than individual statements. However, it
shows, as Table 8.1, that *Hämeen Yhteistyö* criticized mainly the Social
Democratic Party, while *Kansan Lehti* criticized the FPDU, the Independent Social Democrats, and the Agrarians, and *Aamulehti* was negative toward the FPDU and the Agrarians.

According to Figure 8.A, the content of the campaign had a somewhat
different emphasis at the local and national levels. For example, anti-
Communist material was continuously more typical of the non-Communist papers in Tampere than in Helsinki (see p. 145). On the other hand,
the Helsinki papers did not give up, even during the campaign, their
normal anti-Agrarian content. The strength and keen competition among
the left wing parties and the relative weakness of the Agrarian Union,
which were characteristics of the Northern Häme constituency, thus were

significant in the campaign material of its local newspapers. Regarding the Helsinki papers, we find further that, compared with *Helsingin Sanomat,* the number of negative statements on other parties was almost tenfold in *Suomen Sosialidemokraatti.* Yet the objects of the critique were almost alike in distribution. Even the conservative *Uusi Suomi* did not differ much, although it was slightly more concerned about the Agrarians and slightly less about the left wing. Only *Kansan Lehti* treated the Independent Social Democrats as special opponents in 1958, while the Communist organs were the only papers read in Tampere that presented much criticism of the Social Democratic Party.

THE TOPICS OF THE CAMPAIGN MATERIAL

A study of the newspapers has revealed that the total number of statements criticizing other parties increased as election time drew near, and that parts of this critique were turned in new directions. Let us next examine whether a new emphasis also appeared in the topics of statements made about parties during the campaign.

The Critique of Other Parties

In Chapter 6 (pp. 145–47), there was a brief description of the critique published in seven newspapers about the parties during the normal weeks of April and May. In the following, the content of the papers during this period (April 14 to May 11) will be compared with the equally long campaign period (June 9 to July 6). The quantitative basis of the comparison is a classification of the statements published in criticism of other parties by the three Tampere papers (Appendix Tables 15 and 16).

Some general trends can be observed in the content of the critique. The most typical aspect during the campaign was the frequent criticism of political leaders. During the four-week normal period, the three papers made only ten personal remarks, but they contained 129 during the four campaign weeks. Such critique became important then, because the candidates of rival parties had finally been announced. The editorial staffs and the speakers reported in the papers also began to react to the arguments of the candidates of other parties.

However, let us point out that the Tampere newspapers began to criticize chiefly the leaders of the three left wing groups and of the Agrarian Union. Even during the campaign not many critical statements were published about the FPP and Conservative leaders.

Appendix Tables 15 and 16 show a decreasing tendency to accuse others of the "playing party politics tactic." Even actual campaign tactics were mentioned less now than normally. The decrease in the former topic is understandable through the theoretical position of this study, that the approach of an election interrupts the normal political process and shifts the major attention of political powers toward the electorate. References to "party games" belong to normal semantics which now decreases. Even abuse of actual campaign tactic was shown above as a means used before the campaign to depreciate the activity of other parties (p. 188).

These inexact statistical comparisons also point to separate trends in the statements on the various parties. Thus normal references to the lack of patriotism among the FPDU increased in *Kansan Lehti* and *Aamulehti,* but labeling the FPDU destructive, bold, and prevaricating was more typical of the campaign. In addition, *Kansan Lehti* began to call the FPDU anti-labor, and *Aamulehti* began to write about its party tactics.

The existence of the Independent Social Democratic electoral union had most impact on the content of *Kansan Lehti.* This newspaper especially criticized its new rival as a deviate and, in addition, as a fact-twisting and anti-Social Democratic group. *Hämeen Yhteistyö* also made critical statements about the candidates of the Social Democratic Opposition, but it no longer presented it as a weak and quarreling group. *Aamulehti* was almost quiet about this electoral alliance. Even the Social Democratic Party was criticized by the Conservative newspaper only because of its economic policy, whereas *Hämeen Yhteistyö* wrote heatedly about the SDP leaders, foreign policy, and their untrustworthiness.

Talk about the internal quarrels of the Agrarian Union and about its party tactics decreased before the campaign. At the same time the Tampere papers increased their criticism of the Agrarian economic policy and its anti-labor attitude. A critique of the Agrarians in the field of foreign policy increased in two papers, but decreased in *Hämeen Yhteistyö.* The Finnish People's Party was called weak in Tampere, and votes cast for it were said to be wasted. Even *Hämeen Yhteistyö* now began to use this theme, although it otherwise decreased its mention of the FPP. The two other papers began to call the FPP untrustworthy and power hungry. In *Hämeen Yhteistyö* criticism of the Conservatives did not change much as far as its quantity and content are concerned, but it began to call the right wing in general destructive, overbearing, and anti-Communist. *Kansan Lehti,* on the other hand, published a three-fold number of statements criticizing the Conservatives and began to call the National Coalition, for example, a class party, war loving, and anti-Social Democratic.

Thus the critique published by the Tampere papers showed not only general changes in topics but also specific ones connected with the parties. They began to emphasize certain aspects dealt with in the campaign platforms, and to use topics linked in a general way to the election itself. Statements of the latter kind were, for example, the warnings that ballots cast for a weak electoral alliance would be wasted.

TABLE 8.3. Classification of Statements in Three Tampere Newspapers about Their Affiliated Party (1) between June 9 and June 22, and (2) between June 23 and July 6, 1958

Central idea	(1) June 9–June 22			(2) June 23–July 6			Total		
	HY	KL	AL	HY	KL	AL	HY	KL	AL
Prolabor activity	12	2	–	21	18	–	33	20	–
Support of middle class interests	–	–	–	–	–	3	–	–	3
Fair-minded, middle of the road	–	–	1	–	2	1	–	2	2
Fatherland, interest of the whole	–	–	–	4	2	11	4	2	11
Foreign policy of party	–	–	3	3	8	4	3	8	7
Social policy of party	14	1	–	18	16	2	32	17	2
Reduction of unemployment	4	6	–	6	5	8	10	11	8
Other economic policy	4	11	9	9	22	32	13	33	41
Party conduct	4	8	11	14	20	20	18	28	31
Ability, party leaders	3	6	1	9	18	14	12	24	15
Candidates of party	16	45	36	35	30	60	51	75	96
Unity, clarity of party	1	4	–	5	21	4	6	25	4
More cohesive party system	–	–	3	–	2	5	–	2	8
Other positive statements	5	4	3	14	42	15	19	46	18
Total number of positive statements	63	87	67	138	206	179	201	293	246
Number of positive statements per issue	7.9	7.2	5.6	13.8	15.8	12.8	11.2	11.7	9.5

Changes in Presenting One's Own Party

A comparison of Tables 6.1 and 8.3 is a quantitative basis for observing the trends in the topics used by the three Tampere newspapers to praise their own party.

The nominated candidates brought the most significant additions to the positive material concerning one's own party, just as it had to the critiques of other parties. This was most typical of the third and fourth weeks before the election. Actually, the presentation of candidates was then the only reason for the increase in statements about one's own party. More than one half of all statements about their party in both *Kansan Lehti* and *Aamulehti* belonged in this category.

The percentage of the most typical, normal statements remained constant. *Hämeen Yhteistyö* and *Kansan Lehti* continued their emphasis on the interests of the labor, and *Aamulehti* its emphasis on the fatherland and the interests of the whole. In addition, *Hämeen Yhteistyö* and *Aamulehti* concentrated on the kinds of topics used when writing about their own party. The former increased especially its statements dealing with the social policy of the FPDU. This theme also occupied a central position in the so-called demands for economic policy in the FPDU campaign platform. *Aamulehti* concentrated mainly on the presentation of Conservative economic policy, which also was the focal issue of the election according to the Conservative platform. At the same time, however, *Aamulehti* praised more than normally the Conservative procedures and those leaders who were not candidates in the election.

Along with the concentration on certain themes in *Hämeen Yhteistyö,* there was an actual decrease in other topics. For example, fewer references to party procedures and foreign policy might again indicate the temporary diminishing of normal topics and their replacement by campaign topics. The concentration on themes in both newspapers seems to follow the repetition requirement of effective propaganda.[8]

Kansan Lehti showed an opposite trend. No topic was given up, but many new ones were added. We might say that the presented themes of the SDP were scattered and not concentrated. Additional praise was given, for example, to the social and economic policy and to the leaders of the party, and it seemed important in this campaign to emphasize

8. Our measurement is not detailed enough to show to what extent the repetition was accompanied with variations in the style of presentation. It has been found that especially "repetition with variations" increases the persuasive power of propaganda; Joseph T. Klapper, *The Effects of Mass Communication* (Glencoe, The Free Press, 1963), pp. 119–20.

the unity of the split party. An illustrative detail is that *Kansan Lehti* did not write about the foreign policy of its party normally, nor in the beginning of June, but it was dealing with this topic, too, by the end of the campaign.

Such a dispersion of campaign items seems to be connected with the difficult position of *Kansan Lehti,* and the Social Democratic Party in general, in this election. The paper had three important main opponents, while the other papers had only one or two (Table 8.1). Obviously, it was impossible to focus on the presentation of one's own party, when it was necessary to reply to arguments from many directions, all of which deserved attention.

Selected Items of Political Debate

Let us turn to opinions expressed on selected items of political debate (Table 8.4), and analyze the same details which were studied for Table 6.6. "The People's Capitalism" is an additional item in this section.

It seems that arguments presented by others really caused reactions in the campaign. This can be seen in the attitudes toward the people's capitalism issue. After the Conservative *Aamulehti* had begun to write about it during the second to last week of the campaign, the two leftist papers expressed their opposition during the last campaign week. After the demand for industrialization by the SDP had been presented more and more often in *Kansan Lehti,* at the end of the campaign *Aamulehti* began to repeat that the Conservatives, too, were in favor of industrialization.

A comparison of Tables 6.6 and 8.4 leads again to observations about the impact of the campaign period on the content of political material.

1. Even these selected items were dealt with more often during the campaign than normally. The tables contain eighteen examples of this and only two exceptions.

2. The general flavor of the opinions seems to have changed to some extent in the two leftist papers. The Communist paper became more moderate in a way than normally, as is seen in the increased number of neutral statements (points c, d, e, g in the tables). On the other hand, the Social Democratic paper presented its leftist and anti-Communist opinions more sharply now than normally (points a, d, g), and its sharpness was still obvious during the final hot phase of the campaign. A possible interpretation of such opposing trends is the FPDU's need to gain its new voters from the supporters of more moderate parties,

Table 8.4. Attitude of Three Tampere Newspapers toward Selected Platform Items: Number of Statements Pro and Con (1) between June 9 and June 22, and (2) between June 23 and July 6, 1958

	(1) June 9–June 22			(2) June 23–July 6			Total		
	HY	KL	AL	HY	KL	AL	HY	KL	AL
(a) Socialization									
Pro	2	2	–	1	7	–	3	9	–
Neutral	–	2	–	1	–	–	1	2	–
Con	–	–	–	–	–	8	–	–	8
(b) Government regulation of economy									
Pro	–	–	1	2	4	–	2	4	1
Neutral	1	2	–	–	–	2	1	2	2
Con	–	–	1	–	–	2	–	–	3
(c) Industrialization									
Pro	3	35	3	7	38	17	10	73	20
Neutral	4	8	5	4	6	5	8	14	10
Con	–	–	–	–	–	–	–	–	–
(d) Size of farms									
Many small ones	1	3	–	5	10	–	6	13	–
Neutral	3	2	3	4	–	8	7	2	11
Larger ones	–	–	3	–	–	9	–	–	12
(e) Lower taxes									
Pro	1	13	23	5	6	73	6	19	96
Neutral	2	3	–	--	1	5	2	4	5
Con	–	2	–	–	–	–	–	2	–
(f) Increased social support									
Pro	2	2	–	3	3	–	5	5	–
Neutral	–	2	–	–	3	2	–	5	2
Con	–	–	3	–	–	3	–	–	6
(g) Communist participation in government									
Pro	1	–	–	5	–	–	6	–	–
Neutral	2	–	–	–	–	–	2	–	–
Con	–	–	–	–	5	7	–	5	7
(h) People's Capitalism									
Pro	–	–	–	–	–	16	–	–	16
Neutral	–	–	–	–	–	–	–	–	–
Con	–	–	–	3	2	–	3	2	–

whereas the SDP campaigned in Tampere mainly on its left frontier. The changing flavor may also indicate that these two papers were now responding to arguments presented by their opponents about the cruelty of Communism, and the right wing character of the Social Democrats.

3. *Aamulehti* kept rather quiet about these selected items from May through a good part of June. Only demands for lower taxation became more common than was normal as early as the beginning of June, and it was this topic that finally became as focal in *Aamulehti* as in the Conservative platform. During the last week of the campaign *Aamulehti* opposed high taxes an average of eight times in each issue.

A comparison of Tables 6.6 and 8.4 thus indicates that even the treatment of separate items of political debate received a special campaign flavor. Some quantitative changes can be interpreted as obvious results of tactical considerations and of the emphasis on campaign platforms.

Campaign Speeches

This analysis of themes and opinions was based on the content of three local newspapers. The material, thus analyzed, included more than editorials and political articles, yet the analysis covered only that part of the campaign which was conducted or reported in the local newspapers. We shall pay attention to the campaign of individual candidates later. However, in this connection, let us briefly mention campaign speeches.

The speakers repeated many points made in party platforms, but, in addition, they had time to amplify and to explain the arguments and demands. Moreover, in speeches, it was possible to deal with new matters or to specialize in some given ideas. Examples of platform amplifiers were those Communist candidates who not only described the recent legislative term, but criticized the whole unhappy decade since the "good government of Mr. Pekkala" (1945–48). Many also emphasized the concern of the FPDU for the unemployed, and the "legality fight to save the children's allowances" in the 1957 Parliament. An example of new ideas was a speech about the destructive effect of increased radioactivity of the air on the teeth of school children; and examples of specialization were the concern of female candidates over the role of women in politics, the analysis of Arvo Tuominen about Communism,[9] and the criticism by Artturi Tienari of the Finnish People's Party.

9. Tuominen (a former member of the Executive Committee of the Communist International but noncommunist since 1940) summarized his message by saying "what good does bread do before you have protected your neck?"

The Special Character of the 1958 Campaign

We should emphasize that, when the campaign in the press was compared quantitatively with the normal content of the newspapers, it was
not done with the purpose of describing the typical aspects of the 1958
campaign. The content of campaign issues was discussed to some extent
when the platforms were presented. Let us point out a few topics that
were utilized in other propaganda of this campaign:

1. A new way of grouping the political parties appeared in 1958. Instead of the left wing and the bourgeois, one now spoke about "the
popular front" and the "unified right wing." According to *Kansan Lehti*
the "popular front included, under the leadership of the country's largest bourgeois party, the Finnish People's Party, the so-called Independent
Social Democrats and the FPDU." According to the Agrarian Union, the
SDP fought with "abusive slogans against the small farming population
. . . together with the Right Wing." Correspondingly, it was stated by
Hämeen Yhteistyö that "Väinö Leskinen (an SDP leader) has been mentioned as the strong man for whom the Conservatives have been longing,"
but on the other hand, "the Finnish People's Party will collapse after
the election in the easy chair of the Conservatives." [10]

2. The eight-column headline in *Kansan Lehti*: "The People's Democracy Showed Its Own Color—Imre Nagy and Three Others Were Exe-
cuted" is an example of the numerous references to the 1956 upheaval
in Hungary that were typical of the anti-Communist campaign of 1958.
It was stated that Finnish Communists, too, are expecting a suitable
"Kadar angle," toward which they have even been encouraged from
abroad, and it was also stated that "the old Stalinists again had been
nominated to their lists." [11] In Tampere, the anti-Communist campaign
was not only lively but also very sharply worded. The Communist
counterpropaganda also utilized foreign topics. The birth of the fifth

10. *KL*, July 5, 1958, p. 7; *10 toimenpidettä, jotka autioittavat maaseudun* (Ten Measures Which Would Desert the Countryside) (Kokemäki, 1958), p. 11; *HY*, June 13, 1958,
p. 3 and July 6, 1958, p. 3.

11. *KL*, June 18, 1958, p. 1; Poika Tuominen, "Suomalaiset kommunistit odottavat
Kadar-kulmaa" (Finnish Communists Are Waiting for the Kadar-angle), *HS*, June 29,
1958, p. 7; *KL*, June 30, 1958, p. 2, July 2, 1958, pp. 3–4 and July 4, 1958, p. 3;
AL, June 18, 1958, p. 7. Additional examples of anti-Communist propaganda are the page
of *Kansan Lehti*, headlined "Communism is forced power" (June 27, 1958, p. 5), the
page of *Aamulehti* headlined "This is the road of Communism" (July 5, 1958, p. 9); the
special issue of *Savon Kansa* titled "Where has Communism led to" (June 28, 1958); and
the FPP booklet *Kommunismin todelliset kasvot* (The real face of Communism).

French Republic was a proof of right wing danger, and the "revealing report of the Ambassador of Nazi Germany proved that Arvo Tuominen had been employed by the propaganda machine of Hitler's Germany." [12] Simultaneously, the FPDU stressed in Tampere how it had to defend itself alone against the joint attacks of all other parties.

3. Foreign policy became finally one of the main themes of the campaign. Yet the debate concerned only which parties were disqualified in this field and the necessity of discussing even this aspect. According to *Aamulehti* "the Agrarian Union and the Communists attempt to stamp everybody who does not have their membership card as dangerous and untrustworthy in foreign policy." According to *Maakansa,* in turn, the Finnish unanimity in foreign policy "is not furthered by neglecting the bustling of Soini, Junnila, and other such right wing leaders." [13]

4. Printed material on agricultural policy was distributed over the countryside, but press coverage in this field lost both the timeliness and the factual content that had been evident in April and May (especially after the lack of confidence vote for the von Fieandt government concerning the double-price system of cereal). In Tampere, only *Aamulehti* continued to carry a great deal of material on agricultural policy.

5. Social security was dealt with abundantly in speeches and articles. The unemployment problem was mentioned most often and was discussed in the spirit of the campaign platforms. The FPDU campaign speakers had a good opportunity to tell about their visits to the unemployment camps. The Social Democrats emphasized the importance of industrialization for employment, and the Agrarian Union the necessity to stay away from uncertain labor markets, while the Conservatives emphasized the significance of easier taxation for better employment.

6. Slogans advocating participation in the election came into prominence about ten days prior to the election, and finally became the leading theme of the campaign. *Helsingin Sanomat,* for example, considered a high turnout as a goal in itself: *Nothing But One Line—The Finnish Line!* The activating propaganda of the Agrarian Union was directed only at the rural areas: *The Ballots Will Answer the Ridiculers of the Countryside!,* whereas the sharp anti-Communist attitude of two Tampere newspapers was revealed even in their activating attempts: for ex-

12. "Even there (in France) the rise of fascists into power was preceded by slandering the Parliament, fanning the flame of chauvinism among the army and youth, and agitation which prepared the ground for raising a superman, a dictator, into power." *HY*, June 13, 1958, p. 3, and July 3, p. 1.

13. *AL*, June 12, 1958, p. 6; *MK*, July 1, 1958, p. 9.

ample, *A Lost Ballot Is a Ballot for the Communists* and *Remember Hungary—Look Out for Communism.* But the FPDU press directed its activating efforts one step further than other papers with the slogan, *Have You Also Educated Your Neighbors?* [14]

Two parties were still voicing reminders to vote in the papers of the second election day. *You Did Not Vote Yesterday—Do It Today!* was suggested by the Agrarian *Maakansa,* and, according to *Kansan Lehti, The Working Man Will Have a Bad Deal If There Is Nonvoting Today.* An experienced functionary of the Social Democratic district organization, Kustaa Alanko (M.P.), had already doubted in his campaign speeches that many Social Democrats would abstain from voting in this election.

The background of the 1958 election was a general discontent (see Chapter 1), and its main characteristics the repeated accusations of other parties. Actually there was no one in Tampere to defend the policies of the closing legislative term. The FPDU and the Conservatives presented themselves as the only parties free of responsibility. Each of them demanded a new—although different from the other—political line. Especially the FPDU argued that it had attempted to achieve improvements in the old Parliament. Even the SDP, having been outside the Cabinet for the last year of the four-year term, now considered itself a part of the Opposition.

THE PROPAGANDA OF INDIVIDUAL CANDIDATES

Some citizens in Tampere thought that, in order to change the line of policies, it would be more instrumental to replace members of Parliament with other politicians than to change the power relations of political parties (according to Q. 60.C). "New faces" were wanted in the Parliament; some people even considered it "useless to vote because the same names seem to be nominated again." However, change of personality was seldom demanded in the individual candidates' campaign.[15] Perhaps it was considered improper treatment of Parliament members. Also, it would have run against the main theme of the personal campaigns, which emphasized political experience.

14. *HS,* July 6, 1958, p. 5; *MK,* July 6, 1958, p. 4; *AL,* June 29, 1958, pp. 6–7 and July 6, 1958, p. 1; *KL,* July 6, 1958, p. 7; *HY,* June 28, 1958, p. 2. Examples of earlier ways to increase interest were the so-called election bets, arranged by the papers for their readers.

15. This aspect does not concern new parties, for example: "The new man of the new party to the new Parliament!!" (Advertisement of Popular Center candidate U. J. Lehtinen, *Tamperelainen,* July 3, 1958, p. 16.)

There are two reasons for advertising Finnish candidates: (1) it is possible that the individual candidates' personal support and the general image of the composition of the party list may have an effect on the total number of votes cast for the party; and (2) within each party, individual candidates compete with each other to get elected to Parliament and sometimes also to secure other kinds of chances for future political activity.

Because of the former reason, it is not possible to separate candidate propaganda entirely from the rest of the campaign. For example, campaign speeches advertise both the party and the speaker himself. Even the forms of candidate propaganda are parallel to those of the party campaign: individual candidates utilize the textual content of newspapers and newspaper advertisement, outdoor posters, campaign letters, and other campaign material. Only radio programs were denied the candidates (with the exception of a few leading representatives of the parties). Some candidates were able to activate their personal supporters to do campaign work they might not have done for the party as a whole.

After the formal nomination papers had been left with the central election board of the constituency in May, *Aamulehti* published the names of all the seven electoral alliances, while *Hämeen Yhteistyö* and *Kansan Lehti* mentioned only the candidates of their own party and of the Social Democratic Opposition. In the beginning of June, the three local newspapers presented each candidate of their own party with articles and picture. The other electoral alliances did not have such an opportunity.[16]

As the campaign progressed, the advertising of candidates appeared in an increasing proportion. Among the circulated posters there were more presentations of candidates than general posters of parties. Corresponding examples can be given about newspaper advertising. For example, *Aamulehti* carried, on the day preceding the election and on the first voting day, a total of 700 column inches of campaign advertising. The space was distributed as follows:

	Percentage
12 general Conservative advertisements	27
2 joint advertisements of Conservative candidates	19
17 advertisements of Conservative candidates	31
7 advertisements of FPP candidates	15
6 advertisements of Agrarian candidates	8
	100

16. However, Antti Linna of the FPP placed in *Aamulehti* a paid advertisement, which was reminiscent of the presentations of Conservative candidates, *AL,* June 20, 1958, p. 9.

In two issues of the free weekly, *Tamperelainen* (June 26 and July 3), there were 690 column inches of campaign advertisements. They divided space as follows:

	Percentage
3 general advertisements of the SDP and the Popular Center	17
1 announcement of the Social Democratic Opposition campaign rally	1
7 joint advertisements of FPDU, SDP, Agrarian, FPP, Conservative and Popular Center candidates	40
24 separate advertisements of Social Democratic Opposition, SDP, FPP, Conservative, and Popular Center individual candidates	42
	100

In both cases two thirds of the campaign advertisements presented individual candidates, which occupied 54 per cent of the advertising space in *Aamulehti* and 42 per cent in *Tamperelainen*. Candidates were also mentioned in other advertisements. The 35 advertisements in *Tamperelainen* contained only two which mentioned just the parties.

Such personal campaigning emphasized four aspects mainly: the candidates were presented as (1) worthy of the trust of specified groups; (2) experienced; and (3) able persons; and (4) seemingly well-known personally to the voters.

1. The female candidates of the constituency campaigned for women voters only, but in only one case did a man appeal to the men of Northern Häme. But many other groups of voters were designated. The ultimate example of this was the activity of the Social Democratic Opposition. It had nominated, in addition to the general candidate of Northern Häme: candidates for women; rural small farming and wage-earning population; Karelian displaced persons; labor union members; small farmers; textile workers; career women and those active in sports; the population earning its living from agriculture; wood and paper workers; sportsmen; retail workers and housewives; and the white collar employees and sporting youth.[17]

Candidates for the displaced Karelians were nominated by other parties as well. Special groups aimed at in the publicity of the FPDU candidates were, for example: the small farmers and the rural working population; the progressive intelligentsia; young voters; shoemakers; and forest workers. The Conservative candidates turned their advertising toward the agricultural population; the youth; the church-going population;

17. The definitions are quoted from a party pamphlet, but they were also used in joint newspaper advertising.

small entrepreneurs, savers, taxpayers and home builders; the peasantry; busy and happy people; the middle class; and professional and business people. T. A. Wiherheimo (Conservative M.P.) was the only one to appeal to the Swedish-speaking inhabitants of Tampere.[18] The candidates of the SDP said they represented, for example, the working class. The FPP candidates named the middle classes. Most candidates of the FPP and Conservatives did not name any particular group of voters.

There were different ways of connecting the name of the party to an individual's campaign. The party was always visible in the advertisements of the Agrarian and the FPP candidates, but the Conservative candidates began to mention their party only during the last two of the campaign weeks. Mr. Wiherheimo never mentioned his party. The candidates of the Independent Social Democratic electoral alliance always advertised themselves as Social Democrats, thus indicating an attempt to gather their votes from the ranks of the permanent supporters of the SDP. Some Conservative candidates may have been seeking personal support from outside their own party.

The candidates hoped to succeed over a wide area, because they rarely emphasized local interests. However, the Agrarian candidates appealed mainly to the rural population. Many other candidates did mention their place of residence, but there seemed to be only two examples of an attempt to localize support. The Communist, Jalo Lepola, campaigned as the candidate for the Northeastern corner of the constituency, and the Conservative, Toivo Hietala, was mentioned several times as a "real Tampere man."

2. Those candidates who already had been in Parliament reminded people of their legislative experience and used the title, Member of Parliament. Experience has proved that incumbents hold a favorable position among the candidates.[19] The campaign also emphasized other public positions held by the candidates (a few were ministers and many held municipal trusteeships). Emphasis was put on leading positions in private associations and organizations, as well as on sports performance, decoration for bravery during the war, etc. In general, a legislative career begins only after a variety of other meritorious accomplishments.[20]

18. Between June 13 and July 4, 1958, the *Tammerfors Aftonblad* had six advertisements of Wiherheimo's electoral association and, in addition, published the declaration of the local branch of the Swedish People's Party about his nomination as the Swedes' candidate in Tampere.

19. Noponen, *Social Background*, pp. 73–75, 277–90.

20. Noponen and Pesonen, "The Legislative Career in Finland," in Erik Allardt and

3. In addition to their accomplishments, the candidates presented their potential: the lists of candidates included able, balanced, responsible, brave, honest, efficient, loyal, straight-backed, and good men. Suitable training and expertness in some certain field were also displayed as qualifications which were to be desired for the representation of specific groups.

4. A description of the candidate's family and home is not typical of Finnish election campaigns. But the personal characteristics of the candidates are often presented, and photographs are an essential part of candidate propaganda. In 1958, they were used in posters, and many a newspaper advertisement contained nothing but the name, picture, party, and list number of the candidate. It has been shown in England that photographs of party leaders are an essential means of creating favorable images, even of the parties, and not just of the individual candidates themselves, because voters tend to personify their party.[21] A local attempt to get close to the electorate in Tampere was, among others, the slogan used by the FPP candidate Antti Linna: *Yours and Mine = Our Man.*

Specific individual legislative goals were so few that it seems unnecessary to include them as the fifth point of the above list. Many legislative demands were printed in the advertisements of FPDU candidates, but they were direct quotations from the party platform. Other candidates, too, appropriate ideas from the platform of their party for their own campaign. In addition, very general goals were mentioned, such as retaining the mutual trust of citizens, bringing the rural population and wage-earners closer to each other, or "achieving a change in the disastrous governmental and economic policy." Also, candidates might promise to further some promotional activity, such as, temperance, youth, and adult educational work. Few economic reforms were proposed which were not included in the party platforms.

We can conclude that the candidates' individual goals for legislative work were closely connected with the general line of their party, and that, on the whole, the candidates were presented to the electorate as experienced, able, and trustworthy persons, who knew well the problems of a certain group of voters.

Yrjö Littunen, ed., *Cleavages, Ideologies and Party Systems* (Transactions of the Westermarck Society, Vol. X, Turku, 1964), pp. 452–58.

21. Mark Abrams, "Party Politics after the End of Ideology," in Allardt and Littunen, *Cleavages,* pp. 60–61.

One technique which all parties used was the distribution of posters and the publication of corresponding advertisements, presenting the entire group of thirteen candidates nominated by the party. Among the characteristics typical of specific parties, on the other hand, we might mention the uniformity in the advertising of all the FPDU candidates. They and especially the SDP candidates, received plenty of publicity in the newspaper announcements of their coming speeches. And while the Conservative candidates advertised a great deal in papers, their advertisements were quite unlike each other. The candidates of the Independent Social Democratic electoral alliance and of the Finnish People's Party used mainly letters, pamphlets, and posters.

TABLE 8.5. Attention Paid to the Campaign Material of Individual Candidates (Electors' Associations) in Tampere, 1958

Candidate	Party	Number of posters on the main street	Per cent recalling poster	Per cent receiving pamphlet	Per cent receiving letter	Per cent experiencing any one of three
Aarre Simonen	S.D. Opp.	71	24	24	26	50
Antti Linna	FPP	63	17	5	7	22
T. A. Wiherheimo	Cons.	90	8	4	2	11
Arvo Tuominen	SDP	34	5	2	2	7
Kaisa Hiilelä	S.D. Opp.	85	5	0	1	6
Sulo Typpö	SDP	135	4	0	0	5
Artturi Tienari	Cons.	4	3	2	2	5
Toivo Hietala	Cons.	–	2	3	1	5
Leo Suonpää	FPDU	108	4	–	0	4
Elli Stenberg	FPDU	104	2	0	–	2
Valdemar Liljeström	S.D. Opp.	62	1	1	1	2

Because of the large differences in the quantity and quality of candidate advertising, we might presume that the citizens also perceived differences in the presentation of the candidates. Table 8.5 summarizes the percentages of the sample who remembered seeing the poster and receiving the pamphlets or letter of eleven candidates (QQ. 44.D and 66.A-B). These were the only candidates whose material was recalled by at least one out of fifty persons at the time of the second interview.

Aarre Simonen's propaganda had been noticed the most. His posters, pamphlets, and letters were mentioned by one quarter of the sample and one half remembered at least one of the three kinds of material. In 1958, Mr. Simonen was a widely advertised and debated person; he was also the only candidate whose opponents printed a pamphlet aimed at creating a negative image. The posters of Antti Linna, the leading candidate of the Finnish People's Party, were also well remembered, but his other material did not reach as many persons.

Table 8.5 shows the number of posters distributed on the main street of Tampere. These figures also indicate roughly the relative numbers of posters in the whole city.

When the number of posters is compared to how well they were remembered, the two factors seem unrelated. Actually the respondents did not mention many candidates whose posters were numerous on that street.[22] Obviously the citizens remembered best the material of the candidates who were already well known. Some even mentioned a candidate whose name and picture had been printed only on the general party poster. Obviously those means of campaigning that were mentioned in Table 8.5—and in addition, for instance, newspaper advertising—are not perceived as separate sources of political material when they attempt simultaneously to influence people. It is even more difficult to distinguish between them in the later recollections about the campaign. But it is also obvious that many of the objects of the campaign remembered best the advertising of those candidates who had been "the talk of the day" before the election.

INTERPERSONAL DISCUSSIONS ABOUT THE ELECTION

The final aspect of the content of the campaign at the grass roots level depends, in a way, on the discussions of the various small groups. No less than 70 per cent of the Tampere sample mentioned having discussed the election with other people. Two Conservative respondents referred to their discussions in "internal party meetings," but, in general, such discussions were "everyday talks" at home, among friends, and at the place of work. The distribution of the main environments for such campaign discussions was as follows:

22. Among others, the following candidates had posters on the main street: Saima Kankare (SDP, 135 posters), Erkki Nieminen (FPDU, 116), Erkki Puustinen (SDP, 100), Anna Flinck (SDP, 99), and Väinö Virtanen (FPDU, 84).

| | Percentage of: | | |
	Men	Women	Total
In the family	8	25	18
Among friends	8	17	13
On the job	57	22	36
No discussion, don't know	27	36	33
	100	100	100

Men had discussed the election mainly with their co-workers, and women, more in the family and with friends.[23]

According to the responses, it is obvious that the main themes of the campaign were often repeated in the discussions of the electorate about the election. Let us mention a few responses which support this:

> I had a quarrel with an FPDU voter who said that if I don't vote I'll starve to death. A good talker, I won that argument. (Printer, male, 28, nonvoter)

> The Social Democrat wanted more factories and the others said where do you get the money to construct those factories. The People's Democrats said there are no possibilities for getting loans to workers. (Construction worker, male, 40, FPDU)

> I remember a discussion at home about the pros and cons of children's allowances. (Locomotive fireman, 33, FPDU)

> Because everything goes all wrong. Money is wasted too much on all kinds of subsidies and other such things. (Machine operator, male, 24, Conservative)

Although the approaching election may have activated political discussions in general, the subject matter reverted often to the normal topics which people were accustomed to discussing before the campaign:

> When talking things over towards the evening, we discussed the earlier Pekkala cabinet, how it almost ran everything down. (Carpenter, male, 26, SDP)

> What I remember was the blaming of the Agrarian Union. (Widow, 60, Conservative)

> My friend said that should Jesus come, then she would vote for him. At home my religious daughter and I figured that we wouldn't vote. (Dressmaker, female, 63, nonvoter).

23. $\chi^2 = 69.678$, $v = 3$, $p < 0.001$.

It is true, however, that the events of the campaign opened many discussions, and the campaign itself was then also a frequent topic:

> Our family used to have such discussions when we listened to the
> election debate on the radio. (Shoeworker, female, 41, SDP)

> He told about a campaign meeting which gathered only a handful of
> people, and even he didn't want to stay there. (Textile worker, fe-
> male, 55, S.D. Opp.)

> We were blaming the Communists and we suspected that all Com-
> munists will vote. We were talking about the posters on the Häme
> Bridge, especially the Communist poster referring to American race
> riots. It was next to the Social Democratic poster—an arrow pointed
> to the other and it stated that 'did you forget Hungary?' It was one
> of the best there can be. (Molder, male, 21, FPP)

Two interesting aspects were connected especially with the approaching
election. The citizens began to evaluate the candidates nominated by the
parties:

> Yes, I remember one discussion criticizing the bustle of Simonen and
> that Opposition group in general. (Inspector, male, 47, Conservative)

> At my job the men talked almost every day and praised Hertta
> Kuusinen. (Factory worker, female, 52, nonvoter)

And secondly, guesses were hazarded as to how the different parties would
succeed in this election:

> There was some small betting, one forecast that the Conservatives
> win and the other that the Agrarians will win votes and the Social
> Democrats will lose. (Housewife, 49, Conservative)

> I bet that the People's Democrats will win more than the Popular
> Center and I won my bet. There was talk at the plant. Although
> there were conflicting opinions, in bigger matters we were of the
> same opinion. The big fights take place higher up in the hierarchy.
> (Ironplate worker, male, 36, FPDU)

> We were just betting on the success of women candidates in our
> constituency. (Truck driver, male, 30, FPDU)

Persons who were engaged in discussions also thought about their own
voting behavior and tried to influence their friends. We shall return in
Chapter 10 to the effect of personal influence. Let us now first point out

that these discussions emphasized the "importance of the turnout percentage." Closely linked to this were those discussions in which like-minded persons strengthened each other's convictions.

> There were so many of those discussions, but the most important was that everybody has got to vote. That we urged the most. (Worker, male, 37, FPDU)
>
> There once were five farmers and five workers and our common opinion was that the FPDU must not lose a single seat, but it would need more, at least two seats, otherwise the life of the people would get worse. (Stone worker, male, 45, FPDU)
>
> I remember a discussion at work that we really should wake up the nonvoters. (Bank employee, female, 37, FPP)
>
> We talked on the job that otherwise we can't accomplish anything unless our party gains 67 seats, or one third. (Ironplate worker, male, 21, FPDU)

On the other hand, there was unwillingness to vote, which was connected with insecurity about party choice and the feeling of uselessness and alienation:

> Everybody was complaining that they don't know who to vote for, because everything is so quarrelsome. (Taxation clerk, female, 59, Conservative)
>
> Many said that they don't go to vote at all, because the Social Democratic Party is split, and they don't want to vote for the FPDU. (Factory worker, female, 42, SDP)
>
> A friend of mine said that when they get their well-paid job they forget all promises, and he didn't go to vote. (Park worker, female, 54, FPDU)
>
> Many were unaware of whether they should vote or not. There was more feeling of confusion than ever before. (Bookbinder, female, 54, SDP)

Finally, we might conclude that in many discussion circles the general climate of the 1958 election was perceived similarly, and that there was a rather general expectation of an FPDU success:

> I heard some talk that the FPDU gets many more votes, because there has been unemployment. (Widow, 61, SDP)

A few times I heard some unemployed say that I guess now the people know how to vote. (Metal worker, male, 47, FPDU)

In one discussion we really thought about the Communist victory, which we feared may come. (Division director, male, 37, FPP)

We have paid attention to the variety of topics that were dealt with when the citizens talked about the election. But differences existed also in the tone of the discussions. Some groups were conciliatory and made a deliberate attempt to avoid quarrels, but others carried on heated arguments.

We happened to talk about all sorts of things. Nothing very serious because we are not party people, in other words nothing. (Midwife, 51, Conservative)

I hardly touched on those matters. Everybody was so at odds that I didn't want to wrangle. (Bakery worker, female, 28, S.D. Opp.)

My brother demanded a vote for the FPDU and he got mad when we did not say so. (Housewife, 32, S.D. Opp.)

When it was asked in the interview, "Did you usually agree or disagree in the discussions?" (Q. 60.B) almost equally as many respondents gave both answers (43 and 40 per cent). Whether the discussion groups were likeminded or not was related to the milieu of the election discussions: the home, friendly groups, or working groups (Q. 60.A). There was most harmony within families and most disagreement at the places of work.[24]

THE COMPARISON GROUP

In some respects the campaign has the same content in both cities and rural communes. Radio programs are national, and the same material is distributed throughout the whole constituency. Yet the general tone of the campaign is different. The inhabitants of Korpilahti were exposed in 1958 to a different kind of campaigning than were people in Tampere, because:

1. Campaign speeches were more typical of the rural commune, but pamphlets and campaign letters more typical of the city (pp. 197–99).

2. The Agrarian Union, which had only been criticized in the city, was so central in Korpilahti that it organized more than one half of all

24. Per cent who "usually disagree" was: if discussed at home, $20(n = 85)$; among friends, $30(n = 63)$; among co-workers, $53(n = 173)$. $\chi^2 = 29.688$, $v = 4$, $p < 0.001$.

campaign meetings there (p. 197), and its press organ, *Keskisuomalainen,* occupied a dominant position, corresponding to the Conservative *Aamu-lehti* in Tampere (p. 56).

3. Four political parties had nominated their local candidates in Kor-pilahti to act in a focal way as representatives of their party in the com-mune.

4. The local circumstances were generally taken into account for cam-paign speeches, and often for the choice of material to be distributed as well.

The Agrarian speakers praised regularly the accomplishments of their party on behalf of agriculture and the countryside. To this they added criticism of other parties, whose candidates "circle around before the elec-tion fishing for rural votes," although they themselves keep away from the cities. Other useful topics were obtained from the concrete goals of the Agrarian platform. Two goals of the economic policy were stressed. The speakers explained that the butter problem was "due to anti-rural Popular Front, Conservatives, Socialists, and Communists voting too low protective tariffs on foreign fats." The other topic dealt with firewood. According to the speakers, the main cause of unemployment was the loss of markets for wood and chips because of coal and oil. This theme was also supported by one poster: *Prevent Unemployment—Tariffs on Foreign Fuel.*

The fourth central theme of Agrarian speakers was foreign policy. Here they were supported not only by the corresponding poster, but also by the content of *Keskisuomalainen.* It was the only newspaper, widely read in Korpilahti, which dealt much with foreign policy.[25] The basic idea of the paper and the speakers was that "the Paasikivi-Kekkonen line stands or falls together with the Agrarian Union."

The name of the FPDU was not as visible in Korpilahti as in Tampere. For instance, the outdoor advertising of the FPDU meetings referred more to the movies to be shown than to the election or the party. Even here the FPDU speeches criticized the economic policy of the past ten years, and the main reason for the difficulties was considered to be the capitalist economic system of the "20 families." Special emphasis was put on the

25. Paavo Hoikka counted 31 goals for the future in *Keskisuomalainen* between May 18 and July 7, 1958. Of these, 48 per cent dealt with foreign policy. In other papers read in Korpilahti, the percentage was considerably lower: *Hämeen Yhteistyö* 18 per cent (*n* = 93), *Jyväskylän Sanomat* 8 per cent (*n* = 47), and *Työn Voima* 4 per cent (*n* = 72); Hoikka, "Election Campaign, Rural Commune," pp. 55, 66.

merits of the People's Democrats as "savers" of children's allowances and old age insurance. The campaign movie of the FPDU, called "Good News," described those benefits which could be attained if the farmers joined skilled and unskilled workers in cooperation. The inhabitants of Korpilahti linked this message of the movie with the rumors they had heard about the Popular Front which, according to the observer, caused some confusion among Agrarian supporters.

The Finnish People's Party candidate, Antti Linna, deviated in his June speech from the central theme of Agrarian speakers when he spoke about leveling out the class differences, as he believed that the cleavage between cities and the country could be abolished. As elsewhere, the Conservative meetings in Korpilahti concentrated on economic policies. The central call was for "fixing the bankrupt condition of the state." Speakers of the Independent Social Democratic electoral alliance also limited themselves to topics dealing with economic policy, but mainly to criticize the present leadership of their mother party, which was "too close to the extreme Right." The central themes of the SDP platform, industrialization and the crisis of parliamentarism, were dealt with in those speeches which the candidates of the party gave in Korpilahti.

At the end of many meetings, the supporters of different parties began to debate politics. The Conservative supporters called the Finnish People's Party "a satellite of the Agrarians," but the supporters of the FPP did not want to be "satellites of the Conservatives." The Social Democrats and the People's Democrats may have first discussed economic policies, but they were bound to conclude with arguments about the upheaval in Hungary. When the Agrarian Union was criticized for failure, their speakers, in turn, criticized others for blackening the situation.

The topics and the tone of the campaign speeches fluctuated according to the audiences. Thus the Social Democrats spoke of social security and the significance of industry for the future of the country in the central church village, but in the remote places they talked more about foreign policy and about the importance of a high turnout in the election. The Agrarian speakers dealt with internal policies and the foreign policy of parties in the leftist village of Heinosniemi, but in Saukkola, a more remote place, they discussed forest work and the price of standing timber. A meeting of the FPDU in Moksi was concluded with the question raised by a farmer: "Do you promise to industrial workers the same benefits, a 10-penny rise in milk prices and the unconditional increase in subsidies to agriculture?"

Korpilahti was located far from the center of Northern Häme constituency, and many candidates did not speak there at all. Due to its location, a great deal of campaign material in the newspapers was irrelevant to the constituency. This was apparent in the text as well as in the advertising. The leading newspaper, *Keskisuomalainen,* was used primarily as the campaign media of the Eastern Vaasa constituency. During the last week of the election 54 per cent of all the advertising did not even concern the voters of Northern Häme constituency. The Conservative *Jyväskylän Sanomat* also had more advertising for the Eastern Vaasa constituency than for Northern Häme, although no less than one half of all the advertising in that paper was composed of such general Conservative advertisements as would be equally relevant in any constituency.

In order to measure roughly the trends in the political content of newspapers, we can use entire articles or news items as our units of measurement. The two above-mentioned newspapers published per issue the following number of articles praising their own party and criticizing other parties:

May 12 through June 8	*Keskisuo-malainen*	*Jyväskylän Sanomat*
Favorable articles about own party	1.5	1.0
Critical articles about other parties	0.4	0.7
June 9 through June 22		
Favorable articles about own party	2.5	2.1
Critical articles about other parties	1.2	0.6
June 23 through July 6		
Favorable articles about own party	12.5	7.9
Critical articles about other parties	1.6	2.4

The amount of criticism of other parties seems rather small because many critical statements were included in articles praising the party of the newspaper. But it might be a reason to conclude that *Jyväskylän Sanomat* began its campaign in June by increasing presentations of its own (Conservative) party. *Keskisuomalainen,* in turn, carried at the end of the campaign many separate small items about the Agrarian Union, and thus added essentially to the increasingly favorable presentation of the Agrarians.

A couple of observations are in order about the objects of the criticisms.

In both newspapers, we find changes again in those objects. *Keskisuomalainen* seems to have paid increasing attention to the Social Democratic Party. Of all critical articles in May and June, 36 per cent dealt with SDP, but in the following period it rose to 43 per cent, and finally to 59 per cent. During the last two weeks, two articles criticized both the Social Democrats and the Conservatives. *Jyväskylän Sanomat,* in turn, began to criticize just before the election "the planned Popular Front government." It was also new in this newspaper when, during the last weeks, two articles were devoted to the critique of the Finnish People's Party.

Keskisuomalainen did not publish Social Democratic advertising that would have balanced its critical articles about this party. The only exceptions were the presentations of a few SDP candidates of the Eastern Vaasa constituency, whose personal advertising looked similar to that of the Independent Social Democratic electoral alliance in the Northern Häme constituency, and who did enter the Opposition group in Parliament after the election when the SDP group was split.

According to our data on the amount of how much candidate propaganda was remembered in Korpilahti (not shown), there had been efficient distribution of pamphlets and letters only on behalf of the candidates of the Independent Social Democrats, and therefore, as in Tampere, Simonen was the most noticed candidate. However, three of the five local candidates ranked before him with their outdoor posters.

The candidates and their chances were one of the central topics when rural people began to discuss the election:

> I talked with my neighbor. He was a hot People's Democrat. We discussed the chances of the candidate Lepola to get elected. (Farmer, forest worker, 34, Agrarian)

> In Agrarian circles we talked that we shouldn't vote for Pakkanen. He gets enough votes otherwise, too. (Teacher, female, 32, Agrarian)

Also, the general outcome of the election campaign themes and the usual political topics were discussed in Korpilahti, as in Tampere:

> Jussi said the Agrarian Union will win, but I said that is hardly so. (Small farmer, 65, Conservative)

> After the speech of Kivimäki we argued with the Left Wing about ownership of native margarine industry. (Farmer, 28, Agrarian)

One worker said about the price of milk that 'now remember who you vote for'. (Wife of unskilled worker, 30, FPDU)

Yes, they try to bring some light to us, the Communists try to talk heatedly, but I remember more the discussions about religious matters. The tent of Jehova's witnesses will appear here. Some people maintain that now the Communists begin to take care of their own interests only and don't understand the good of everybody. I wish they wouldn't quarrel and be fanatical. (Farm laborer, female, 55, S.D. Opp.)

Some people used to joke about the election:

The only thing is that I teased other old women that I will cast my ballot for my old sweetheart. (Washer, female, 47, FPDU)

I was asking what everybody now promised. And with a neighboring farmer we talked about Ryömä. He said that now Ryömä also took a doctor's job, he probably was afraid that he would be kicked out of the Parliament when the FPDU loses the election. I said that he started his medical career because there is so much to be fixed in the Conservatives after they get shocked by the election outcome. (Small farmer, 30, FPDU)

According to the responses, it also seems that the 1958 campaign was perceived as more moderate than the earlier ones, and that there existed a great deal of unwillingness to vote:

Because no one even breathed about it, it was like there wouldn't be any election. (Farmer's wife, 61, nonvoter)

Ordinarily they have tried to urge me toward just about every direction. This year no one came to talk such nonsense. (Salesman, 27, FPDU)

The neighboring farmer said that he doesn't go to vote, because there is no such list. Actually one should vote for the losing side to keep up the balance. (Wife of a farmer, 34, Agrarian)

The rural people were engaged in discussions about the election: for example, "at the mill with the miller"; "when neighbors assembled in the evening"; when "visiting the town"; and "in places where more men gathered". The primary groups of such discussions were distributed as follows:

	Percentage of:		
	Men	Women	Total
In the family	13	20	16
With friends	35	26	31
On the job	21	6	14
No discussion, don't remember	31	48	39
	100	100	100
Number of cases	*48*	*46*	*94*

There was an equal amount of discussion of the election among the men, but women discussed it less in Korpilahti than in Tampere. Even the comparison group shows that men discussed more at their place of work, but women more with their husband and other family members. Because of the predominant type of work, there was in general more discussion with friends in Korpilahti and more with workmates in Tampere. Let us finally mention about the tone of the discussions that with friends and at work people were equally often in like-minded and different-minded discussion groups. But within the family, mainly similar opinions were exchanged.[26] This was the case in Tampere too.

Summary

Attention has been paid here to the content that filled the frame of the 1958 election campaign. We have (1) described the topics used in the campaign; (2) compared the campaign with the preceding normal political communication; and (3) compared the city with the rural commune.

1. The campaign debate dealt more with economic policy than with anything else. The starting point was dissatisfaction and the accusation of others, although there was no uniform opinion among the parties as to which ones belonged to the opposition. Only the Agrarian Union was considered by all to be politically responsible. This was the only party whose propaganda emphasized the positive aspects of recent policies. When other parties proposed new goals for economic policy, the Agrarian Union occupied the role of "the defender of the countryside."

Discussions concerning internal policy dealt with the way the cabinet had been formed, and with the possible cooperation of the FPDU in the cabinets. These topics included discussions about "the Popular Front

26. In two subgroups, those discussing with friends and on the job, the distribution was as follows: agreed 38 per cent, disagreed 38 per cent, don't know 24 per cent ($n = 29$ and $n = 13$); of those discussing in the family, only 27 per cent ($n = 15$) disagreed.

tactic." Foreign policy was also drawn into the debate, and other current items were unemployment, industrialization, and Communism. Some considered the 1958 campaign unusually moderate. This might have been related to the so-called campaign truce agreement of the four nonsocialist parties.

Some parties named in their campaign platforms the groups whose support they sought. But it was even more typical for individual candidates to appeal to particular groups of voters. Individual campaigning also presented the merits and potentialities of the candidates, but it did not refer much to personal legislative goals. In the lively final stage of the campaign, individual advertising occupied the largest proportion. However, the population exposed to it did not perceive or remember many details of this campaign.

2. Increasing praise of one's own party and criticism of others is a feature typically added to the normal political content of the press by the campaign. The same is true of writing about the campaign itself and of the intense urging to action at the end of the campaign.

A quantitative analysis of the changes which occurred in the content of the newspapers after the actual campaign phase had started involved mainly the examination of three Tampere papers. The analysis considered the papers as a whole and comprised editorials, news items on speeches, and campaign advertising. Criticism of other parties got livelier before the election and simultaneously the direction of the critique tended to change. Generally, the political rivals closest to the party of the newspaper now became its main competitors. Such changes in emphasis may have been determined by the tactical aims of the party. The anti-Communist or antiright wing attitude was apparently considered so obvious by some that, in order to criticize another party, it was enough to blame it for cooperation with the FPDU or with the right wing. Changes in the direction of the criticisms seem to support the basic hypothesis of this study, according to which a campaign turns the attention of political powers temporarily to the electorate. Thus the obvious main campaign tactic is to emphasize the differences between one's own party and its close rival.

In addition, the quantitative analysis showed that general and party-bound changes appeared in the critical statements about other parties. Positive statements about one's own party changed as well: *Hämeen Yhteistyö* and *Aamulehti* concentrated their themes, but *Kansan Lehti* diversified even more than earlier. Dealing with selected items of political debate also became noticeably livelier and began to acquire the special label of the campaign.

3. The local campaigning in Tampere, in comparison with that conducted in the capital city, showed an obviously sharper treatment of Communism and its brutal behavior. There were also many differences between Tampere and Korpilahti. Because of the political effect of the Agrarian Union's being the strongest party there, the local conditions in the rural commune differed from those in the city. An organized campaign was brought closer to the inhabitants of the rural commune than to those of the city. Moreover, the local candidates gave a very special flavor to the campaign in their rural commune. There were only four candidates in the constituency whose personal propaganda was remembered both in the city and in the rural commune. These were Simonen (Soc. Dem. Opposition) and Linna (FPP), and, to a lesser extent, Arvo Tuominen (SDP) and Kaisa Hiilelä (Soc. Dem. Opposition). In Korpilahti, people paid most attention to the posters of their local candidates.

Campaign speeches in the rural commune were aimed at rural people. Agricultural policy was thus the focal theme, but the Agrarian Union's emphasis on foreign policy there made it the second main topic of the campaign. Which party was justified in "fishing for rural votes" was also a topic of discussion.

In a way, the campaign was given its final content by those discussions which the electorate carried on about campaign themes, their own participation, the outcome of the election, and the campaign in general. Many seemed to expect a Communist victory. Certain discussions revealed an exceptional uncertainty and lack of desire to vote. Perhaps this was related to the "feeling of confusion" which was said to be "in the air."

9. Participation in the Election

The Finnish electorate numbered 80,000 more persons in July 1958 than it had in March 1954, yet 65,000 fewer voters went to the polls. The national turnout was 75 per cent of the enfranchised citizenry.

However, the 1954 turnout of 79.9 per cent had set a new record, and furthermore the proportion of the electorate to cast their ballots has been almost always smaller in summer than in winter elections, administered in October or January through May. In the February 1962 parliamentary election, 85.1 per cent of the qualified Finns participated.

In Tampere, in 1958, ballots were cast by 59,480 persons, or 77.6 per cent of the inhabitants entitled to vote (82.4 per cent of the men, 73.9 per cent of the women). Here, too, the previous turnout had been higher (82.3 per cent). Korpilahti's turnout in 1958 was 74.8 per cent (79.6 per cent of the men, 70.1 per cent of the women).

In this chapter, observations on electoral participation are not limited to the citizens' official act of voting, but include such other participation as the electorate's attention to the campaign and their actual campaign activities (see Chapter 7). The timing of two other aspects of voting behavior is interesting to note. First, it is important to know when the voting decisions that are finally confirmed at the polls take place, and, secondly, since the polling stations in Finland are kept open for two days, one might observe the time when different voters choose to exercise their franchise.

PARTICIPATION

Among the postelection interviewees, 88.0 per cent reported that they had participated in the election. There was some (2.3 per cent) discrepancy, however, between this report and actual voting behavior as recorded in the registers of the respective election boards. Also, relatively more voters than nonvoters were interviewed in the study. The corrected turnout percentages are as follows:

Re-interviewed (July) sample	85.7 $(n = 476)$
May sample	84.0 $(n = 501)$
Whole sample entitled to vote	81.0 $(n = 574)$
Original sample	79.8 $(n = 583)$

The "whole sample entitled to vote" excludes those cases from the original sample who were deceased or who had permanently immigrated, but whose names remained in the official register. They, of course, count as nonvoters. Therefore, the official statistics give turnout percentages which are slightly lower than the actual ones.

On the other hand, let us note that (a) most turnout figures in the following presentation are likely to be higher than those of the universe of the study, which still does not prevent a comparison of voters and nonvoters; and (b) the first interview itself may have increased interest in the election enough to add a couple of percentage points to the turnout of the sample.[1]

Activity According to the Two Interviews

We have shown previously that in July 1958 many persons followed their former practice of either voting or remaining nonvoters (p. 65). We find also that most persons correctly anticipated in May whether or not they would vote in July (see Table 4.10). Of persons who definitely intended to vote, 89 per cent ($n = 345$) actually turned out at the polls, as compared with 29 per cent ($n = 31$) of those who had decided not to vote. And 57 per cent ($n = 21$) of the persons who still felt uncertain in May actually voted in July. Therefore, it seems that the intention to participate was dropped less often than was the intention to abstain. Unwillingness to vote was so rare in May that this activation phenomenon does not much alter the general conclusion that promises to vote were easier to make than to keep. Among the sample, 94 per cent intended to vote while only 84 per cent voted.

Because persons who were interested in politics were the most likely to give these promises (p. 84), it is now reasonable to assume that the normal interest expressed in May had a decided impact on the turnout in July.

Table 9.1 presents data on the normal interest of voters and nonvoters. Every comparison within the total sample corresponds to our expectations, usually very significantly. In May the July voters had been more interested,

---

1. The turnout percentages of the original sample and the universe of the study differed 3.2 percentage units, or more than the standard error of the turnout of the sample (1.66). It is possible that some wasted extracts from the register of voters are raising the corrected turnout of the sample (because all persons obtaining such an extract had to be considered voters, whether they actually did or did not cast an absentee ballot). However, a slight activating effect seems the natural explanation for part of the difference.

TABLE 9.1. Relationship of July Voting and Nonvoting in Tampere to Interest in Politics Revealed in May, and to Earlier Voting Participation (in percentages)†

	Total		Men		Women	
	Voters	Non-voters	Voters	Non-voters	Voters	Non-voters
Estimated themselves very or rather interested in politics	32	15***	45	38	21	4***
High exposure (scale values 4 or 5) to political mass communication	36	15***	47	27*	27	9***
Good knowledge of politics (scale values 3 or 4)	25	15*	41	15**	14	15
Willing to give reasons for their opinions (scale values 3 or 4)	51	27***	47	38	54	22***
Party members	12	4***	19	8°	7	2*
Recalled participation in all previous elections	82	55***	84	62*	79	51***
Number of cases	421	80	179	26	242	54

† The level of significance for each difference is given in the table as denoted in Table 4.1. The two youngest age groups do not affect percentages of previous voting.

better informed, more willing to give reasons for their opinions, and more active in party organizations than the nonvoters. The intention to vote thus endured through the campaign. Generally these differences also prevailed separately between the sexes. However, self-estimated interest apparently predicted the participation of females better, while knowledge about politics was more related to the participation of males.

Table 9.1 also repeats the above-mentioned finding that former voters were more likely to cast a ballot in 1958 than former nonvoters. Consequently, the official electoral participation of 1958 correlated with both the earlier official participation and with the normal, informal participation.

In Chapter 7 (Table 7.5) we presented some forms of that political participation which are made possible by the election campaign. It now seems reasonable to assume that: (1) the various forms of informal campaign activity were sufficiently interrelated to justify the expression, interest in the election;[2] (2) normal interest in politics also continued as

2. For data on mutual correlations of various forms of active behavior during a campaign, see Berelson, Lazarsfeld, and McPhee, *Voting*, pp. 241–42; Lazarsfeld, Berelson, and Gaudet, *The People's Choice*, pp. 41–42, 79–80; Pesonen, *Student Voters*, pp. 122–25, 135.

interest in the election;[3] and furthermore, (3) the persons most interested informally in the election were the most likely to take the formal role of voters in it.[4]

1. Figure 9.A shows one example of the many positive correlations

FIGURE 9.A. Relationship of Exposure to Campaign Articles in the Newspapers to Number of Recalled Party Posters (QQ. 64.B and 44.A) (in percentages)

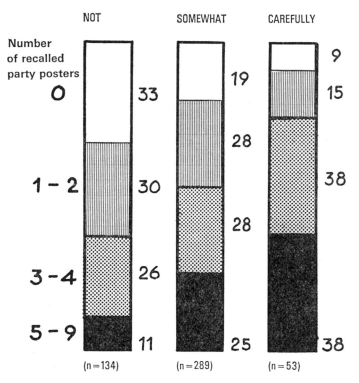

3. The panel method is essential in studies of these relationships. For previous data, see Benney, Gray, and Pear, *How People Vote*, pp. 157, 161, 165–66; Berelson, Lazarsfeld, and McPhee, *Voting*, p. 243; Morris Janowitz and Dwaine Marvick, *Competitive Pressure and Democratic Consent* (Ann Arbor, The University of Michigan, 1956), pp. 20, 62–64; Korchin, *Psychological Variables*, p. 160; Lazarsfeld, Berelson, and Gaudet, *The People's Choice*, pp. 41–42, 79–80, 95, 167; Pesonen, *Student Voters*, pp. 140–147.

4. In many scales and indexes which have been formed in order to measure interest in the election or campaign activity, the easiest qualification has been participation in the election. See for example Campbell, Gurin, and Miller, *The Voter Decides*, pp. 30–31; Milbrath, *Political Participation*, p. 51; Pesonen, *Student Voters*, pp. 147, 219.

among the various forms of exposure to campaign communication. We find that the more carefully people read the campaign content of their newspapers, the more posters they noticed.[5] Although some persons who did not care about the election articles paid attention to party posters, in general the persons exposed to one were likely to have been exposed to both propaganda media.

TABLE 9.2. Relationship of Exposure to (a) the Presentation of Parties on Radio, and (b) Campaign Advertisements in Newspapers to Other Campaign Activity (in percentages)†

| | (a) Radio presentations of parties | | (b) Campaign advertisements | |
	Yes	No	Yes	No
Remembered a party poster	85	75**	80	75
Remembered a candidate's poster	56	49	56	44*
Listened to neutral election program on the radio	52	16***	32	23*
Listened to the great election debate	68	38***	52	43°
Read articles on the election in newspapers	78	69*	85	49***
Received campaign pamphlets	88	84	86	85
Went to a campaign meeting	11	6*	7	9
Number of cases	170	306	305	171

† The level of significance for each difference is given in the table as denoted in Table 4.1.

Table 9.2 presents more corresponding interview data. We do find that some people are specific radio listeners and others newspaper readers. Yet frequent listeners to election broadcasts also showed an above average interest in the campaign content of the newspapers, while the persons exposed to campaign advertisements had a tendency to listen to the election programs on the radio. Even more generally, this table shows differences in the expected direction. The only exception shows that attendance of campaign meetings bore no relationship to looking at advertisements. And pamphlets were, of course, distributed in mail boxes regardless of the receivers' exposure to other campaign propaganda.

2. Interest in the campaign was a consistent extension of the preceding normal interest in politics. This can be seen, for example, if the self-estimate is used as a measure of normal interest. According to Appendix Ta-

5. $\chi^2 = 15.16$, $v = 6$, $p < 0.02$.

ble 17, the higher the population estimated their interest in May, the more they were exposed during the campaign to posters, newspapers, and political radio programs. The very interested especially also liked to hear campaign speeches and to do campaign work for their party, while the little or not interested discussed the election less than the others did. Thus, the self-estimate predicted both the turnout and actual unofficial campaign activity.[6]

TABLE 9.3. Relationship of Voting and Nonvoting to Campaign Activity in Tampere, 1958 (in percentages)†

	Total		Men		Women	
	Voters	Non-voters	Voters	Non-voters	Voters	Non-voters
Worked for his party	13	4**	16	14	9	–*
Knew a campaign worker	21	16	27	36	17	7*
Discussed the election	69	60	72	82	66	50*
Remembered four or more party posters	54	38*	68	64	44	26***
Identified one poster or more	80	68*	86	82	76	61*
Remembered the poster of at least one candidate	53	43	62	55	47	37
Received pamphlets	86	84	82	86	88	83
Listened to the entire election debate on radio	17	9*	19	14	15	7°
Listened to the presentation of some party	37	28	35	36	39	24*
Read carefully election articles in newspapers	13	3***	18	9	8	–*
Looked often at campaign advertisements	26	13**	27	23	25	9***
Went to a campaign meeting	9	1***	11	–*	7	2°
Listened to election results past midnight	14	9	15	9	13	9
Number of cases	*408*	*68*	*176*	*22*	*232*	*46*

† The level of significance for each difference is given in the table as denoted in Table 4.1.

3. Finally, Table 9.3 presents comparative data on the unofficial campaign activity of voters and nonvoters. Within the whole sample, the differences are again in line with the expectations. Those who attended a campaign meeting were very likely to vote. Also, the voters had paid more attention than the nonvoters to posters, radio programs, and the

6. The Finnish student study showed also this relationship between self-estimated interest in politics and later campaign activity; Pesonen, *Student Voters,* pp. 146–47.

campaign content of newspapers. Some differences, however, do not reach statistical significance, and a few might be considered surprisingly small. This is especially true of the men. Their voting seemed to bear little relationship to their looking at posters, listening to the radio, discussing the election, or even to active campaign work. However, the small number of male nonvoters in the sample warns against daring conclusions. Moreover, it is possible that the differences might have been larger in a winter election. Possibly the season of summer vacations affected some expressions of the potentially higher interest in the campaigning among the voters.

The special character of the campaign period differentiates the electoral interest from normal political interest, and the coverage of legislation defines official political participation separately from the unofficial one. We thus have four conceptually different categories of citizen participation in politics. Three of these four were discussed above. But obviously a high interest in any area reflects the same basic characteristic—a general interest in politics.

A Comparative Study

In addition to interviewing people, there are other means of discerning relationships between turnout and other political activity. When the names of those people whose political activity differs interestingly from that of others are known, one can also make certain whether or not they have voted. All addresses, essential for determining the voting districts, are filed with the city police, and, after the election, the registers of the voting districts reveal who voted (or obtained an absentee ballot).

Thus, in order to supplement the interview data, we verified the turnout of these 1,765 inhabitants of Tampere who had played an official role in the nominations by signing some list of candidate, and of these 448 persons who were in a position of high normal, unofficial activity as chairmen or secretaries of local political associations.[7] The turnout percentages were as follows:

7. The material for the comparative study was collected as follows: (1) from the register of associations, kept by the Ministry of Justice, was obtained a list of all political associations headquartered in Tampere; (2) the last announced chairmen and secretaries were marked down; (3) the names and occupations of all signers of the candidates' petitions residing in Tampere were copied; and (4) the address files of the city police provided the address and the voting district of each person (some party office holders had moved away from the city, and a few persons had to be excluded because other persons had the same name; however, the occupation generally helped to find the correct person from that register); (5) because the register was derived from the situation on January 1, 1957, many married women could be found only from a separate register of marriages

94.8 per cent of the persons who had signed a list of candidate but did not hold important party office participated. The turnout of male signers was 96.3 per cent ($n = 819$) and of females 93.2 per cent ($n = 844$). As for the signers' spouses, 93.0 per cent ($n = 718$) of the wives and 95.2 per cent ($n = 519$) of the husbands voted.

98.5 per cent ($n = 346$) of those local party leaders who had not signed a list of candidate voted.

100 per cent ($n = 102$) of the persons who were both signers and important office holders participated in the election.

Furthermore, all the candidates with a residence in Tampere and their spouses voted. Also, among the voters were the Helsinki candidates of the Northern Häme constituency.[8]

This information provides us with three conclusions which confirm our survey findings: (1) the turnout of each of the politically active groups was well above the average for the city; (2) those highly motivated persons who qualified for both groups turned out most frequently; and (3) the greater interest of men than women was obvious even at this high level of political activity; it can be seen that women signers actually voted with a lower frequency than their nonsigning husbands. An additional finding shows that a signature in a candidate's petition does not necessarily prove that the person will definitely vote. The official role of a signer is actually a less reliable indication of true voting participation than is a focal attachment to a political association.

The importance of party organization can also be observed indirectly if the turnout figures are counted separately for the signers of each party's lists of candidates. Included are only those signers who were residents of Tampere. Their turnout was the following:

	Total	Percentage of: Men	Women
FPDU	98.6	99.2 ($n = 245$)	98.1 ($n = 262$)
Conservatives	96.6	100.0 ($n = 105$)	94.8 ($n = 191$)
SDP	95.6	97.9 ($n = 140$)	92.6 ($n = 108$)
FPP	92.8	95.0 ($n = 180$)	90.3 ($n = 155$)
S.D. Opp.	89.7	90.8 ($n = 120$)	88.5 ($n = 104$)
Popular Center	76.9	82.8 ($n = 29$)	69.6 ($n = 23$)

and deaths; (6) the next step was to check for each person, whether or not he had voted (the poll books gave additional information about the sex, marital status, occupation, spouse's occupation, and place and time of birth); (7) furthermore, for every married person in this study, information was also obtained concerning the participation of the spouse.

8. The method described above was used to check the participation of candidates residing in Tampere and in Helsinki.

We find that the official supporters of those three parties, whose supporters were the most organized and the most involved in campaign work (pp. 48, 176), were most apt to turn up at the polling places. Obviously the well-rooted and highly institutionalized party organizations found the necessary signers easily within organizational ranks. The FPP may have had more difficulty, whereas the Social Democratic Opposition, which had to create a campaign organization at the last moment, apparently collected any signatures they could get. Evidently the petitions of the Popular Center were simply forgotten by their signers, since the official supporters of this new party did not turn out with any more frequency than the rest of the Tampere electorate.

THE TIME OF VOTING DECISION

Participation in an election and the choice of one party, rather than one of its rivals, are analytically different concepts, but they are inseparably interlinked in actual behavior. Obviously, a preference is needed for participation. Only the time of the choice varies greatly.

Without yet considering the content of the final choice, we can here observe how the time of party choice was related to the respondents' participation potential, that is, to both their interest and their actual voting turnout. Certain previously mentioned findings lead us to presume that an early awareness of preference was connected with high interest and high turnout.

There are two means of measuring the time of voting decision. The question can be asked directly in a post election interview,[9] or the development of voting intentions can be followed by repeated interviews of the same persons. The former method does not give wholly dependable information because the respondents' memory may be inaccurate; the latter is handicapped by the necessity to limit the number of successive interviews.

Both methods are used in this study, and both provide the same basic finding: most voters had made their decision before the campaign (see Figure 9.B). No less than 80 per cent of the voters of Tampere recalled that they knew at least by the beginning of the election year which party to support in July; only 15 per cent recalled having made a choice during the actual campaign. The panel method, in turn, revealed that 74 per cent of the voters had expressed an intention in May which was consistent with

9. For example, Campbell, Gurin, and Miller, *The Voter Decides*, pp. 18–20, and Campbell and Kahn, *People Elect a President*, pp. 9–12.

FIGURE 9.B. (a) The Recalled Time of Final Choice and (b) Relationship of Final Choice to Voting Intention in May 1958 (voters only) ($n = 386$)

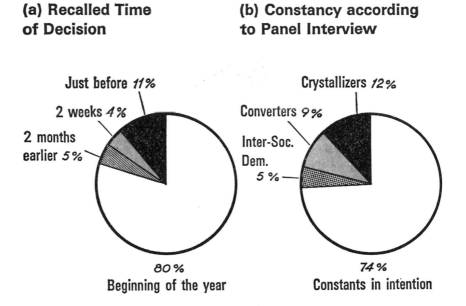

(a) Recalled Time of Decision

Just before *11%*

2 weeks *4%*

2 months earlier *5%*

80% Beginning of the year

(b) Constancy according to Panel Interview

Crystallizers *12%*

Converters *9%*

Inter-Soc. Dem. 5%

74% Constants in intention

their actual vote. The proportion rises to 79 per cent, if changes between the two Social Democratic wings are not considered party conversions. In that case only 9 per cent changed, while 12 per cent delayed their decision on either preference or participation beyond May.

Table 9.4 compares the information obtained through these two methods. Most voters belong to just one entry of this table, as 65 per cent were consistent in their intentions and also recalled a ready preference in the beginning of the year. Four additional observations summarize the remaining content of this table:

1. The panel method did not reveal all the changes which occurred between the first interview and the voting. Of those persons who voted as they had intended in May, 7 per cent recalled a final decision within the last two weeks of the campaign. Some actually said that they had temporarily intended to support another party but then returned to the party of their earlier preference.

2. Changing from one Social Democratic wing to the other obviously was not perceived as a party conversion.

3. On the other hand, the other party converters and those persons who

TABLE 9.4.   Relationship of Discovered Constancy in Voting Intention to Recalled
Time of Final Party Choice (July voters only) (in percentages)

Recalled time of decision	Constancy of voting intention				
	Con-stants	Inter-Soc. Dem.	Con-verters	Crystal-lizers	Total voters
Knew half a year earlier	87	83	51	49	79
A couple of months in advance	5	–	3	12	5
A couple of weeks in advance	3	11	17	2	4
Just before election	4	6	29	30	10
No information	1	–	–	7	2
Total	100	100	100	100	100
Number of cases	*287*	*18*	*35*	*43*	*408*

Constants = Sure voting intention in May concurred with final choice.
Inter-Soc. Dem. = Conversions from SDP to opposition, and vice versa.
Converters = Sure intention in May, voted for another party in July.
Crystallizers = Voters who were uncertain in May about participation or party choice.

delayed their decision clearly differed from the two former groups of
voters; a good many more of them recalled a late decision.

4. Yet this table also demonstrates how unreliable such recollections
are, as one half of both types of changers believed that their decisions
had already been made in the beginning of the year.

Table 9.5 repeats some previous comparisons between voters and nonvoters with a further classification of the voters according to the time
of their final party choice. The measure is the recall, although it is inaccurate as stated above. We hypothesize that the largest differences are to
be found when the nonvoters are compared with the early deciders only,
and, consequently, that the late deciders are most reminiscent of the nonvoters. We can make the following observations:

1. Those voters who made an early decision really had been consistently
most interested in politics in May. It even seems that the two groups of
late deciders were closer to nonvoters than to those early deciders. This is
especially true of those who joined a party organization. But normal political interest was no longer related to just how late the choice was postponed.

2. Table 9.5.b corresponds to our expectations, too, but it differs from
the previous table in one respect. Those 1958 voters who postponed their

TABLE 9.5. Relationship of the Recalled Time of Party Choice and Nonvoting to (a) the Interest in Politics Revealed in May, (b) Earlier Voting Participation, and (c) Campaign Activity (in percentages)

	Half a year	2 weeks to 2 months	Just before	Nonvoters
(a) Normal interest				
Very or rather interested	35	19	22	15
High exposure to mass communi-				
cation	40	22	24	15
Knew that the election was due				
in July	69	56	54	46
Party members	15	3	2	4
*Number of cases**	*321*	*36*	*41*	*80*
(b) Earlier participation				
Recalled participation in all				
previous elections	83	85	74	55
(c) Campaign activity				
Worked for his party	12	14	7	4
Knew a campaign worker	25	22	12	16
Remembered four or more party				
posters	56	47	56	38
Identified one poster or more	83	83	63	68
Listened to the entire election				
debate on radio	17	25	10	9
Listened to the presentation of				
some party	38	34	32	28
Read carefully election articles of				
newspapers	12	17	12	3
Looked often at campaign				
advertisements	25	33	27	13
Went to a campaign meeting	10	6	–	1
Listened to election results past				
midnight	16	8	10	9

* The numbers of cases for Table (a) are given. The two youngest age groups are excluded from Table (b), and the nonvoters, who were not re-interviewed, from Table (c).

decision until very nearly election day were the same voters who had been inactive in earlier elections. Even so, their previous turnout had been higher than that of 1958 nonvoters.

3. As expected, the time of party choice correlated with campaign interest too. For example, the latest deciders were no more willing than nonvoters to do campaign work, attend campaign meetings, or listen to the

radio debate. And despite seeing numerous posters, they did not remember their message. After the ballot places were closed, only the very early deciders had a special interest in the outcome of the election. An obvious continuum is seen in the exposure to the presentations of parties—the later the decision occurred, the closer the interest level sank to that of nonvoters.

4. As far as newspaper reading is concerned, Table 9.5.c runs contrary to our expectations. The voters and nonvoters were different, but no difference of the expected kind existed between the early and the late deciding voters.

In general, however, we can conclude that nonvoting looks almost like an extreme case of a delayed decision. The more inactive the people were, the more they tended first to postpone their final party choice and then to give up voting entirely.

The Time of Casting a Ballot

Still another link can be attached to this chain of events. Because inactivity is related both to delayed decisions and to the tendency to abstain entirely, it would seem to follow that such inactive persons also "wake up" relatively late on polling days and cast their ballots after the more eager voters have already accomplished the task. This matter is of special interest in Finland, a country with the rare custom of two-day polling. An earlier study has pointed toward the tendency of the politically inactive persons to delay their participation as well as their decision, while they tend also toward a below average turnout.[10] Of course, the time of actual participation is not without interest in countries of one-day polling as well, for this still leaves the voter a period of several—as many as fifteen —hours to do his duty.[11]

Two methods can be used to study the time of casting a ballot: a direct question can be asked in a postelection survey, or alternatively, information on this kind of behavior can be obtained by observation.

10. Pesonen, *Student Voters*, pp. 142–44.

11. For example, in the United States the polling stations are kept open from four hours (minimum in rural Massachusetts) to fifteen hours (in Louisiana, when voting machines are used); Bertram M. Bernard, *Election Laws of the Forty-Eight States* (New York, Oceana Publications, 1950), pp. 86–87. In Great Britain, the voting stations are open during one day for fourteen hours (7 A.M. to 9 P.M.). The Soviet Union and Romania have a record long voting day, which lasts for eighteen hours (from 6 A.M. to midnight); Deutsches Institut für Rechtswissenschaft, *Das Wahlrecht der sozialistischen Staaten Europas* (Berlin, VEB Deutscher Zentralverlag, 1958), pp. 38, 250.

Interview Data

The recalled participation in Tampere was distributed as follows (Q. 51.A):

| | Percentage of: | | |
	Men	Women	Total
First election day	48	38	43
Second election day	38	43	41
Voted abroad	1	–	0
Did not vote	13	19	16
	100	100	100
Number of cases	202	286	488

Again, the difference between the two sexes catches our attention.[12] Not only did fewer females vote, but they also more often postponed their voting until the second day of polling. Analysis of the interview data discloses this difference with fairly consistent regularity.

Table 9.6 has been prepared for general analysis. The voters have been grouped according to the time of their participation, not that of decision. To present the conclusions, we can proceed as we did in connection with Table 9.5:

1. The more interested the voters had been in politics prior to the campaign, the greater the likelihood that they voted on the first election day. We found this to be true for the entire sample. Among women there were two exceptions: their time of voting was not related to their exposure to political mass communication, nor to their membership in a party. On the other hand, the male party members rushed to the polling stations.

2. The time of voting was obviously in no way connected with the turnout in previous elections.

3. Table 9.6.c repeats the data of Table 9.3. Without pointing to details, one is justified in making the general observation that, whenever the voters and nonvoters differed in some specific kind of campaign interest, the highest interest was to be found among the first day voters.

4. An exception, however, again concerns newspaper readership. The time of voting did not correlate, as had been expected, with attention paid to the campaign content of newspapers. It is possible either that newspaper readership was too widely customary to be a discriminating factor, or that it actually stimulated potential nonvoters to become late participants.

12. The difference is symptomatic: $\chi^2 = 5.85$, $v = 2$, $p < 0.10$.

TABLE 9.6. Relationship of Choice of Polling Day or Nonvoting to (a) the Interest in Politics Revealed in May, (b) Earlier Voting Participation, and (c) Campaign Activity (in percentages)

	Total			Men			Women		
	First day	Second day	Non-voters	First day	Second day	Non-voters	First day	Second day	Non-voters
(a) Normal interest									
Very or rather interested	40	28	15	56	45	38	25	18	4
High exposure to mass communication	40	32	15	54	40	27	28	27	9
Good knowledge of politics	29	22	15	42	40	15	16	11	15
Willing to give reasons	53	45	27	52	42	38	55	47	22
Party members	17	8	4	28	9	8	7	7	2
*Number of cases**	*207*	*200*	*80*	*97*	*78*	*26*	*110*	*122*	*54*
(b) Earlier participation									
Recalled participation in all previous elections	81	81	55	83	84	62	79	79	51
(c) Campaign activity									
Worked for his party	12	13	4	15	18	14	9	10	–
Knew a campaign worker	24	19	16	32	21	36	16	18	7
Discussed the election	72	65	60	69	74	82	73	60	50
Remembered four or more party posters	57	51	38	68	68	64	48	40	26
Identified one poster or more	83	77	68	88	83	82	79	73	61
Remembered the poster of at least one candidate	56	51	43	65	59	55	47	46	37
Received pamphlets	86	85	84	85	80	86	87	89	83
Listened to the entire election debate on radio	19	14	9	23	15	14	16	13	7
Listened to the presentation of some party	39	35	28	35	35	36	42	36	24
Read carefully election articles of newspapers	13	12	3	16	20	9	9	7	–
Looked often at campaign advertisements	26	26	13	23	31	23	28	23	9

Table 9.6 (*Continued*)

	Total			Men			Women		
	First day	Second day	Non-voters	First day	Second day	Non-voters	First day	Second day	Non-voters
Went to a campaign meeting	12	5	1	15	5	–	9	5	2
Listened to election results past midnight	15	13	9	16	14	9	15	12	9

* The numbers of cases for Table (a) are given. The two youngest groups are excluded from Table (b), and nonvoters, who were not re-interviewed, from Table (c).

And there is also a new exception: persons who did campaign work were not prone to vote on the first day.

In any case, Table 9.6 does give additional support to our hypothesis that the early voters include especially many of those who are interested in politics. A late entrance to the balloting station seems to indicate the same vague but focal characteristic as a late decision does, namely a lack of interest in politics.

Just as late party choice goes along with unwillingness to vote, active participation is not likely to result in late choice. However, the previous conclusions regarding the correlation between the time of voting decision and the time of voting participation, based on their relationship to political activity, have been indirect. There is further reason to verify the direct correlation of the two variables, and for this purpose we might also abandon the recalls of Table 9.5 and group voters again according to the information revealed by the panel method.

The correlation can be seen in Figure 9.C, and the previous conclusions are justified.[13] Most voters cast a ballot to carry into effect the intention they had in May, and a 55 per cent majority of these voted on the first day of polling. A newly converted preference was put into practice more slowly: only two out of five voted on Sunday. There was no hurry either if there had been no intention in May: only one out of three crystallizers voted on the first election day. Thus two out of three voted on the second day, and from there the step to nonvoting was not long.

Observation of Voters

Observation has been previously mentioned as the other method of collecting information about time of voting. A few election boards kindly

13. $\chi^2 = 8.14$, $v = 3$, $p < 0.05$.

Figure 9.C. Relationship of Constancy in Voting Intention to Day of Voting Participation (in percentages)

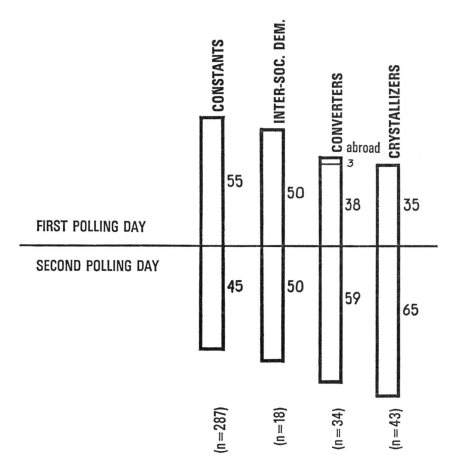

agreed, upon request, to change at a certain time the mark used to check off the names of voters from the register. Consequently, these registers now contain information about the time of participation as well as about the exact turnout. Again the hypothesis is that early voters differ most from nonvoters.

In examining the register of the 13th Voting District of Tampere, which contained 1,414 names, we found that the turnout was 78.9 per cent. The relationship of sex and marital status to turnout was as follows, in percentages:[14]

14. Marital status is inferred here on the basis of the same name and living together; it has not been further verified from other population registers. Therefore, it is also

Married men	86.3 ($n = 364$)
Married women	82.7 ($n = 365$)
Single men	62.8 ($n = 195$)
Single women	74.7 ($n = 480$)

These differences are in accord with previous findings that indicate that men turn out in greater numbers than women and married persons more frequently than single ones, but single men less often than single women.[15]

TABLE 9.7. Relationship of Sex and Marital Status to Time of Participation in the 13th Voting District of Tampere, 1958 (in percentages)

	Married		Not married		
	Men	Women	Men	Women Single	Widows
Obtained an absentee ballot	6	7	9	7	7
July 6, from noon to 4 P.M.	16	12	13	14	12
July 6, from 4 to 8 P.M.	18	16	12	13	12
July 7, from 9 A.M. to 4 P.M.	32	32	23	25	27
July 7, from 4 to 8 P.M.	14	16	11	16	17
Did not vote	14	17	32	25	25
Total	100	100	100	100	100
Number of cases	*364*	*365*	*195*	*325*	*165*

Table 9.7 shows the time of participation for these groups. The single women category has been further broken down to specify widows and unmarried women. The election time has been divided into four periods, dividing each day at 4:00 P.M.

The first impression is that Table 9.7 contains scarcely any differences of the expected kind. However, the hypothesis is supported somewhat by the fact that 39.7 per cent of the married persons, who voted in their own district, voted on the first day, but only 37.6 per cent of the single ones did likewise. As expected, the behavior of husbands and wives was also different. Forty-three per cent of the participating husbands and 37 per cent of the wives cast their ballots during the first election day.

---

impossible to make a distinction between single men and widowers in this analysis; the group of widows also includes divorced women (the maiden name differentiating both groups from unmarried women). In this connection, the author wishes to thank the Election Board of the 13th Voting District for their cooperation, as well as those Election Boards which helped to get similar material to be analyzed later.

15. For example, Allardt and Kettil Bruun, "Characteristics of the Finnish Non-Voter," *Transactions of the Westermarck Society,* Vol. III (Åbo/Copenhagen, Ejnar Munksgaard, 1956), p. 65. See also Milbrath, *Political Participation,* pp. 134–36.

In this connection, it is reasonable to assume that many married couples go to the polls together. Therefore, couples who voted at the same time form a separate group in Figure 9.D, which illustrates the data on married persons voting in their own district. Literally, voting together here means voting during the same half-day period. Using this definition, 81 husbands and 65 wives voted alone.

This voting station was entered by a relatively even flow of married

FIGURE 9.D. The Time of Participation of Married Couples Voting Together and Husbands and Wives Voting Alone in the 13th Voting District, Tampere, 1958 (in cumulative percentages)*

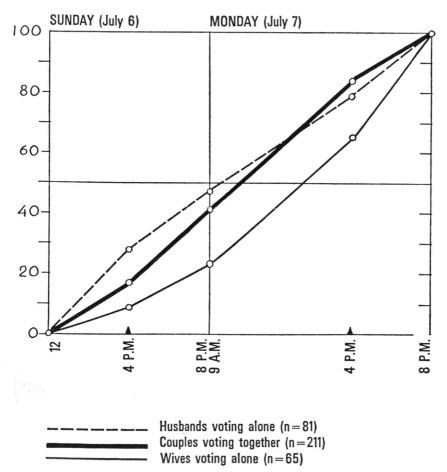

—————————— Husbands voting alone (n = 81)
————————— Couples voting together (n = 211)
————————— Wives voting alone (n = 65)

*Voting together is here defined as voting during the same half of the day. Information was obtained through the cooperation of the Election Board. The turnout of all married men in the District was 86.3%; that of married women, 82.7%.

voters; but the three groups were different. A comparison of married men voting alone, or with their spouse, suggests that married men were anxious to cast a ballot soon after the opening of the station, but that many of them waited to accompany their wives. The difference got smaller by Sunday evening and the last voters on Monday included more married men voting alone than with their wives. The ladies who voted alone were quite different. If not brought by their husbands to vote, they were more quiescent, thus accounting for the larger number of unaccompanied wives who voted on Monday evening. Moreover, a large group of these ladies remained nonvoters.

The longer the balloting continues, the more the politically indifferent persons begin to narrow the lead which the more interested persons have gained with their higher turnout in the beginning of the balloting. Yet they do not catch up by the time the polling stations close and the counting of the votes begins.

THE EXTERNAL RESTRAINTS ON VOTING

The Tampere nonvoters were asked to explain why they did not participate in this election (Q. 50.A). They gave the following reasons:

	Percentage of:		
	Men	Women	Total
Sickness, infirmity, or old age	–	25	18
Working	7	–	2
Lack of absentee ballot, uninformed about voting district	20	17	18
Other external restraints	20	10	12
Lack of interest	33	27	29
Unable to choose between parties	13	2	5
Religious conviction	–	17	12
Don't know	7	2	4
	100	100	100
Number of cases	*15*	*41*	*56*

We might further condense these responses into two basic reasons: some were prevented from voting because of an external difficulty, while others were not willing to vote. Let us quote a few respondents who were classified in the former group:

"It didn't work because I was then taken to bed and had no desire to bother an ambulance," said the wife (52) of an industrial worker, who had intended to vote for the SDP.

"It just was beyond my strength, I was sick," responded a pensioner (80), who had answered in May to the question about voting intentions, "You never know. You don't even know about tomorrow whether you'll still be alive."

An engineer (46), who had also intended to vote for the Social Democrats, told us, "I had a chance to spend a nice, free weekend, but then I was on duty all day Monday."

The wife (28) of an auto mechanic, who intended to vote, although she did not know for which party, did not participate "because the husband had to work overtime and I could not leave my baby"; while the wife (24, FPDU) of a grinding-machine operator told us that "the summer vacation just started and there was a surprising hurry to leave for the summer cottage on Sunday morning; in that fuss nothing came of the voting. I didn't have any absentee ballot either because we did not intend to leave that day." The widow of a stockkeeper (70, FPP) simply responded that "You don't feel like going in these backwoods."

"I had no time to get an absentee ballot because there was such a long line waiting; why didn't they have more people giving out those ballots," said a female worker (53) who supported no party in May. The widow of an electricity meter inspector (70, Agrarian) said in May, "I'm not able to go anywhere. When a person gets over seventy it really does not matter how this world stands," but in July she responded that "I really should have obtained those absentee ballots but I didn't remember, I was not feeling well then. After my husband passed away I just had no strength to follow things."

External Restraints and Willingness to Vote

In many studies and explanations of nonvoting, the exterior restraints and the unwillingness to vote have been mentioned as alternatives, as if either is sufficient cause by itself.[16] However, it seems necessary to observe them simultaneously. For example, Campbell has stated that "if the political institutions interpose barriers to the act of voting . . . the psychological cost of voting is increased and the level of motivation necessary to overcome this cost is also raised." [17] This concerns whole electorates,

16. For example, this was the basic classification of nonvoters in the first interview study of nonvoting, concerning the Chicago mayoralty election in 1923: Charles Edward Merriam and Harold Foote Gosnell, *Non-Voting, Causes and Methods of Control* (Chicago, The University of Chicago Press, 1924).

17. Campbell, *Acta Sociologica, 6,* 19.

but one might think as well that the voting of an individual is handicapped by external barriers of different magnitudes; and, consequently, a different level of desire to vote is needed to clear those barriers. Each ballot is cast with some minimal inconvenience. The more willing a citizen is to vote, the worse a physical condition, the rougher a trip to the ballot booth, the more compelling the household duties must be, before the cost of participation becomes impossibly high.

Many aspects of the Finnish electoral system have been specifically planned to make voting easy.[18] In addition to the two-day balloting, there are the large number of voting districts and the privilege to vote with absentee ballots (p. 11). It is of special significance that the electorate does not need to guarantee its right to participate before the election; the registers are prepared automatically. In many states of the U.S.A., for example, approximately one person out of ten loses the chance to participate because of failure to register within a fixed time.[19] International comparisons have shown that the turnout is higher under automatic registration than under systems which require the initiative to register of the potential voters.[20]

In a way, however, the obtaining of an absentee ballot is similar to pre-election registration. A potential voter has to guarantee by a personal act his later opportunity to exercise the right to vote, although this concerns only persons who will not be at home on election day. It now seems a reasonable assumption that the registration requirement sifts out the most passive elements of the electorate before the election. To test this, we

18. Kai Korte, "Äänioikeuden käyttämistä helpottavat pyrkimykset vaalilainsäädännössä" (Legislative Attempts to Make It Easier to Use the Right to Vote), *Lakimies ja Yhteiskunta,* 2 (1958).

19. The percentages of eligibles whose names were in the register of voters in 1960, in selected states of the U.S.A., were the following (in parentheses are the turnout percentages in the presidential election): Louisiana 62.0 (45.7), Arizona 64.8 (58.5), New Mexico 73.4 (63.4), Indiana 81.7 (76.7), Michigan estimated 83.0 (73.4), Massachusetts 83.8 (76.4), Delaware 87.0 (74.3), Rhode Island 87.2 (76.2), Illinois 87.6 (76.2), Washington 88.9 (72.9), Maine 92.6 (73.5), New Hampshire 94.8 (80.6). The total population on which the percentages are based includes persons who did not fulfil all the suffrage requirements. Data obtained from: U.S. Bureau of the Census, *Statistical Abstract of the United States: 1963* (Washington, D.C., 1963), Tables 506 and 507; *The Book of the States: 1962–1963,* Vol. XIV (Chicago, The Council of State Governments, 1962), p. 30. See also Milbrath, *Political Participation,* pp. 93–95, and the President's Commission, *Report on Registration and Voting Participation* (Washington, U.S. Government Printing Office, 1963).

20. Stein Rokkan, "The Comparative Study of Political Participation: Notes toward a Perspective on Current Research," in Austin Ranney, ed., *Essays on the Behavioral Study of Politics* (Urbana, University of Illinois Press, 1962), pp. 47–90.

TABLE 9.8. Relationship of Voting and Registration in the 1952 Election in the United States to Self-estimated Interest in Politics (in percentages)

		Nonvoters			
Interest	Voters	Regis-tered	Not registered	Unneces-sary to register	Total Sample
Very interested	44	23	16	16	38
Somewhat interested	35	32	33	26	34
Not interested	21	45	51	58	28
Total	100	100	100	100	100
Number of cases	*1,181*	*86*	*289*	*19*	*1,575*

DATA SOURCE: Survey Research Center, The University of Michigan, *Study No. 400*. Political interest according to the following question: "Some people don't pay much attention to political campaigns. How about you? Would you say that you have been very much interested, somewhat interested, or not much interested in following the political campaigns so far this year?"

can use the data collected by the Survey Research Center of The University of Michigan in 1952, because in that year its national postelection interviews included a question about registration. Table 9.8 shows the well-known difference between voters and nonvoters: the voters are more interested. But apparently the nonvoters were also different; at least within the sample, the registered persons who did not vote were more interested than other nonvoters.[21] On the other hand, persons who failed to register and those few nonvoters who did not have to register were equally uninterested. Obviously, persons who had at one time visited election authorities were more interested than those who had never gone to meet them.

In Finland, the necessity of obtaining an absentee ballot can be considered a similar kind of barrier, that is more easily overcome by the politically active than by the inactive. Thus the absentee voters who clear two formal barriers should be, on the average, more eager to vote, and generally more interested in politics, than the majority of voters whose participation only costs one visit to the authorities.

The interview data support this hypothesis. However, the differences lack statistical significance (Appendix Table 18). A partial reason might be the small number of absentee voters interviewed. Within the sample, at any rate, absentee voters did have a higher self-estimated interest and

21. $t = 1.52$, $0.10 < p < 0.20$.

they were more likely to be party members. Although they noticed fewer posters, they remembered better the messages of those to which they were exposed. We can generalize two differences: absentee voters received fewer pamphlets but knew more campaign workers than did the rest of the voters.[22] The first is not surprising because of their travels; the latter might hint that many absentee ballots were obtained at the suggestion of a friend, and not because of a high personal interest. If this be the case, large differences in interest are hardly to be expected.

Vacationing and Participation

More absentee ballots are needed in the summer than in the winter elections in Finland.[23] But whatever the date may be, large sections of the electorate find the schedule of elections inconvenient. After frequent arguments comparing the relative significance of the summertime vacationing of city inhabitants, and the occasional severe weather conditions of rural areas in the wintertime, the issue was recently settled in the favor of March (p. 11). There is little doubt that vacations kept many people from the Tampere polls in 1958. Continuous absence from midsummer until after the election lowered the turnout of these vacationers by some 30 per cent (Table 9.9.a). The highest turnout, however, was shown by those inhabitants who had been away from home for an extended period, but who returned for polling days.[24] Perhaps they were generally more active than those who had remained in the city.[25]

Obviously, July was not a convenient time to vote in Tampere. After the election, only 7 per cent felt that future elections should be administered in July (Q. 52). The urban population much preferred March (21 per cent), the month in which the 1954 parliamentary election had been held and which was adopted in 1965, or October (19 per cent), when local elections take place. Moreover, these opinions were related to vacationing (Table 9.9.b). July was not popular, even among the non-vacationing persons, but many of them did not object to it because they found the issue unimportant.[26]

22. $t = 2.10$, $p < 0.05$ and $t = 1.90$, $p < 0.10$.

23. The number of absentee ballots used in other constituencies and abroad was 44,850 in 1954 and 70,613 in 1962 (both were winter elections), but 86,760 in the summer election of 1958.

24. $t = 2.12$, $p < 0.05$.

25. In May their regular readership averaged 2.0 newspapers and 33 per cent of them were well informed about politics (those who were away during the election, 1.7 papers and 24 per cent; the others, 1.5 papers and 20 per cent).

26. When nonvacationers are compared with others, $t = 2.74$, $p < 0.01$.

TABLE 9.9. Relationship of Vacationing* of the Tampere Electorate to (a) Turnout and (b) Opinions on the Most Desirable Time for Future Elections, July 1958 (in percentages)

	All Vacationing			Men Vacationing			Women Vacationing		
	Not	Some	Polling days	Not	Some	Polling days	Not	Some	Polling days
(a) Turnout									
Voted	87	93	61	91	95	66	85	92	59
Did not vote	13	7	39	9	5	34	15	8	41
	100	100	100	100	100	100	100	100	100
(b) Most desirable time (Q. 52)									
July	8	3	8	11	5	11	6	1	6
October	17	25	14	24	29	8	12	22	18
January	7	9	10	3	6	8	10	11	12
March	19	22	27	15	23	34	22	22	21
Other month	11	13	19	11	14	12	11	12	25
Makes no difference	36	26	19	35	21	23	36	31	15
Don't know	2	2	3	1	2	4	3	1	3
Total	100	100	100	100	100	100	100	100	100
Number of cases	*281*	*136*	*59*	*110*	*62*	*26*	*171*	*74*	*33*

* Vacationing concerns the time of two weeks between the midsummer holiday and the election. The first group stayed in Tampere the whole period, the second was away for some time, and the third was away some time which included the polling days (Q. 48).

The effect of vacations on turnout can also be studied without interviews. For this purpose, one needs a basic list of names comprising large and homogeneous groups, which includes information on the vacationing habits of each individual. Four textile factories in Tampere provided such information to this study through access to their payrolls, which were grouped according to the starting dates of summer vacations.[27] Information on turnout was then obtained for random samples of these workers. Turnout percentages were the following:

	Working	On Vacation
Office employees	94 ($n = 50$)	80 ($n = 15$)
Male factory workers	84 ($n = 59$)	82 ($n = 162$)
Female factory workers	81 ($n = 121$)	81 ($n = 329$)

27. The method of the study is described in Antti Pullinen, "Kesävaalit, loma ja

Among office employees and male factory workers we thus find differences consistent with the interview data, but even the former difference lacks statistical significance.[28] On the other hand, a closer study of female workers showed that the time of their vacation played an important role in their behavior. If the beginning of the vacation coincided with the polling days, the turnout remained smaller than if the vacation had started at least one week earlier.[29] No such difference existed among the males. Perhaps the women had not remembered the necessity of obtaining an absentee ballot before departing, and the beginning of their annual vacation might at that time have been such an exciting event that it created too high a cost to be overcome by their desire to vote.

THE MOTIVATION TO PARTICIPATE

The permanent level of motivation may meet barriers other than external ones. For example, the current political situation and the content of the campaign might prevent some persons from voting. It is conceivable that the level of motivation is then lowered only temporarily, and would return to its earlier level in another political situation.

Elections themselves differ and provide the electorate with diverse kinds of motivation. First of all, there are various types of elections. One segment of the United States electorate that turns out for presidential elections refrains from voting in the congressional race two years later; participation in municipal elections in Finland, Sweden, and many other countries has been lower than participation in parliamentary elections. Secondly, even elections of the same character frequently arouse varying degrees of interest. Turnout increases if the election appears to be important (p. 84), but decreases if it is perceived as a routine procedure.

Some political situations may interest or discourage only certain individuals or groups. One group in question consists of the supporters of a party. If the political wind is blowing against a party, the habit of voting for it, as opposed to its present disfavor, may make the choice unusually difficult for its supporters. An additional assumption is that arduousness of party choice considerably increases the psychological cost of participation and that a substantial number of party supporters remain nonvoters.

In Tampere the respondents were not asked directly whether they con-

---

äänestysvilkkaus" (Summer Elections, Vacation, and Voting Frequency) (unpublished master's thesis, University of Helsinki, 1961), pp. 35–38.

28. $t = 1.29$, $p \sim 0.20$.

29. 73 per cent ($n = 112$) and 85 per cent ($n = 217$), $t = 3.00$, $p < 0.01$.

sidered the 1958 choice more or less difficult than usual. But fortunately other interview material provides data for testing the assumption. The Finnish Gallup Institute asked a national random sample: "Last July we had a parliamentary election. Did you feel the choice among parties easier then or more difficult than earlier?", and the party preference and reported voting participation were also asked. An easier choice was reported by 16 per cent, a more difficult by 11 per cent. The percentage of persons with an easier choice and the turnout of the different groups of party supporters were the following:[30]

	Per cent who considered this voting decision easier than usual	Per cent who voted
FPDU	26	$90(n = 178)$
Social Democrats	9	$85(n = 171)$
Agrarians	16	$88(n = 195)$
Other nonsocialists	20	$92(n = 181)$
Nonpartisans	7	$67(n = 137)$

The assumed correlation did exist: an easy choice encouraged participation, a difficult one lowered the turnout.[31]

In this connection, let us cite two examples which describe the relationship between ambivalence and turnout. A young lady who, like her father, preferred the Agrarian Union had married a Communist in Tampere. In a postelection interview, she said she had changed her mind at the last minute and voted for the FPDU. In reality she did not vote at all.[32] A worker, who had been an uncertain supporter of the Social Democratic Party, mentioned after the election that he had found it extremely difficult to choose between the SDP and the Communists. He was still undecided on his way to the polling place. After considerable time in the voting booth, he folded, stamped, and dropped into the ballot box his empty ballot.[33] The girl was faced with a difficult choice because of her transfer to a small group of different influence; the latter's choice was obviously

30. Data obtained through the courtesy of the Finnish Gallup Institute.

31. When calculated from the four political groups, $r = + 0.81$.

32. According to the poll book marked by the election board.

33. In Tampere, 251 ballot papers were disqualified (0.4 per cent of the ballots cast), and many may have been spoiled on purpose. Thus, 47 were empty, 57 were marked incorrectly, and 110 were too unclear to read the number voted for. Other reasons for disqualification were: number on the wrong side of the ballot (28 cases), vote for numerous candidates (2), and unstamped (7). Information from Mr. Mauri Nieminen, secretary of the Central Election Board. In the whole country, 10,162 ballots (0.5 per cent) were disqualified (Table 4 of the 1958 Official Election Statistics).

burdened by the troubles of the sdp. These difficulties raised the psychological cost of participation too high.

In Chapter 5, in comparing weak and strong party identifiers, we found that conflicting experiences had weakened party preferences prior to this campaign. Thus uniform family groups tended to strengthen party identification (p. 110), and a long lasting party preference was often perceived firmly (Tables 5.9 and 5.10).

There are now two reasons to assume that a strong party identification, in turn, tended to increase the frequency of voting. First, the stronger the party identification had been before the campaign, the higher the interest in politics (Figure 4.A, Table 4.3). It would seem natural then that an interest in the campaign, early voting decisions, and a high turnout were related to a strong party identification, because they also correlated with normal political interest. Secondly, in addition to raising the level of motivation, a strong party identification may also have protected people from those voting barriers caused by conflicting pressures. The latter problem will be analyzed later.

Figure 9.E presents a comparison of party identification with the voting

FIGURE 9.E. Relationship of Party Identification to Constancy in Voting Intention (in percentages)

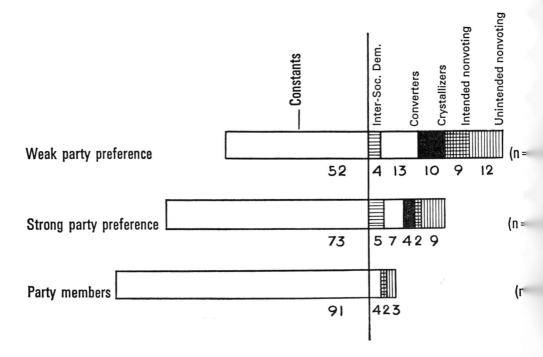

decision, and we find that party members, other strong supporters of parties, and people with a weak preference differed very significantly.[34] The stronger the party identification had been in May, the more likely the precampaign voting decisions were to be realized. A weak party preference had four different kinds of impact on the voting decision: (1) it involved a weak desire to vote in May, which was followed consistently by a low turnout; (2) even the precampaign decisions to vote were dropped easily; (3) the time of the decisions, however, tended to be postponed; and (4) a good many precampaign party choices were converted.

This information is similar to our earlier findings about participation in the election. Low turnout was connected with two kinds of tendencies to delay the voting decision, whereas a strong motivation to vote overcame those barriers to participation which would discourage a lower level of motivation.

FIGURE 9.F. Relationship of Firmness of Party Preference in May 1958 to Recalled Time of Final Party Choice in the July Election (QQ. 21 and 53, in cumulative percentages)

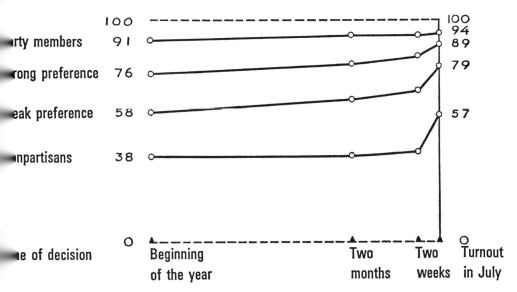

In Figure 9.F, the recollections of the interviewees are used to measure the time of final voting decisions. It is impossible to observe party conversions separately from the first crystallizations of voting intentions. But memory might provide a means (although not a very precise one) for making observations at more than just two moments.

34. $\chi^2 = 34.45$, $v = 5$, $p < 0.001$.

First of all, the figure depicts the correlation between turnout and party identification. Ninety-four per cent of party members voted, but only 57 per cent of nonpartisans went to the polls. The turnout of the other two groups was in between these extremes. In addition, we see the tendency of strong party identifiers to make early voting decisions. The curves are shaped differently: a weakening party identification obviously brought about a delay in the final party choice. This can be shown numerically as well. If we base our percentages on only those persons who did vote but did not recall the time of their party choice as earlier than two months before the election, we find among them the following percentages of latest deciders:

Party members and other strong identifiers	$37(n = 30)$
Weak party identifiers	$50(n = 30)$
Nonpartisans	$88(n = 8)$

Consequently, the relationship of a low desire to vote to a tendency to delay the decision is again displayed in Figure 9.F. But now let us stress that the group of nonpartisans obviously belonged to the same dimension of party identification as the extreme opposite to party members. They had the least desire to vote, and they were the slowest to make up their minds. Moreover, we might add that when they went to the polls they were most likely to vote among the late participants.[35]

The desire to vote correlated with party identification before the campaign (Figure 9.E). Another factor that had an impact on precampaign intention to participate has also been mentioned previously; that is, the citizens' perceived importance of the election. Therefore, it is not surprising to find that the more important a citizen considered the 1958 election, the stronger his party identification was apt to be. For example, only 24 per cent of the nonpartisans, but 62 per cent of the party members agreed in May with the statement: "The future management of the country's affairs depends decisively on the outcome of the election."

By now it is obvious that turnout also correlates with the importance attached to the election. Therefore, it is of special interest to find out whether or not party identification and perceived importance of the election played a separate role in bringing voters to the polls. The necessary data are given in Table 9.10, according to which:

35. First day voters comprised the following percentages: of party members 69 $(n = 191)$, of weak identifiers 47 $(n = 112)$, and of nonpartisans 33 $(n = 27)$; $\chi^2 = 10.98, v = 3, p < 0.02.$

1. As expected, perceiving the election as important increased, and considering it useless decreased, the turnout.

2. The average turnout of the city was reached only when the non-partisans considered the election to have decisive importance, as otherwise their turnout was lower.

3. In turn, weak party identifiers voted with the average frequency, if they considered the election to have at least some importance.

4. The strong identifiers distinctly had a high turnout, regardless of their opinion on the importance of the 1958 election.[36]

TABLE 9.10. Relationship of Firmness of Party Affiliation and Precampaign Opinion on the Importance of the Election to Voting Turnout: Tampere, 1958 (in percentages)

Importance of the Election (Q. 34)	Firmness of Affiliation									
	Non-partisan		Weak preference		Strong preference		Party members		Total	
	%	No.	%	No.	%	No.	%	No.	%	No.
Decisive importance	83	12	82	51	93	86	94	34	90	183
Some importance	62	13	83	66	85	99	94	19	84	197
Useless, don't know	50	24	64	28	94	35	..	2	73	89
Total	61	49	79	145	90	220	95	55	84	469

Thus we find two factors in this table which have a separate impact on the motivation to vote: namely party identification and the perceived importance of the election. The former definitely affects the basic level of motivation to vote, which might remain constant for a long period. The latter, in turn, may be partly the result of the current political situation. If the nonpartisans and the weak party identifiers consider the election important, they are activated enough to reach the average level of turnout; but they never seem to vote more frequently than the average, no matter how decisive they perceive the election. Disregarding the political situation, a high level of turnout presupposes an established belief that one is casting the ballot for a right cause.

36. The last-mentioned finding may be connected with the tendency of the most interested people to belittle the importance of the election, see p. 84.

The Comparison Group

It was no surprise that the turnout remained three percentage units lower in Korpilahti than in Tampere. The voting frequency had been lower in previous elections as well,[37] and we found more uncertainty about voting intentions in the comparison group than in Tampere. Of those persons in the rural sample who expressed a sure voting intention, 83 per cent ($n = 76$) voted, but the turnout was only 57 per cent ($n = 21$) of those who in May intended to remain nonvoters, or were uncertain about their voting intention.[38] However, the activation of many persons whose voting intention had been uncertain compensated in Korpilahti for the abstention of those nonvoters who had expressed a sure intention.[39] In Tampere, the final turnout was lower than had been expected on the basis of intended voting (p. 246).

The normal interest in politics and campaign activity in Korpilahti has been compared with Tampere in Chapters 4 and 7, especially in Tables 4.9 and 7.4. On the polling days the rural sample turned out as follows:

| | Percentage of: | | |
	Men	Women	Total
First day of voting	55	28	42
Second day of voting	31	40	35
Nonvoters	14	32	23
Total	100	100	100
Number of cases	49	47	96

This turnout percentage of the comparison group deviates from the correct figure for the Korpilahti population in the same direction, but not as far, as in the Tampere sample.[40] The two sexes favored different days in Korpilahti, just as in Tampere.

37. The turnout has been the following in the parliamentary elections from 1945 to 1966:

	1945	1948	1951	1954	1958	1962	1966
Tampere	86.2	81.6	79.6	82.4	77.6	87.3	85.3
Korpilahti	79.4	74.3	68.3	76.4	74.8	83.3	85.2

38. $t = 2.17$, $p < 0.05$.

39. The Korpilahti sample ($n = 97$) can be classified as follows: 65 per cent had sure voting intention and participated; 12 per cent had uncertain intention but participated; 13 per cent had sure intention but did not vote; and 9 per cent had uncertain intention and were nonvoters.

40. In the comparison group 77 per cent of the May sample ($n = 97$) voted, and 79 per cent of the July sample ($n = 94$)

The comparison group also tended toward unidimensional interest in the campaign and in the election. Appendix Table 19 supports consistently the findings presented in Table 9.2. For example, campaign articles in newspapers were read in Korpilahti by 85 per cent of those people who listened to the party programs on the radio, but by only 62 per cent of others. The great radio debate was listened to by 35 per cent of those who looked at campaign advertising in newspapers, but only by 14 per cent of the others. Likewise, the correlation shown in Figure 9.A was obvious in the comparison group.

Furthermore, many comparisons show a correlation between campaign activity and normal political interest, which, in turn, supports the findings in Appendix Table 17. To illustrate, let us mention that campaign work was done by 22 per cent ($n = 18$) of the very or rather interested persons, but by only 7 per cent of the little or not interested. The campaign material of newspapers was read carefully by 22 per cent of the former, but only by 3 per cent of the latter.

The comparison group also corresponds to the above findings concerning the interrelationship of the two means of measuring the time of voting decision (Table 9.4). Among those voters, who, according to the panel interview, did not change the intention expressed in May, 78 per cent ($n = 50$) remembered that their final choice was made in the beginning of the year. The same answer was given by only 35 per cent ($n = 20$) of those voters who had made their choice during the campaign.

Table 9.11 repeats for the rural sample those findings which were presented in Tables 9.1, 9.3, 9.5 and 9.6. The table suggests the following three conclusions about participation, time of decision, and day of voting in Korpilahti:

1. The 1958 voting behavior reflected participation in earlier elections; consequently, either voting or nonvoting seem relatively constant modes of behavior. In May, the July voters had been more active than nonvoters regarding their exposure to mass communication and their membership in party organizations. Differences in campaign activity are also in line with expectations. Only newspaper advertising seems to offer an exception.

2. Furthermore, when the Korpilahti voters are classified according to those who remembered an early or a late party choice, the differences between the two groups concur with the Tampere findings. The early deciding voters had been more interested in politics in May than the late deciders. However, campaign activity differed enough to be mentioned only as far as party work, exposure to posters, and perhaps exposure to

TABLE 9.11. Relationship of (a) Political Interest in May 1958, (b) Participation in Previous Elections, and (c) Campaign Activity in 1958 to Participation in the Election, Recalled Time of Final Party Choice, and Day of Voting on July 6 and 7, 1958, in Korpilahti (in percentages)

	Voters	Non-voters	Time of decision Begin-ning of year	Time of decision Close to election	Day of voting 1st day	Day of voting 2nd day
(a) Normal interest						
Very or rather interested	19	22	21	8	27	6
High exposure to mass communication	28	14	32	16	35	18
Party members	15	–	21	4	15	15
(b) Earlier participation						
Recalled participation in all previous elections	75	33	77	72	75	74
(c) Campaign activity						
Worked for his party	11	5	15	4	17	3
Knew a campaign worker	23	10	21	24	32	12
Remembered four or more party posters	45	25	53	38	55	32
Identified one poster or more	73	60	77	68	77	68
Remembered the poster of at least one candidate	43	25	38	44	55	29
Received pamphlets	49	30	49	48	47	50
Listened to the entire election debate on radio	16	10	19	12	17	15
Read carefully election articles of newspapers	37	25	36	40	42	32
Looked often at campaign advertisements	28	25	28	28	27	29
Went to a campaign meeting	25	–	28	24	32	18
Listened to election results past midnight	8	–	9	8	10	6
Number of cases	75[a]	22[b]	47	25	40	34

a. In Table (a), $n = 74$.
b. In Table (b), $n = 21$ and in Table (c), $n = 20$.

radio were concerned. Yet differences contrary to expectations were few or nonexistent.

3. The first-day and second-day voters also seemed to differ as expected. A new exception, however, is the equal tendency of party members to vote

on both days. On the other hand, it seems that early voters were more active attendants of campaign meetings, and more active viewers of the posters of candidates.

It is true that Table 9.11 is based on very few cases only, but nevertheless it seems to support the above conclusion that an early party choice, high probability of participation, and the tendency to vote on the first day of polling are mutually correlating characteristics of those persons who were interested in politics.

Let us add that in the comparison group, too, the time of decisions was directly related to the day of voting. Among the first-day voters, it was the following:

Those who decided in the beginning of the year	$60(n = 47)$
Those who decided 2 months/2 weeks before the election	$56(n = 9)$
Those who decided just before the election	$37(n = 16)$

The other method of measuring the time of decision shows very weak differences only, but they are in line with Figure 9.C.[41]

When nonvoting people in Korpilahti explained why they did not vote, a natural grouping of their responses is again into two basic classes. The reason was either (1) an exterior obstacle or (2) lack of desire to vote.

1. People fell sick, were prevented by work, or failed to obtain absentee ballots in time in Korpilahti as in Tampere. And awkward transportation was an additional difficulty in the rural commune:

> The old woman and I were sick and weak, and the trip without a motorboat would have been difficult. (Small farmer, 73, Agrarian)
>
> Just then I was so sick that it was impossible to vote even with a taxi ride. (Wife of small farmer, 78, FPDU)
>
> I was sick and I'm too weak to walk. It would have been three miles by boat or rocky path over the mountain. (Unskilled worker, female, 70, nonpartisan)
>
> It was a rainy day and my legs had been hurting all the summer. I was not able to bicycle either. (Wife of farmer, 41, Agrarian)
>
> It was a real busy time in work. I worked both days overtime. (Carpenter, 43, FPDU)

2. On the other hand, we were told that lack of interest or difficulty in choosing were reasons for nonvoting. In this connection, the impact of religious convictions was not mentioned in Korpilahti:

41. The percentage of first-day voters was 54 per cent of the constants in intention ($n = 50$) and 50 per cent of others ($n = 22$).

I was so very unwilling about the whole business and I just didn't happen to go. (Widow, 34, Conservative)

I was at home and looked after the cows. I had a cold and didn't feel like going. (Small farmer, female, 39, Agrarian)

There was no reason, I just didn't happen to go. Because I don't know finally which is the best one. (Servant, female, 33, SDP)

I did not know who to vote for, Communists or Social Democrats. (Wife of shopkeeper, 41, nonpartisan)

The rural people traveled less for vacation than city people: 84 per cent of the comparison group was in the commune the two weeks before the election, but only 59 per cent of those in Tampere. In the comparison group, too, the travelers were less content with the time of the election, yet their turnout seems to have been higher than that of the nontraveling majority.[42] Generally, the population felt differently about the time of election in the two places. One out of two inhabitants of the rural commune thought it made no difference when parliamentary elections took place, and in addition there were more persons (18 per cent) who favored the month of July than there were in Tampere.

In Korpilahti, people were apt to estimate the 1958 election more important if they identified more closely with their preferred party. The same was found in Tampere too. The time of voting decision seems to correlate in Korpilahti with the degree of party identification, because the percentages of those who remembered an early party choice were the following:

Party members	$91(n = 11)$
Other strong identifiers	$64(n = 25)$
Weak identifiers	$55(n = 38)$

The difference between strong and weak identifiers seems to exist also if the time of voting decision is measured by the panel method.[43]

Thus the turnout in Korpilahti also correlates with party identification and estimated significance of the election. In addition, the comparison

42. Of those who stayed at home ($n = 79$), 20 per cent preferred July and 77 per cent voted; of those who had been traveling ($n = 15$), 7 per cent preferred July and 87 per cent voted. The difference in turnout may correspond to the higher turnout of those in Tampere who had been away from the city.

43. Of party members and other strong identifiers ($n = 41$), 71 per cent voted as intended, 2 per cent changed inter-Soc.Dem., 7 per cent switched parties, 7 per cent were crystallizers, and 12 per cent did not vote. Of weak identifiers ($n = 30$), the corresponding distribution was 57, 3, 13, —, and 27 per cent.

group supports the interpretation, based on Table 9.10, that party identification increased the motivation to vote more than the perceived significance of the election. Among strong identifiers in Korpilahti, 88 per cent ($n = 41$) voted, and this figure was not lowered by the opinion that the election was unnecessary. The turnout of other persons (70 per cent, $n = 56$) varied according to the opinion expressed in May about the significance of the election. It was 79 per cent ($n = 19$) if the election was considered to be of decisive importance, and 72 per cent ($n = 18$) if it was considered to have some importance, but remained as low as 56 per cent ($n = 19$) if this election was seen as having no impact on the policies of the country.

SUMMARY

The dissimilarity found in the citizens' political interest before the election (Chapter 4) was later reflected in their official and unofficial electoral activity. In May the desire to vote already correlated with interest. Furthermore, a comparison of the July voters and nonvoters showed that the former had been normally more interested, more knowledgeable, more willing to give reasons for their opinions, and more willing to join political parties. Unofficial electoral activity—especially exposure to campaign communication and campaign work—were, in turn, linked to precampaign interest and to the July voting. According to this, a normal interest in politics, actual voting, and unofficial electoral activity are expressions of nearly the same basic dimension, namely, a general interest in politics. The differences in the degree of interest also were found to be rather constant, because the 1958 nonvoters had been infrequent voters previously as well.

Many findings based on the Tampere sample were supported by the comparison group, and furthermore the findings got additional support from recorded sources. An above average turnout was because of the high unofficial political interest represented by a leading position in the local party organization, on the one hand, and an official electoral activity represented by signing a candidate's petition, on the other. Yet a signature on a list of a new, completely uninstitutionalized party had no impact on voting participation.

The two preconditions for the act of voting are making a choice and going to the polling station. Information about both aspects of voting should be added to the study of participation. In studying the time and stability of party choice, we found that early decisions led to high turnout.

And when the polling day itself was studied, differences were again found. Interested persons, who tended to make early choices and to vote frequently, also tended to vote on the first day of polling. Early participation was linked to an early decision, and nonvoting looked as if it were an extreme case of inactivity and delayed decision. Nonvoting was a delay extended longer than the polling stations remained open.

These findings got some support from the comparison group as well. Moreover, it was arranged in Tampere for the time of voting to be observed, and these observations concurred with some of the interview findings.

Generally, it is believed that nonvoting is caused either by an external obstacle or by the unwillingness to vote. However, neither explanation is adequate alone, because participation requires both a motive to vote and the overcoming of some inconvenience. Therefore, the nonvoters' motives are too weak to outweigh the trouble of voting or, conversely, the obstacles are so great that the motives do not help to overcome them.

We found, accordingly, that the easier participation is made technically, the smaller the interest that may stimulate potential nonvoters. In American interview data, the lowest level of interest was represented by two kinds of nonvoters: those who failed to register and those whose names were registered automatically. Between these groups and the voters ranked the interest of such nonvoters as had registered. Correspondingly, in the Tampere sample, voting on an absentee ballot seemed to require more interest than voting in one's own voting district. An analysis of recorded data showed further that the beginning of the summer vacation caused an additional obstacle to the participation of female workers.

The difficulty of choice was found to be one psychological barrier which could lower the desire to vote. According to a comparable national sample, the turnout in Finland was related to the perceived ease of the 1958 party choice.

Two motives, which added to the desire to vote in Tampere and in Korpilahti, were a close party identification and the opinion that this was a significant election. Both factors had been measured in the May interview. A very low turnout was typical of those nonpartisans who had considered the election useless. If they thought the election was of decisive importance, their activity reached the average level of the city. But the turnout of strong party identifiers was high, even if they did not consider this election important. Their desire to vote was based on the permanent belief that their vote supported the right party.

10. The Choice of Party and Representative

The failure of former voters to turn out in the 1958 election had little effect on either the extreme left or the right, both of which were in opposition to the government coalition. The FPDU gained 17,000 and the Conservatives 40,000 more votes than in the 1954 election. The latter increase was greater than that party's share of the increase in the size of the electorate. In contrast, the total number of votes polled by the Social Democratic groups was 43,900 less than in the previous election; the Finnish People's Party lost 43,700; the Agrarian Union and its Opposition, 30,500; and the Swedish People's Party, 9,200 votes.

But, even so, there were no large changes in the relative support of the Finnish parties. The share of the FPDU in the ballots increased from 21.6 to 23.2 per cent, and that of the Conservatives from 12.8 to 15.3 per cent. However, the parliamentary group of the FPDU, which had contained 43 representatives in 1951 and 1954, became, with their 50 members, the largest one in the new Parliament. The Conservatives gained five new seats and the Swedish People's Party gained one. But both the Agrarian Union and the FPP lost five seats in Parliament, and the SDP lost six seats, three of which went to those Opposition candidates who ran on separate slates (See Table 1.2).

The election surprised many observers. Perhaps the Communist victory was greater than expected and the Agrarian loss and a leftist majority (101 to 99) in the new Parliament also may have surprised many persons. It is characteristic that the Agrarian Party Secretary said, in a radio interview after the polling, but before the counting of ballots, "the Agrarian Union won this election." The press even referred to a "shock election."[1]

THE ELECTION RESULTS IN TAMPERE

Because the distribution of votes cast in different elections in Finland does not vary much, and because most of our respondents did not remember any change in party choice, there was no reason to expect a big political upheaval in the Northern Häme constituency in the summer of 1958.

1. For example, " 'Chockvalet' i Finland," *Nordisk kontakt*, 1958, pp. 566–68.

On the other hand, experience has shown that political trends in any limited area tend to follow national trends.

The election outcome in the Northern Häme constituency corresponded to that in the whole country (Tables 1.2, 10.1). Of the thirteen seats,

TABLE 10.1. Electoral Alliances and Their Votes and Seats in Northern Häme Constituency in 1958, with Vote Distribution in Tampere and Korpilahti

	Constituency Votes	Seats	Tampere	Korpi- lahti
A. The Electoral Alliance of the Agrarian Union (candidates 2–14)	16,404	1	348	1,270
B. The Independent Social Democratic Electoral Alliance (candidates 15–27)	10,941	1	4,622	313
C. The Electoral Alliance of the Finnish People's Party (candidates 28–39)	6,347	–	2,512	108
D. The Electoral Alliance of the Popular Center (candidates 41–45)	554	–	320	9
E. The Electoral Alliance of the National Coalition—Conservatives (candidates 46–58)	30,524	3	14,777	229
F. The Electoral Alliance of People's Democrats—FPDU (candidates 59–71)	41,631	5	18,818	931
G. The Social Democratic Electoral Alliance (candidates 72–84)	33,082	3	13,615	264
Total	139,083	13	55,012	3,124

nine went to the left as before, but the FPDU captured a fifth seat from the Social Democrats. The SDP was more popular than its Opposition. Sufficient votes were cast for the latter to elect one candidate, and the party itself seated three representatives. The four seats of the nonsocialist parties were distributed as before. The Agrarian Union did receive in this constituency 400 more votes than in 1954 (Table 1.1), but it still would have needed 250 more votes to win its second seat from the Communists (the last seat was won by the FPDU with the average $41,631/5 = 8,326$; its closest rivals were the SDP with the average $33,082/4 = 8,270$, and the Agrarians with $16,404/2 = 8,202$; see pp. 7–8). The electoral alliance of the Conservatives elected three members, and the number of votes received increased by 5,200. Thus the Finnish People's Party did not recapture the seat it had won in 1954 but lost later in Parliament.

The inhabitants of Tampere comprised 42.5 per cent of the enfranchised population of this constituency and exactly the same proportion of its July voters. More than half the Conservative votes in the constituency were won in the city of Tampere; the FPDU ranked as the second most urban party in the constituency. Only 2 per cent of the votes cast for the Agrarian Union were from the city.

TABLE 10.2.   Results of the 1958 Election in Tampere

Parties	Votes received	Increase or decrease from 1954	Votes	Estimate, including absentee ballots* (per cent)	July sample
FPDU	18,818	+643	24.5	25.6	24
Soc. Dem. Opposition	4,622	+4,622	6.0	6.4	6
SDP	13,615	−5,768	17.7	18.6	23
Agrarian	348	+106	0.5	0.7	1
FPP	2,512	−3,361	3.3	3.8	4
Conservative	14,777	+2,005	19.3	21.6	22
Others and disqualified ballots	571	+371	0.7	0.8	0
Additional absentee ballots*	4,217	+3,166	5.5	.	.
No answer	.	.	.	.	6
Nonvoters	17,313	+4,914	22.5	22.5	14
Total	76,793	+6,678	100.0	100.0	100

* The absentee ballots cast by the Tampere electorate have been distributed among the parties in relation to absentee ballots cast in the entire constituency.

Table 10.2 compares the result of the election in Tampere with that of the 1954 election and with our sample. Because most absentee ballots are counted in the statistics for the constituency only and not according to the residence of the voters, it is not possible to give exact information about the city. But, in any case, the Conservatives gained most new votes; an increase was also scored by the FPDU and to a lesser extent by the Agrarians. The FPP lost votes in this election. Similarly, the two Social Democratic electoral alliances combined received less votes in Tampere than the party had gained alone in 1954. These trends are in line with the results of the whole constituency.

Interview data are essential for a detailed analysis of changes in party support. Let us now first repeat two percentage figures from the sample that show that party preference was relatively constant. In May 1958, 83 per cent of the inhabitants of Tampere favored the same party which they had voted for in 1954. This percentage concerned only those persons who recalled and revealed their party choice in the previous election (see Table 5.8). On the other hand, 74 per cent of the persons who voted in July 1958 had behaved as they had decided before the campaign in May (Figure 9.B.b). If we disregard the switches between the two Social Democratic wings, the corresponding percentages were 89 per cent for the four years, and 79 per cent for the campaign period. Only 9 per cent were converted from their sure voting intention, while the 12 per cent of crystallizers included also those voters whose intention had been uncertain concerning only their participation, but not their party choice (p. 254).

In order to study the impact of the campaign on the outcome of the election, it is first necessary to compare party changes during the campaign with those changes which had occurred earlier during the normal era. Table 10.3 presents the necessary information. In a way it describes how the trends shown in Table 5.8 continued until the election. Table 10.3 concerns only those persons who voted in 1958. They are grouped according to their vote in July, and not according to their party preference in May. Of the 76 per cent who had voted in 1954 and whose choice is known, three quarters had remained constant supporters of the same party. The remaining quarter included more voters whose party preference had changed before the campaign (8 per cent of the sample) than those who were converted later during the campaign (6 per cent). In addition, there were people who had changed their affiliation twice (5 per cent); however, at the election most of these simply returned back to their 1958 position. And some voters had been nonpartisan in the beginning of the campaign.

The conclusion of some studies in other countries has been that more party changes occur before the campaign than close to the election.[2] Let us remember, however, that such comparisons are inaccurate; and that this is true of the Tampere study too. Later changes are measured with the panel method, but information on precampaign changes depends on the memory of the respondents. There has been one American panel study, the span of which extended from one election year to another. Even this study supports the conclusion that there are more conversions before than during the campaign.[3]

Furthermore, the sheer percentage of party converters does not indicate

2. Berelson, Lazarsfeld, and McPhee, *Voting*, p. 138; Lazarsfeld, Berelson, and Gaudet, *People's Choice*, p. 102.

3. Communication from Philip E. Converse.

TABLE 10.3. Relationship of Voters' Party Choice in the July 1958 Election to Voting Behavior in 1954 and Party Preference in May 1958 (in percentages)

| | | Party choice in July | | | | |
| | | S.D. | | | | Total |
	FPDU	Opp.	SDP	FPP	Cons.	voters
Voters in 1954*						
1954 = May 1958 =						
July 1958	55	.	70	30	53	54
1954 = May 1958 ≠						
July 1958	2	50	–	10	5	6
1954 = July 1958 ≠						
May 1958	3	.	6	–	3	3
1954 ≠ (May 1958 =						
July 1958)	6	19	3	15	12	8
1954 ≠ May 1958 ≠						
July 1958	3	4	–	–	3	2
Nonpartisan	3	4	3	5	1	3
No information	9	4	3	5	11	8
Nonvoters in 1954						
May 1958 = July 1958	6	4	11	10	4	7
May 1958 ≠ July 1958	1	7	1	10	4	3
Nonpartisan	1	–	–	–	–	0
21–24 years of age						
May 1958 = July 1958	10	4	3	5	–	4
May 1958 ≠ July 1958	–	4	–	5	3	1
Nonpartisan	1	–	–		1	1
No information	–	–	–	5	–	0
Total	100	110	100	100	100	100
Number of cases	*115*	*26*	*111*	*20*	*103*	*379*

* = Party choice remains same.
≠ Party choice changes.

the full impact of changes on the outcome of the election. Their direction is decisive too. There are three possibilities in a two-party system. The trends in the gains and losses of parties may continue during the campaign in the same direction, or they may reverse direction; the third possibility is simply that there is no net change in the relative support of the parties because individual changes cancel each other's effect. The multiparty system may experience many combinations of these basic types.

Figure 10.A indicates how the voting intentions expressed in May in Tampere developed during the campaign. The corresponding detailed figures are given in Appendix Table 20.

FIGURE 10.A. Voting Decisions in Tampere on July 6 and 7, 1958; Voting Intentions in May 1958; and Consequent Changes in Intentions during the Campaign*

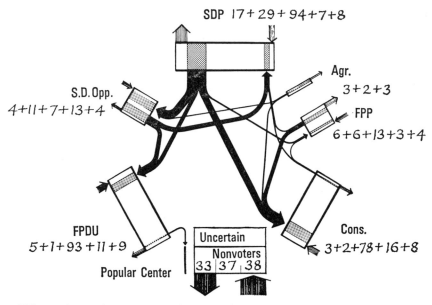

* The numbers under party names denote the following (see Appendix Table 21):
(1) Unintended nonvoters,
(2) (shaded) Intended voters who voted for another party,
(3) Constant voters,
(4) (shaded) Voters converted from other parties, and
(5) Voters whose intention was uncertain in May.

We find first that those party conversions, which were seen in Table 5.8 (and Figure 5.D) before the campaign, continued also after the May interview. The most frequent conversions were the switches of the SDP supporters to the Opposition or the FPDU, and the conversions of FPP supporters to vote for the Conservatives. To a lesser extent, we find that the FPP continuously gained support from the left and from the right, and that the SDP gained from the right. On the other hand, it seemed as though all roads away from the FPDU were blocked before the election.

However, there emerged three new channels for conversions, two of which followed the appearance of new parties: (1) the Social Democratic Party regained some supporters who had been lost to the Opposition earlier in the spring; (2) on the other hand, many earlier supporters of the Social Democratic Opposition had found in this group only a temporary haven on their way from Social Democracy to Communism; (3)

an almost new phenomenon was the opening of the gates from the left to Conservatism. During the 1958 campaign the SDP lost more voters to the National Coalition than it had lost, according to the recall of the sample, in all previous elections combined.

The outcome of the election is not decided just by party changes which occur during the peaceful era after an election or later during the new election campaign. To some extent, the electorate itself changes as new generations replace earlier ones. In Tampere the FPDU and the FPP had the most support among the young in May 1958 (Table 3.2). After May, even the Conservatives gained some first-time voters. Yet it seems that the FPDU and the FPP captured during the balloting as well more support from young voters than did the Social Democrats and the Conservatives (Table 10.3).

A study on just one community has to take migration into account as an additional renewer of population. This does not concern the campaign period, because the register of voters is based on precampaign circumstances. In 1958, the enfranchised Finns voted where they had dwelled on January 1, 1957, and therefore the newly enfranchised inhabitants of Tampere were those persons who had moved to the city during 1953–1956. It is possible that migration creates a potential tendency to party conversion that is not realized until nearly election time. This may explain why there seemed to be a continuous loss of Agrarian support in Tampere. According to the interviews, the Agrarian Union lost support in the city not only before the campaign, but even during it. On the other hand, the election statistics show that the number of votes cast for this party in the city increased slightly from 1954 to 1958 (Table 10.2). These data are not controversial, because there had been so much migration from the country that Tampere had gained almost alone the entire increase in the population of the constituency.

It was shown above that the citizens' tendency to change their voting intention correlates with the sureness of their party preference. The more closely they identified with their supported party in May, the more likely they were to cast their ballot for the same party (Figure 9.E). Now we might ask whether the precampaign interview also included information that might have predicted—in addition to the tendency to change—the most likely direction of the conversion. The rank ordering of the parties is a possible way of answering the latter question (Q. 19, Table 6.4).

Both the FPDU and the Conservatives won votes from some persons who intended to vote for the SDP or its Opposition. The following distribution shows which parties the FPDU and the Conservative converters preferred in May as their second choice after the Social Democrats:

	Percentage of:	
		Conservative
	FPDU voters	voters
FPDU	64	20
Agrarian	–	10
FPP	36	30
Conservative	–	40
	100	100
Number of Cases	*11*	*10*

Even such a small sample proves that the two groups had ranked parties differently before the campaign.[4] In May the FPDU converters had inclined more strongly toward the left wing, while the Conservative converters had ranked parties like the Social Democrats in general and perhaps placed the Conservatives even more favorably (see p. 142). Let us add that those interviewed voters who were won by the Conservatives from the Finnish People's Party or the Agrarians had ranked their future party in second place even before the campaign.

Consequently, the outcome of the election was implicit even before the campaign began. The party choice of the majority was the same as in the previous election. Most party conversions obviously took place before the campaign, and, finally, many of the later converters had already ranked their party as number two when the campaign began. Yet there were some individual conversions to vote for a party which had been considered very remote before the campaign.

Finally, let us also remember that party choice alone does not determine the outcome of an election. Activity is the other decisive factor, because the desire to vote might vary among the supporters of different parties.

First, it is possible that a party could earn exceptionally many votes among persons who had remained nonvoters in previous elections. However, in the Tampere sample there were no such differences. About an equal number of voters in each party recalled nonvoting in 1954 (Table 10.3). Moreover, it seems that voters who had not decided by May were distributed among the parties in relation to the final vote (Figure 10.A, Appendix Table 20). And the reason for indecisiveness had been in many cases simply uncertainty about participation. About two thirds of the

4. The line FPDU: $t = 2.26$, $p < 0.05$. Third preference is counted for those whose second preference was the other Soc. Dem. group.

voters, who had been uncertain in May, did favor some party, and a majority of them turned out to vote for that party.[5]

On the other hand, it is possible that exceptional unwillingness to vote could appear among the supporters of certain parties. The national Gallup sample showed that (1) the turnout of Social Democratic and Agrarian supporters was lower than that of others; and that (2) the low turnout groups perceived party choice as most difficult (p. 271). Moreover, according to Figure 10.A, the SDP and the FPP in Tampere lost many persons, who had intended to vote for them, to the group of nonvoters. Thus a defeat in the election consisted of two kinds of losses: intended votes were converted to other parties, or they were not cast at all. Similarly, an election victory was brought about by new voters as well as the high voting frequency of a party's own supporters.

TABLE 10.4. The Turnout Percentage in Tampere in 1958 by Age and Party Preference*

	FPDU	S.D. Opp.	SDP	Agr.	FPP	Cons.	Total
21–42 years of age	95	82	72	50	86	91	82
43 years and over	95	86	82	33	62	93	85
Total sample	95	84	78	43	74	92	84
Number of cases, 21–42	*61*	*17*	*58*	*4*	*14*	*43*	*222*
Number of cases, 43 and over	*60*	*14*	*84*	*3*	*13*	*69*	*266*

* The total number of supporters was obtained by adding to the voters, first, 35 nonvoters according to Q. 50.C (or Q. 54.A), and, secondly, 27 nonvoters according to Q. 19.

One half of the nonvoters did not lose interest during the campaign, but were uncertain about participation in May, even though many of them had a party preference. Therefore, they should not be neglected in a comparison of the unused reserves of voters of the parties. Such a comparison among the 1958 nonvoters in Tampere shows more Social Democrats than supporters of all other parties combined.[6] We can also calculate

5. Same party 40 per cent, inter-Soc. Dem. changers 12 per cent, other party 12 per cent, nonpartisans 30 per cent, no answer 6 per cent ($n = 33$). In this group, most changes were conversions of Social Democrats to vote for their party opposition or the FPP.

6. The party preference of nonvoters: FPDU 8 per cent, Soc.Dem. Opposition 6 per cent, SDP 39 per cent, Agrarian 5 per cent, FPP 9 per cent, Conservative 11 per cent, no answer 5 per cent, nonpartisan 17 per cent ($n = 80$). Party preference (as in Table 10.4) according to QQ. 50.C, 54.A, and 19.

roughly the turnout percentages of the supporters of different parties (Table 10.4). According to this, too, the extreme left wing and the right wing turned out with high frequencies, while the middle of the party scale was less active.

In addition, Table 10.4 shows these turnout figures separately for the young and old supporters of the parties. As such, they are inaccurate, and the differences lack statistical significance. Yet the supporters of the losing parties call for attention. It seems that among the Social Democrats the turnout of the old supporters was exceptionally higher than that of the young; the oldest seemed as eager to vote as the supporters of the winning parties.[7] But in the Finnish People's Party the old supporters seemed unwilling to vote.[8] If this difference is generalized for the universe of the study, it indicates the significance of established activity for a party which gets "the wind against it." The guardians of an old party are its faithful veterans, whereas a new party finds it exceptionally difficult in such a situation to activate those supporters who have affiliated with it after being voters in another party.

The Reasons Given for Party Choice

The Usual General Themes

The most favorable aspect of the different parties had been presented and perceived differently before the campaign (Tables 6.1 and 6.2). Moreover, it seems that the campaign did not change much the favorable images held by the voters about their party (Q. 54.B, Appendix Table 21). Thus, the FPDU was voted for especially because it was thought to work in the interest of labor:

> It is the vital necessity for the working people, well, at least it is for them. (Unskilled worker, male, 51)

> Because it is the party of the workers and all are equal in it, pulling in the same direction. (Wife of warehouse worker, 23)

> I consider that it is the most realistic advocate of the interests of the working people. I'm a worker myself. This party advocates the separation of the church and the state. (Janitor, male, 30)

7. $t = 1.35$, $0.10 < p < 0.20$; the turnout of Social Democrats 65 years of age or more was 93 per cent ($n = 14$), of all others 77 per cent ($n = 128$), $t = 2.08$, $p < 0.05$.
8. $t = 1.47$, $p < 0.20$.

Many voters of the Social Democratic Party as well considered their party the champion of labor interests. In addition, its voters gave reasons repeating many other images expressed in May:

> It is a party that favors the interests of the worker and it is more reasonable than the FPDU. (Former construction worker, male, 73)

> Because it's the party of labor and it's moderate. It doesn't always succeed well, but I don't think the others can do any better. (Plumber, male, 33)

> It furthers labor ideas moderately, the others try by force. They make progress in social security and they have always started social improvements for workers. (Female, 59)

> If they would take better care of the old. At least they promise beautifully. (Bricklayer, male, 69)

> It fits a person like me who doesn't own stone-houses. (Seamstress, 56)

The reasons expressed by the voters of the Independent Social Democratic electoral alliance were again similar to the previous ones:

> It's a working man's party, however, not as sharp as the FPDU. (Wife of industrial worker, 42)

> It has in general taken care of the working men, children's allowances, old age pensions, etc. (Wife of crane operator, 32)

> It's everybody's own business. You know if one starts from such a cottage one doesn't vote for Conservatives. (Seamstress, 55)

The voters of the Finnish People's Party again considered their party as the advocate of white collar interests and an unbiased and restrained party:

> It fits students well and it's more the party of office personnel, not too extreme to either direction. (Student, male, 21)

> It takes care of our interests mainly in wages and other things. (Foreman, 51)

> Because the party I voted for stands for the rule of the golden mean. (Machine operator, female, 54)

And the voters of the Conservatives again considered their party the one which advocated the interests of the whole, or those of white collar groups, and still retained the image of good economic policy and good party leadership.

> The constructive, patriotic and widely comprehensive principles of the party and feeling of responsibility for common affairs were my reasons. (High school teacher, male, 27)
>
> It has a straight Finnish direction and a backbone. It doesn't sway here and there, it is not only the party of the capital, although that is often mentioned. (Skilled worker, male, 34)
>
> It's the only party that does not exploit the class of owners. (House owner, female, 63)
>
> Other parties have wasted the money of the people too much and in vain. (Electrical mechanic, male, 68)

The Voters of the Parties Compared

In May, people usually praised some very general aspect or principle of their party. And, as is obvious from the citations above, "the main reason why you chose that party" was also often a general image. The votes seemed to be cast to support a general principle rather than such goals as would have borne specific connection to the tasks of the new Parliament or to the current political situation. Neither did the voters mention as reasons for their choice any propaganda or other external stimuli; they seemed to consider their behavior mainly as a result of individual thinking.

Such is the nature of 65 per cent of all answers given to Question 54.B. Only 14 per cent related current considerations to their choice. On the other hand, 19 per cent considered their old habit to be a sufficient reason for party choice. A small sector of the electorate said that the reason for their vote was a suggestion received from an information source. Table 10.5 shows how the voters of different parties in Tampere were distributed into the four classes.

Current considerations were reasons most frequently mentioned by voters of the victorious parties.[9] The People's Democrats wanted to help their party out of the opposition position of the past decade.

> Maybe the workers are better able to conduct the affairs of the country than others, because the others have failed. (Wife of industrial worker, 30)

9. $t = 3.66, p < 0.001$.

TABLE 10.5. Classification of Reasons Given for Party Choice by the Voters of Five Parties in Tampere (QQ. 54.A and 54.B; see Appendix Table 21) (in percentages)

	FPDU	S.D. Opp.	SDP	FPP	Cons.	Total sample
General reason based on personal deliberation	75	57	60	94	56	65
Own decision based on the situation	14	9	8	–	26	14
Voting habit	10	24	30	6	16	19
Advice by another person	1	10	2	–	2	2
Total	100	100	100	100	100	100
Number of cases	*100*	*21*	*105*	*17*	*98*	*344*

They attempt to get into the cabinet and it would be good to try if they have any better means than the others. The others are broken, FPDU in integral. After all the FPDU also is a national party. (Painter, male, 35)

It takes best care of those things which touch me, like national pension, children's allowances—and the most important is that it would stop the quarrels in the plants. There would be no striking if the FPDU would be in the Cabinet. Then we would respect the governments. (Construction worker, male, 64)

Even some Conservative voters wanted to increase the influence of their party in the current situation:

If it would be easier to find jobs again and the affairs of the country would be mended, because the Agrarian Union always only raises the price of bread. (Wife of carpenter, 53)

It would be more able to take care of the country's affairs if it would be allowed to take care of them. (Bus driver, male, 43)

But two other aspects played a role in their thoughts at the time. Especially the National Coalition seems to have gained voters because of its candidates; and it was also supported by persons who would have chosen the Swedish or the Finnish People's Party in other circumstances:

I voted after thorough thinking. Earlier I have been a Social Democrat, but I have not been content with its representative. I thought the one I now voted for was more educated and more able. (Seamstress, 40)

Because my cousin was a candidate. (Taxation clerk, female, 59)

Because there was no corresponding Swedish party and because this is a bourgeois party. (Correspondent, female, 40)

A person like me really should not vote for the Coalition, but if I would have voted for the Finnish People's Party, it would have been lost. (Wife of technician, 39)

On the other hand, exceptionally many Social Democrats gave the reason that this was their traditional party choice:[10]

It's my position which I have inherited, and it will not change. (Forest foreman, 63)

Dad and mother have always been Social Democrats. That's why there is no reason to change now either. (Unskilled worker, male, 28)

The decision made since 1919 has not changed a single time. Social Democracy is my conviction. I have earlier belonged to its youth organization. When it was divided in 1919 to socialists and communists, I chose the socialists and since then I have not troubled my head about the matter. My choice then was due to the advice of a friend. (Former industrial worker, female, 62)

There were some responses which deviated from the general trend. Even some Social Democrats voted "to keep the Communists from winning" (warehouse foreman, 61), and because "the affairs of Finland have to be mended" (electrician, male, 64). On the other hand, the FPDU received votes because "it is so close to my habitual thinking I learnt at home" (pharmacist, female, 21), and the Conservatives were supported "because that's what I always voted for and I belong to it and I sort of grew into it" (widow, 77). This kind of quantitative analysis based on Table 10.4 generally requires cautious conclusions. But despite the reservations, we might conclude that in 1958 voting habits and traditions motivated especially the voters of the SDP, which now was in a "position of defense." Electoral victories, in turn, owed more to motivation connected with the political situation, such as the desire of voters to empower the leftist or rightist opposition, in their turn, to try to rule the country.

We might presume further that, as late as during the campaign, force of habit was preventing conversions to a new position, and that reasoning connected with the situation, in turn, was characteristic of those persons who changed their precampaign voting intention.

10. $t = 3.57, p < 0.001$.

TABLE 10.6. Relationship of Party and Constancy in Voting Intention to the Reason Given for Party Choice (in percentages)†

	FPDU		Soc.Dem. Party and Opposition		Nonsoc.		Total	
	C	N	C	N	C	N	C	N
General reason based on personal deliberation	80	79	65	41*	61	61	68	56°
Own decision based on the situation	8	21	6	14	19	28	11	21°
Voting habit	11	–	28	35	19	4*	20	16
Advice by another person	1	–	1	10*	1	7	1	7°
Total	100	110	100	100	100	100	100	100
Number of cases	*83*	*14*	*97*	*29*	*90*	*28*	*270*	*71*

C = Voters whose precampaign intention did not change.
N = New voters whose intention changed or who were uncertain before the campaign.
† The significance of the differences is determined by the *t*-test, as denoted in Table 4.1.

To verify this presumption, we have to show the distribution of Table 10.5 separately for the new voters of the parties and for their constant supporters. This is done in Table 10.6. Because of the small number of cases, the voters of the two Social Democratic electoral alliances are combined as are all nonsocialist voters. Neither group contains mutually inconsistent material.

We find that the new voters of each party gave more current reasons for their party choice than those who had made their final decision already in May. It thus seems that motives connected with the situation caused changes in voting intentions during the campaign. It was also according to expectations that the constant supporters of the FPDU and the nonsocialist groups considered it unnecessary to think out their habitual party choice. However, voting habit was given as the reason by the SDP voters even if they had changed their precampaign voting intention. But this factor does not contradict the hypothesis, because changes in voting decisions among the Social Democrats were not quite comparable to the changes among others. In Table 10.6 the changers include among others: (1) those Social Democrats who in May planned to vote for their Party Opposition, but who then returned to their old position; (2) those voters of the Party Opposition who did not notice a change in their position; and (3) the permanent Social Democrats who made a late decision to participate.

Events Affecting Decisions

After the respondents had given reasons for their party choice, they were also asked: "Did anything happen before the election which affected your voting decision?" (Q. 54.C). Only 7 per cent gave an affirmative answer. If we classify the sample according to the constancy of voting intentions, the percentage mentioning such events was the following:

Constants	5($n = 287$)
Inter-Social Democratic changers	6($n = 18$)
Party converters	21($n = 34$)
Crystallizers	9($n = 43$)
Nonvoters	4($n = 68$)

Again it seems that the inter-Social Democratic changes were not generally perceived as party conversions. On the other hand, other converters were the group most likely to remember those events which had an impact on their decision.[11]

It is noteworthy how few events that affected voting decisions were remembered. Although in the case of the majority, "the conviction said everything" (widow, 66, SDP), the smallness of the percentages was caused at least in part by false memories. We have found (Table 9.4) that one half of the converters thought that they had made their final decision in the beginning of the year.

The following are some basic features of the content of responses to Question 54.C, grouped according to the source of information mentioned by the respondents:

1. A group of voters "attempted to follow the situation all the time," without specifically mentioning where the information was obtained. Unemployment experiences, "the conduct of legislative matters, like children's allowances" and "this downward trend of the Finnish economy" led Social Democrats to switch their votes to the FPDU, and also strengthened the position of constant People's Democrats. Yet there were also anti-Communist changes before the election:

> Because everybody fusses about the Communist victory, I decided to vote for the Social Democrats. (Wife of electrician, 46, SDP)

> It was in the interest of the fatherland that the Communists would not win. (Warehouse foreman, 61, SDP)

The split of the Social Democratic Party was also mentioned as an event

11. In the comparison of converters and constants, $t = 2.18$, $p < 0.05$.

which strengthened the Communist position and, in addition, decreased the desire of Social Democrats to vote at all. "The conduct of the state until now" converted some people to voting for the Conservatives.

2. Mass communications had, according to the responses, affected voting decisions only in two ways. Some said that it made their voting intention more firm:

> A week before the election we had a meeting in the plant which enforced my decision. (Carpenter, male, 35, FPDU)

> At least the speech by that engineer on radio assured me of my position. (Unskilled worker, male, 41, FPDU)

> There was all kind of advertising which strengthened my decision. (Former industrial worker, female, 71, SDP)

But other persons mentioned that the campaign annoyed them so much that they lost their desire to vote:

> Because they spoke so much and don't do nothing and they always offer the same old candidates and not new ones. (Typographer, male, 28, SDP nonvoter)

> Because there was such a quarreling before the election. (Truck driver, 54, FPP, spoilt the ballot)

3. Discussions with peers were recalled as factors which changed party choice, but they were never mentioned as factors strengthening the permanent position or decreasing the desire to vote:

> I was of the same opinion as everybody else round here that it's time to change the party. (Dependent of municipal old age institution, female, 74, SDP–FPDU)

> Actually nothing of that kind happened. My brother asked me to vote for the Conservatives and so I did. In the meantime I thought I might vote for the Social Democratic Party, but then I switched to the Conservatives again. (Widow, 65, SDP-Conservative)

Table 10.6 showed correspondingly that the desire to follow a friend's advice was a reason offered especially by those voters who had converted to a new party.

The Direct Impact of the Campaign on Voting Decisions

Although most voters perceived their party choice as a result of independent reasoning, and not as a product of mass communication, it is still possible that mass communication had a direct impact on voting behavior by increasing and biasing the grounds for such independent reasoning. Even in this sense the opposite of direct mass communication would be person-to-person communication in small groups.

The Effect of Direct Communication

The main purpose of an election campaign is to increase the number of voters in the party. Accordingly, the success of various media in realizing this should be observed by comparing the communication experiences of the parties' old and new voters. For this purpose, Table 10.7 summarizes the data concerning the attention paid by constant and converted voters to the campaign. The group of converted voters in the table comprises both actual party changers and those voters who still were uncertain in May. The number of cases is in many points too small for reliable generalizations.

Nevertheless, the basic finding is quite obvious: people who carried into effect their precampaign voting intention were more exposed to the propaganda of their party than were those who were converted during the campaign to vote for a particular party. These constant supporters especially identified their party posters and evaluated them as the best ones. The constant voters of the leftist parties had listened to the radio presentations of their party more than had the new ones. And the audiences at campaign meetings had consisted mainly of persons whose voting intention did not change during the campaign.

There may have been some exceptions to this basic finding. It is possible that the Independent Social Democratic electoral alliance won new votes with its rally held in the sports stadium. It is also possible that the programs of the FPP on the radio gained new voters for that party. Table 10.7 also hints at such a possibility as that the new voters of the leftist parties began to read their party newspaper as often or even more often than did their constant voters. But the general conclusion is that direct mass communication does not seem to obtain new votes for the parties.

Because Table 10.7 actually shows only one line of each of nine different tables, this conclusion would be false if the new voters of the parties had tended to pay no attention to the propaganda of other parties either. But it seems that the converted voters were equally or even more exposed to communication from other parties than constant voters were.[12]

12. For example, a poster of another party was ranked best by 34 per cent of the constant supporters but by 46 per cent of the converted voters, $t = 1.97$, $p \sim 0.05$.

TABLE 10.7. Relationship of the Voters' Party and Constancy of Voting Intention to Attention Paid to the Campaign in Tampere (in percentages)†

	FPDU		S.D. Opp.		SDP		FPP		Cons.		Total voters	
	C	N	C	N	C	N	C	N	C	N	C	N
Recalled own party poster	62	65	14	41	56	40	79	43	55	42	57	46°
Identified own party poster	70	65	14	12	59	33*	46	43	75	54°	65	42***
Saw poster of candidate of own party	21	5°	43	18	22	27	46	43	25	21	24	19
Ranked own party poster best	54	40	14	6	26	–*	46	29	50	25*	42	20***
Listened to radio program of own party	38	25	43	24	22	14	30	43	34	39	31	25
Recalled own party representative in radio debate	12	5	–	–	12	13	8	29	8	–	10	6
Received campaign letter from own party	5	5	43	36	18	26	23	–	17	16	14	18
Went to a meeting of own party	18	10	–	12	2	–	–	–	3	–	7	5
Adopted a paper of own party	20	25	–	6	10	13	–	–	4	–	11	9
Number of cases	93	20	7	17	94	15	13	7	78	24	288	84

C = Constants in voting intention.

N = Voters whose intention changed or who were uncertain before the campaign.

† Differences between percentages according to the *t*-test, level of significance denoted as in Table 4.1.

It has been shown in other studies, too, that the direct exposure of voters to mass media does not provide sufficient explanation for changes in voting decisions,[13] nor even for changes in the images of parties.[14] Mass communication may have increased political knowledge and activated voters;[15] on the other hand, the appearance of a new important medium has been found quite insignificant in this respect.[16] And scholars have been surprised when the data they have gathered has not proved that mass communication has exerted the expected influence.[17]

The Amount and Choice of Material

Two basic reasons have been shown why mass media do not directly convert many voters to the position attempted by the communicator. (1) Often the campaign reaches least those persons most likely to change their intentions;[18] and (2) exposure to the campaign is selective, so that most attention is paid to the communication which specifically strengthens earlier positions.[19] Furthermore, it has been found that the more exposure there is the more selective it becomes.[20] Let us now observe whether corresponding relationships exist in the Tampere data.

1. The late deciders had not been as interested in politics normally as those voters who recalled an early voting decision. This was apparent in the smaller amount of attention given to mass communications by the late

13. Herbert A. Simon and Fredrick Stern, "The Effect of Television upon Voting Behavior in Iowa in the 1952 Presidential Election," *American Political Science Review,* 49 (1955), 470–77. Trenaman and McQuail, *Television,* pp. 186–90.

14. Trenaman and McQuail, *Television,* pp. 191–92.

15. Berelson, Lazarsfeld, and McPhee, *Voting,* pp. 248–51; Trenaman and McQuail, *Television,* p. 188.

16. Simon and Stern, *American Political Science Review, 49,* 474.

17. "In the present (Erie County) study, face-to-face contacts turned out to be the most important influences stimulating opinion change. To the worker in a political machine this is probably not surprising, but to the social scientist it is a challenge." Lazarsfeld, Berelson, and Gaudet, *People's Choice,* xiii–xiv.

18. Benney, Gray, and Pear, *How People Vote,* p. 177; Berelson, Lazarsfeld, and McPhee, *Voting,* pp. 248–49; Milne and Mackenzie, *Straight Fight,* p. 97; Milne and Mackenzie, *Marginal Seat,* pp. 103–04. In Sweden, the difference concerned radio listening in 1960, but not TV viewing, Sjödén, *TV Election in Sweden,* p. 110.

19. Berelson, The Effect of Print upon Public Opinion, Douglas Waples (ed.), *Print, Radio, and Film in a Democracy* (Chicago, University of Chicago Press, 1942), pp. 49, 51, 60; Benney, Gray, and Pear, *How People Vote,* pp. 155–56, 162–63; Lazarsfeld, Berelson, and Gaudet, *People's Choice,* pp. 89–90; Pesonen, *Student Voters,* p. 126. See also Berelson and Gary A. Steiner, *Human Behavior* (New York, Harcourt, Brace & World, Inc., 1964), pp. 529–33.

20. Lazarsfeld, Berelson, and Gaudet, *People's Choice,* pp. 90, 167.

deciders (Table 9.5.a). During the campaign they had a special tendency toward not listening to election programs on the radio and not attending campaign meetings. In the case of newspaper reading, however, these differences existed only between voters and nonvoters and not between persons deciding at different times (Table 9.5.c).

If we now measure the time of decision with the panel method, the findings correspond to those mentioned in Chapter 9. For instance, the constancy of the voting decision correlated with the knowledge of politics

FIGURE 10.B. Relationship of Political Knowledge to Constancy in Voting Intention (in percentages)

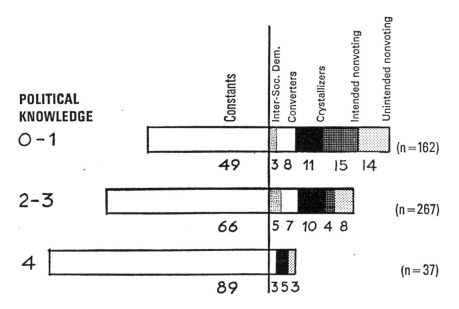

revealed in May, which, in turn, can be considered a consequence of a different exposure to normal political mass communication. Figure 10.B shows—in line with expectations—that the less the persons had been informed about politics, the more easily voting intentions changed during the campaign.[21] Appendix Table 22 offers data on exposure to campaign communication. Even that indicates that constant voters paid most attention to the campaign and nonvoters the least. The latter group can be further subdivided into two more groups: those persons who had no voting intention in May and did not participate were less exposed to the cam-

21. $\chi^2 = 19.92$, $v = 5$, $p < 0.01$.

paign than those nonvoters who failed to realize their earlier intention to vote. There were also differences in the activity of those voters who made their final decision during the campaign. The converters were in many respects as exposed to the campaign as the constant voters; they saw only posters less.[22] On the other hand, crystallizers paid relatively little attention to the campaign. For example, radio programs and campaign meetings had little chance to affect their position.[23] The campaign material of newspapers was read about equally by constant and converted voters, but less by the crystallizers.

It thus seems that those voters who would have needed information on which to base their changing, and especially their crystallizing, decisions tended to avoid all kinds of campaign communications. Yet they had been the least knowledgeable even earlier. Those inhabitants of Tampere who gave up their intention to vote paid equally much or even more attention to the campaign than did those who now crystallized their delayed decision.

2. Regarding the selection of normal political material, we have mentioned the tendency of many persons to follow their own party paper in order to supplement the information offered by the leading local newspaper (Table 3.5). Some conclusions about the selective exposure during the campaign can be based on Table 10.8.

Because the FPDU organized most campaign meetings in Tampere (Table 7.2), its supporters had the best opportunity to hear speeches by their own party candidates. Thus the selective attendance of campaign rallies was seen in the Communist majority of the total audiences. Of those people who assembled in the FPDU meetings, no less than 81 per cent had been FPDU supporters in May. We might mention, however, that the interviewed Social Democrats had visited more meetings of other parties than of their own, and that some of them indeed became voters for their Party Opposition or the FPDU.

Contrary to expectations, Table 10.8 does not reveal any other significant tendency toward favoring the propaganda of one's own party. Supporters of all parties preferred to hear the first party presentation on the radio. It was the time the FPDU, Finnish People's Party, and Conservatives

22. On the average, the converters remembered 0.55 fewer posters and identified 0.66 fewer posters than the constant voters; $t = 2.74$, $p = 0.01$ and $t = 4.41$, $p < 0.001$.

23. The presentation of one's own party was listened to by 41 per cent of constants and 19 per cent of crystallizers ($t = 3.40$, $p < 0.001$); campaign meetings were attended by 10 per cent of the former and 2 per cent of the latter ($t = 2.67$, $p < 0.01$).

TABLE 10.8. Relationships of Party Preference in May to Attention Paid to the Campaign of One's Own Party and Others in June and July 1958 (in percentages)

		S.D.					
	FPDU	Opp.	SDP	Agr.	FPP	Cons.	Total
(a) Recalled party posters (Q. 44.A)[a]							
Own party only	3	–	2	–	7	7	3
Own and other	60	29	51	11	59	51	52
Other party only	16	46	18	67	15	13	19
No poster	21	25	30	22	19	29	26
(b) Poster ranked best (Q. 44.C)							
Own party	51	17	30	11	26	49	38
Other party	19	54	42	44	41	33	35
Don't know	30	29	28	45	33	18	27
(c) Party presentations on radio (Q. 47)[b]							
Evening of own party	21	8	4	11	11	12	11
Both evenings	14	17	17	11	7	21	16
Evening of other parties	6	25	13	33	7	7	11
Did not listen	59	50	66	45	74	60	62
(d) New newspaper adopted during campaign (QQ. 5 and 63)							
Paper of own party	19	17	7	11	4	3	10
Own and other	6	–	4	–	–	3	4
Paper of other party	10	25	21	22	18	13	17
No new paper	75	58	68	67	78	81	70
(e) Campaign meetings (Q. 58)							
Own party	15	–	2	–	–	2	5
Own and other	3	–	1	–	–	1	1
Other party	1	4	4	–	–	2	3
No campaign meeting	81	96	93	100	100	95	91
Total	100	100	100	100	100	100	100
Number of cases	*105*	*24*	*159*	*9*	*27*	*92*	*416*

a. Two posters shown in Q. 44.A are omitted in order to have each party represented by one poster only.

b. The program of the SDP is considered the "own" program of the Independent Social Democrats, too.

were speaking. It is possible that these parties simply had a more favorable evening than the Swedes, Agrarians, and SDP. It seems, however, that the Social Democrats showed, even in this connection, their special interest in the two parties which now had "the political wind behind them." It may be indicative of a corresponding indifference of attitude toward one's own party material that the Social Democrats did not like their party poster as much as the FPDU supporters and Conservatives liked theirs.

As election time neared, newspaper readership increased to some extent, and the percentage of people reading at least three papers rose in Tampere from 14 to 20 per cent. An increasing number of People's Democrats began to read in June their party papers, *Kansan Uutiset* and *Hämeen Yhteistyö*. Their third new favorite was the Social Democratic *Kansan Lehti*. Were *Helsingin Sanomat* not classified in Table 10.8.d as an organ of the Finnish People's Party, we would find that the Social Democrats and Conservatives seldom began to read papers of other parties either. This would give additional support to the hypothesis concerning partisan choice of campaign material.

The Dominance of a Conservative Paper

The dominant role of the Conservative organ *Aamulehti* does not seem to concur with the finding that the inhabitants of Tampere chose their newspapers in accordance with their party preference. In order to state that other papers were read especially for political reasons, we ought to show that non-Conservative persons paid relatively little attention to the political material in *Aamulehti,* but followed politics in other newspapers.

Table 10.9 concerns interview data about normal political communication which can be used to test the hypothesis. Both sections of the table bring out the tendency of the people in Tampere to have a more nonpolitical attitude toward *Aamulehti* than toward their own party papers. (1) The interest of leftist supporters increased if they read another paper in addition to *Aamulehti*. However, the most interested were those supporters of leftist parties who also read their own party organ,[24] and especially those leftist supporters who read two papers of their own party. (2) Quite a few Conservative supporters read another Conservative paper in addition to *Aamulehti,*[25] whereas other additions to *Aamulehti* were

24. $\chi^2 = 8.15, v = 2, p < 0.05$.
25. $\chi^2 = 6.50, v = 2, p < 0.05$.

TABLE 10.9. Relationship of Newspaper's Party Affiliation to Attention Paid to Political Content, by (a) Readers Supporting the FPDU, S.D. Opp., or SDP, and (b) Readers Supporting the Conservatives (QQ. 5.B and 5) (in percentages)

| | Political material | | | Total | |
	Not	Some-times	Often	Per cent	Number of cases
(a) Supporters of FPDU, S.D. Opp., and SDP*					
Aamulehti only	24	34	42	100	153
Numerous papers of others	17	36	47	100	42
Also one paper of own party	11	35	54	100	80
Two papers of own party	–	15	85	100	13
(b) Conservative supporters					
Aamulehti only	24	33	43	100	37
Aamulehti and papers of others	18	41	41	100	32
Two papers of own party	14	14	72	100	22

* SDP papers were also classified as "own" papers of people supporting the Social Democratic Opposition.

not related to their political interest. On the other hand, what seems surprising in Table 10.9 is that there was no difference related to party choice among the readers of *Aamulehti* only. Among these one paper readers, leftist supporters were as interested in political material as Conservative supporters. This finding does not contradict our hypothesis if even the Conservative supporters perceived their dominant local paper as an unpolitical means of communication.

The information contained in Table 10.10 about the supporters of three parties concerns actual campaign time. In the sample, 28 per cent began to read in June a newspaper which they did not follow regularly in May (see Table 10.8.d). Moreover, exposure to campaign advertising cor-

TABLE 10.10. Relationship of Party Affiliation of New Newspaper Adopted by Supporters of the FPDU, SDP and Conservatives to the Attention Paid to Campaign Advertising in the Papers (QQ. 64.A, 5, and 63) (in percentages)

| | Campaign advertising | | | Total | |
	Not	Sometimes	Often	Per cent	Number of cases
No new paper	34	43	23	100	256
Papers of other party	41	33	26	100	49
Own and other party	19	44	37	100	16
Papers of own party	26	40	34	100	35

related with the party position of the new paper. Those persons, who began to read an organ of another party, were not exposed to campaign advertisements any more than those who read in June only the same papers they had read in May. But those persons who adopted their own party paper paid more attention to campaign advertising.[26] This seems to indicate that new papers were adopted during the campaign in order to get the kind of information about the election which would support the reader's political thinking.

Thus the party preference expressed in May had an impact on the later choice of campaign material. This was apparent in attendance at campaign meetings and interest in newspapers. And it gives a partial explanation of the constant party supporters' tendency to pay more attention to the campaign of the party of their choice than did those voters who were converted during the campaign to voting for another party.

PARTY IDENTIFICATION AND THE CHOICE OF CAMPAIGN MATERIAL

The quantity and quality of newspapers read in May was also related to the strength of party identification: the stronger the identification, the more newspapers were read regularly (p. 67), and the greater tendency to this was revealed in the reading of one's own party paper, especially its main organ (Table 4.4). Correspondingly, we might hypothesize also that strong party identifiers tended during the campaign to be more exposed to and more selective of mass communications than were other persons.

The data of Table 10.8 are repeated in Appendix Table 23 separately for the weak and the strong party identifiers. The hypothesis concerning the quantity of material is better supported than is the hypothesis about the choice of material. The strong identifiers of all parties proved to be loyal in their preference for their own party posters.[27] Especially among the Conservative supporters, the sure identifiers preferred their own party's radio program, and the weak, other party programs. Similarly, the strong supporters of the FPDU and the Conservatives appeared to have a tendency to go to their own party meetings. One third of the total audiences of the FPDU meetings were members of the organizing party and more than two thirds were strongly identifying People's Democrats. However, at least within the sample, strongly identifying Social Democrats were the most

26. The percentage of looking often or sometimes at advertisements was 79 of those adopting own party paper, but 59 of those adopting other paper only, $t = 2.25$, $p < 0.05$.
27. In the whole sample, $\chi^2 = 8.48$, $v = 2$, $p < 0.02$.

typical representatives of their party in a surprising fashion: they were the most interested in the propaganda of other parties.

The campaign activity of people with a strong identification and their apparent tendency toward partisan choice of campaign material were consistently connected with the strong desire to vote, which caused their high turnout and was related to the early time of their final voting decision (see Figure 9.E).

Additional examination of Table 10.8.a and Appendix Table 23.a seems in order. They do not support the conclusion about selective attention to propaganda, because the inhabitants of Tampere recalled outdoor posters irrespective of their party choice or their degree of party identification. But we might use the ability to recall the message of the posters as measure of exposure to them (Q. 44.B; see Tables 9.5.c and 10.7). This measure shows the following exposure of weak and strong party identifiers to the posters:[28]

	Percentage of:	
	Weak identifiers	Strong identifiers
No poster	24	19
Identified posters of other parties	26	20
Identified posters of own and other parties	44	53
Identified only own party poster	6	8
	100	100
Number of cases	*158*	*262*

In both groups one's own party poster was identified more than a random choice would explain.[29] At the same time the difference between weak and strong party identifiers is in line with the hypothesis, although it is not statistically significant.[30]

Let us return to the direct relationship of mass communication to voting. We might examine whether the relationship of constancy in voting intention to exposure to campaign posters still exists if the effect of party identification is controlled. The data are presented in Figure 10.C. This examination cannot concern nonpartisan people, but it includes persons who had an uncertain voting intention but did have a party preference in

28. Two posters, Nos. 5 (FPDU) and 7 (Agrarian) are excluded from the analysis, and nonpartisans are omitted from the sample.

29. Relation of "only own" to "other parties" would be at random 1:6, but among weak party identifiers it is 1:4 and strong identifiers 1:2.5. One's own party poster was identified by 50 per cent of all weak and 61 per cent of strong party identifiers.

30. $\chi^2 = 4.26$, $v = 3$, $0.20 < p < 0.30$.

FIGURE 10.C. Relationship of Party of Identified Posters and Precampaign Party Identification to Constancy in Voting Intention (in percentages)

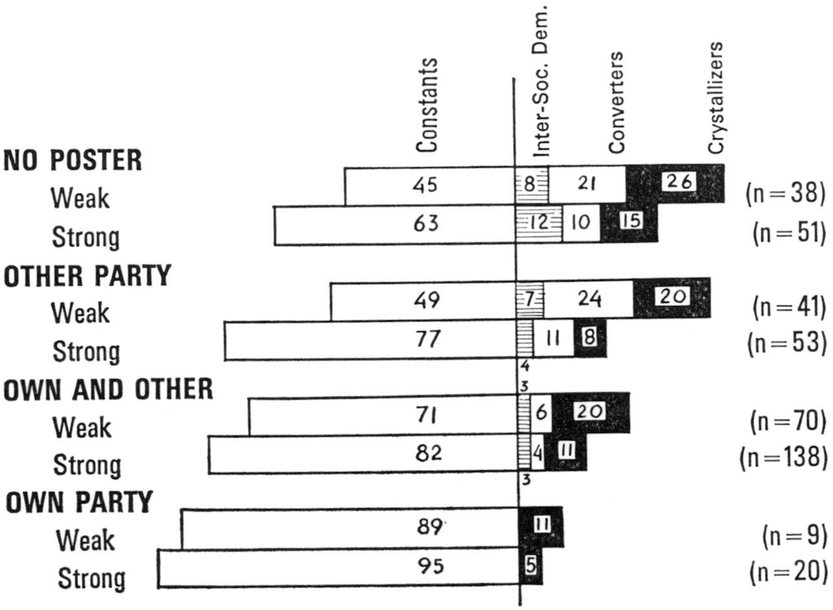

May. Figure 10.C indicates three correlations which have been noted above:

1. Participation in the election was least frequent among those people who did not identify a single poster (see Table 9.5.c). In this sample their turnout was 80 per cent, whereas the turnout of those who identified their own party poster only was 93 per cent.

2. The more selective exposure to posters had been, the more constant was party choice (see Table 10.7).

3. The strength of party identification was related to turnout and to party choice.

But we can also point out two additional findings:

4. The relationship of exposure to posters to the constancy of voting decision exists to some extent even when party identification is controlled.[31]

5. Even posters of other parties seem to have prevented the conversion of strong SDP identifiers to voting for the Social Democratic Opposition.

31. Among weak identifiers, $\chi^2 = 15.71$, $v = 2$, $p < 0.001$; among strong identifiers, $\chi^2 = 9.55$, $v = 3$, $p < 0.05$.

It thus seems that those persons who had identified with their party before the campaign were selective about the posters in such a way that led to constancy in party choice. Correspondingly, persons with a weak preference tended to be less exposed to posters or to notice posters of other parties. Yet party identification alone does not explain the relationship of this mass communication to voting decision.

Now it would be possible to interpret the information of Figure 10.C in two opposing ways: (1) Perhaps posters really increased the desire to vote among their audiences and—in case only strange posters were perceived—also persuaded people to abandon their existing party preference. But if people were exposed to their own party posters, too, such strange appeals were turned aside. (2) On the other hand, it is possible that strange posters were no longer strange during the days preceding the election. Perhaps the beginning temptation toward a new party was already drawing attention to its campaign material, while a constant party choice was continuously supported by the material in line with the permanent preference, and if there was no desire to vote there was no desire to look at the posters either.

According to the former interpretation posters did have direct impact on voting decision. This influence may have extended even to people who had a sure voting intention in May. However, the latter interpretation is again in line with the idea that people followed the campaign selectively, as if they would have sought support for a position which had been adopted for some other reason.

PERSONAL INFLUENCE

A direct exposure to newspapers, radio, campaign material, and campaign meetings was not the only way of getting information about the election. Other sources of information are, of course, the people with whom politics are discussed. Some voters even considered the advice of a friend the most important reason for their party choice (Table 10.5). Respondents who gave such reasons trusted greatly the judgment of other people:

> I can't think so independently. Maybe my husband influenced me. Earlier I've voted for the Social Democrats. (Wife of taxi driver, 28, S. D. Opp.)
>
> My husband voted for the same and it had a candidate whom we think might help the interests of metal workers. Maybe there had been some suitable women, but because I can't hold my job long any-

way it's more important that my husband gets good working conditions. (Industrial seamstress, 24, S. D. Opp.)

My son advised me to vote for the Social Democratic Party. Maybe
he knows more than I do. I'm not interested in these things. (Wife
of an electrician, 56, SDP)

I suppose it is the friends who draw me toward that party. (Saleswoman, 25, Conservative)

This study uses three methods to make observations on personal influence. First, the respondents were asked to evaluate where they obtained
before the election "the most and the most reliable information on the
election," and what was their second-best source of information (Q. 67).
The answers were distributed as follows:

	Best		Second		Total
		Percentage:			
Newspapers	52	+	28	=	80
Radio	30		30		60
Discussions with friends	7		4		11
Posters	1		5		6
Other party material	1		3		4
Campaign meetings	1		2		3
Periodicals	1		1		2
Other	2		0		2
	95	+	73	=	168

We can thus extract from the sample one group who considered discussions to be their most important source of information. By comparing
them to the audiences of mass media, we can get information about personal influence. It is true, however, that the two normal mass media were
considered by far the most important sources of campaign information:
more than one half considered newspapers their primary source, and most
of the others considered it to be their second best source. The only significance of actual campaign media seems to have been the supplementation
of primary sources of information.[32]

32. When student voters were interviewed in Helsinki in connection with the 1956
presidential election, an almost equal percentage (54 per cent) considered newspapers their
most important source of information. Discussions were mentioned by 11 per cent (an
additional 6 per cent together with newspapers), but radio by only 6 per cent (7 per cent
more with newspapers). Even students very seldom considered the campaign material of
parties to be a primary source of information; Pesonen, *Student Voters,* p. 127. Concerning studies in other countries, see Lazarsfeld, Berelson, and Gaudet, *People's Choice,* p.

The second method of studying personal influence is to observe how the respondents participated in political discussions. As is explained in Appendix 3, 22 per cent were classified as opinion leaders and 33 per cent as outsiders in discussions. Between the two groups there remain 45 per cent who are called in the following "ordinary discussers."

TABLE 10.11. Relationship of Most Important Source of Campaign Information to the Type of Participation in Political Discussions: Tampere, 1958 (in percentages)

	All			Men			Women		
	Opls.	Disc.	Outs.	Opls.	Disc.	Outs.	Opls.	Disc.	Outs.
Newspapers	52	49	55	55	56	61	48	45	52
Radio	38	31	25	37	27	29	40	33	23
Discussions	4	9	6	3	7	–	5	10	9
Campaign material	1	2	3	2	2	2	–	2	4
Campaign meetings	–	1	–	–	1	–	–	2	–
Magazines	1	1	–	–	2	–	3	–	–
Other	2	2	1	2	4	2	2	1	1
Don't know	2	5	10	1	1	6	2	7	11
Total	100	100	100	100	100	100	100	100	100
Number of cases	*105*	*212*	*159*	*65*	*85*	*48*	*40*	*127*	*111*

Opls. = Opinion leaders.
Disc. = Ordinary discussers.
Outs. = Outsiders.

These two methods are consistent only in case those people whose main source of information was discussions were neither opinion leaders nor outsiders, but mainly ordinary discussers. According to Table 10.11 this seems to be the case. Within the sample we find that ordinary discussers mentioned more often than opinion leaders and outsiders personal discussions as their major source of information. However, quite a few women, even if classified as outsiders, called discussions their most important source. Let us remember, however, that Table 10.10 does not concern the quantity of attention paid to the various media. It is possible that a few women were exposed so little to the campaign that discussions still had relative significance for them.

The third method is simply the identification of actual campaign work-

127; Sjödén, *TV Election in Sweden*, p. 78; Westerståhl and Särlvik, *Svensk Valrörelse*, p. 59; and V. O. Key, Jr., *Public Opinion and American Democracy* (New York, Alfred A. Knopf, 1961), p. 346.

ers. A common feature of the third and the second method is that attention is paid mainly to the influencers and not to the influencees. But we can separate from the sample that 11 per cent minority who said that they worked for their party during the campaign (Q. 68, see Tables 9.3 and 9.5.c). Some of the campaign workers were also opinion leaders: 48 per cent ($n = 54$) belonged to the group of opinion leaders. But more than one half did campaign work without being an opinion leader. A classification of the sample according to campaign work and the way of discussing gives the following six groups, and the following distribution of the sample into the groups:

	Did campaign work	No campaign work	Total
		Percentage:	
Opinion leaders	5	17	22
Ordinary discussers	4	41	45
Outsiders	2	31	33
Total	11	89	$100(n = 476)$

In many studies of personal influence, the role of political opinion leaders and a person's desire to promote his own party have been considered as almost the same thing. Between the two, however, there is a noteworthy conceptual difference. An attempt to further the goals of the party organization is based mainly on the party worker's own initiative, whereas the role of opinion leader presupposes, in addition to the desire to present one's opinions, a desire of other people to ask for those opinions.[33]

According to Table 9.5.c, campaign workers recalled that their voting decision happened before the final stage of the campaign. Let us now compare the time of voting decision with the most important source of information and with opinion leadership in Tampere. Table 10.12 contains the recalled times of final party choice. We find that there were three exceptions to the average time of decision: (1) people who were informed in discussions tended to decide late;[34] (2) relatively many outsiders recalled

33. In both the Erie County study of 1940 and the Elmira study of 1948 opinion leaders were defined by means of two questions, one dealing with the attempt to influence others, the other inquiring whether the opinions of the respondent had been asked for. On the other hand, Sjödén defined opinion transmitters ("opinionsförmedlarna") so that he mentioned six kinds of campaign activity, all of which were based on one's own initiative, and classified those giving three positive responses as opinion transmitters; see also Pesonen, "The Role of Influentials in Political Communication," *Asla*, 2 (1965), 21–30.

34. $\chi^2 = 16.36$, $v = 2$, $p < 0.001$

TABLE 10.12. Relationship of (a) Most Important Source of Campaign Information and (b) Type of Participation in Political Discussions to the Recalled Time of Final Party Choice (in percentages)

Final party choice	(a) Main source			(b) Type of discussion		
	News-papers	Radio	Discus-sion	Opls.	Disc.	Outs.
Beginning of year	70	73	49	84	68	59
2 months before voting	5	3	–	5	4	3
2 weeks before voting	5	1	9	3	4	4
Just before voting	8	7	24	1	8	16
Did not vote	12	16	18	7	16	18
Total	100	100	100	100	100	100
Number of cases	*242*	*142*	*33*	*103*	*211*	*152*

Opls. = Opinion leaders.
Disc. = Ordinary discussers.
Outs. = Outsiders.

a late decision; whereas (3) opinion leaders decided almost without exception before the campaign and also voted with the highest turnout.[35]

The activity and early decisions of opinion leaders seems to concur with the findings of some earlier studies.[36] If we consider the outsiders to be at the opposite pole of the same dimension, their late decisions, perhaps also their low turnout, were in line with the expectations. But the late decisions of those people who were informed in discussions would seem to suggest that personal influence had caused changes in voting intentions.

Answers to open-ended questions also suggest that discussions in small groups changed voting intentions relatively more effectively than direct mass communication. This was true of the reasons given for party choice (Table 10.6) and of the answers which were given to the question about events influencing voting decisions (p. 299).

Figures 10.D and 10.E can now be used to examine the hypothesis about the persuasive influence of personal discussions. According to Figure 10.D, it seems that people who were informed in discussions changed their voting intention more often than did people relying on the two mass media. If this statistically symptomatic difference can be generalized,[37]

35. $\chi^2 = 22.39$, $v = 4$, $p < 0.001$.
36. Regarding the political activity and political competence of opinion leaders, see Lazarsfeld, Berelson, and Gaudet, *People's Choice*, p. 51, and Berelson, Lazarsfeld, and McPhee, *Voting*, p. 112. Neither work reports data on the opinion leaders' time of voting decision, but their other characteristics suggest that they belonged to the early deciders.
37. $t = 1.72$, $p < 0.10$.

FIGURE 10.D. Relationship of Main Source of Campaign Information to Constancy in Voting Intention (in percentages)

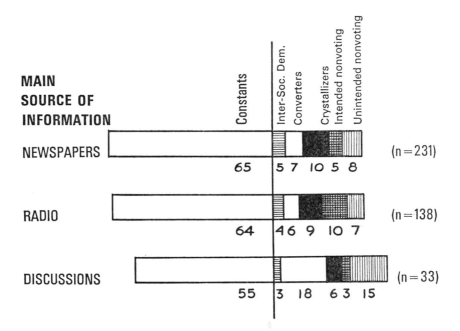

discussions were most effective in changing the precampaign party choices. And there would seem to be another way of influencing voting intentions, because people who relied on discussions tended to give up entirely their intention to vote. If we can generalize the latter finding, it emphasizes either the activating effect of mass media or the disruption of some party changes to the point of nonvoting.

Figure 10.E seems to show that, although the outsiders and the people informed in discussions recalled late voting decisions, these decisions were not of the same kind. The outsiders did not tend to change their intentions. Instead, they had been uncertain in May and thus delayed their decisions until close to the election.[38] In this sense they were a less political group than the discussers. Their other characteristics, too, were typical of politically inactive persons.

According to the panel interview, many people forgot that they had changed their intentions (Table 9.4). Comparing Figures 10.D and 10.E with Table 10.12, we can now make two additional conclusions about the voters' memory. In case discussions were the main source of information,

38. $\chi^2 = 17.72$, $v = 8$, $p < 0.05$ when the three classes of Figure 10.E are compared.

the decision was not easily forgotten. The memory of outsiders may have been weaker. Opinion leaders especially tended to forget changes in their party choice. Although they did recall early voting decisions (Table 10.12.b), and although they tended to remain constant in preference, Figure 10.E shows that opinion leaders changed their party as frequently as others in Tampere. According to the panel interview, their only special characteristics were the desire to vote and the precampaign certainty about voting intention.[39] The corresponding finding was also made about the other group of influencers, the campaign workers.[40]

According to the changes in voting intentions and the recollection of such changes, personal discussions were relatively more influential and

FIGURE 10.E. Relationship of Type of Participation in Political Discussions to Constancy in Voting Intention (in percentages)

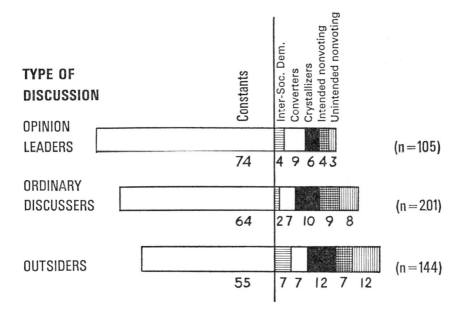

39. In the student sample of 1956, opinion leaders also changed their intention as often as others; Pesonen, *Student Voters,* p. 188. Let us note that there are others besides political influencers who have been found to be the first to adopt new innovations rather than just defenders of their old habits; see James Coleman, Elihu Katz, and Herbert Menzel, "The Diffusion of an Innovation," *Sociometry,* 20 (1957), 253–70.

40. Distribution of campaign workers ($n = 53$): constants in intention 79 per cent, converters 11 per cent, crystallizers 4 per cent, nonvoters 6 per cent. Distribution of others ($n = 398$): constants 62 per cent, inter-Soc. Dem. 5 per cent, converters 7 per cent, crystallizers 10 per cent, nonvoters 16 per cent.

persuasive than direct mass communication. Such effectiveness of personal influence has been found and accounted for in many previous connections.[41] Let us now emphasize that in Tampere this source of information was used mainly by the politically inexperienced persons who were awakened by the approaching election to improve their poor knowledge of politics through the advice of their friends. Among the people informed mainly in discussions, there were mostly young voters and people not knowledgeable about politics in May.[42] The following percentages support this:

Most important source of information:	Age 21–25	Poor knowledge of politics (0 or 1)
Newspapers	5	29($n = 246$)
Radio	9	29($n = 145$)
Discussions	27	61($n = 33$)

The corresponding percentages should be shown also for people grouped according to their manner of participation in political discussions:

Type of participation:	Age 21–25	Poor knowledge of politics
Opinion leaders	7	17($n = 105$)
Ordinary discussers	8	31($n = 212$)
Outsiders	9	44($n = 159$)

Here we find that ordinary discussers were not necessarily younger than opinion leaders or outsiders. The relationship of opinion leadership to political knowledge[43] was to be expected because of the general correlation between political knowledge and political activity. Even outsiders did not seem to be as poorly informed in May as those persons who got most of their information from other people.[44] Therefore, the latter percentages emphasize the lack of experience and lack of knowledge among the people relying on discussions.

Comparing the other group of influencers with the rest of the sample, we get the following percentages:

Campaign work:	Age 21–25	Poor knowledge of politics
Campaign workers	7	13($n = 54$)
Other persons	8	35($n = 422$)

41. See Klapper, *The Effects of Mass Communication*, pp. 68–72, 106–09.
42. $t = 2.66$, $p < 0.01$ and $t = 3.60$, $p < 0.001$.
43. $\chi^2 = 21.40$, $v = 2$, $p < 0.001$.
44. $t = 1.77$, $p < 0.10$.

In accordance with expectations, we find that those people who did work for their party, like opinion leaders, were better informed of politics in May than were the rest of the population.

Although people who relied on discussions lacked experience and knowledge, many other characteristics show that they were just ordinary inhabitants of the city. For example, there was nothing exceptional about their distribution in the various occupational groups. However, there may have been more women than men among them.[45] In the opinion leader class there were more males than females,[46] which has also been observed in countries other than Finland.[47] Generally, we might conclude that opinion leaders existed in every segment of the population. The ordinary discussers were the approximate average of opinion leaders and outsiders as far as sex was concerned, but the occupational structure and nonpolitical organizational activity of the discussers did not differ from those of opinion leaders. Only the outsiders tended to stay outside other associations as well.

The few responses quoted above told about the event of influencing decisions. Some general observations or assumptions can yet be drawn from Table 10.13. (1) Newspaper readers and radio listeners again did not differ. (2) Again it seems that discussions were remembered best. However, only those discussions which had been conducted with workmates and other people outside the family were recalled as the best sources of information. Discussions with strangers had been carried on mainly by campaign workers. (3) It also seems that many people who were informed in discussions voted in the company of other people. Thus it is not impossible that some decisions were influenced on the way to the voting place. Opinion leaders liked to vote with their spouse and other members of the family. Let us repeat in this connection that campaign workers, although active, did not hurry to vote on the first voting day (Table 9.6, p. 260).

Thus it is obvious that personal influence prevailed upon voting decisions more effectively than direct mass communication. We should remember, however, that the intentions of most people did not change during the campaign. We should also take into account that mass commu-

45. The percentage of women among respondents mentioning newspapers, 54 per cent, radio, 58 per cent, and discussions, 76 per cent.

46. The percentage of women among opinion leaders was 38 per cent, but 59 per cent of ordinary discussers and 70 per cent of outsiders.

47. Berelson, Lazarsfeld, and McPhee, *Voting,* p. 112; Katz and Lazarsfeld, *Personal Influence* (Glencoe, The Free Press, 1955), p. 276.

TABLE 10.13. Campaign Activity in Tampere Related to (a) Most Important Source of Campaign Information, (b) Type of Participation in Political Discussions, and (c) Campaign Work for Party (in percentages)

	(a) Main Source			(b) Type of Discussion			(c) Campaign work	
	News-papers	Radio	Discus-sion	Opls.	Disc.	Outs.	yes	no
(Q. 54.C)								
Recalled an incident affecting decision	6	6	12	5	8	6	7	6
Did not recall	94	94	88	95	92	94	93	94
(Q. 60)								
Discussed the election outside family	49	52	55	60	57	34	69	47
Discussed with family	20	17	6	13	16	23	20	18
Did not discuss	31	30	39	27	27	43	11	35
(Q. 51.B)								
Voted with outsiders	5	7	15	5	8	5	9	6
Voted with spouse	38	36	24	39	36	35	44	35
Voted with family	12	12	15	19	9	11	11	12
Voted alone	33	29	28	30	31	32	30	31
Did not vote	12	16	18	7	16	17	6	16
Total	100	100	100	100	100	100	100	100
Number of cases	246	145	33	105	212	159	54	422

Opls. = Opinion leaders.
Disc. = Ordinary discussers.
Outs. = Outsiders.

nication and personal influence may have been linked together as inseparable components of the same communication process.

THE JOINT INFLUENCE OF CAMPAIGN PROPAGANDA AND PERSONAL DISCUSSIONS

One of the purposes of this study was to attempt to test the hypothesis concerning the two-step flow of communication (p. 29). The hypothesis is supported if (1) people whose main source of information was discussion did not pay much attention to mass communications; and if (2) opinion leaders, in turn, heeded mass communications more than people who otherwise participated in political discussions; (3) additional conclusions may be possible if we compare opinion leaders and campaign workers.

TABLE 10.14. Interest in the Campaign in Tampere Related to (a) Most Important Source of Campaign Information and (b) Type of Participation in Political Discussions (in percentages)

	(a) Main source			(b) Type of discusser		
	News-papers	Radio	Discus-sion	Opls.	Disc.	Outs.
High interest in precampaign mass media (scale values 4–5)	33	36	21	52	34	19
Recalled at least 4 posters	45	41	52	41	45	47
Identified at least 1 poster	81	77	79	89	81	67
Listened to the whole campaign debate	15	21	6	31	13	9
Listened to a party presentation	30	49	39	53	44	35
Read campaign items in newspapers	50	41	27	61	50	26
Looked often at campaign advertisements	31	21	9	36	24	17
Went to a campaign meeting	7	7	6	15	6	4
Listened to election results past midnight	11	19	18	21	14	9
Were told by friends about campaign meetings	15	17	12	27	15	9
Knew a campaign worker	14	14	18	25	8	7
Number of cases	*246*	*145*	*33*	*105*	*212*	*159*

Opls. = Opinion leaders.
Disc. = Ordinary discussers.
Outs. = Outsiders.

1. Table 10.14.a again classifies the sample according to the main source of information. We find no differences between newspaper readers and radio listeners other than the tendency of radio listeners to expose themselves most to given radio programs, and the tendency of those who mentioned newspapers as a source of information to read most of the campaign material in the papers. But those people who considered discussion as their main source of information were a clearly different group. In May they had been least interested in political mass communication. During the campaign, too, they paid the least attention to the campaign material of the newspapers and almost as little to the election programs on the radio. Apparently they were as exposed as others only to some specific means of campaign communication, such as meetings or outdoor posters.

Because during the campaign the normal media reached those persons who were mainly informed in discussion less than they reached others,

Table 10.14.a emphasizes the importance of discussion as the source of information of this group. This was expected on the basis of the two-step hypothesis.

2. Table 10.14.b, in turn, verifies the expectation that opinion leaders were most exposed to mass communication. Already in May they had paid more attention to the mass media than other people, and later, too, they were more exposed to the campaign than other inhabitants of Tampere. Let us emphasize specifically that this difference existed also between opinion leaders and ordinary discussers. Thus the direct political mass communication reached most effectively those persons who, as political opinion leaders, further advised their small groups.

However, Table 10.14.b also contains information that cannot be satisfactorily incorporated into the simple model of a two-step flow of communication. First, we find that opinion leaders not only paid the most attention to political mass communication, but they also were told most about meetings which they themselves did not attend. According to this, even opinion leaders were not satisfied with the impersonal mass communication directed at them. It seemed to be completed by a kind of horizontal communication among opinion leaders.

The other step presumed by the hypothesis seems to have left many persons outside the total flow of communication. When the respondents are classified into opinion leaders and others, not all the others were followers of the opinion leaders. One third appeared to be outside any personal communication. Table 10.14.b shows that these outsiders were at the opposite pole from opinion leaders even in their interest in mass communication. They paid the least attention to all political mass communication. The only exception is that they may have looked at posters as much as others, but they forgot even their content the most easily. Because persons who were outside personal discussion did not pay much attention to the mass media either, this part of the electorate tended to remain outside the reach of all communication.

Three simple models of the flow of communication can be based on the above discussion (Figure 10.F). The direct communication (Figure 10.F.a) did not reach the whole population nor did it look very efficient. Our material favors the newer hypothesis of the two-step flow (Figure 10.F.b), which was discovered in the original panel interview study of voting behavior.[48] But Table 10.14.b seems to require two corrections of this

48. Lazarsfeld, Berelson, and Gaudet, *People's Choice*, pp. 151–58; this has been the point of departure for many later studies.

FIGURE 10.F. The (a) Direct, (b) Two-step, and (c) Two-and-a-half-step Flow of Communication

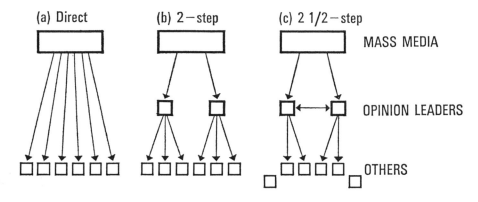

model. (1) The first step of communication, that from the media to the opinion leaders, is complemented by a horizontal exchange of information among equal opinion leaders. Therefore, we might add a horizontal step to the model. (2) We have to consider the communication flow in personal discussion as only half a step. Instead of a classification of the electorate either into opinion leaders and others, or into discussers and others,[49] any simplified presentation requires the study of at least three classes simultaneously. The third class is left outside the discussions and is not easily within the reach of other communication. To emphasize these findings, we should add another step to the two-step model, but then deduct half a step, which gives us the hypothesis of the two-and-a-half-step flow of communication (Figure 10.F.c).

3. Table 10.15 was prepared in order to compare opinion leaders and campaign workers. The sample is classified according to campaign work and the type of participation in political discussions.

The differences between opinion leaders and outsiders found in Table 10.14.b increase when we compare only those opinion leaders who also did campaign work with those outsiders who did not work for their party. This, of course, was to be expected. But in the comparison of those people who functioned in only one influential role, the last two lines of the table attract attention. It seems that opinion leaders were informed by their friends about campaign speeches, regardless of their own initiative in

49. Examples of the dichotomy opinion leaders/others have been given above; the classification into discussers/others is presented by Trenaman and McQuail, *Television*, p. 194. Sjödén, *TV Election in Sweden*, p. 32, has used the three classes as far as opinion transmitters are concerned.

TABLE 10.15. Interest in the Campaign Related to Campaign Work and Type
of Participation in Political Discussions: Tampere, 1958 (in percentages)

	Did campaign work			No campaign work		
	Opls.	Disc.	Outs.	Opls.	Disc.	Outs.
High interest in pre-campaign mass media	62	53	9	49	21	20
Listened to the whole campaign debate	42	24	18	27	12	8
Read campaign items in newspapers	77	65	55	56	48	24
Went to a campaign meeting	31	24	9	10	5	4
Were told by friends about campaign meetings	31	18	9	25	15	9
Knew a campaign worker	54	53	18	22	22	9
Number of cases	*26*	*17*	*11*	*79*	*195*	*148*

Opls. = Opinion leaders.
Disc. = Ordinary discussers.
Outs. = Outsiders.

working for their party. Campaign workers, in turn, knew other campaign workers, regardless of their role as opinion leader or ordinary
discusser. The pure opinion leaders did not tend to know people who were
engaged in campaign work.

Both of the last-mentioned findings support the view that the sources
of information utilized by the influencers included—in addition to mass
media—other persons functioning in a similar role. We consider this the
horizontal stage in the total process of communication flow. At the same
time it seems justifiable to conclude that there were different kinds of
people functioning as opinion leaders or as campaign workers active upon
their own initiative. The chance for parties to influence voting decisions
depended much on how many of each kind of influencer was taking their
campaign message to the ordinary voters.

THE CHOICE OF CANDIDATE

In each Finnish constituency, the ballots cast in the parliamentary election determine first the number of seats won by each electoral alliance.
After this is known, the ballots decide who are the elected individuals
(pp. 7–10).

This presentation of voting choice, and of factors which influence it,
concerns the choice of party and not that of an individual candidate. However, it is necessary to verify whether the voters themselves consider party

choice the main purpose of the election. To some extent, this is connected with the question of the importance of the nominations to the total number of votes won by each party.

In Tampere, the choice of candidate was not generally considered the main purpose of the election. Two findings support this:

1. One third of the sample (35 per cent) did not mention which candidate they had voted for (Q. 55). This percentage included people who refused to answer, because the respondents were less willing to reveal the choice of candidate than that of party. The percentage especially proves that there were persons among the voters who either did not remember whom they had chosen or simply did not pay attention to the choice of candidate:

> I don't remember. Why didn't you ask on the same day, maybe I would have remembered then. (Saleswoman, 25, Conservative)
>
> I don't remember the name, but she was a woman candidate. (Foreman, 32, SDP)
>
> Let's not talk about that. I didn't even tell it to my husband. (Wife of builder, 32)

2. Respondents were also asked: "Did you first choose the party and then the candidate, or did you primarily choose a person without regard to the party?" (Q. 56). The responses were distributed in the following percentages:

	Men	Women	Total
Voted for party	78	82	80
Voted for candidate	18	13	15
Don't know	4	5	5
	100	100	100

These answers show that, in general, the election of representatives to Parliament concerned political parties primarily. The choice of candidate was of secondary importance.

Images of the Representatives and Other Candidates

The thirteen candidates, who were elected to Parliament in the Northern Häme constituency in 1958, received the following number of personal votes:

		In Tampere	Elsewhere
FPDU:	Elli Stenberg, Tampere	5,191	3,077
"	Leo Suonpää, Tampere	4,759	3,037
"	Usko Seppi, Ruovesi	316	4,078
"	Kuuno Honkonen, Tampere	3,327	955
"	Väinö Virtanen, Nokia	487	3,377
S. D. Opp.:	Aarre Simonen, Helsinki	1,619	2,199
SDP:	Arvo Tuominen, Tampere	3,763	4,089
"	Kustaa Alanko, Tampere	2,224	4,248
"	Anna Flinck, Tampere	2,340	2,197
Agr.:	Atte Pakkanen, Helsinki	75	3,732
Cons.:	T. A. Wiherheimo, Helsinki	2,470	2,376
"	Toivo Hietala, Tampere	3,763	775
"	Mikko Asunta, Ruovesi	197	3,465

Only three candidates who received at least 3,000 personal votes were not elected. They were: Kaisa Hiilelä, a former Member of Parliament and a candidate of the Independent Social Democrats (3,172); and two Conservative candidates, Eero Kivelä (3,316) and Leena Perttula (3,262).

The responses show that positive images of these members of Parliament were attached to them personally. Thus Stenberg was, in the opinion of her voters, "an appropriate person" and "such a good speaker," who "belongs to us and favors the interests of women," and who "as a woman has on her heart also the interests of children and old aged persons." She received votes "because of the party" and "as a representative of women." Suonpää was "an extremely good man to occupy this position," "the only one whom I can trust perfectly," "closest to us metal workers," and "an inhabitant of my own place of residence and interested in the affairs of this region." He "had been long enough in the Parliament to know all those things" and "he would push the matters of our own city, at least employment matters." Seppi "just happened to be chosen" in Tampere, "because he belongs to my party." Honkonen received votes "because he is a champion athlete, an educated man, who wants to be close to the working man," and "because he is young" and "an educated, well-informed man," who "has made good speeches." Virtanen was "as a social worker well-informed about social affairs."

Simonen of the Independent Social Democrats was "at least in my opinion a good man," "such a pleasant man" and at the same time "a strong and courageous man," who had "performed exemplary things in Parliament." He was voted for because "they advertised him so much" and "because I voted for him previously, too." The Social Democrat, Alanko, "spoke to the point and was an old-fashioned Social Democrat, none of those waverers," and "an experienced legislator" who "does not have as many occupations as many others and therefore has found time to stand his ground in Parliament, so that he has not sat there with his mouth closed." He was, on the one hand, "one of us in this Nekala suburb and proved to do good work in Parliament," but, on the other hand, also "the first number in that electoral alliance, I don't remember the name." Tuominen was voted for "because I have liked his books and he is a brave man," and "mainly because he knows what communism is like and can stand against it." In addition, he was "an intelligent man, has been editor of the *Kansan Lehti*," who "at least is a newcomer in politics and appears to be trustworthy." Flinck was "an able and moderate representative of women," "a former Member of Parliament," "a woman and a Social Democrat," and "a popular and true-blue person," who "takes care of women's interests and sports affairs" and "is able to open her mouth in the Parliament as elsewhere in suitable places."

The Conservative Wiherheimo was, in the opinion of his voters, "an economist and a real intelligent man, because he has been in Parliament previously," "a reliable man," and "the candidate of the Swedish-speaking people," who "makes the impression of an intelligent and educated person," and who "as an old and experienced legislator should be able to take care of things." Hietala, in turn, was "a peaceful and understanding man" and "a precise man" and "a strong banker," "a well-known economist in Tampere," who "furthers the interests of small savers and is a member of the Taxpayers' Association," and "should be able to take care of fiscal affairs because he is a bank director." Asunta received votes in Tampere "because he is a friend since my childhood," and because "we more or less knew who would get through and who would not."

A total of 60 per cent of the voters gave reasons for their choice of candidate. Two general conclusions can be based on the quotations. (1) Although the choice of candidate generally occupied a position secondary to party choice, at least one half of the voters considered this decision significant too. (2) The images of the different candidates corresponded in many respects to the themes used in the personal campaigns of the candidates.

These two conclusions are by no means limited to the thirteen candidates who were elected, but the quotations here have been selected only from the responses given by those who voted for them.

Candidate Propaganda and the Choice of Candidate

In studying the nominations (Chapter 7) and the content of candidate propaganda (Chapter 8), we found that the parties and the candidates (their so-called electors' associations) paid special attention to (1) local representation; (2) group representation; (3) experiences; and (4) potential; and, to some extent, (5) familiarity of their candidates. These aspects had their counterparts in the voting behavior of citizens and in the reasons given for voting.

TABLE 10.16. Percentage Distribution of Votes Cast for the Seven Parties (a) in Tampere, (b) Elsewhere in the Constituency, according to Residence of Candidates (in percentages)

		S.D. Opp.	SDP	Agr.	FPP	Cons.	Popular Center	Total sample
	FPDU							
(a) Votes in Tampere								
Candidates from Tampere	93	44	89	–	61	77	28	81
Elsewhere in the same constituency	7	2	11	78	2	2	72	7
Other constituency	0	54	–	22	37	21	–	12
(b) Votes elsewhere								
Candidates from Tampere	34	35	63	–	57	43	15	37
Elsewhere in the same constituency	58	13	37	72	6	34	85	44
Other constituency	8	51	–	28	37	23	–	19
Votes in Tampere	*18,818*	*4,510*	*13,615*	*384*	*2,512*	*14,777*	*320*	*55,012*
Votes elsewhere	*21,687*	*10,589*	*19,009*	*15,759*	*3,289*	*13,190*	*211*	*78,617*

1. A comparison of the thirteen elected members show that the Conservative, Hietala, who was advertised as "the real Tampere man" received the largest relative share of personal votes in the city itself, whereas the elected members living in Ruovesi and Nokia received very few votes in the city. This—like some responses quoted above—reminds us of the sig-

nificance of local considerations in the choice of a candidate. Table 10.16 shows how the urban and rural votes cast for each party were distributed among the candidates living in Tampere, elsewhere in the constituency, and in other constituencies. According to the table: (a) city people liked to vote for candidates residing in their own city and gave very few votes to candidates residing elsewhere in the constituency; while (b) the Tampere candidates had generally less appeal elsewhere in the constituency; and (c) candidates from outside the constituency gained equal support from the city and from the rest of the constituency.

Many rural candidates depended even more on the personal votes given in their own locality. Thus the only FPDU candidate from outside the constituency succeeded well outside the city because he—Mr. Lepola, residing in Jyväskylä—was especially nominated for the northeastern corner of the constituency. The Independent Social Democratic electoral alliance cast almost its entire vote for candidates from outside the constituency. This resulted in the re-election to Parliament of its Helsinki candidate Simonen. The same was true of the Finnish People's Party, which had nominated the three outside "power engines."

Among the candidates residing in Tampere, seven (23 per cent) were elected to Parliament. On the other hand, only three (8 per cent) of the candidates residing elsewhere in the same constituency were elected; and although the number is the same, it is relatively less than the number of representatives elected from outside the constituency (23 per cent of the candidates). In general, urban centers have gained over-representation in the Finnish Parliament.[50] However, some respondents equated local representation with their former place of residence, with their current part of the city, perhaps even with their place of work.

2. An obvious example of group representation was the nomination of female candidates and the orientation of their campaigns to women voters. In the Northern Häme constituency, all three leftist parties and the FPP nominated a woman member of Parliament. And it was the parties on the left that gave female candidates the largest percentages of their total votes:

The FPDU (2 female candidates)	35
Soc. Dem. Opposition (3)	39
Social Democratic Party (3)	31
Agrarian Union (1)	7
Finnish People's Party (3)	24
Conservatives (2)	14

50. Noponen, *The Social Background,* pp. 220, 231.

A female candidate was elected to Parliament from two leftist parties, and, in a third, Kaisa Hiilelä lost a rather close contest to Simonen. As a whole, the fourteen female candidates in the constituency received 15,073, or 27 per cent, of the votes cast in Tampere.

Voters for female candidates represented 30 per cent of the sample. The distribution was the following:

| | Percentage of: | | |
	Men	Women	Total
Voted for man	91	52	69
Voted for woman	7	47	30
No answer	2	1	1
	100	100	100

We find that men voting for women candidates were exceptional, whereas one half of the women voters cast ballots for female candidates. This corresponds to the attempt of parties to offer their female candidates mainly to women voters.

Other group connections of the candidates were also mentioned in the responses. The FPDU voters referred to the workers, the youth, children and old aged persons, sportsmen, shoeworkers, metal workers, forest workers, and labor unions. The voters of the Independent Social Democrats noted representatives of labor and Karelians; and the voters of the SDP mentioned workers, such as working-class mothers, underprivileged people, anti-Communists, and a representative of their sport club. Groups mentioned by Conservative voters included small savers, taxpayers, Karelians, Swedes, nurses, teachers, widows of clergy, the nation, and the Finnish people. And among the voters in each party, there were some who supported the candidate who best personified their party.

3. The significance of experience in public life was revealed in this connection by the greater success of candidates who sought re-election than of those who had no legislative experience. But some voters wanted to support new faces, either to encourage a new candidate likely to receive few votes, or to satisfy a specific desire for change in the composition of the parliament. However, many more references were made to the legislative experience than to the newness of chosen candidates.[51]

Some voters chose "an oldtime politician" who was not a member of

51. Among the responses, specific references to experience in Parliament comprised 11 per cent, and to the newness of candidate 6 per cent; other reasons amounted to 87 per cent ($n = 230$).

Parliament. Participation in politics was not considered the only way to gain qualifications for the parliamentary mandate. Many voters mentioned the education and occupational experience of their candidate. Many also emphasized the importance of experience gained in nonpolitical trusteeships, or simply chose "a well-known name." Corresponding themes had been typical of candidate propaganda.

4. The potentialities of the candidates included not only their experience but also their character, general ability, and popularity. Many responses referring to such qualifications have been quoted. Let us add a few. The voters' image of their candidate was described, among others, by such words as well-educated; intelligent; ready with an answer; energetic; able; well-liked and matter-of-fact; peaceful and reliable; an all-around able man; regular and responsible; understanding, socially minded person; intelligent, peaceful and moderate; and pleasant, honest, and patriotic.

But the most central reason that was often repeated, was the desire of voters to elect a representative whom they trusted.

5. A horseman chose his candidate because of "our old friendship and the confidence based on it." Generally, personal acquaintanceship affected the choice: votes were cast for cousins, "a boy from our village," and a "childhood friend," or for a workmate and a trustee of workers, sometimes even for "a friend of my husband." Often acquaintance with the candidate increased the confidence in him, but sometimes the voters also felt a kind of pride about their famous acquaintances. A vote for a relative was considered so natural that other reasons did not seem necessary for such a choice.

Thus it is obvious that (1) the voters gave such reasons for their choices as had been emphasized in candidate propaganda, but, on the other hand, (2) the campaign had only limited chances to affect the base of these choices. Sometimes public speaking and the abundance of campaign material as such made the candidate well-known, but it seems that the voters paid favorable attention mainly to the propaganda of those candidates whose names they knew from previous connections. Let us point out that only one out of ten persons in Tampere mentioned before the campaign (and the final nominations) the persons for whom they finally voted. Three quarters (74 per cent) were not able to mention in May a single person from the constituency whom they hoped would be elected to Parliament.

Voters for the Party and Voters for the Candidate

These observations about candidate choice apply to the voters who perceived this choice only as an intraparty one as well as to those who considered it the most important choice in the election. But it is also possible that the total number of votes cast for the party was affected by nominations and the propaganda of individual candidates. To examine this, the majority voting for a party should be compared with that minority who considered candidate choice more important.

Table 10.17.a shows that there was a difference between the parties.[52] The SDP especially received votes as a party. The voters for a candidate, on the other hand, were above average supporters of the Independent Social Democrats and the Conservatives. These are the very electoral unions whose voters tended to mention candidates as the reason for their party choice (Appendix Table 21). Correspondingly, the campaign of the Independent Social Democrats had been built largely on the personal support of its candidates, especially Hiilelä and Simonen; whereas the supporters of the Conservatives tended even normally to give able leaders as their reason for party preference (Table 6.2). Concerning the FPDU, we might point out that its candidates attracted as many women as men, although as a party it was more popular among the men.[53]

Two points in Table 10.17 refer generally to the additional vote getting ability of the candidates: (1) Those people who voted for a candidate recalled a later choice than the ones who voted for the party.[54] This was to be expected, as it was not possible to choose a candidate before the nominations were announced. (2) The candidate voters gave up their precampaign voting intention and switched their vote to another party more easily than party voters.[55] The natural explanation for this difference —that party voters were more sure of their party than candidate voters— is not supported by the data.[56] Obviously, parties gained new voters because of an attractive list of candidates and an appealing candidate propaganda. But Table 10.17.c shows further that only female voters could be

52. $\chi^2 = 12.11, v = 4, p < 0.02.$
53. In the latter comparison $t = 3.32, p < 0.002.$
54. $\chi^2 = 22.58, v = 2, p < 0.001.$
55. Among the converters, $t = 1.76, p < 0.10$; among converters and inter-Soc. Dem. changers, $t = 2.18, p < 0.05.$
56. Precampaign voting intention was realized by 70 per cent ($n = 88$) of the weakly identifying party voters, but by only 59 per cent ($n = 34$) of the strongly identifying candidate voters.

TABLE 10.17. Relationship by Sex of Choosing Primarily Party or Candidate to (a) Party Choice, (b) Recalled Time of Final Party Choice, (c) Constancy in Voting Intention, (d) Day of Voting, and (e) Campaign Work (in percentages)

	All Party	All Candidate	Men Party	Men Candidate	Women Party	Women Candidate
(a) Party choice						
FPDU	28	26	38	26	21	27
Soc. Dem. Opp.	6	12	2	10	8	13
SDP	29	13	28	19	30	7
Agrarian	1	–	–	–	2	–
FPP	5	5	5	3	5	7
Conservative	25	31	22	29	27	33
Popular Center	–	2	–	–	–	3
No answer	6	11	5	13	7	10
(b) Time of choice						
Beginning of year	84	56	91	58	79	53
2 months before	4	10	1	13	6	7
2 weeks or closer	10	29	7	19	13	40
Don't know	2	5	1	10	2	–
(c) Constancy in intention						
Constants	79	63	84	78	74	48
Inter-Soc. Dem. change	4	7	2	7	5	7
Converters	7	17	7	4	8	30
Crystallizers	10	13	7	11	13	15
(d) Day of voting						
1st day	51	51	58	42	46	60
2nd day	49	49	42	58	54	40
(e) Campaign work						
Did campaign work	13	11	20	3	8	20
Did not	87	89	80	97	92	80
Total	100	100	100	100	100	100
Number of cases	327	61	137	31	190	30

converted in this fashion. (3) Apparently the Independent Social Democratic electoral union received exceptionally many votes cast primarily for individual candidates.

It may seem natural that strong party identifiers thought the election concerned mainly parties and that weak identifiers preferred to vote for a person rather than for a party. The data, however, do not support this. The following percentages of people, classified according to the degree of party identification, voted primarily for a candidate:

	Total	Men	Women
Party members	10	$6(n = 34)$	$18(n = 17)$
Other strong identifiers	16	$21(n = 76)$	$13(n = 118)$
Nonpartisans and weak identifiers	14	$18(n = 49)$	$12(n = 83)$

Even those persons who had been uncertain in May generally voted for a party, and not for an individual candidate. According to expectation, however, almost all male party members were party voters.[57] On the other hand, among women, the difference may have been in the opposite direction: party members perhaps tended more than other women to vote primarily for a candidate. No other differences existed between the strong and weak identifiers.

On the basis of Table 10.17.d, we may finally observe whether a primary vote for a candidate was related to an exceptional electoral activity, or to a tendency to favor either day of balloting. Even here we find no difference when considering the sample as a whole. However, there were differences among men and among women, although their direction contradicted each other. The men who voted primarily for a party tended to do party work and to vote on the first day. Women tended to be similarly activated when they considered candidate choice the main purpose of the election.[58] Consequently, the election related strongly to individual candidates in the opinion of politically inactive men, but politically active women.

It is possible that this difference between the sexes corresponds to the difference we found in the impact of party identification. Moreover, women voters seemed most willing to do campaign work if they were strong party identifiers and yet voted primarily for a candidate. The difference between the two sexes in Table 10.17.e is perhaps because strong party identification of women voters, and their consequent desire to do campaign work, presupposes a candidate who personifies the party enough to make the women perceive the person as more important in the election

---

57. $t = 275$, $p < 0.01$.

58. Among the men, (d) $t = 1.66$, $p < 0.10$ and (e) $t = 3.59$, $p < 0.001$. Among the women, the differences are not significant: (d) $t = 1.47$, $p < 0.20$ and (e) $t = 1.54$, $p < 0.20$.

than the party. Often such a candidate may have been well-known before the campaign.[59]

THE COMPARISON GROUP

The rural communes of the Northern Häme constituency had 89,295 enfranchised inhabitants in 1958 (1,099 more than in 1954). The number of voters was 68,925 (77.2 per cent), or 519 less than in 1954 (78.7 per cent). More rural votes were cast for the Conservatives (+1,639), the FPDU (+820), and, contrary to the general trend in the country, also for the Agrarian Union (+211) than in the previous election. A loss was suffered by the Social Democrats combined (−1,224) and by the Finnish People's Party (−1,099).

TABLE 10.18. Results of the 1958 Election in Korpilahti

Parties	Votes received (number)	Increase or decrease from 1954 (number)	Votes	Estimate including absentee ballots (per cent)	July sample
FPDU	931	−170	21.8	22.0	22
Soc. Dem. Opposition	313	+313	7.3	7.4	7
SDP	264	−341	6.2	6.4	16
Agrarian	1,270	−69	29.7	29.8	23
FPP	108	±0	2.5	2.6	2
Conservative	229	+38	5.4	6.0	6
Others and disqualified ballots	28	−8	0.6	0.6	−
Additional absentee ballots	57	−69	1.3	.	.
No answer	.	.	.	.	1
Nonvoters	1,076	−12	25.2	25.2	23
Total	4,276	−343	100.0	100.0	100

In Korpilahti commune, 3,200 votes were cast, which was 434 less than in 1954. The turnout was thus lowered from 76.4 per cent to 74.8 per cent. Table 10.18 presents the results of the election in this commune. The Conservative and the Agrarian vote followed the trend of all rural communes in the constituency, but some changes were contrary to the general trend

59. 5 per cent of the women voting for the party, but 17 per cent of the women voting for the candidate named already in May the candidate they voted for; $t = 1.72$, $p < 0.10$.

(see p. 52). The number of votes for the FPDU decreased there, whereas it increased slightly for the two Social Democratic groups combined. The number of votes cast for the FPP remained unaltered.

Appendix Table 25 compares the precampaign voting intentions with the behavior in July (see Figure 10.A and Appendix Table 20). Let us again remember that 94 interviews are too small a sample for statistically significant differences between subgroups. Nevertheless, at least they suggest how the opinions of the inhabitants of the commune had developed.

The following distribution summarizes the information of Appendix Table 24:

| | Percentage of: | | |
	Men	Women	Total
Constants in voting intention	69	39	54
Inter-Soc. Dem. changes	2	2	2
Converters	10	4	7
Crystallizers	4	22	13
Intended nonvoters	4	15	10
Unintended nonvoters	11	18	14
	100	100	100
Number of cases	*48*	*46*	*94*

If voters only are considered, 73 per cent ($n = 72$) realized their precampaign intention. This percentage includes the inter-Social Democrat changers. Ten per cent were converted to vote for another party, and 17 per cent delayed their decision. These percentages are similar to the findings in Tampere, except that it seems the comparison group had more crystallizers, just as it showed more uncertainty in May.

An extension of the timespan of the comparisons indicates that, even in Korpilahti, the changes may have been more numerous before than during the campaign. In a comparison of three points of time, the voters were distributed in the following percentages:

Nonvoters in 1954 or did not recall the 1954 vote	29
Same party in 1954, May 58 and July 58	40
1954 = May 58 ≠ July 58	7
1954 = July 58 ≠ May 58	3
1954 ≠ (May 58 = July 58)	10
1954 ≠ May 58 ≠ July 58	3
No party preference in May 1958	8
	$100(n = 72)$

The direction of the changes in party choice, which were recalled in Korpilahti until May 1958, has been presented (p. 126). According to Appendix Table 24, the conversion of Social Democrats to FPDU supporters continued during the 1958 campaign, and the SDP won no compensation for these losses. The Tampere findings are further confirmed by the position of the Party Opposition as a rest area between Social Democratic and the Communist affiliation, and parallel findings might be the changes from the FPP to the Conservatives. But deviating aspects were the conversion from the FPDU to vote for the Agrarians, the votes cast for the Independent Social Democrats by crystallizers, and the absence of any avenue from the supporters of the SDP toward the right wing in Korpilahti.

Even in Korpilahti, party conversions followed the direction which had attracted future converters before the campaign. Almost all the respondents in the comparison group who changed parties had mentioned their final choice as their second choice in May. Only one person had been unable to rank any party in the second place. For example, most constant Social Democrats differed from the changers to the left in that they had ranked the Agrarian Union, and not the FPDU, as their second choice in May.

The data also give some hints about the reserve who did not vote. The turnout percentages of all supporters of the four parties was the following:

FPDU	$88 (n = 24)$
Social Democrats	$75 (n = 20)$
Agrarians	$79 (n = 28)$
Conservatives	$86 (n = 7)$

According to the figures above, nonvoting was most damaging to the Social Democrats and the Agrarians. FPDU supporters appeared to be the most active. Although their turnout was below that of the Tampere People's Democrats, nonvoting does not seem to explain why Korpilahti experienced decreasing Communist support. Even changes in party preference do not explain this local phenomenon. Therefore, we have to refer to the uncertainty of conclusions again, perhaps also to the possibility that many FPDU supporters had migrated during the previous four years.

When the respondents in the comparison group gave reasons for their party choice, they often repeated ideas expressed in May. For instance, the FPDU and both Social Democratic electoral alliances won votes "because we somewhat belong to the workers and they are for us." The Agrarian Union received votes because "it has been the tactic here in the country"; the FPP "because of its ideological activity"; and the Conservatives "because it furthers better the interests of the world and is a bourgeois party."

It seems, however, that current reasons appeared more frequently in the responses of the FPDU voters in Korpilahti than in Tampere. According to one nonskilled worker, "it has promised to look out for the interest of the working men. Some years ago the employment situation was better and the FPDU has now promised to improve it." And in another opinion, "at least a year ago the children's allowances were a good thing to do, otherwise I don't quite know what they are about." One farmer's wife voted for the FPDU: "Maybe things would begin to run better. The poor dweller will be lost if things won't change."

Correspondingly, the Independent Social Democrats activated a farmer's wife to vote, "if the bread of the poor folks would get thicker"; and the Conservatives were voted for "in the hope of lower taxes." A former voter of the FPP now supported the Agrarians, because "this time it is the best party." Otherwise, the nature of reasons given by Agrarian voters was very general, for example: "I haven't earned marks anywhere else but from agriculture."

An established voting habit was given as another reason for party choice. The Communist preference of a sawmill worker's wife "originated from the war years; I am tired of fighting and that party promised to stop the war and since then my support has continued." An Agrarian preference of a 51-year-old farmer was "an inheritance from my old man"; and a 39-year-old sawmill worker voted for the SDP, because "I've been there since my boyhood years." The most references to traditions, however, were made by the voters of the Independent Social Democrats: a 72-year-old farmer voted for it "from old memory"; and in the opinion of a 55-year-old housewife "the reason is that I have considered all through my life that they have tried to stick to the interests of the workers and they don't know how to be fanatic, they like to negotiate."

Again it seems that direct campaigning did not convert people. Indicative of this were the differences between constant and converted voters, especially in their exposure to posters. The poster of the party voted for was recalled by 67 per cent ($n = 51$) of the constant, but by 51 per cent ($n = 21$) of the new voters; and it was identified by 48 per cent of the former, but only by 19 per cent of the latter.[60] The man who

60. Percentage remembering: $t = 1.50$, $p < 0.20$; percentage identifying: $t = 2.89$, $p < 0.01$.

had represented one's own party in the election debate on the radio was recalled by 22 per cent of the constant and by only 10 per cent of the new voters.

The party biased selection of campaign material might again be one explanation of the inefficiency of direct communication. Such selectiveness had already existed before the campaign, for example, in the attention paid to political material in the newspapers. If we divide the sample into supporters of Agrarians and other parties, and further into the readers of the Agrarian *Keskisuomalainen* and people who read another paper in addition to, or instead of, this dominant paper, we get four classes. Among the readers of *Keskisuomalainen* only, the Agrarians were more interested in the political material than were other groups. The nonpolitical attitude of the supporters of other parties, who read only the Agrarian newspaper in Korpilahti, corresponds to the feelings in Tampere about the locally dominant Conservative newspaper. However, in Tampere even Conservative supporters perceived *Aamulehti* as a relatively nonpolitical means of communication. In Korpilahti, *Keskisuomalainen* alone seemed to satisfy the Agrarian readers' need to get political information.

Such a normal impact of party preference continued in the choice of campaign material. Thus campaign meetings of one's own party were visited by 14 per cent, but those of other parties by only 5 per cent, and of both parties by 4 per cent. The SDP and Agrarian supporters were equally exposed to both radio programs presenting the parties, while the supporters of other parties did not listen at all when the Swedes, Agrarians, and Social Democrats were on the air.

Exposure to posters did not appear to correlate with party preference, but even here the precampaign degree of party identification had an influence. A poster of one's own party only was seen by 20 per cent of sure supporters, but by 8 per cent of uncertain supporters. One's own party poster was considered best by 29 per cent of the former and 8 per cent of the latter.[61] An example of selective exposure was a farmer's wife supporting the Agrarian Union, who identified the Agrarian poster she had seen in the central village, but did not recall which party had been advertised by the (FPDU) poster hanging on the wall of her own drying house.

The responses given in Korpilahti to the question about the best and second best source of campaign information were as follows:

61. $t = 1.57$, $p < 0.20$ and $t = 2.63$, $p \sim 0.01$.

	Best		Percentage: Second		Combined
Newspapers	41	+	32	=	73
Radio	38		22		60
Discussions	1		7		8
Posters	3		2		5
Party material	1		–		1
Periodicals	1		1		2
	85	+	64	=	149

The responses were almost the same as those in Tampere. The only difference was that radio was more important in the rural commune, where it ranked close to the newspapers. These answers are of no use in observing personal influence, because only one respondent considered discussion the most important source of information.

As might be expected, this respondent happened to belong to the ordinary discussers, in the classification of the type of participation in discussions. Ordinary discussers comprised 38 per cent of the sample, while only 14 per cent were opinion leaders and 48 per cent outsiders. Because the difference in exposure to the mass media was small between these three classes, the comparison group does not consistently support the hypothesis on the two-step flow of communication.

Instead there is support for our interpretation concerning the horizontal exchange of information. No less than 62 per cent of the opinion leaders said that they were told by others about campaign speeches; the corresponding percentage among ordinary discussers was 19 and among outsiders 13. Another campaign worker was known by 67 per cent of the campaign workers ($n = 9$), but by only 15 per cent ($n = 85$) of other people. It also seems that opinion leaders communicated with each other as did campaign workers. Yet both of them tended to identify strongly with their preferred party.

Let us finally say a few words about the choice of candidate. The five local candidates who had been nominated, of whom one now lived in Jyväskylä and one in Helsinki, succeeded in Korpilahti as indicated on page 341. These five candidates received no less than 66 per cent of the total number of votes cast for their four parties in Korpilahti (and 58 per cent of all the votes in the commune). Such an outcome is descriptive of the strong tendency in rural areas to cast a ballot for "a man of our own commune." In addition, they indicate the considerable significance of

	Number of votes in Korpilahti	Per cent of party vote in Korpilahti	Per cent of all personal votes
Lepola (FPDU)	776	83	41
Vallenius (Soc. Dem. Opposition)	188	60	49
Laukkala (Agrarian)	462	36	63
Salonen (Agrarian)	274	22	42
Ratia (Conservative)	108	47	41
	1,808	66	46

local votes toward the total number of votes received by candidates who are not known generally in the constituency.

A local candidate's attraction of the voters, and the desire to vote for an experienced candidate who has good chances to be elected, are obviously contradictory reasons for a candidate choice. For example, among the Agrarian candidates, Veikko Laukkala was voted for because he was "one of our local men and furthers local interests," but Atte Pakkanen, a Member of Parliament, was voted for because "he is the one bound to get to the Parliament from the old ones, I thought the new ones are uncertain." In the FPDU electoral alliance, Jalo Lepola collected most local votes, because "I think one should vote for the man of one's own commune" and "because we were fighting in the same group during the war," although Kuuno Honkonen was voted for because "he makes the most fair impression among those I've seen; I didn't elect him because he is a sportsman but because I think he might respect his opponent and play a fair game."

In other parties, too, votes were cast for acquaintances and representatives of one's own occupation. But, in Korpilahti, women did not like to vote for a woman: only 142 votes (4.6 per cent) were cast for female candidates. In the sample, the distribution was in the following percentages:

	Men	Women	Total
Voted for man	93	94	93
Voted for woman	2	6	4
No answer	5	–	3
	100	100	100
Number of cases	*42*	*33*	*75*

Obviously the small popularity of female candidates was partly because of the lack of them among the local candidates.

Yet the parliamentary election was considered mainly a party election. The following answers were given by the Korpilahti sample:

	Percentage of:		
	Men	Women	Total
Voted for party	69	79	73
Voted for candidate	21	12	17
Don't know	10	9	10
	100	100	100

Again most reasons for the choice of candidate were of a secondary nature, preceded by party choice. It seems, however, that there was one exception to this in Korpilahti. Taito Vallenius, nominated by the Independent Social Democrats and without a local competitor in the Social Democratic Party, seemed to convert voters from the mother party by his personal campaign. Therefore his group polled more votes in Korpilahti than the SDP. However, according to the responses, the voters for the Independent Social Democrats did not vote against the SDP. Instead they thought they were supporting "that old democracy."

SUMMARY

The two successful parties in the 1958 election were the FPDU and the Conservatives. The former gained its fifth seat in Northern Häme and increased its total parliamentary group from 43 to 50, while the latter retained in Northern Häme its third seat and elected a parliamentary group of 29 members, five more than in 1954. One of the three members who were elected from the lists of the new group, the Independent Social Democratic electoral alliance, came from the Northern Häme constituency. A nationwide defeat was experienced by the Social Democratic Party, the Finnish People's Party, and the Agrarian Union, although the last mentioned did not lose in the constituency studied here.

The most unstable voting decisions were those made by supporters of the Social Democratic Opposition. A majority of them switched after May further to the FPDU or back to the SDP, but the Opposition also gained voters from the Party. In addition, a considerable number of SDP supporters were converted to the Conservatives.

However, a majority of the voters repeated their 1954 party choice. Changes in party preference were more frequent before than during the campaign. Moreover, most converters had ranked their new party second in May. Thus electoral victories were based largely on the loyalty, and also on the turnout of the precampaign supporters, whereas an unwillingness to participate decreased the vote for the Social Democrats and the Finnish People's Party in Tampere, and the vote for the Agrarians in the comparison group.

The favorable images people held of their preferred parties did not change much during the campaign. But, in addition, relatively many voters for the winning parties gave current reasons for their party choice. The People's Democrats wanted to help to get their party away from the opposition, and the Conservative voters wanted to increase the influence of their party or to support its candidates. On the other hand, the Social Democrats especially gave voting habits as their reasons for party choice. Stimuli connected with the situation seem to have caused changes in voting intentions that voting habits, in turn, were preventing.

People whose vote was consistent with their precampaign intention had been more exposed to the propaganda of their party than those persons who converted to a new party during the campaign. Thus the direct campaign strengthened earlier intentions more than it converted new voters for the party. Such inefficiency seemed to be caused in two ways by the kind of attention paid to propaganda: (1) Campaign material was followed least by the new voters of parties, especially by those crystallizers who had not been much interested in politics in May; (2) furthermore, exposure to political communication was somewhat selective. For instance, in May, people in Tampere, even Conservative supporters, considered their dominant Conservative paper to be a nonpolitical means of communication, rather than a source of political information. In Korpilahti, people who supported another party than the Agrarian Union, may have considered their locally dominant Agrarian newspaper equally nonpolitical. Later during the campaign, party preference was most influential in the selection of campaign meetings attended and in the readership of newspapers; however, it did not influence the interest in all campaign materials.

Exposure to campaign material correlated, in addition to precampaign party preference, with the degree of party identification. The stronger the identification had been, the more attention was paid to the campaign. The strength of party identification also influenced the selection of material, although less consistently than its total quantity. Moreover, party identification did not explain the relationship between mass communication and voting decision as far as outdoor posters were concerned. Perhaps posters activated voters in Tampere and also caused conversions without reference to party identification, but it is equally possible that the strange posters had become one's own before the time they were on display, and were supporting the newly adopted preference.

It seems that mass communication activated voters. On the other hand, party choice was more effectively changed by personal discussion than by the mass media. Discussions were the main source of information for the youngest voters, and for persons who were least knowledgeable about politics. Influencers functioned everywhere. They were either opinion leaders, who were approached by others, or campaign workers, who functioned upon their own initiative. Even some influencers may have changed their intentions, but they hardly perceived it themselves.

In the total flow of communication, mass media and personal influence are intertwined. The two-step flow of communication combines these factors in the same process of communication. The hypothesis concerning this was supported by the Tampere data. The influencers were most exposed to mass communications, and those depending on discussion were the least exposed. On the other hand, people who were outsiders in discussion did not show any tendency to compensate the lack of personal contacts with exposure to mass communication. Thus the influence of the campaign depended to a large extent on the functioning of opinion leaders and campaign workers who mediated the message of mass media to other people.

Moreover the data suggested a new hypothesis, the two-and-a-half-step flow of communication. The additional step would be the equal or horizontal exchange of information among influencers, to some extent separately among opinion leaders and among campaign workers. This was supported by the data of the comparison group. The final step of communication is here called only a half step, because mass communication and personal influence do not reach everyone.

It is reasonable to consider that voting decisions concern—in addition to the decision to participate—the choice of a party. Most voters did cast their ballot primarily for a party, and not for an individual candidate. But, after this basic limitation, many voters also paid attention to the place of residence, group connections, experience, and personal characteristics of their candidates, and perhaps also to their being personally acquainted with the candidate. Similar things had been emphasized in candidate propaganda, and many images expressed about the candidates repeated such propaganda. Yet individual campaigning and nominations had relatively little chance of changing party affiliations, although this was not quite impossible; people who voted primarily for a candidate changed parties more often than voters for a party. But, in general, when conversions were stimulated by candidates, the voters perceived the difference between their old and new party as very small or nonexistent.

Despite the fact that the Finnish variety of the list system of proportional representation emphasizes individual candidates to a unique extent, parliamentary elections were found to be party elections in Finland. Women voters, however, were most attached to their party if there was someone to personify it.

11. Some Aspects of Elections and the Political System

A political system consists of the interaction of all political powers and the use of such power as will create generally authoritative political decisions. Voting days provide the people themselves, that is, the enfranchised citizens, with the opportunity to participate in official decision making. In Finland's indirect democracy, the people do not make detailed political decisions, but their voting behavior in elections has a focal impact upon the conditions of decision making. On polling days the electorate, the basic holders of political power, decide which 200 persons will be given the mandate to legislate during a specified legislative term.

The Election Campaign

This general conception of the political system implies that, as an election approaches, the attention of all other political powers turns from other decision makers toward the people in an attempt to influence the outcome of the election. During the final stage, they concentrate their efforts on the decision of voters. Therefore this study considers an election and preparations for it a period of activity that partly interrupts the other political process and can be distinguished as having its own entity. To clarify this point, the normal political process and campaign activity have been treated as two separate concepts.

In Finland, the weeks preceding an election are usually called an election fight. But the word campaign obviously has a wider and more neutral connotation. This campaign is distinguishable from normal political communication insofar as both its framework and its content are concerned.

Political parties enjoy an advantage in their campaign, if they have a strong, institutionalized organization and a newspaper of their own. In 1958, in Tampere, this was the case with the FPDU, the Social Democratic Party, and the Conservatives. The Communist Party organization was the strongest, and the Conservative newspaper had the widest local circulation. The lack of a newspaper and the weakly established party machine were obviously handicaps to the local campaign work of the Social Democratic Opposition, the Agrarian Union, and the Finnish People's Party.

The normal organization of most parties was expanded into a campaign organization. But, in the widest sense, their campaign organization included all those persons who did something among their peers to further the success of their party. The better established a machine and the more numerous the membership of the parties, the larger was the proportion of their supporters who did campaign work.

The normal organizational activity of the parties was changed easily into arranging campaign meetings. The first apparent change in many newspapers was a new regular section reserved for election material. Eventually the election began to overshadow the entire political content of the press, and finally the advertising as well. The radio broadcast a few propaganda programs. In addition to these normal mass media, the campaign utilized its own propaganda methods, such as posters, pamphlets, and letters. These means and commercial advertising were most significant for those parties which did not have a daily newspaper of their own, and for some individual candidates as well.

The duration of the actual campaign can be determined by such things as certain official decisions, observation of the campaign activity, and the quantity of campaign material. But the results are not consistent. Thus the internal campaign preparations continue in party organizations while some campaign activity already is being directed at the electorate. Between the closing ceremonies of the Parliament's legislative session and the election, there were thirty days, but the campaign could not reach its final form until the delivery of posters on the sidewalks and the political radio programs. This phase lasted only ten or eleven days. The editorial campaign of the newspapers lasted approximately two to four weeks, but their advertisers campaigned only during one or two weeks.

The increased political material in the newspapers dealt more than normally with party leaders, for example parliamentary candidates, with the campaign itself, and with the importance of voting. This, of course, was to be expected.

The theoretical background of the study led also to another hypothesis about trends in the content of the material. If the political system undergoes a real change as the attention of political powers—in this case mainly of parties—turns from other decision makers toward the people, the impact should be felt in the content of the newspapers, as well as in quantitative changes and the adoption of new issues. Changes could be expected in the relative emphasis put on different issues.

A content analysis indicated that such changes did occur in at least two of the three local newspapers and also, apparently, in the national newspapers and in the house organs of the parties. Criticism tended to be directed more than previously at the parties from whom one's own party could expect the strongest competition for voters. The changes were reflected in the way certain issues were handled, in the topics used in criticizing other parties, and in the praise of one's own party. Speculation on campaign tactics helped to interpret many of the findings.

In some form, the campaign reached almost every citizen. However, in general, the citizens had an indifferent attitude toward the propaganda and were in many respects critical, even annoyed by it. Perhaps this experience was the reason why the parties labeled many moves of their opponents as campaign propaganda long before the campaign. On the other hand, their own volunteer organizations were effective help only close to the election. Perhaps this is why the parties later pepped up their own organizations by announcing repeated starting signals for the final spurt of their own campaign fight.

When the parties prepare for the campaign, they make a numerically much larger choice than that left to the voters. The nomination stage eliminates 99.96 per cent of all the eligible people. The voters choose from only 0.04 per cent.

Voting

The choice of a candidate was not generally considered the most important aspect of the election. The election of Parliament was a party election. Only one out of four voters knew before nominations whom he wanted as his representative, and in the election a majority gave the legislative mandate primarily to a party, and not to a candidate. This limitation duly considered, however, the voters were not indifferent concerning the person to whom they entrusted the Parliament. And the campaign proper had very little chance of obtaining such a trust for a previously unknown name.

The two principal components of voting are participation and party choice. These are realized in the polling place, but a study of voting behavior has to consider the time dimension too. And the campaign weeks are a very short time indeed to change the relative interest or to effect changes in party affiliations.

Interest in politics is revealed in behavior normally as well as in connection with the election. In this study measures of normal interest were such things as the attention paid to political events and political knowledge, the latter interest was indicated by active attention to the campaign. The original reasons for political interest can often be traced back to times prior to voting age, although women tended to become involved at other times as well, if some break occurred in their political world. Those persons who were not interested in politics were normally indifferent and uninformed, and later unwilling to vote. The last mentioned characteristic included not only the likelihood of abstaining from voting, but also the tendency to delay decision making and even to delay going to the polling station.

Unwillingness to vote and certain exterior handicaps are usually mentioned as if they were alternative reasons for nonvoting. However, this study employed the concept that in the case of every citizen these two components should be weighed to show that the stronger the desire to vote the greater the likelihood that exterior handicaps would be overcome by it. This concept was supported by a comparison of those people who, in order to vote, had to visit the officials twice with those who only had to visit the polling place.

Some elections are exciting enough to increase collectively the electorate's desire to vote. On the other hand, such willingness was decreased by the difficulty of the choice—in certain groups as well as among individuals. Factors which motivated people to vote were a strong party identification and the belief that this was a significant election.

All voters put their party choice into effect when marking the number of one candidate in the circle reserved for this purpose in the ballot[1] (except those few who vote for a person not officially nominated). But the party, from whose candidates the one number is chosen, is elected with a varying amount of firmness. Normally the parties had strong and weak supporters. The strength of party identification proved to be a significant factor in actual voting. Interest in politics correlates with party identification; strong identifiers were the most typical supporters of their party as far as certain characteristics, opinions, and the tendency to select propaganda material were concerned; selection of campaign material later on was also more partybound, if the party identification had been strong

1. However, each Finnish voter thus must make a genuine choice between individual candidates, which is a rather unique version of the list system of proportional representation; see page 10.

prior to the campaign; and a strong identification was related to an early voting decision, a stable position, high exposure to the campaign, and a willingness to vote.

In general, party affiliation proved to be so durable that it is not possible to understand the final party choice without attention to its development. Especially in two-party systems, but apparently in the Finnish multi-party system also, many voters always support the same party, which in many cases is the very one which has been supported by their parents.[2] Some changes did occur, but since last election there had been more changes during the normal period of four years than during the campaign of 1958. Moreover, changes during the campaign were usually the shortest step, a vote for that party which had been the second preference before the campaign. Very few people who had changed their party, even a long time ago, had become strong identifiers with their new party.

The campaign conducted by a party may work toward four kinds of impact on the result of the election. The supporters of one's own party must remain faithful, and turn out in high numbers. Simultaneously, a party should win support from other parties, or at least discourage the desire to participate on the part of supporters of other parties.

Because of the rigidity of party choice, the main outcome of the campaign was the activation of one's own supporters and the reaffirmation of their position. Direct communication did not win many new voters. This was particularly because of the uneven distribution of the quantity and the content of propaganda among the electorate. The campaign reached least its most desired objects, those citizens who were uncertain about their decision and who were poorly informed about politics.

But the campaign was complemented by opinion leaders in various small groups and by those persons who did campaign work on their own initiative. They formed two partially separate activist subcultures, who shared their own observations and interpretations of the content of mass communication with others in their surroundings.

The Political Situation and Political Traditions

The count of ballots showed that the two opposition parties, the FPDU and the Conservatives, were winners in the 1958 election. The Social Democrats, Agrarians, and the Finnish People's Party were on the losing

---

2. Tauno Hellevuo, "Poimintatutkimus säätykierrosta" (A sample survey of social mobility), *Suomalainen Suomi* (1952), 96 and Pesonen, *Student Voters,* pp. 97–102; Herbert Hyman, *Political Socialization* (Glencoe, The Free Press, 1959), pp. 69–84.

side. The newly established Social Democratic Opposition competed in four constituencies, and its three elected members were later joined by eleven other Social Democrats in the new Parliament. The Communist success brought about a leftist majority in the new Parliament.

It seems that the political situation of the 1958 election leads to the most natural explanations when one tries to interpret certain findings about the influencers and other people in Tampere.

Let us first examine the influencers. Attention was paid above to the correlation between the strength of local party machines and the number of campaign workers. In Appendix Table 25, the supporters of the parties are classified into both kinds of influencers and into the group remaining outside these classes. According to this table, the supporters of five parties in Tampere included the following percentages of campaign workers and opinion leaders (in the same connection, the percentages of members and all strong identifiers are repeated):

	Campaign workers	Opinion leaders	Members	All strong identifiers
FPDU	18	33	21	69
Soc. Dem. Opposition	8	25	4	32
SDP	12	18	12	64
FPP	4	19	3	47
Conservatives	11	28	10	64

These percentages draw attention to the fact that the occurrence of opinion leaders, unlike that of campaign workers, was not related to how well established the parties were locally. Instead it seems that opinion leaders were most numerous among the supporters of the winning parties, and least numerous among the supporters of losing parties.[3]

To understand this difference in the proportion of influencers, we have to return to their principal difference by definition (see p. 314). As campaign workers were defined, they functioned only because of their enthusiasm and on their own initiative. On the other hand, in the classification of opinion leaders, not only was their own desire to express opinions considered, but the desire of their friends to ask for their opinions was also significant. In other words, opinion leaders were people who were in demand.

It is feasible that citizens were most interested in those parties whose support was increasing at the moment. Therefore, one might also think

3. FPDU and Conservatives 31 per cent; SDP and FPP 18 per cent; $t = 3.06$, $p < 0.01$.

that in the various small groups special demand was put on the opinions of friends and acquaintances who were known to support a party now sailing with the wind behind it.

TABLE 11.1. Relationship of (a) Campaign Work and (b) Recollection of Campaign Discussions to Desire to Influence Others and Desire of Others to Ask Opinions: Tampere, 1958 (QQ. 61 and 62)

	(a) Per cent campaign workers		(b) Per cent recalling discussions		Number of cases
Friends don't ask					
I listen	7		57		159
I take part		10		70	93
I try to convince		22		53	19
Friends ask sometimes					
I listen	4		75		44
I take part		9		72	81
I try to convince		(50)		(63)	8
Friends like to ask					
I listen	8		75		24
I take part		24		88	34
I try to convince		44		86	14

The definition of opinion leaders provides one possibility for verifying the bases of this interpretation. Two questions were used, one about the opinion leaders' own activity, and the other about the desire of others to hear their opinions. It would be consistent to expect that the former question brought into the class of opinion leaders more people who also did campaign work, but especially the latter question spotted influencers whose opinions were desired by their friends. For the sake of comparison, Table 11.1 classifies the sample according to answers given to both questions.

In Table 11.1.a each of the nine cells gives the percentage of campaign workers. And, as expected, campaign work was related more to the desire of people to express their opinions than to the desire of others to listen to them.[4]

Table 11.1.b shows how large a percentage of the interviewees belonging to each cell remembered discussing the election with others. Of the total

4. In a comparison of campaign workers and others by type of participation in discussions, $\chi^2 = 22.99$, $v = 2$, $p < 0.001$. In a comparison of the same groups by desire of others to ask their opinions, $\chi^2 = 13.49$, $v = 2$, $p < 0.01$.

sample, 68 per cent mentioned discussions concerning the campaign. The percentages vary again, but now in a different direction.[5] People remembered campaign discussions almost without regard to their desire to influence others, but they remembered discussions more clearly, the more they thought their friends wanted to hear them. Again the correlations concur with expectations.

This internal analysis of the class of opinion leaders shows that the difference and separateness of the roles of campaign worker and opinion leader were to some extent a result of the attitudes of the friends or influencees. However, it still has not been explained why campaign workers desired to further their position even if their opinions were not sought after.

A strong party identification might be a good explanation. According to the previously presented figures, people were more likely to work for their party, the more strongly they identified with it. But if it is true that party identification motivated people to work for the party, then campaign workers should identify more strongly with their party than opinion leaders.

TABLE 11.2. Relationship of Precampaign Strength of Party Identification to Campaign Work and Opinion Leadership in Tampere, 1958 (in percentages).

| | Campaign work | | No campaign work | |
	Opinion leaders	Others	Opinion leaders	Others
Party members	39	21	14	8
Other strong identifiers	42	50	47	44
Weak identifiers, nonpartisans	19	18	34	42
No answer	–	11	5	6
Total	100	100	100	100
Number of cases	26	28	79	343

Table 11.2 gives separately the party identification of both kinds of influencers. According to this table, party identification was weakest in the majority who did not belong to either class of influencers, and it was strongest among those people who functioned in both influencer roles. But it is remarkable that the strong identifiers had a greater tendency

5. When discussers and others are compared by type of participation in discussions, $x^2 = 6.69$, $v = 2$, $p < 0.05$; by desire of others to ask, $x^2 = 13.80$, $v = 2$, $p < 0.01$.

to do campaign work than to function as opinion leaders.[6] As expected, it thus seems that a strong party identification motivated people to speak for their party on their own initiative, even if their advice was not wanted.

According to Appendix Table 25, the supporters of the victorious parties, FPDU and the Conservatives, included many pure opinion leaders, whereas there were few opinion leaders among SDP supporters, outside of their campaign organization (in the wide meaning of the term). The sample did not happen to include any campaign workers of the FPP who belonged to the group of opinion leaders as well.

Thus it is obvious that in 1958 the political situation and local political circumstances alike approved the personal influences which favored the Communists: their campaign was backed by a well organized group of supporters and by numerous opinion leaders as well. The Conservative and the SDP campaign depended upon an equally well organized group of supporters, but apparently there was more demand for Conservative opinion leaders. The organization of the Finnish People's Party seems to have been too weak to provide enough campaign workers to compensate for the small number of opinion leaders.

So far political opinion leaders have not been studied from the point of view of the change in demand for them that might correlate with a changing political situation. Obviously, this approach could lead to fruitful studies, combining research on the macro and micro levels of the political system. The above observations seem to suggest the following preliminary hypothesis for such studies: Some opinion leaders who transmit and color information are always created by the current situation, because there exists a special demand for such opinions as are expressed by supporters of the political views on the upswing.

This idea would not be contrary to the unexpected finding that relatively many opinion leaders also changed party during the campaign. Almost all of them did have an affiliation in May and almost all did cast a ballot. Moreover, we might conclude that, in general, the situation and current factors favored the victorious parties in the election. This was found in the comparison of the reasons given by voters of the different parties for their party choice. On the other hand, it is obvious that the political wind does not blow any party very far. Traditions and voting habits are the effective counterforce of a changing political situation.

And, in addition to the current factors, the reasons given for party

6. Only the two columns in the middle do not differ on a significant level ($\chi^2 = 2.91$, $v = 2$, $p < 0.30$).

choice hinted at the significance of traditions. Many voters of the Social Democratic Party mentioned habit as their reason for party choice. It seems obvious that well established party activities had strengthened locally such voting habits. The importance of local party activities could be observed from the official lists of candidates. An analysis of those petitions revealed that the stronger the party organization, the more certain the signers of the lists were to vote on election day (p. 253). On the other hand, an analysis of the party preferences of nonvoters seems to show that a contrary wind did not decrease the desire to vote of the longtime supporters of an old party, the SDP. Yet such an adversity eliminated from the group of voters of a new party—the FPP—numerous older persons who had previously voted for another party.

THE IMPORTANCE OF THE ELECTION

The results of the 1958 shock election surprised people in Tampere. Answers to the question: "Did the outcome of the election surprise you or was it according to your expectations?" (Q. 42) were distributed as follows:

| | Percentage of: | | |
	Men	Women	Total
Surprised	54	58	56
According to expectations	41	31	35
Don't know	5	11	9
	100	100	100

The answers given by the comparison group were distributed in almost the same way: 50 per cent were surprised and 32 per cent said that the outcome was according to their expectations.

What was considered expected in Tampere, was especially "such a victory for the People's Democrats" (Female, 44, FPDU) and "the victory of the left because of the unemployment and the split of the Social Democratic Party" (Female, 34, SDP). However, the "turn to the left was surprisingly strong" (Male, 45, Conservative). No less than 43 per cent of the population (or 81 per cent of the surprised, $n = 252$) was surprised by "the tremendous victory of the FPDU" (Male, 61, FPDU); "the awful victory of the Communists" (Female, 34, Conservative); or "the fact that the FPDU gained the leading post" (Female, 65, SDP):

> Well, because that party of ours has always been the third and now it became the first. (Unskilled worker, male, 51, FPDU)

First the outcome startled me. The Communists have taken good care of their business. (Wife of engineer, 30, SDP)

I did guess the direction, but the size of it surprised me. (Plumber, male, 35, SDP)

It was a surprise that the Communists gained so many votes although they quarrel and cause confusion on jobs. (Houseowner, female, 65, Conservative)

After all, I didn't believe that the FPDU would win." (Market seller, male, 52, nonvoter)

The election caused other surprises too. Some were astonished because "the Agrarians lost so much and the Communists won; the Opposition Socialists gained so little" (Male, 45, FPDU); and people wondered about "the loss of the Social Democratic Party" (Male, 44, SDP); "the defeat of the Finnish People's Party" (Female, 38, FPP), and "the increase of the Conservative representation" (Female, 54, FPDU). Also mentioned were "the victory of both extremes" (Male, 25, Conservative), and "the defeat of the Agrarians—it's good that they were hit" (Female, 61, SDP); and criticism was directed at "the low turnout in voting" (Female, 30, FPP) without which "the outcome would have been different" (Female, 62, Conservative).

Before the election both the FPDU and the Conservatives had stressed their intention to change the direction of policies and their desire to get into the Cabinet to realize their intentions. As usual, forming the new Cabinet was a vital decision soon after the election. Let us now observe whether the outcome of the shock election had changed the Cabinet coalitions which were desired by the electorate. One might expect that the opinions had become more favorable toward the victorious opposition parties, and perhaps more negative concerning Cabinet participation of the losing parties.

The table below shows the percentage of Tampere inhabitants mentioning each party as a desired Cabinet party in May and in July. The percentages for May are also counted for the re-interviewed July sample, as indicated on page 357.

This comparison shows that the expectations were wrong. Obviously the winners' right to step in at this moment was not recognized. The only outcome in accordance with the expectation was the continuously rare reference to the Social Democratic Opposition and to the Finnish People's Party, whereas the decrease in the don't know group might be

	Percentage:		
	In May	In July	Difference
All parties	26	27	+1
FPDU	22	27	+5
Soc. Dem. Opposition	13	14	+1
Social Democratic Party	43	51	+8
Agrarian Union	29	35	+6
Finnish People's Party	22	21	−1
Conservatives	27	36	+9
Swedish People's Party	11	16	+5
Nonpolitical Cabinet	1	1	0
Don't know	18	12	−6

connected with the increasing political knowledge due to the campaign. Contrary to expectations, both the most desired group in the city, the SDP, and the victorious Conservative Party were mentioned more often than previously, while additional choices were given to the losing Government Party, Agrarian Union, as well as the now victorious opposition party, FPDU.

When the corresponding development of the opinions is studied separately for the supporters of each party, the basic finding is the tendency of people to consider their own party the most suitable to the Cabinet (data not shown). This was apparent in May as well as in July, and it did not appear to be related to the outcome of the election. As additional single trends, we might mention that relatively many supporters of the FPDU and the SDP had begun to approve of the Conservatives, and that the supporters of the Finnish People's Party mentioned the SDP and the Agrarians more often than previously. The voters for the Conservatives now began to remember the Cabinet potentiality of the Swedish People's Party. On the other hand, the voters for the Conservatives—perhaps also those of the FPP—were as reluctant as previously to include the Communists in the Cabinet.

The general conclusions are that citizens wanted to include their own party in the Cabinet and, consequently, expressed opinions on Cabinet coalitions that were hardly related to electoral victories and losses.

Let us take a corresponding look at the opinions of the citizens concerning the significance of the parliamentary election. Before the campaign, two out of five had considered the election to be of decisive importance for the country, and only one out of five thought it useless. The development of the opinions was as follows:

| | Percentage: | | |
	In May	In July	The change
Decisive importance	39	9	− 30
Some importance	42	62	+ 20
Useless, don't know	19	29	+ 10
	100	100	

After the excitement cooled down, the election did not seem as important as before the campaign. Forty-five per cent of the sample considered the election now less significant than previously, and only 14 per cent considered it now more important.[7]

Even this opinion has developed, in general, without relationship to party preference. Only three groups seemed to have developed contrary to the general trend. Voters for the Social Democratic Opposition began to belittle the election more than the others, whereas the Conservative voters considered the election as important as earlier and the nonvoters thought it even more important now than they had considered it in May.[8]

Before the campaign, there had been a tendency to consider the election the more important, along with more interest in politics and closer party identification. Yet none of these three factors gave sufficient explanation for the variation between any two given factors. The data are presented in Table 11.3, which also takes into consideration the dynamics of the opinion concerning the importance of the election.

We find that the importance attached to the election correlates separately with political interest and with party identification. One half of those persons who were both interested and sure of their party considered the election important all the time, but only one out of eleven considered it useless. A comparison of those persons who changed their opinion shows only small differences. Thus, the focal finding of Table 11.3 is that the interest which people estimated in May and their precampaign party identification influenced separately, and almost equally, their opinion on the importance of the election.

7. Correspondingly, 41 per cent had maintained their earlier opinion. Because QQ. 34 and 43 are worded differently, the answers are not strictly comparable. However, the substance of the two questions is the same. Again, both distributions are calculated for the same persons, $n = 476$.

8. The conclusions were obtained in a comparison of those persons who began to consider the election useless (20 per cent of total sample) with those who now thought the election more important than in May (14 per cent of the sample). In the subgroups the difference of these percentages was as follows: FPDU 7, Soc.Dem.Opp. 19, SDP 9, FPP 10, Cons. 1 and nonvoters −5 (in total sample 6).

TABLE 11.3. Relationship of Precampaign Interest and Party Identification to the Opinions Expressed in May and July about the Importance of the Election (QQ. 34, 43, 14, and 21) (in percentages)

Importance of the election*	Not interested			Interested			Total sample
	Weak	Strong	Mem-bers	Weak	Strong	Mem-bers	
Useless	30	16	–	12	11	6	18
Some importance	26	34	30	32	24	11	28
Decisive importance	21	24	35	24	48	50	28
Began to consider useless	19	19	29	28	15	19	20
Began to consider decisive	4	6	6	4	2	14	5
Total	100	100	100	100	100	100	100
Number of cases	*159*	*160*	*17*	*50*	*54*	*36*	*476*

* The class "useless" also includes "don't know" responses. Included in the first line are those who answered "useless" in the first and "useless" or "some importance" in the second interview. Correspondingly, line three includes those who answered "decisive" in May and "decisive" or "some importance" in July.

CONTINUITY

On the other hand, one should remember that the opinion expressed in May 1958 on the importance of the election correlates with the July turnout, even when party identification is kept constant. Generally, one of the focal conclusions of this study has been the significance of the normal precampaign characteristics for the behavior realized on voting days.

The earlier voting experiences, recalled in May, showed consistencies in voting behavior from one election to the other, and during whole lifetimes. Yet we have to be careful about conclusions concerning earlier voting experiences because the information is based only on memories, which might be unreliable.

Therefore, repeated interviewing of the same sample was the method of this study. We could extend the time period of data collection over the campaign without having to rely too much on the memory of the respondents. But it is also possible to follow reliably some voting behavior of the sample beyond the second interview. If, for example, the inhabitants of Tampere are classified according to the opinions they expressed concerning the importance of the 1958 election, we know that these groups participated in the two elections of 1962, namely the normal election of the presidential electors on January 15–16, and the parliamentary election of February 4–5, after the dissolution of the Parliament, in the following percentages:

Opinions in 1958	Presidential election 1962	Parliamentary election 1962
Unnecessary	81	81($n =$ 78)
Some importance	88	92($n =$ 114)
Of decisive importance	92	94($n =$ 111)
Began to consider it useless	88	89($n =$ 84)
Began to consider it decisive	96	96($n =$ 23)

The opinions which had motivated people to vote in 1958 were still effective almost four years later.

Information concerning the participation of the sample in the 1962 elections has been obtained in principle by the same method as used in checking the 1958 participation, following which comparative studies of participation were carried out. The changes in addresses, and the subsequent changes in voting districts, were first found from the police register of addresses, after which the voting registers of the two elections were examined for those who had been checked out as voters (or issued absentee ballots).[9]

Of the 501 persons interviewed in May 1958, 23 were deceased and 48 had moved away from the city.[10] Thus the additional data concerning voting in 1962 were obtained for 430 persons, and 410 of these had been interviewed twice in 1958. This sample no longer represents the whole enfranchised population of the city, because it does not include those born between 1937–40, nor those who had moved to the city between 1957–60. The Tampere electorate had a net gain of 7,300 persons in four years, from 76,800 to 84,100.

Yet 13,500 more people voted in the city in 1962 than in 1958. The number of nonvoters decreased from 17,300 to 6,300 and the turnout percentage rose to a record breaking 86.8 per cent in this winter election. Another record was reached by the participation in the presidential elec-

9. The same method could be applied to an analysis which would follow the participation of the same sample in numerous elections. The 1958 Tampere sample cannot be used for such an extended study because the interviewees were guaranteed anonymity, and consequently the questionnaires and punchcards are no more identifiable.

10. Let us mention that a desire to move away was expressed in May 1958 by 33 per cent of later movers, but only by 11 per cent of those who stayed in the city and by 13 per cent of those who died during the four years after 1958.

tion which was 85.5 per cent. The corresponding turnout percentages were also higher than previously: for the whole country it was 85.1 and 81.5, and for the Northern Häme constituency, 86.9 and 84.9.

The explanation for the increased turnout is not so simple as that former voters were joined by such 1958 nonvoters as had become activated since that time. Following the development by means of one sample only, we find that even in this respect there were changes which compensated each other and that the change in the turnout was the net result. The following percentage distribution shows the comparison of 1958 and 1962 for the sample:

	Voted in 1958	Did not vote in 1958	Total
Voted twice in 1962	77.4	7.0	84.4
Only presidential election	1.6	1.2	2.8
Only parliamentary election	3.5	1.6	5.1
Nonvoters in 1962	3.3	4.4	7.7
Total	85.8	14.2	$100.0(n = 430)$

Persons who did not vote in 1958 had a very significantly greater tendency than others to abstain in 1962 as well.[11] Yet only 81.8 per cent behaved consistently in the three elections, and 18.2 per cent were both voters and nonvoters. The latter percentage is much higher than those differences in turnout which show net changes only.

In spite of this, factors which were measured in May 1958, and which correlated with the July 1958 turnout, still had an impact on the participation in the 1962 elections. Table 11.4 has a few comparisons which prove this. We find that differences between the groups were consistently in the same direction in 1962 as they had been four years before. Only some mild leveling of differences had taken place. The difference between the highest and lowest turnout percentage was smaller, which was natural in an election livelier than the previous one. Thus normal interest in politics, measured in May 1958, and of no direct concern in the election, predicted not only a high turnout, in July 1958 but also the desire to vote in an election which took place four years later in a very different political situation.

The 1962 turnout of the 1958 voters and nonvoters has already been

11. 49 per cent of the former and 90 per cent of the latter voted in all the elections, $t = 6.23, p < 0.001$.

shown to be different. The following comparisons test three other factors which were related to participation and campaign activity in 1958:

		Percentage in:	
		Presidential election 1962	Parliamentary election 1962
(a)	Did not vote in 1958	57	61($n =$ 61)
	2nd voting day 1958	87	90($n =$ 175)
	1st voting day 1958	98	99($n =$ 180)
(b)	Had always voted	91	94($n =$ 328)
	Remembered some incidence of nonvoting	72	73($n =$ 86)
	Born in 1935–36	81	94($n =$ 16)
(c)	Had decided in the beginning of the year	95	97($n =$ 282)
	Had decided two months or less before the election	68	72($n =$ 65)

TABLE 11.4. Relationship of (a) Political Interest in May 1958, (b) Party Identification in May 1958, (c) Attention Paid to Mass Communication in 1958, and (d) Political Knowledge in May 1958, to Turnout in the Parliamentary Election of July 1958, in the Presidential Election of January 15 and 16, 1962, and in the Parliamentary Election of February 4 and 5, 1962 (in percentages)

		Turnout percentages in 1962			
May 1958	1958 Election	Both	January 15–16	February 4–5	Number of cases
(a) Interest					
Not interested	66	66	72	77	83
Little and rather interested	90	88	90	92	309
Very interested	97	97	97	100	35
(b) Party identification					
Nonpartisan	68	68	78	76	37
Weak identifiers	81	86	87	92	120
Strong identifiers	93	88	91	95	191
Party members	98	96	96	96	46
(c) Mass communication					
Scale value 0 (low)	72	66	70	77	61
1–2	83	85	89	89	168
3–4	89	89	91	94	151
Scale value 5 (high)	100	92	92	98	50
(d) Political knowledge					
Scale values 0–1 (low)	76	78	82	84	135
2–3	89	88	91	93	256
Scale value 4 (high)	97	97	97	97	35

Participation in the 1962 elections thus correlated on a very significant level, not only with voting in 1958, but also with the day of voting in 1958, the regularity of previous participation, and the time of final decision remembered in 1958.[12]

The mutual consistency of these comparisons might be explained as being due to the intercorrelation of these four factors in 1958. But we can attempt to determine whether the 1962 participation also showed a separate influence of these four factors. For this purpose, in Table 11.5 the sample has been classified simultaneously according to four variables. Because of the small number of cases some groups have been combined.

TABLE 11.5. Relationship in Tampere of Participation and Day of Voting (July 6 and 7, 1958), Recalled Constancy in Earlier Participation, and Recalled Time of the 1958 Party Choice to Turnout in the Presidential Election of January 15 and 16, 1962, and in the Parliamentary Election of February 4 and 5, 1962

| | Turnout percentages in 1962 | | | |
Participation in 1958 and earlier	Both	January 15–16	February 4–5	Number of cases
Voted in 1958 and always before				
Early decision, first day	100	100	100	122
Late decision, first day	96	96	96	23
Early decision, second day	88	89	94	144
Late decision, second day	78	85	89	27
Voted in 1958, not previously*				
First day of voting	92	92	97	36
Second day of voting	74	82	79	34
Nonvoters in 1958				
Voted always before	68	74	74	31
Previously nonvoting	30	40	47	30

* This class contains 85 respondents who mentioned some previous nonvoting (Q. 29) and 15 respondents too young to be entitled to vote in 1956.

These comparisons give an obvious result: the four factors which are included and which correlated with the 1958 turnout exerted perhaps a different, but in any case also a separate, influence upon the 1962 turnout. A verbal description of the content of Table 11.5 follows:

> Very high turnout in 1962 was typical of these persons who had always voted before 1958, who had made an early decision in 1958, and who had participated on the first day of voting.

12. When comparing the percentages voting in both 1962 elections, we get (a) $t = 4.77$, $p < 0.001$, (b) $t = 6.38$, $p < 0.001$ and (c) $t = 4.74$, $p < 0.001$.

High turnout was typical of other persons who participated in 1958 on the first day of voting.

Moderate turnout was shown in 1962 by those previously consistent voters who had made an early decision and participated on the second day in 1958.

Rather low participation characterized in 1962 others who had voted on the second day of balloting.

Low participation was typical in 1962 of those 1958 nonvoters who had always voted previously.

Very low turnout was typical in 1962 of those 1958 nonvoters who had also neglected to participate previously.

In other words, Table 11.5 gives an example of a certain scaleability: the more characteristics correlating with inactive behavior citizens had revealed in 1958, the more they tended not to vote in 1962.

However, in this connection one must explain not so much why this scale of active behavior classifies people in groups whose turnout was different, but why many individuals belonging to these groups still behaved differently in different elections. We have shown that the gross changes in participation were much greater than the net changes in turnout percentages, and we must remember that most groups compared in Table 11.5 turned out 100 per cent in 1958 despite their different characteristics.

As an interpretation, we might repeat the view of this study, that participation in elections has to be studied as a joint result of the desire to vote and the exterior restraints on voting, in other words as a kind of difference between these two dimensions. We might presume that random restraints on voting in 1962 occurred equally often in all the groups of Table 11.5. We might also assume that the number of random restraints increased at that time among the 1958 voters and decreased among the 1958 nonvoters. Our observations have shown that these restraints in 1962 did not decrease the participation of those persons characterized in 1958 by a very high desire to vote, yet they prevented as many as one quarter of those persons who had voted in 1958 despite a relatively low desire to vote.

An inverse interpretation can be used when the two groups of 1958 nonvoters are compared. It is possible that some people who had always voted previously did not vote in 1958 because of some random restraint. But the lack of the said restraint freed them to vote again in 1962, whereas many persons who had not voted previously continued having a low desire to vote, and consequently showed the lowest turnout in 1962.

This observation has led to a general interpretation which considers the desire to vote a relatively constant characteristic. The special character of a certain election might increase the general level of desire to vote among the citizens, but even that does not seem to eliminate the relative differences between individuals.

However, one should consider this interpretation only a general rule, to which there are exceptions. For example, personal influence may activate individuals who otherwise would not be willing to vote, while the difficulty of choice in the 1958 situation lowered the desire to vote among the supporters of certain parties. This study has no information concerning new factors which might have activated some groups in 1962 and lowered the motivation of others. But we might look for experiences in connection with the 1958 election that were then new factors influencing the desire to vote, the impact of which might have been preserved over four years. We have noted above that such an activating impact might have been exerted by a new opinion that the election had been of decisive importance.

Party choice was generally considered the main component of voting. Of the people in Tampere who had voted for different parties in 1958, the following percentages participated in the 1962 election:

	Both elections 1962	Presidential election	Parliamentary election
FPDU	93	94	95 $(n = 104)$
Soc. Dem. Opposition	74	78	87 $(n = 23)$
SDP	93	95	97 $(n = 93)$
FPP	94	94	94 $(n = 17)$
Conservatives	90	92	95 $(n = 87)$
Nonvoters	49	57	61 $(n = 61)$

This comparison shows that the voters of four different parties turned out equally in the new elections. However, one group, the voters for the Social Democratic Opposition, tended more than others not to vote in 1962.[13] It is possible that the voters of this new group had been disappointed by the lack of success of their party, or that they were simply unable to distinguish between it and the Social Democratic Party. These

13. $t = 1.98$, p < 0.05, when the percentages of voting twice are compared (S.D. Opp. 74 per cent, others 92 per cent).

disappointments might then have caused alienation from politics and decreasing motivation to participate which was still effective in 1962.

The data of this study do not show whether the Social Democratic Opposition, since 1959 the Social Democratic League of Labor and Small Farmers, had already collected its own group of Tampere supporters in 1958. If this had happened, the passive behavior of its supporters was one obvious explanation for its poor showing in 1962. In 1958, the SDP and the Agrarian Union lost the election mainly because of their supporters' lack of motivation to vote. However, it seems that they were able to activate their supporters once again four years later.

Let us finally stress that changes in party affiliation alone do not cause differences in election outcomes. New generations of voters may change the centers of gravity, which is of special significance in those changes in the desire to vote which depend on the citizens' party affiliation. In no situation is the total support of the parties revealed by the number of votes cast for them.

A low motivation to vote is sometimes considered the first step toward changing party affiliation.[14] On the other hand, nonvoting might also be a result of a temporary desire to punish one's own party. In such a case it might correspond to votes cast for the opposing party in a United States presidential election when the voters still do not perceive giving up their own party identification.

Partly because voting for another party in the American presidential elections does not always mean a change in party affiliation, an electoral victory has been almost regularly followed there by a defeat of the winning party in the midterm election of the House of Representatives.[15] Great electoral victories—like that of the Republicans and Dwight D. Eisenhower in 1952—have been called surges and deviating elections. They are thus differentiated from the more usual and less colorful maintaining elections. But the most unusual elections have been those which, in addition to changing the relative strength of the parties, have also shaken the foundations of party identification among the population, thereby creating political generations of a particular nature. Such realigning elec-

14. For example, Rantala, "Äänestäjän siirtyminen puolueesta toiseen" (The Party Conversion of Voters), *Valtio ja Yhteiskunta, 16* (Vammala, Finnish Political Science Association, 1957), 84.

15. During the century after the American Civil War, the election of 1934 has been the only exception to this rule. Campbell, "Surge and Decline: a Study of Electoral Change," *Public Opinion Quarterly, 24* (1960), 408, 417.

tions occurred in the United States in the 1930s and in England in 1945.[16]

In Finland, the 1958 parliamentary election differed so much from the maintaining elections of 1951 and 1954 that it, too, might be called an electoral surge. However, low motivation to vote is largely the explanation for the outcome of this election, which otherwise did not cause any large changes in the party situation. Therefore, it does not belong in the same class as the Finnish realigning election of 1945.

This classification, which helps to label and interpret elections in two-party systems, must be used with caution when describing an election under the Finnish type of multiple party system. Even if an election as a whole is only of the maintaining type, it still might include some significant realignments as far as single parties are concerned. Some details of breaking with tradition were apparent in the 1958 election. One of these was the grouping of the parties in campaign propaganda into "the popular front" on one hand, and "the right wing" and "the right wing socialists," on the other. The panel interview revealed one trace of a corresponding nature in the voting behavior in Tampere: the cleavage between the left wing and the right wing, which had been continuous for forty decades, was abolished precisely during this campaign.[17] Moreover, a comparison of different age groups showed, in the city as well as in the rural commune, the results of some earlier political realignments.

16. Campbell, "Voters and Elections: Past and Present"; Stokes, lectures at the University of Helsinki on February 21 and 24, 1964. Campbell's terms are "electoral surge" and "realignment." In Campbell, Converse, Miller, and Stokes, *The American Voter*, pp. 531–38, the noncritical elections are called either "maintaining" or "deviating" elections. The theory on critical elections was first suggested in 1955 by V. O. Key, Jr., in "A Theory of Critical Elections," *Journal of Politics, 17,* 3–18.

17. Similar conversions before the 1958 election were shown in the national sample of the Finnish Gallup Institute, but they were weaker than in the analyzed Tampere sample.

Appendixes

APPENDIX TABLE 1. Number and Type of Registered Associations in Tampere Belonging to or Cooperating with the FPDU, by Year of Registration*

| Year of Regis-tration | Communist Party | | | | FPDU and the Democratic Youth League | | | | | Total |
	Ward	Plant	Field of Work	Other	Ward etc.	Field of Work	Women	Youth	Pioneers of Democ-racy	
1944	–	–	–	1	2	–	–	4	–	7
1945	5	–	5	1	6	–	3	5	6	31
1946	3	5	1	–	1	1	1	1	4	17
1947	–	9	3	–	3	1	1	–	1	16
1948	–	2	–	1	2	–	–	2	–	7
1949	25	2	–	–	–	1	2	1	–	31
1950	1	3	–	–	–	–	1	1	–	6
1951	2	3	–	–	–	–	5	1	–	11
1952	–	1	–	1	1	1	2	1	–	7
1953	6	–	–	–	–	–	3	–	–	9
1954	1	1	–	–	–	1	1	–	–	4
1955	2	–	–	–	2	–	1	–	–	5
1956	1	–	–	–	1	–	–	–	–	2
1957	2	1	–	–	–	–	1	–	–	4
1958	–	–	–	–	–	–	–	–	–	–
1959	2	–	–	–	3	–	–	–	3	8
Total	50	27	9	4	21	5	21	16	14	167

* Information obtained from the register of associations, Ministry of Justice.

APPENDIX TABLE 2. Relation of Political Knowledge to (a) Sex and Marital Status and (b) Strength of Party Preference: May 1958 (in percentages)

	Knowledge of Politics					Total	
	0 (low)	1	2	3	4 (high)	Per cent	Number of cases
(a) Sex and marital status							
Men, not married	19	19	37	25	–	100	16
Men, married	5	15	41	26	13	100	174
Men, widowers and divorced	13	7	53	14	13	100	15
All men	6	15	41	25	13	100	205
Women, not married	11	24	43	14	8	100	65
Women, married	11	50	48	9	2	100	166
Women, widows and divorced	17	29	40	5	8	100	65
All women	12	29	45	9	5	100	296
(b) Strength of preference							
Nonpartisan	24	20	48	4	4	100	46
Uncertain	10	32	39	14	5	100	145
Sure preference	6	22	48	17	7	100	217
Party members	4	10	38	25	23	100	56
No information	22	19	40	16	3	100	35
Total sample	10	23	43	16	8	100	501

APPENDIX TABLE 3. Relation of Perception of the Importance of the Election to (a) Interest in Politics and (b) Exposure to Political Mass Communication: May 1958 (in percentages)

	Decisive	Somewhat important	Needless	Don't know	Total	
					Per cent	Number of cases
(a) Interest						
Not interested	31	27	23	17	100	99
A little interested	33	49	11	6	100	255
Rather interested	55	38	7	–	100	104
Very interested	54	24	17	5	100	41
(b) Mass communication						
0 (Low)	23	36	18	23	100	74
1	27	50	16	7	100	89
2	48	36	13	3	100	98
3	41	41	13	5	100	78
4	51	41	6	2	100	99
5 (High)	43	38	16	3	100	63
Total sample	39	41	13	7	100	501

APPENDIX TABLE 4. The Percentages Exposed Often to Selected Topics in Newspapers and to Certain Radio Programs in Korpilahti: May 1958; and Correlations of Exposure with Self-estimated Interest in Politics†

Communication Media and Selected Topics	Men	Women	Total Sample	r_{bis}
NEWSPAPERS				
Government and Parliament	44	15	30	−0.59***
Economy	46	26	36	.60***
Sports	50	30	40	.55***
Movies	4	15	9	.30***
Literature	16	17	16	.33***
Public Speeches	12	26	19	.17*
RADIO				
News broadcasts	92	85	89	−0.04
Radio theatre	48	60	54	−0.03
Talks about parliament	48	34	41	.30***
Press review	54	55	55	.06
"In the focus" (current)	40	28	34	.40***
"The Social Mail Box"	38	34	36	−.05
Sports reports	58	34	46	.25**
Religious services	62	85	73	.16*
Agricultural lectures	50	43	46	.18*
Number of cases	*50*	*47*	*97*	

† Level of significance indicated in the table is determined by the *t*-test. The levels of significance are indicated and denoted as follows: * almost significant, $p < 0.05$; ** significant, $p < 0.01$; *** very significant, $p < 0.001$.

APPENDIX TABLE 5. Party Preference in Tampere, May 1958, by (a) Own and (b) Own or Higher Salaried Spouse's Income Tax Rate for 1957 (in percentages)

	Total sample	FPDU	SDP and Opp.	Non-soc.	SDP	S.D. Opp.	Agr.	FPP	Cons.	Non-part.
(a) Own Taxable Income	25	19	23	30	24	16	40	30	30	38
1–1999	8	10	9	6	10	4	10	–	8	7
2000–3999	35	38	41	20	40	48	40	17	18	41
4000–5999	22	26	19	25	17	32	10	33	24	12
6000–7999	5	6	6	5	7	–	–	7	5	2
8000–	5	1	2	14	2	–	–	13	15	–

APPENDIX TABLE 5 (*Continued*)

	Total Sample	FPDU	SDP and Opp.	Non-soc.	SDP	S.D. Opp.	Agr.	FPP	Cons.	Non-part.
(b) Own or Spouse's Taxable Income	11	5	13	11	14	4	20	13	10	19
1–1999	8	6	9	7	10	–	20	4	8	12
2000–3999	34	42	38	19	40	28	50	13	17	41
4000–5999	31	37	29	31	25	52	10	30	30	21
6000–7999	9	9	8	10	8	12	–	10	11	7
8000–	7	1	3	22	3	4	–	20	24	–
Total	100	100	100	100	100	100	100	100	100	100
Number of cases	*501*	*108*	*189*	*136*	*164*	*25*	*10*	*30*	*93*	*42*

APPENDIX TABLE 6. Party Preference in Tampere, May 1958, by (a) Satisfaction with Income and (b) Unemployment Experiences (in percentages)

	Total Sample	FPDU	SDP and Opp.	Non-soc.	SDP	S.D. Opp.	Agr.	FPP	Cons.	Non-part.
(a) Income (Q. 9)										
Satisfactory	60	38	60	78	59	60	90	77	78	64
Perhaps too small	24	33	25	15	24	28	10	10	17	24
Definitely too small	14	28	13	6	13	12	–	10	4	10
Don't know	2	1	2	1	3	–	–	3	1	2
(b) Unemployment (Q. 12)										
Never (self or spouse)	76	54	77	93	76	84	70	94	95	79
Currently	4	10	4	1	4	4	10	–	–	–
Partially in 1957–58	7	11	6	2	6	8	20	3	–	7
Earlier	13	25	13	4	14	4	–	3	5	14
Total	100	100	100	100	100	100	100	100	100	100
Number of cases	*501*	*108*	*189*	*136*	*164*	*25*	*10*	*30*	*93*	*42*

APPENDIX TABLE 7. Relationship of Party Preference in May 1958, and Income Tax Rate (in new marks) for 1957 to (a) Satisfaction with Subsistence, and (b) Unemployment Experiences (in percentages)

	Tax rate below 4,000				Tax rate above 4,000			
	FPDU	SDP and Opp.	Non-soc.	All	FPDU	SDP and Opp.	Non-soc.	All
(a) Satisfaction								
Got along satisfactorily	17	50	70	49	53	77	85	74
Income perhaps too small	37	29	19	30	28	20	13	20
Income definitely too small	36	21	11	21	19	3	2	6
(b) Unemployment								
No unemployment experience	40	71	85	67	67	85	96	85
Present or earlier unemployment	60	29	15	33	33	15	4	15
Total	100	100	100	100	100	100	100	100
Number of cases	*62*	*103*	*46*	*251*	*43*	*81*	*85*	*236*

APPENDIX TABLE 8. Relationship of Sex and Strength of Party Identification to Consistency of Own and Father's Party Preference (in percentages)

	Men			Women			Total sample
	Weak	Strong	Total	Weak	Strong	Total	
Same party	29	42	37	30	40	35	36
"Left" of father	21	28	25	11	18	15	19
"Right" of father	11	4	7	5	12	9	8
Nonpartisan	9	.	3	26	.	12	9
No information	30	26	28	28	30	29	28
Total	100	100	100	100	100	100	100
Number of cases	*76*	*119*	*195*	*136*	*148*	*284*	*479*

APPENDIX TABLE 9.   The Percentage Distribution of Inhabitants of Tampere according to the Occupation of Main Supporter of Family and That of Father* (in percentages)

	Occupation of Main Supporter				
	Farmer	Labor	Lower white collar	Top-ranking position	Total
Father's Occupation					
Farmers	1	16	2	2	21
Agrarian labor	0	7	1	0	9
Labor and services	1	36	6	6	49
Lower white collar	0	4	3	2	9
Top-ranking position	–	1	2	3	6
No information	0	5	1	0	6
Total	3	69	15	13	100

* Father was also main supporter of 2 per cent. Most often the supporter was respondent (64 per cent) or spouse (30 per cent).

APPENDIX TABLE 10.   The Content of Statements about Other Parties Published in Seven Newspapers from April 14 to May 11, 1958 (see Table 6.5)

	FDPU	S.D. Opp.	SDP	Agr.	FPP	Cons.	Swedish	Right wing	Total
Unpatriotic	45	–	2	17	1	14	1	4	84
Antilabor	9	11	16	7	1	14	–	6	64
Class party, selfish	23	3	3	45	4	12	–	3	93
Economic policy, subsidies	4	1	33	148	3	15	6	14	224
Opposes own party	5	6	7	11	3	6	–	–	38
Warlike	15	1	2	1	–	8	–	–	27
Divisive, categorical	18	1	–	1	–	1	–	–	21
Weak	3	12	7	6	11	–	1	–	40
Unreliable	15	17	15	48	7	21	2	–	125
Politically calculating	7	7	34	71	6	16	1	–	142
Election calculations	3	12	23	87	3	14	–	1	145
Desire for power	12	4	6	38	1	4	–	–	65
Inner controversies	1	33	54	78	2	1	–	–	169
Critical of leaders	5	29	32	80	–	12	4	–	162
Other	27	21	37	64	11	18	11	5	194

APPENDIX TABLE 10 (*Continued*)

	FPDU	S.D. Opp.	SDP	Agr.	FPP	Cons.	Swed-ish	Right wing	Total
Total									
Negative statements	194	158	271	712	53	156	26	33	1603
Neutral statements	24	46	60	58	47	53	56	–	344
Positive statements	2	7	13	9	6	7	6	–	50
Total	220	211	344	779	106	216	88	33	1997

APPENDIX TABLE 11. Relationship of Most Disliked Party to Most Negative Opinion on That Party: May 1958 (in percentages)

	FPDU	S.D. Opp.	SDP	Agr.	FPP	Cons.	Swed-ish	Total sample
Unpatriotic	22	7	–	–	–	–	5	12
Antilabor	1	29	30	12	25	43	3	10
Class party, selfish	1	–	–	36	–	23	2	8
Economic policy, subsidies	1	–	–	29	–	2	–	3
Too radical	3	–	–	3	–	–	–	2
Opposes own party	1	7	10	–	–	5	–	2
Warlike	–	–	–	–	–	7	–	1
Divisive, categorical	41	7	–	12	12	2	–	22
Swedish	–	–	–	–	–	–	55	9
Poor platform	4	–	–	–	–	4	–	3
Weak, useless	–	7	–	–	25	–	13	3
Unreliable	5	14	–	–	–	–	–	3
Inner controversies	–	7	30	6	–	–	–	2
Critical of leaders	2	–	10	3	–	–	–	1
Other	6	–	10	3	–	5	8	6
Everything	3	–	–	3	–	–	–	2
No answer	10	22	10	3	38	9	14	11
Total	100	100	100	100	100	100	100	100
Number of cases	*176*	*14*	*10*	*34*	*8*	*56*	*62*	*360*

APPENDIX TABLE 12.   Relation of Party Preference to (a) Second and (b) Last Ranking Party in Korpilahti: May 1958 (in percentages)

Parties	FPDU	SDP	Agr.	FPP + Cons.	Non-partisan	Total sample
(a) Second						
FPDU	.	20	–	–	–	6
S.D. Opp.	11	(12)*	7	12	–	5
SDP	28	.	36	–	–	16
Agrarian	11	44	.	25	–	16
FPP	–	4	25	25	–	10
Conservative	–	–	7	25	–	4
Don't know	50	32	25	13	100	43
(b) Last						
FPDU	.	16	56	88	7	28
S.D. Opp.	–	–	4	–	–	1
SDP	–	.	–	–	–	–
Agrarian	6	–	.	12	–	2
FPP	6	–	–	–	–	1
Conservative	22	24	7	–	–	13
Swedish	22	28	7	–	–	14
Don't know	44	32	26	–	93	41
Total	100	100	100	100	100	100
Number of cases	*18*	*25*	*28*	*8*	*14*	*97*

* For these, the third preference has been substituted.

APPENDIX TABLE 13.   Relationship of the Carefulness of Attention Paid to Campaign Material in Newspapers (Q. 64.B) to the Frequency of Advertisement Readership (Q. 64.A): Tampere, 1958 (in percentages)

Advertisements	Campaign articles				
	Not	A little	Some attention	Careful attention	Total sample
Hardly ever	65	34	18	19	36
Sometimes	28	50	52	11	40
Often	7	16	30	70	24
Total	100	100	100	100	100
Number of cases	*134*	*132*	*157*	*53*	*476*

APPENDIX TABLE 14. Negative Articles Published in Seven Newspapers on Other Parties (a) May 12–June 8, 1958, and (b) June 9–July 6, 1958

(a) May 12–June 8   (b) June 9–July 6

Parties	FPDU		SDP		Cons.		Ind.	Total	FPDU		SDP		Cons.		Ind.	Total
	HY	KU	KL	SS	AL	US	HS		HY	KU	KL	SS	AL	US	HS	
FPDU	·	·	12	41	6	6	–	65	·	·	38	130	46	13	15	242
S.D. Opp.	3	–	3	30	4	1	–	41	3	4	29	55	7	–	2	100
SDP	9	16	·	·	2	–	–	27	31	32	·	·	6	1	–	70
Agrarian	3	11	14	64	15	7	8	122	7	23	18	156	22	30	19	275
FPP	–	–	–	–	5	–	–	5	–	7	2	6	7	7	1	30
Conservative	5	10	1	4	·	·	–	20	6	15	1	29	·	·	1	52
Swedish	–	–	–	–	–	–	–	–	–	–	–	3	1	–	–	4
Agr. + FPDU	–	–	–	–	–	–	–	–	–	–	4	–	4	3	–	11
Agr. + S.D. Opp.	–	–	–	–	–	–	–	–	–	–	2	–	–	2	–	4
Agr. + Left	–	–	–	–	1	–	–	1	–	–	–	–	2	–	–	2
Agr. + Cons.	–	1	–	–	–	–	–	1	–	–	–	–	–	–	–	–
SDP + Cons.	1	4	–	–	–	–	–	5	–	6	–	–	–	–	1	7
Left	–	–	–	–	–	–	–	–	–	–	–	–	–	–	1	1
Right	6	4	1	10	–	–	–	21	12	5	1	19	–	–	–	37
Total	27	46	31	149	33	14	8	308	59	92	95	398	95	56	40	835

APPENDIX TABLE 15. The Content of Negative Statements about Other Parties Published in the Three Tampere Newspapers from April 14 to May 11, 1958 (see Appendix Table 10)

	FPDU		S.D. Opp.			SDP		Agrarian			FPP			Con-servative		Swedish			Right wing
	KL	AL	HY	KL	AL	HY	AL	HY	KL	AL	HY	KL	AL	HY	KL	HY	KL	AL	HY
Unpatriotic	12	13	–	–	–	2	–	5	–	3	–	–	–	7	–	–	–	–	2
Antilabor	4	1	3	1	–	11	–	2	–	–	1	–	–	6	2	–	–	–	–
Class party	7	6	–	–	–	1	–	1	6	–	2	–	–	2	–	–	–	–	2
Economic policy	2	–	2	–	1	18	3	19	24	22	1	–	1	7	2	1	–	1	6
Opposes own party	2	3	–	–	–	–	1	–	3	1	–	–	1	–	–	–	–	–	–
Warlike	3	2	–	–	–	–	–	–	–	–	–	–	–	–	–	–	–	–	–
Divisive, categorical	7	4	–	–	–	–	–	–	–	–	–	–	–	–	–	–	–	–	–
Weak	–	3	2	–	3	2	1	1	3	–	–	1	3	–	–	1	1	–	–
Unreliable	4	1	1	1	–	5	2	5	9	7	1	–	3	4	–	–	2	–	–
Calculating	4	–	–	–	2	10	3	6	9	12	2	2	–	4	4	1	–	–	–
Election calculations	1	3	–	1	2	3	2	4	10	18	–	1	1	2	1	–	–	–	–
Desire for power	3	4	–	3	1	3	–	4	9	5	1	–	–	1	–	–	–	–	–
Inner controversies	–	1	6	–	4	12	4	1	14	11	–	–	2	–	–	–	–	–	–
Criticism of leaders	2	–	–	2	–	6	4	2	7	14	–	–	–	2	3	–	3	–	–
Other criticism	3	8	1	3	4	11	5	4	4	10	5	1	2	2	2	1	3	–	3
Total	54	49	14	10	18	84	25	58	98	104	11	5	13	41	14	3	6	1	13

APPENDIX TABLE 16. The Content of Negative Statements about Other Parties Published in the Three Tampere Newspapers from June 9 to July 6, 1958 (see Appendix Tables 10 and 15)

	FPDU		S.D. Opp.			SDP		Agrarian			FPP			Con-servative		Swedish			Right wing
	KL	AL	HY	KL	AL	HY	AL	HY	KL	AL	HY	KL	AL	HY	KL	HY	KL	AL	HY
Unpatriotic	58	45	–	–	–	24	1	1	4	11	–	–	–	5	–	–	–	–	4
Antilabor	18	2	1	74	2	25	1	9	8	7	–	–	–	7	7	–	–	–	2
Class party	6	7	–	–	–	4	–	8	2	10	–	–	1	3	6	–	–	–	–
Economic policy	4	4	5	2	4	23	18	23	39	56	2	1	3	9	8	–	–	1	10
Opposes own party	6	5	–	11	1	12	3	3	10	5	–	2	1	7	5	–	–	–	6
Warlike	11	5	–	1	1	1	–	–	1	1	–	–	–	–	2	–	–	–	–
Divisive, categorical	36	25	–	1	–	4	–	1	–	2	2	–	–	3	–	–	1	–	7
Weak	–	–	–	4	–	2	2	–	–	–	3	9	7	–	–	–	–	1	–
Unreliable	28	21	–	15	5	21	2	11	16	17	3	5	5	3	–	–	–	–	2
Calculating	–	8	–	6	–	1	1	2	4	6	–	–	3	–	–	–	–	–	–
Election calculations	4	7	1	5	2	9	3	4	9	18	–	–	1	2	2	–	–	–	–
Desire for power	5	7	–	5	–	1	–	–	11	19	–	6	3	1	1	–	–	–	1
Inner controversies	–	1	–	–	–	8	5	–	3	2	–	–	2	–	–	–	–	–	–
Criticism of leaders	3	15	39	19	6	64	3	17	16	26	–	–	1	3	4	–	–	–	5
Other criticism	13	17	5	11	2	22	7	8	14	15	2	6	7	9	8	–	3	3	8
Total	181	169	50	155	23	221	46	87	137	193	10	29	34	49	43	–	4	5	45

APPENDIX TABLE 17. Relationship of Self-estimated Interest in Politics in May to Later Campaign Activity (in percentages)

	Not	Little	Rather	Very
	interested in politics			
Worked for their party outside family	2	3	6	18
Discussed the election	44	67	81	78
Remembered a party poster	62	77	91	93
Remembered the poster of at least one candidate	35	53	56	80
Listened to a nonpartisan election program	20	29	34	35
Listened to a partisan program	27	38	33	50
Read campaign articles	23	40	63	78
Looked at campaign advertisements	16	23	28	43
Went to a campaign meeting	2	6	8	28
Number of cases	*91*	*242*	*101*	*40*

APPENDIX TABLE 18. Relationship of Absentee Voting in July 1958 to Political Interest in May, Earlier Voting Participation, and Campaign Activity (in percentages)

	TOTAL		MEN		WOMEN	
	Own district	Absentee ballot	Own district	Absentee ballot	Own district	Absentee ballot
Very or moderately interested	31	42	44	59	21	25
Willing to give reasons	49	52	48	41	50	63
Party members	12	21	18	29	7	13
Recalled participation in all previous elections	81	76	85	67	78	86
Worked for their party	13	12	16	18	9	6
Knew a campaign worker	20	36	25	47	17	25
Remembered four or more party posters	55	45	69	59	45	31
Identified one poster or more	79	88	85	94	75	81
Remembered the poster of at least one candidate	55	39	63	53	48	25
Received pamphlets	87	70	83	77	90	63
Listened to the presentation of some party	38	30	37	18	38	56
Read carefully election articles of newspapers	12	18	17	29	8	6
Number of cases	*374*	*33*	*158*	*17*	*216*	*16*

APPENDIX TABLE 19.   Relationship of Attention Paid in Korpilahti to (a) the Presentation of Parties on Radio and (b) Campaign Advertisements in Newspapers to Other Campaign Activity, 1958 (in percentages)

	(a) Presentation of parties		(b) Campaign advertisements	
	Yes	No	Yes	No
Remembered a party poster	88	77	83	76
Remembered a candidate's poster	41	33	40	28
Listened to neutral election program on the radio	47	13	26	24
Listened to the great election debate	41	22	35	14
Read articles on the election in newspapers	85	62	78	52
Received campaign pamphlets	53	40	43	48
Went to a campaign meeting	24	18	23	14
Number of cases	*34*	*60*	*65*	*29*

APPENDIX TABLE 20.   A Comparison of Voting Intentions and Voting Decisions in the Tampere Sample (see Figure 10.A)

Voting in July	Intentions in May								Total in July
	FPDU	S.D. Opp.	SDP	Agr.	FPP	Cons.	Uncertain	No answer	
FPDU	93	6	5	–	–	–	9	2	115
S.D. Opp.	–	7	12	–	1	–	4	2	26
SDP	–	5	94	1	–	1	8	2	111
Agrarian	–	–	–	–	3	–	–	–	3
FPP	–	–	2	13	–	1	4	–	20
Conservative	–	–	10	5	1	78	8	1	103
Popular C.	1	–	–	–	–	–	–	–	1
Nonvoters	5	4	17	6	3	3	37	5	80
No answer	3	–	3	1	–	–	10	12	29
No interview	2	–	3	1	–	1	4	2	13
Total in May	104	22	146	27	8	84	84	26	501

APPENDIX TABLE 21. Party Choice of 1958 Voters in Tampere and Expressed View about the Main Reason for Party Choice (Q. 54.B) (in percentages)

Main Reason	FPDU	S.D. Opp.	SDP	FPP	Cons.	Total
Favors labor or some other own group	66	28	34	18	5	34
Fatherland, interest of the whole, middle of the road	–	–	9	52	16	10
Social policy	2	–	–	–	–	0
Party program	2	–	3	6	9	4
Accomplishments	7	5	2	–	2	4
Party conduct	–	5	5	6	3	3
Candidates, leaders	–	9	–	–	12	4
Dependable, can mold the affairs	–	–	9	–	11	6
Inherited or habitual vote	10	24	28	6	19	19
New faces, opposition	7	5	–	6	4	4
Other statements	6	24	10	6	19	12
Total	100	100	100	100	100	100
Number of cases	*100*	*21*	*105*	*17*	*98*	*344*

APPENDIX TABLE 22. Relationship of Constancy in Voting Intention to Attention Paid to the Campaign (in percentages)

	Constants	Inter-Soc. Dem.	Converters	Crystallizers	Intended non-voting	Unintended non-voting
Listened to the entire election debate on radio	19	11	24	5	9	8
Listened to the presentation of some party	41	41	41	19	25	31
Read carefully election articles of newspapers	13	–	15	9	–	6
Looked often at campaign advertisements	27	18	32	21	3	22
Listened to election results past midnight	16	24	9	9	–	17
Attended a campaign meeting	10	12	6	2	–	3
Average of remembered posters*	3.92	3.65	3.37	3.79	3.03	3.56
Average of identified posters	2.92	2.23	2.26	2.58	1.75	2.44
Average of newspapers read regularly in June	1.90	1.59	1.76	1.37	1.19	1.58
Number of cases	*288*	*17*	*34*	*43*	*32*	*36*

* Max. = 9 posters (QQ. 44.A-B).

APPENDIX TABLE 23. Relationship of Party Preference and Party Identification in May to Attention Paid to the Campaign of One's Own and Other Parties in June and July 1958 (in percentages)

	Total*		FPDU		SDP		Cons.	
	Weak	Strong	Weak	Strong	Weak	Strong	Weak	Strong
(a) Recalled party posters (Q. 44.A)								
Own party only	3	3	3	3	–	2	3	9
Own and other	51	52	64	58	53	49	58	47
Other party only	20	18	15	17	17	19	9	15
No poster	26	27	18	22	30	30	30	29
(b) Poster ranked best (Q. 44.C)								
Own party	29	43	40	57	24	32	39	54
Other party	40	32	24	17	46	40	39	29
Don't know	31	25	36	26	30	28	20	17
(c) Party presentations on radio (Q. 47)								
Evening of own party	9	12	18	22	5	3	3	17
Both evenings	11	20	6	18	16	18	15	24
Evening of other parties	12	10	3	7	11	15	12	5
Did not listen	68	58	73	53	68	64	70	54
(d) New newspaper adopted during campaign (QQ. 5, 63)								
Paper of own party	7	11	15	21	7	7	–	5
Own and other	3	4	3	7	3	5	6	2
Paper of other party	16	17	6	12	16	23	9	15
No new paper	74	68	76	60	74	65	85	78
(e) Campaign meetings (Q. 58)								
Own party	15	7	9	18	2	2	–	3
Own and other	–	2	–	4	–	1	–	2
Other party	3	2	3	–	3	5	3	2
No campaign meeting	94	89	88	78	95	92	97	93
Total	100	100	100	100	100	100	100	100
Number of cases	*160*	*256*	*33*	*72*	*57*	*102*	*33*	*59*

* Includes six parties.

APPENDIX TABLE 24.   A Comparison of Voting Intentions and Voting Decisions
in the Korpilahti Sample

| Voting in July | Intentions in May | | | | | | | | Total in July |
	FPDU	S.D. Opp.	SDP	Agr.	FPP	Cons.	Uncer-tain	No answer	
FPDU	14	1	3	–	–	–	3	–	21
S.D. Opp.	–	–	2	1	–	–	4	–	7
SDP	–	–	13	–	–	–	2	–	15
Agrarian	1	–	–	18	–	–	2	1	22
FPP	–	–	–	–	2	–	–	–	2
Conservative	–	–	–	–	1	4	1	–	6
Nonvoters	3	–	4	5	–	1	9	–	22
No answer	–	–	–	–	–	–	–	1	1
No interview	–	–	–	1	–	–	–	–	1
Total in May	18	1	22	26	3	5	21	2	97

APPENDIX TABLE 25.   Relationship of Party Preference in May to Campaign
Work (Q. 68) and Opinion Leadership: Tampere 1958 (in percentages)

	FPDU	S.D. Opp.	SDP	FPP	Cons.	Non-partisan	Total sample
Opinion leaders who did campaign work	10	4	6	–	5	–	5
Other campaign workers	8	4	6	4	5	6	6
Other opinion leaders	23	21	12	18	23	3	17
Ordinary discussers and outsiders who did no campaign work	59	71	76	78	67	91	72
Total	100	100	100	100	100	100	100
Number of cases	*105*	*24*	*159*	*27*	*92*	*32*	*476*

1.   Personal data
1.A.   Sex and marital status
1.B.   Year of birth
1.C.   Number of children, year of their birth
2.   How many different places have you lived, and how long did you live at each place?
2.B.   Would you like to or would you not like to move away from Tampere/Korpilahti?
        Where? And why?
3.   How many persons are living with you, and how are they related to you?
4.   Do you live in your own house (apartment), do you rent your home, or are you living in a shared room?
4.B.   Do you have a radio? How about a telephone?
5.   Which newspapers and periodicals do you read regularly?
5.B.   When reading newspapers, do you notice the following topics often, sometimes, or hardly ever?
            Articles dealing with motion pictures
            "   "   "   literature
            "   "   "   the government and the Parliament
            "   "   "   the economy
            "   "   "   sports
            "   reporting festivals and public speeches
6.   Do you listen to the following radio programs often, sometimes, or hardly ever?
            News by the Finnish News Agency?
            Radio theatre
            "In the focus" (current interest) programs
            Agricultural lectures on Sunday morning
            Religious services
            "The social mail box"
            Press review
            Talks about the Parliament's work
            Sports commentators
7.   Are your father and mother alive?
        If so, where do they live permanently?
8.A.   Who provides the major support for your family?

* Some instructions are not included here. Questions 1–40 were asked in May and 41–70 in July, 1958.

8.B.   What is his (her) occupation?

8.C.   (if other than interviewee)
        What is your main occupation?

8.D.   What is your father's occupation?

9.   Considering your circumstances, do you get along financially satisfac-
        torily, or is yours and your spouse's income somewhat too small or
        definitely too small?

9.B.   If too small, what additional income per month would make your
        livelihood satisfactory?

10.   Which schools and courses have you attended?
        How long in each?
        And what is/was the training of

10.B.   your father?

10.C.   your mother?

10.D.   your spouse?

11.   (if married)
        What is your children's education?
        (if not completed)
        What schooling would you like your children to get?

12.   Were you or your spouse ever unemployed or in unemployment
        works?
        If so, when, and for how long?

13.   Many experts say that there will be unemployment next winter too.
        What do you think the state ought to do to help the situation?

14.   This study will include a few questions about your attitudes toward
        politics.
        How interested are you generally in politics and governmental affairs:
        very interested, rather interested, a little interested, or not at all inter-
        ested?

15.   And are you satisfied or not satisfied with the recent conduct of Finn-
        ish internal politics?
        Would you like to give reasons for being/not being satisfied?

16.   Power to take care of our common affairs belongs primarily to the
        President, the Parliament and labor market organizations. Do you
        think any one of these is too powerful or has too little power?
        Would you like to give reasons for your opinion?

17.   There are many parties in Finland. Do you consider our multi-party
        system a good one, or would you prefer two parties or maybe only
        one?
        Would you like to give reasons for your opinion?

18.   Which parties do you remember as being in the present Parliament?

Please mention those parties you recall, from the biggest to the small-est.

19. This list includes all the parties in Parliament, that is the People's Democrats, the Independent Social Democrats, the Social Democratic Party, the Agrarian Union, the Finnish People's Party, the National Coalition, and the Swedish People's Party. Please arrange these par-ties now so that you mention first the one that appeals to you most, and last one that pleases you the least.

20.A. What displeases you most about the party you placed last?

20.B. And what is best about the party you ranked first?

21. Is it a party that you consider merely closest to the best possibility, or do you have a sure party preference?
(if sure) Are you a member in some of its associations?

22. Then we would like to hear your opinion on a few general problems. The coat of arms of Tampere has been recently discussed, although many inhabitants probably don't remember what the coat of arms looks like. Could you describe it?

22.B. An opinion has also been expressed in favor of renewing it. Do you think a totally new coat of arms should be designed for the city, or should the present one be improved, or would it be best to make no change?
Would you like to give reasons for your opinion?

23. Industrialization is a frequently discussed topic. Should new plants be started in Finland, or do you think there is now enough native in-dustry at least for the next few years?
Would you like to give reasons for your opinion?

24. A part of the Finnish economy is owned by individuals, a part by the state. Is the present ownership right, or should the state take hold of private firms, or perhaps should the stock of state firms be sold to the public?
Would you like to give reasons for your opinion?

25. Opinions are often exchanged about the size of farms. Many would like to have as many (although small) farms as possible, others say that farms should be large enough to be profitable, even if their num-ber would be smaller. Which opinion do you agree with?
Would you like to give reasons for your opinion?

26. Which do you consider more important at the moment: lower taxes or additional state support to the needy?

27. And what do you think about regulating the economy: is the present situation good, is business allowed to function too freely, or does the government give too many orders to business?
Would you like to give reasons for your opinion?

28.   Things of this kind are of course decided in the Parliament. Do you happen to remember when the new Parliament will be elected?

29.   (Not for respondents born in 1935–36)
       On election days many people are not interested in voting and many can't go to the polls even if they would like to. Have you ever happened to be unwilling or unable to vote?
       (if nonvoter)
       Did you not vote once, a couple of times, more often, or in just about every election?

29.B. (if nonvoter)
       Would you like to tell why you have not voted?

30.   To be accurate, the next parliamentary election will be July 6–7, this year. Do you intend to vote?
       (if not)
       Why not?

31.   Suppose the election would take place tomorrow; which party do you think you would vote for?

32.A. Are you satisfied with the way the party has been run until now?
       Would you like to give reasons for your opinion?

32.B. Have you always voted for the party you mentioned?
       (if other party)
       Which party and when?

33.   And which party is/was supported by:

33.A. your father?

33.B. your mother?

33.C. your spouse?

34.   If we consider the importance of this summer election, which of these three opinions is closest to yours?
       1. The future management of the affairs of the country depends decisively on the outcome of the election.
       2. Apparently the election will somewhat clarify the political situation.
       3. Elections are useless, because it does not seem to make any difference who is sitting in Parliament.

35.   After the parliamentary election a new Cabinet will be formed. Which party or parties should be represented in the new Cabinet?

36.   Without regard to your own voting intention, how would you predict the outcome of the next election? Which parties will gain and which will lose?

37.   And could you mention someone in Northern Häme, whom you would especially like to have sent to Parliament?

38.   Still a couple of additional questions about yourself.
       Please mention the clubs and associations in which you are a member.

39.A. And when did you last go to the movies?

39.B. What movie did you see?

40. Finally, I would like you to tell, how you spent the first of May. Did you attend labor festivals, listen to the glee club performances and so on?

.   .   .

41. How did you first get news about the outcome of the election?

42. Did the results surprise you, or were they what you expected?

43. Do you think the changes in the Parliament will affect the management of governmental affairs decisively, somewhat, or not at all? (Possible reasons:)

44.A. Before the election, the parties put up posters. Which of these did you happen to see?

44.B. The names of parties have been eliminated from the pictures. From memory or by guessing please say which party was mentioned in each poster.

44.C. Which poster do you think was best? Why?

44.D. Advertisements for individual candidates were also circulated outdoors. Which do you remember?

45.A. Two days before the election, the radio broadcast a big election debate. Did you hear it all, hear part of it, or did you miss it?

45.B. Do you recall the names and parties of the men who participated in the discussion?

45.C. How did you like the debate?

45.D. Which participant gave the impression of being most reliable?

46. For how long did you listen to the counting of votes on the eve of the second polling day?

47. The radio had some other election programs, too. Did you happen to hear these (show the list) in their entirety, in part, or not at all?

48. To what extent did you spend the time between midsummer and the election out of town or otherwise vacationing?

49. Partly due to vacations, partly for other reasons, more people than usual did not vote. Did you vote this time?

50. If did not:

A. Please tell briefly why you did not go to the polls or get an absentee ballot.

B. Would you have voted if you could have guessed the outcome of election?

C. Which party would you have voted for?

51. If voted:

A. Did you vote on Sunday or Monday? Did you vote in your own voting district or with an absentee ballot?

B. Did you go to the polling place alone or with somebody? With whom?

52. In which month should future elections be held? July, October, January, or March, or does it make no difference to you?

(Questions 53–57 for voters only)

53. (Show list 53–54)

In Northern Häme, the following seven electoral alliances had nominated candidates: Agrarians, Independent Social Democrats, Finnish People's Party, the Popular Center, the Coalition, the People's Democrats and the Social Democrats. When did you know definitely which party would receive your vote: in the beginning of this year, at least a couple of months before the election, around midsummer, or just before the election days?

54.A. Which was your party this time?

54.B. What was your main reason for choosing that party?

54.C. Did anything happen before the election that influenced your voting decision?

55. Which candidate did you vote for and why?

(if refuses to answer)

Maybe you could tell whether you voted for a man or for a woman?

56. Did you first choose the party and then the candidate, or did you primarily vote for a person, with less regard to the party?

57. Would you have voted differently if you had guessed the election outcome beforehand?

58.A. Before the election there were meetings and festivals where the candidates made speeches. Did you attend any of them?

58.B. If did attend:

Whose and what kind of a meeting?

Do you remember who spoke?

59. Did some friends of yours tell you about speeches they had heard?

60.A. With whom did you most often discuss the election?

60.B. Did they usually agree or disagree?

60.C. Do you remember a specific discussion prior to the election about the election and voting?

61. When politics is discussed among your friends, how do you yourself take part in the discussion?

1. Despite my own opinions, I usually only listen.

2. I listen a lot, but also express my opinions now and then.

3. I take part in the discussion like anybody else.

4. I have my opinions, of which I try to convince my friends, too.

62. Do your friends usually like to ask your opinion concerning public affairs?

Like to ask, ask sometimes, don't ask

63. Which newspapers and periodicals did you read regularly in June?

64.A. Did you look at the election ads in the newspapers often, sometimes, or hardly ever?

64.B. How about articles on elections: did you pay careful, some, only a little, or no attention to them?

65. What is your opinion about the campaign propaganda of different parties in the newspapers?

66.A. And what kind of campaign brochures did you receive at your home?

66.B. Did parties or candidates also mail letters to your address? Who and what kind of letters?

66.C. What was your opinion of the campaign brochures?

67. On the whole, from which source did you get the most and the most reliable information about the election:
newspapers, periodicals, radio, posters, printed party material, campaign meetings, discussions with other people, or some other source? And what do you consider was the second best source of information?

68. Did you participate actively in your family, among your friends, or maybe also elsewhere for the electoral success of your party?

69. Did any close acquaintance of yours take an active part in the campaign activity?
Who and how?

70.A. Finally a question about conducting matters from now on. Which do you prefer: frequent changes of Cabinet or one Cabinet for the whole term until the next election?

70.B. Which parties do you think would be most suitable for the Cabinet?

APPENDIX 2: THE SAMPLES

(a) Sampling

A random sample of adults was taken from the 1957 population register of Tampere as representative of the enfranchised population of the city. The first name was drawn by lot and then every 132nd name included. The sex distribution was:

	The Sample		The Electorate	
	Cases	Per cent	Cases	Per cent
Men	245	42.0	31,901	41.5
Women	339	58.0	44,892	58.5
	583	100.0	76,796	100.0

These percentages differ far less than the standard error of the percentages calculated for the sample (2.04).

The sampling procedure provided such personal information about the respondents as sex, marital status, time and place of birth, years of residence in the city, and occupation. Also, the registers gave the addresses used for the interviewing. Eighty-two persons had moved to other addresses in Tampere after the register was drawn up; forty-one had moved out of the city and eight had migrated abroad (through remaining in the Tampere registers for the 1958 election).

(b) The Interviews

The first series of interviews was begun on Saturday, May 10, and completed by May 25, 1958. The post election interview in July lasted slightly longer. The interviewing was performed by 31 local people, experienced in part-time interviewing and especially trained for this study.

To ensure improved response, the study was pinpointed by a local radio program on May 4, and the three local newspapers helpfully published a news item about it on May 10. Only 16 interviewees (2.8 per cent) in May and eight others in July refused cooperation.

(c) Incidence of Incompletion

A total of 82 persons were not interviewed in May; of those, 44 voted in the election. The reasons for noncompliance were:

	Voters	Nonvoters	Total
Death in May	–	1	1
Migration abroad	–	8	8
Migration elsewhere in Finland and			
unavailable for interview	6	7	13
Residence unknown	5	5	10
Abroad	1	2	3
Sickness	6	5	11
Refusal	10	6	16
Unlocated by interviewers	16	4	20
	44	38	82

The two first classes could not be expected to vote. Of the remaining 574 potential voters, 73 (12.7 per cent) were not interviewed. In July, 25 additional persons (4.3 per cent) could not be reached. For them, too, information about participation in the election was obtained from the official registers.

(d) The Accuracy of the Sample

The percentage of men in the first sample of those interviewed was 40.9 ($n = 501$) and in the second 41.6 ($n = 476$). Thus, the incompletion did not change the sex distribution considerably: the proportions were closest to the true ones in the July sample, which was interviewed twice. The age distribution was also very nearly accurate with one exception: the youngest group, ages 21–25, was under-represented in the interviewed samples.

Certain conclusions are possible about the reliability of the answers. Of the original sample, 79.8 per cent voted; that is a figure 2.2 per cent higher than that of the city's enfranchised inhabitants (the standard error being 1.66). It is thus possible that the interviewing had a slightly activating effect on the sample (see p. 246). Of the 476 persons interviewed in July, 12 nonvoters said that they had voted and one actual voter reported abstention. A comparison with the distribution of votes among the parties shows an over-representation in the sample of Social Democratic voters and a slight under-representation of the FPDU voters (Table 10.2).

(e) The Comparison Group

Of the 4,276 enfranchised inhabitants of Korpilahti, a random sample of 101 was taken. The men numbered 2,122 (49.6 per cent) in the electorate and 52 (51.5 per cent) in the sample, the differences being again much smaller than the standard error of the latter percentage (5.05).

A group of students traveled to the rural commune to do the interviewing. Despite difficulty of access to some houses, only four persons were not interviewed: one had died; another one had been disqualified from voting after the sampling; one sick person could not be interviewed; and one refused.

Three others dropped out in July. Then the proportion of men rose to 51.5 per cent ($n = 94$).

The voting turnout was 74.8 per cent in Korpilahti and exactly the same in the original sample. In the sample of potential voters it was 76.8 per cent ($n = 99$), and in that of July interviewees 78.7 per cent ($n = 94$). In the rural sample the support of the SDP was over-represented and that of the Agrarians under-represented (see Table 10.18).

(a) Exposure to Political Mass Communication

Questions 5.B and 6 had eight items dealing with exposure to political mass communication. Their mutual correlations (also that of the number of newspapers, Q. 5) are:

		(p-1)	(p-2)	(p-3)	(r-1)	(r-2)	(r-3)	(r-4)	(r-5)
(p-1)	Government and Parliament	—							
(p-2)	The economy	.49	—						
(p-3)	Reports on public speeches	.20	.16	—					
(r-1)	Daily news broadcasts	.12	.14	.28	—				
(r-2)	"In the Focus"	.40	.24	.10	.46	—			
(r-3)	"The Social Letter Box"	.15	.13	.01	.39	.43	—		
(r-4)	The Press Review	.22	.20	.07	.42	.35	.31	—	
(r-5)	Talks on the Parliament	.30	.30	.08	.44	.33	.43	.49	—
	Number of newspapers read	.16	.15	.11	.06	.15	.06	.04	.13

Items p-1, p-2, p-3, r-2, and r-5 were combined in the scale. They correlated with each other both in the sample as a whole and separately among the men and the women:

		Men				Women			
		(p-1)	(p-2)	(p-3)	(r-2)	(p-1)	(p-2)	(p-3)	(r-2)
(p-1)	Government and Parliament	—							
(p-2)	The Economy	.41	—			.44	—		
(p-3)	Reports on public speeches	.30	.22	—		.23	.20	—	
(r-2)	"In the Focus"	.30	.30	.20	—	.34	.26	.22	—
(r-5)	Talks on the Parliament	.29	.33	.15	.51	.28	.24	.17	.66

The cumulative scale (with R = .94) used the following specific qualifications:

(r-2)	Listened to the "In the Focus" programs often or sometimes	373 cases
(r-5)	Listened often to the talks on the Parliament	275 "
(p-1)	Read often items on the government and the Parliament	219 "
(p-2)	Read often items on the economy	170 "
(p-3)	Read often reports on meetings and public speeches	94 "

(b) Political Opinion Leaders

In the second interview, Question 61 concerned active participation in private political discussions and Question 62 called for an estimate by the interviewees

397

as to the desire of others to hear their opinions. The following were classified as opinion leaders:

41 interviewees who had their opinions of which they "try to convince friends, too,"

50 interviewees who "take part in the discussion like anybody else" and whose opinion friends either like to ask or "ask sometimes,"

14 interviewees who "listen a lot, but also express their opinions now and then" and whose opinion friends like to ask.

Those persons who indicated the lowest level of activity of both kinds were classified as outsiders. The following three groups were thus evolved:

	Men		Women		Total sample	
	Cases	Per cent	Cases	Per cent	Cases	Per cent
Opinion leaders	65	33	40	14	105	22
Ordinary discussers	85	43	127	46	212	45
Outsiders	48	24	111	40	159	33
	198	100	278	100	476	100

(c) The Knowledge of Politics

The answers given to two open-ended questions, QQ. 18 and 28, correlate very significantly:

Question 18 (Parties):   Question 28 (Current events):

	0 Wrong year	1 Summer	2 July	3 Early July	Total
0 Remembered three or fewer parties	48	25	39	6	118
1 Remembered four parties, or five parties but could not name the three largest ones	28	29	54	14	125
2 Remembered five parties and the three largest ones, or remembered six parties	11	23	61	24	119
3 Remembered six parties and the three largest ones, or remembered seven party groups	4	16	79	40	132
Total	91	93	233	84	501

Of these answers, the scale for measuring political knowledge was made up as follows:

0   Parties 0, current events 0   48 cases
1   Parties 0 and events 1, or parties 1–2
       and events 0–2   116   "
2   Parties 0–2 and events 2–3, or parties
       3 and events 0–1 (20 cases)   218   "
3   Parties 3 and events 2   79   "
4   Parties 3 and events 3   40   "
                                                   ―――――――
                                                      501 cases

(d) The Number of Opinions

The sample was dichotomized according to five questions, 23–27 (all dealing with economic policies), into the responsive ones and the "don't knows." The five items showed a significant mutual correlation. A simple sum scale ranging from 0 to 2 measures "the number of opinions" as follows: Scale value 0 (three or fewer responses, 123 cases), scale value 1 (4 responses, 143 cases), and scale value 2 (5 responses, 235 cases).

(e) The Readiness to Give Reasons

Nine questions from the first interview dealing with political opinions were followed by the question "Would you like to give reasons for your opinion?" Those four items (QQ. 15, 23, 24, and 26) chosen all had mutual rϕ values higher than 0.50, and the following sum scale was combined: Scale value 0 (0–1 reasons given, 136 cases), scale value 1 (2–3 reasons, 220 cases), scale value 3 (indicating 4 reasons, containing 145 cases).

1957   The parties were beginning campaign preparations or continu-
ing preparations started in 1956. Reservations were made on
January 15, 1957, for outdoor advertising during June 1958; on
January 21 the Agrarian Union arranged its first course for the
rear guard organization; the improvement of campaign organizations also included special efforts to establish new local party
units; the final campaign and organizational plan was decided
during the autumn by the FPDU national council, for example;
nominations began to be discussed in the meetings of local party
associations, and so-called membership polls were taken; in-
formational journals were founded, and money was collected
for the campaign; some meetings in the country were actually
called election meetings; and in December the public registration officials handed over to the election boards the basic population lists as of January 1, 1957, to be used in preparing the
registers of electors.

1958

January   The municipal councils of the rural communes appointed an
election board for each voting district.

Jan. 16   The decision of the Council of Ministers concerning the distribution of the 200 seats in the Parliament among the country's
constituencies was published in the Statute Book of Finland.

Jan. 19   An extraordinary district convention of the Conservatives
nominated tentatively the 13 candidates of the party.

Jan. 26   A regional meeting of the Agrarian Union decided on local
candidates for Korpilahti.

Feb. 3   The *Helsingin Sanomat* initiated its column, "Toward the
Election."

Feb. 16–17 The Social Democratic Party held its membership primary.

Feb. 23   The district convention of the Finnish People's Party nominated
eight candidates and delegated the power to nominate five
others to the district board.

February   Local units of the FPDU nominated candidates for the organiza-
and March tional vote.

* All local references concern either Tampere, Korpilahti, or the Northern Häme
constituency.

March 4	The first actual campaign advertisement was run in the *Kansan Lehti;* nomination of Agrarian candidates was finalized in a district convention held in Tampere.
March 11	The *Uusi Suomi* began its column, "On the Threshold of the Election."
March 15–21	The registers of electors, now signed by the election boards, were available for public inspection; election cards were mailed in Tampere to each registered elector.
March 25	This was the last day for requesting the elimination of names of unqualified persons from the register.
March 30	National convention of the Finnish People's Party met in Helsinki; the district convention of the Conservatives made a final decision on nominations in Tampere.
March 30 to April 19	Membership elections for FDPU candidate nominations were held.
March 31 to April 1	National meeting of the "communal chiefs" of the Agrarian Union in Helsinki was held.
April 4	All election boards met; this was the last opportunity to request the inclusion of missing names in the register.
April 4–7	National convention of the FDPU met in Turku.
April 10	The *Suomen Sosialidemokraatti* began its column, "Elections are approaching—tighten the lines"; the *Maakansa* began its regular three-column advertisements of campaign meetings.
April 12–26	Conservative posters were displayed in the countryside.
April 14	This was the last day for appealing to the provincial governments against decisions of election boards concerning registration.
April 16	The FPDU started a new saving contest for financing its campaign.
April 17	First campaign meeting of the Agrarian Union was held in Korpilahti.
April 27	Nomination of FPP candidates ended in Northern Häme.
April 29	The Finnish Confederation of Labor issued its election platform.
May 1	May Day festivals of the FDPU and Social Democrats assumed a rather electioneering character.
May 4	The Finnish People's Party had a campaign meeting in Tampere; the local Swedish People's Party association named its candidate there.
May 6	The Finnish Broadcasting Corporation allowed no more parliamentary candidates on its programs.
May 14	Last day for holding the first meeting of the central election board.

May 15	The founding of the Independent Social Democratic Electoral Alliance was publicly announced.
May 19	Four parties signed the "agreement on campaign-peace."
May 27	Last day for the electors' associations to hand their candidates' petitions to the central election boards.
May 28	The central election board held the meeting at which the candidates' petitions were presented and the order of the electoral alliances on the final ballot was drawn.
May 31	The central election board gave new consideration to the candidates' petitions (disqualifying one list in Tampere).
June 3	The first nonpartisan election program in radio; the biggest Social Democratic campaign meeting in Tampere.
June 5	The first campaign advertisement in the weekly advertising paper *Tamperelainen;* an outdoor meeting of the Conservatives in Tampere.
June 6	Conclusion of the 1957 legislative session of the Parliament in Helsinki.
June 7–8	The national convention of the Agrarian Union in Kankaanpää.
June 9	The founding of a local FPP association in Korpilahti.
June 12	The central election board met to make final decisions on the names of electoral alliances and the numbers of individual candidates, and sent the "final combination of the lists of candidates" to be printed.
June 13–16	The Campaign Tour of the Independent Social Democratic electoral alliance was in action in Korpilahti.
June 16	The Ministry of Justice advised election boards on efficient ballot counting.
June 18	The Bench of Magistrates announced the voting districts and balloting places in Tampere.
June 19	Agrarian outdoor posters were distributed in rural communes.
June 23– July 7	Voting was conducted in Finnish embassies and missions and on board Finnish ships.
June 25	Three parties were presented on radio.
June 26	The city of Tampere rented space for outdoor advertising.
June 27	Three more parties were presented on radio; free distribution of posters in Tampere was allowed from 9 P.M.
June 29	First Social Democratic campaign meeting in Korpilahti.
July 2	The FPDU held its biggest campaign meeting in the Tampere stadium.
July 3	"Great election meeting of Tampere partisans" was held by the Social Democrats.

July 5   Last day for obtaining extracts from the register for absentee voting purposes.

July 6   Voting from noon to 8. P.M.

July 7   Voting from 9 A.M. to 8 P.M. and thereafter the opening, inspection, and counting of ballots; the approval of the election protocol by the election boards; sending of the ballots and protocols to the central election board; removing outdoor posters from the streets; and radio news on election results.

July 8   The control count in the central election board was begun.

July   "Thank-you" gatherings were arranged by the parties for their campaign organizations; advertisements and announcements referring to the election results were run in the press.

July 22   The final meeting of the central election board gave official results of the election.

July 29   The Speaker of the new Parliament was elected.

July 30   The 1958 legislative session was opened.

November   The Statistical Central Bureau published the election statistics.

Index